FREUD'S TECHNIQUE PAPERS

COMMENTARY

"The appearance of this book will be welcomed by all therapists who base their technique on psychoanalysis. In a carefully thought out and critical presentation of Freud's papers on technique, the author traces the influence of Freud's seminal ideas as they appear in the writings of psychoanalysts today. The writing is engagingly lucid and the presentation commendably objective. This book represents one of the most comprehensive overviews of the evolution of psychoanalytic technique since the beginning of psychoanalysis."
—Jacob A. Arlow, M.D.

"*Freud's Technique Papers: A Contemporary Perspective* is a didactic and expository tour de force. The volume presents eight of Freud's papers on the psychoanalytic method embedded in discussions of the origins and development of the core concepts and their impact on and reformulations in the contemporary technical perspectives of Brenner, Gill, and Kohut. Ellman's footnotes to Freud's papers are exceptionally lucid and clarifying. He has succeeded in explicating Freud's theory of technique in a manner comparable to what Rapaport achieved for Freud's theory of thought."
—Arnold D. Richards, M.D.

"The book, written by a first-rate thinker and teacher, is an invaluable contribution. The student will get a broad, nonpolemical education. The teacher will find a goldmine of ideas for a fascinating model of teaching. And the advanced professional will encounter a mind-stretching review that will stimulate integration as well as controversy. It is truly a book that is valuable at many levels. I recommend it highly."
—Fred Pine, Ph.D.

"Steve Ellman has written an original, ingenious, and very intelligent book that will be of use to all students of Freud. It contains a careful and scholarly tracing of Freud's development as an investigator of the mind, as a clinician, and as a theorist of psychoanalytic therapy and technique.

"Dr. Ellman also adds a synthetic exposition of current psychoanalytic views on each of the topics he has chosen—such as transference, dream interpretation, beginnings and terminations of treatment, and reconstructions—and compares these widely varying opinions with Freud's own and often very different notions. This book is a coherent, challenging, complex, and yet highly intelligible series of accounts on a number of important intellectual as well as psychoanalytic subjects."
—Steven Marcus, Ph.D.

FREUD'S TECHNIQUE PAPERS
A Contemporary Perspective

by STEVEN J. ELLMAN, Ph.D.

with the research assistance of Peter Kaufmann, Ph.D.

JASON ARONSON INC.

Northvale, New Jersey
London

Production Editor: *Adelle Krauser*
Interior Designer: *Ernie Haim*
Editorial Director: *Muriel Jorgensen*

This book was set in 10/12 Garamond by Alpha Graphics of Pittsfield, New Hampshire, and printed and bound by Haddon Craftsmen of Scranton, Pennsylvania.

For credits see pp. 369-370.

Library of Congress Cataloging-in-Publication Data
Ellman, Steven J.
    Freud's technique papers: a contemporary perspective / Steven Ellman.
        p. cm.
    Includes bibliographical references.
    Includes index.
    ISBN 0-87668-619-6
    1. Psychoanalysis. 2. Psychotherapy. 3. Freud, Sigmund,
1856-1939. I. Title.
    [DNLM: 1. Freud, Sigmund, 1856-1939. 2. Psychoanalysis—history.
3. Psychoanalytic Theory. 4. Psychoanalytic Therapy. WM 460 E49f]
RC506.E45   1991
616.89'17—dc20
DNLM/DLC
for Library of Congress   90-14451

Manufactured in the United States of America. Jason Aronson Inc. offers books and cassettes. For information and catalog write to Jason Aronson Inc., 230 Livingston Street, Northvale, New Jersey 07647.

This book is dedicated
to the tolerance, love, and good humor
shown to me by my wife, Dr. Carolyn Ellman,
and my children, Peter and Lauren.
It is also dedicated
to Dr. Edward Kronold,
a truly extraordinary analyst.

Contents

Preface

Beginning Questions

The idea of writing a book on Freud's technique—or, more accurately, writing a book of commentary on Freud's psychoanalytic method—comes as a natural task to someone who has taught Freudian courses for the last twenty years. I have found during these years that ideas about Freud's technique are as varied as the theoretical positions in the analytic community. It seems to me possible to use opinions about Freud's ideas on technique as a diagnostic test for a given author's or student's theoretical perspective. It would be hard to imagine that this diagnostic test would not be relevant to the present volume; undoubtedly I am reading and writing about Freud through my own theoretical transference reactions. However, in this publication we will have Freud's own words to compare with the views that I introduce: one of the major aspects of this manuscript is the reprinting of many of Freud's technique papers. Since this is an important facet of the text I will give a brief rationale for my selection of papers to reprint. I will also provide an explanation for the inclusion of contemporary psychoanalytic authors and the choice of the various translations of Freud's papers. These explanations will be more understandable after we look at an overview of the book's contents.

Contents and Format of This Volume

Throughout the book we will keep one eye on Freud's work, and one eye on how Freudian concepts have been incorporated into modern or contemporary psychoanalytic thought. The book is divided into six parts. In Part I (Chapter 1) we engage Freud as he is beginning to emerge as a psychoanalytic clinician. In these pages we see Freud beginning to develop a technique (the pressure technique) that is the forerunner of modern psychoanalysis and many versions of dynamic psychotherapy. This section ends with Freud's encounter with Dora (Ida Bauer), one of his most famous patients.[1] This encounter was to prove decisive for his ideas about the importance of transference. I consider this section an introduction to the book, and as such it does not include any of Freud's papers.

In Parts II through V we introduce Freud's papers on technique. These sections of the book have identical formats. To illustrate the organization we can look at Part II, "Transference as a Central Concept." The first chapter in this section (Chapter 2) delivers a historical purview of the evolution and oscillation of Freud's ideas about transference. Chapter 3 includes three of Freud's papers on transference. Throughout the course of Freud's papers I offer commentary in the form of marginal notes; this commentary is distinguished from Freud's footnotes by the symbol ■ . These notes will either attempt to clarify an aspect of Freud's writings, or to briefly show how other analysts have developed or used a concept that Freud originated.[2] In the final chapter in this segment of the book, Chapter 4, I discuss contemporary views of the concepts that Freud has initiated. I have chosen to primarily follow three authors in the discussion of contemporary views: Charles Brenner, Merton Gill, and Heinz Kohut.[3] Throughout most of the book I will summarize these authors' views and compare their positions with Freud's concepts. At times I will also feature other contemporary authors. For example, I include in Chapter 4 Brian Bird's seminal writings on transference.

The third part of the book, Dream Interpretation, presents Freud's views on the place of the dream in psychoanalytic treatment (Chapter 5). The exceptional place of the dream in psychoanalysis is in part due to the importance of *The Interpretation of Dreams* (1900) in the history of psychoanalytic thought. In this chapter we note the changes of Freud's positions on the dream in psychoanalysis. Then, in the two papers of Freud's that I present in

---

[1]Dora's actual name, Ida Bauer, has been known for a period of time, but a recent book (Decker 1991) presents us with both the name and an excellent view of Freud's life circumstances as he was treating this 18-year-old woman. This book appeared after I had finished the present manuscript, but its appearance did not lead me to revise the relatively limited points that I have made about the historical significance of Freud's encounters with Dora. Decker in one aspect of the case has followed Gay's interpretation of why Freud delayed the publication of the case. As the reader will see, I do not completely accept this version.

[2]These notes will not provide formal references but rather refer to authors in a more informal manner. It is my goal to comment in a way that does not take the reader too far away from Freud's essays. Put in other terms, I hope that I do not clutter the Freud papers with excessive notes. I have, however, included a large reference list which includes all of the authors referred to in the marginal notes.

[3]Although I usually follow these authors, at times I depart from this format if I feel that others have commented more extensively on a given topic.

Chapter 6, we see the extent to which he changed his views from 1900. We also see the extent to which he continued to see the dream as a window into the world of the unconscious. The chapter on contemporary views (Chapter 7) features a report from the Kris Study Group (1967) on the place of the dream in psychoanalysis. This report includes accounts of two quite different positions concerning the place of the dream in the psychoanalytic situation.

In the fourth part of the book, Clinical Practice, I summarize and discuss Freud's suggestions on a variety of issues that all clinicians face in their practice (Chapter 8). Freud raises these issues in two papers (Chapter 9), and offers a series of recommendations to analytic practitioners. The issues discussed here range from the question of analyzability to the use of the couch and the fundamental rule of free association. I feature only Kohut, Gill, and Brenner in the chapter on contemporary perspectives (Chapter 10).

Part V, Freud's Final Views, presents Freud's views on termination and on the role of constructions (or reconstruction) in analytic treatment (Chapter 11). The two Freud papers in this part of the book (Chapter 12),[4] are in effect Freud's final views on the psychoanalytic situation. In the chapter on contemporary views of termination we also discuss Novick's views on the termination phase of treatment (Chapter 13). In this part of the book there is a chapter on contemporary views of the role of reconstruction[5] in psychoanalysis (Chapter 14). This chapter features the work of Dr. Jacob Arlow.

In Part VI, Integrating Freud's Legacy with Contemporary Views and Experience, there is first a chapter (15) that concentrates on one of Freud's cases, "Notes upon a Case of Obsessional Neurosis" (1909). Freud's notes on this case have been found and we have an opportunity here to see in some detail how he viewed his interaction with the patient, the Rat Man or Dr. Ernst Lanzer.[6] The next chapter (16), presents some of my thoughts on an aspect of treatment that I believe to be under-represented in Freud's writings. Here I try to show some of the influences that have led to the expanding world of psychoanalysis. In particular I emphasize the importance of the beginning stages of psychoanalytic treatment. The final chapter (17) in this volume is a summary in which the writings of Brenner, Gill, and Kohut are reviewed and compared with those of Freud.

During two of the chapters introducing Freud's work, I present several theoretical issues that are historically relevant to the development of his ideas about the psychoanalytic method. In Chapter 2 there is a section on Freud's ideas about diagnosis; in particular we focus on Freud's use of the diagnostic category of actual disorders. Those readers who are somewhat puzzled by the term "actual neurosis" in Chapter 1 might want to refer to this section of Chapter 2. In Chapter 5 there is a brief overview of Freud's shifting theoretical models.

---

[4]One of the papers, "Analysis Terminable and Interminable," is only partially reprinted.
[5]I will not distinguish between reconstruction and construction in the present volume.
[6]Mahony (1986), as far as I know, is the first author to use the proper name of the patient who is called the Rat Man.

A Rationale for Some Choices

PERSONAL CONSIDERATIONS

Freud, perhaps as much as any author in the last two centuries, elicits extraordinarily powerful reactions. Before I begin the discussion of my choices for this book, it seems relevant to try to give some indication of my attitudes toward Freud's writings. It is hard to be neutral about his theoretical positions. Yet in many ways I value Freud even more for the questions he raises than for the theoretical concepts he provides. One can agree or disagree with some of his positions, but it is rare (it seems to me impossible) that we can read an essay of Freud's without encountering questions that in some important way challenge our image of our inner processes. Even in dealing with seemingly trivial issues, Freud is able to ask the type of question that brings us back to fundamental concepts. In this respect one might say Freud accomplishes, in an off-hand manner, what William James aspired to; that is, the framing of fundamental psychological issues in virtually every essay he wrote.[7] Thus I especially appreciate Freud for the manner in which he is able to conceive of what is required of a theory of human experience. In this volume we follow his thoughts and see him express or posit what he thinks is necessary for a meaningful theory of psychoanalytic technique. In many ways this can be a renewing encounter since often in contemporary psychoanalysis one gets enmeshed in narrow issues without being able to gain a broader perspective. Hopefully, in this volume we can look at the flexibility of Freud's concepts and the depth of his questions, as well as examine some of his more definitive positions.

SELECTION OF FREUD'S TECHNIQUE PAPERS

Let me now turn to some of the rationale for the choices that have been made in writing this volume. Although there are a number of places where Freud mentions technical matters, I decided to include only those papers in which Freud focuses primarily on issues relevant to the psychoanalytic situation. In addition we include only those papers in which we can look at both process and content. For example, in his papers on transference he addresses topics in a specific and pointed manner; we see him struggle with issues and evolve a position in the course of these papers. If one follows the flow of these writings it is possible to get some feel for how Freud arrived at his conclusions; we do not have to read a finished statement of this process. On the other hand I have decided not to reprint sections of either of Freud's Introductory Lectures (1916–1917, 1933). The lectures are by and large summary statements and we can get little feeling of process while we are reading them.

---

[7]This is meant in no way to demean James who I believe was a great psychologist and a fascinating thinker. Certainly James framed many interesting questions, and fundamental ones at that; but from my point of view he did not have the encompassing genius that Freud possessed.

I have decided not to reprint those articles or portions of papers that were written before Freud was an analytic therapist. This decision can be considered at least somewhat arbitrary. Freud, as I point out, became an analyst gradually; there was not a sharp delineation between Freud as a therapist and Freud as an analyst. Moreover, Freud continued to go back to earlier positions even after he developed a fuller analytic position. Thus one could reasonably ask, Why not include his earlier papers? I have quoted extensively from these papers; however, since we are looking at Freudian concepts that have been used in contemporary positions, I decided to reprint those papers that were most directly relevant to this purpose. I believe that in our present selection we see those positions of Freud's that have had the most direct impact on contemporary psychoanalytic practice.

CHOICE OF TRANSLATIONS

An issue closely related to the choice of papers is the choice of the translations that I have utilized. By and large we have used the translations of Joan Riviere because they seem to me to be the most elegant and literary versions of Freud's work that are available. In recent years there have been a number of attacks against the Strachey translations as they appear in the Standard Edition. Bettelheim (1982) and Mahony (1986) have been two of the strongest critics of Strachey's translations. I would agree with Gay (1988) when he considers some of Bettelheim's comments on the "cranky" side. Mahony, it seems to me, is even more extreme in his criticism.[8] There are of course legitimate concerns about how Freud is translated; and while Mahony and Bettelheim raise important issues, the most balanced commentary, in my opinion, is provided by Ornston (1982, 1985). At any rate, we avoid the controversies about the translations in the Standard Edition by using the literary and accurate translations provided by Riviere.

CHOICE OF CONTEMPORARY AUTHORS

In my chapters on contemporary views I have chosen to look at Brenner, Kohut, and Gill, both because they have made substantial contributions and because they present relatively complete and systematic views on technique. In addition their ideas have found a reasonable number of adherents in the analytic community. The substantial disagreements between these authors allow us to explore some of the important controversies in psychoanalytic technique.

A sub-theme in this exploration involves the term "classical analyst." Most analysts use this term to denote practitioners who continue to adhere to Freud's concepts, or concepts closely allied to or derived from Freudian theory. In this context it is intriguing to compare Brenner, a classical analyst, with

---

[8]The full evaluation of his comments is a task for another time. I have assessed some of his substantive arguments about Freud's case reports.

Kohut and Gill, who have explicitly departed from classical concepts. If we restrict ourselves to issues of technique we will see that there is not one author who entirely agrees with Freud. While this is not surprising, it is my view that when we explicitly compare the extent of the agreement with Freud, there will be some unexpected conclusions.[9]

Freud's Analytic Practice

Freud's behavior as an analyst is one that excites a great deal of passion and has been the subject of various recent biographies. At one point in the writing of this book I anticipated including a review of all the literature on Freud's actual conduct as an analyst. There are now many such reports from former patients (see, for example, Kardiner 1977). These reports vary from first-hand statements to third- or fourth-hand anecdotes. In addition, there are various reanalyses of the cases that Freud has published. The literature on Freud's published cases includes not only reanalyses, but the identification of his patients, as well as various types of follow-up reports. After considering all the published comments that I could find from these sources, I decided not to undertake the task of reviewing this literature. I believe that while the issue is certainly of interest it is not directly relevant to the present work.

Freud's ideas no longer rest or fall on his case studies or his behavior with patients.[10] It may well be the case that Freud is an example of a genius who put forth a variety of central concepts about technique but who was not acutely interested in steadfastly following his own suggestions. I believe this was particularly the case later in his career. However, whether or not this is true, his ideas can be evaluated independently of his behavior. Thus the question of Freud's actual practice is one that I will deal with only peripherally in most of the present text, and centrally in only one chapter (15). In reading the comments from former patients (a few comments are presented in Chapter 15) it is clear that Freud practiced analysis in several different ways. In addition to reports from former patients we have Freud's notes from one of his cases (that of Dr. Lanzer, the Rat Man). I am assuming that Freud's notes afford us a clear picture of his analytic behavior. Thus, although we will look at various reports from patients, we will explore in detail the case of Dr. Lanzer.

---

[9]So as not to overstate the impending shock, I should say that the assessment of the scope of agreement is a subjective analysis. It depends on one's own evaluation of the importance of a given concept in Freudian theory. If you believe that the concept of reconstruction is crucial to Freud's ideas, then the conclusion you will reach will be quite different than if you believe that it is most important to understand and interpret conflict in terms of oedipal formulations. The issue of understanding conflict in terms of a given developmental period is not strictly a technical issue, yet a clinician's general theory may be the most important criterion in determining whether or not she is designated as a classical analyst.

[10]This contention is in direct contrast to Mahony's and even Eissler's, who maintain that writings about the cases are crucial to understanding Freudian thought. This idea is at best puzzling to me, since it is clear that the case reports contain many difficulties and are certainly not Freud at his best.

Besides reading the published comments from Freud's patients, I have had the opportunity of seeing some of the unpublished comments that one investigator has collected from eleven of Freud's patients. I do not know whether this person will ever publish these comments. I have briefly discussed with another investigator the interviews that he or she has had with twenty-five of Freud's patients. The numerous reports in the literature (and these unpublished interviews) indicate what we have all known intuitively: Freud was a highly variable analyst who frequently disregarded (or violated) his own suggestions. Neither of these people who have collected reports from Freud's patients has in any way contradicted this impression.

Conclusions

Although Freud may have been variable as an analyst, his thoughts on psychoanalytic technique followed what I consider to be an understandable progression. Of course we must highlight the fact that there are many interpretations of Freud as an analyst and as a technical innovator. I have said that it is my contention that the psychoanalytic method and psychoanalytic practice were not major concerns to Freud after World War I. Others have put forth different interpretations of his development as a psychoanalyst, which illustrates my contention that how Freud is viewed by a given analyst will be largely a function of that analyst's theoretical orientation. Thus it is not surprising that Greenberg and Mitchell (relational analysts) see Freud as essentially having a fully developed technique when he presents the 1905 case of Dora (Greenberg and Mitchell 1983). Since this is a somewhat embarrassing and unsuccessful case, many Freudian analysts think it is not indicative of Freud's mature technique. Kanzer (a classical analyst) sees Freud as evolving into a contemporary classical analyst by the end of his career (Kanzer 1980).[11] On the other hand, I will attempt to demonstrate that Freud—even while he presents new ideas about psychoanalytic technique—never fully leaves behind his earliest thoughts about the treatment situation. In the end he tries to blend his initial understanding with the hard-won insights that he embraces at times, and at times is virtually forced to deal with in his clinical encounters. He is propelled to these conclusions by using his new method of understanding human discourse—that is, the psychoanalytic method. Fortunately, we can continue this discussion in the context of Freud's own words; and so I will end these prefatory comments and begin to look at Freud at the point at which he is starting to develop his revolutionary new method.

[11]Although I disagree with his interpretation of Freud's development, Kanzer's work is of course of interest. The article in which he makes this assertion is one that I quote from profitably for other purposes. One can of course say the same thing about Greenberg and Mitchell's work. While I disagree with some of their contentions their various ideas are stimulating and of interest.

Acknowledgment

A number of friends and colleagues have systematically read this volume and offered advice and suggestions that I probably did not heed with enough care. I must first of all thank Dr. Sheldon Bach and Dr. Michael Moskowitz, not only for reading the book and offering their carefully considered comments, but more importantly for enduring my oscillating moods during the course of the writing of this volume. In their different ways they have both been the type of ideal friends and colleagues that hardly seem possible. If their friendship had not been of such long duration, I would assume that I was in the midst of two idealizing transference states. In addition, Dr. Laurence Gould—who has been a friend and colleague for the last twenty years—was kind enough to read the initial drafts of the present volume. Although several other people have been quite helpful, Dr. Mark Silvan, Dr. Irving Steingart, and Dr. Anni Bergman, in particular, have always been available when I asked for their support.

I wish also to thank the numerous students who have listened to some of the ideas expressed in these pages. If there is any value in this book, all of my students deserve some credit for its positive aspects. In particular I would like to thank a City University Clinical Psychology Doctoral Student, Ms. Melissa Kresch, for her helpfulness in preparing aspects of this volume.

It would be impossible to overlook the contribution of Dr. Jason Aronson. He first suggested that I write such a book and he read the manuscript as it was being developed. It somehow seems to me more appropriate to have an adversarial relationship with one's publisher, but in fairness I have to thank him for his unwavering attention and encouragement.

Dr. Peter Kaufmann, although he was not technically my co-author, was as helpful and dedicated as any co-author could ever have been. Neither he nor any of my other colleagues should be held responsible for the opinions herein, but he was of immense help in compiling the views of contemporary authors, as well as in tracking down the information necessary to finish such a project. He also read the manuscript many times and offered innumerable suggestions about the content and form of the final book. It is hard to imagine how the volume would have turned out without his aid and encouragement.

While I have dedicated this volume to my wife and children, I would be remiss if I didn't note that my wife read this volume more times than any other living person—certainly more times than any person should have been subjected to. Her good humor and gently offered advice and criticism were (almost) always taken as a ray of badly needed sunlight.

Since my German is quite primitive I was always in need of a translator who also was familiar with psychoanalysis. For her help in this endeavor I wish to thank Ms. Bettina Volz, a graduate student in the Clinical Psychology Program at City University. She not only translated aspects of the present text (the first eight sessions of the case of the Rat Man, Dr. Lanzer), but also provided advice on other translations. Her patience and linguistic skill were of immense help. Dr. Edward Kronold was also of direct and indirect assistance in dealing with translations. He suggested to me that the meaning of Freud's words would be apparent in most translations, and also that (paradoxically) only someone who had learned German in Vienna would be sensitive to some of the nuances of Freud's writing style. Since Ms. Volz was born and grew up in southern Germany, I decided that I had to test Dr. Kronold's assertions by consulting him on some of the translations. Inexplicably (and paradoxically), he was right on both counts.

As a final note I wish to thank Ms. Judith McCarthy for her secretarial assistance.

PART I

The Early Years

1

Freud's Early Ideas

We begin this volume at a time when Freud is leaving the hypnotic method,[1] and beginning to listen and talk to patients in a manner that will shake the foundations of Western Society. Although contemporary analysts frequently draw a sharp dichotomy between psychoanalysis and psychotherapy, we will see that Freud's psychoanalytic technique gradually evolved from his work as a hypno- and psychotherapist. In fact, Freud's method will always remain a mixture of his later, more mature psychoanalytic technique, with ideas he developed in his first therapeutic interventions. As Bernfeld has noted (1949), Freud often saw himself primarily[2] as the inventor of the psychoanalytic method and viewed psychoanalysis

> first of all as a new technique by which a whole realm of facts, inaccessible before, can be brought to light. It is a new instrument of observation, a new tool of research. In the second place only is it a body of new knowledge gained by the use of the new instrument. [p. 238]

In this first depiction of Freud as a psychotherapist, we see that he is intent on describing how this new technique provides new *facts*, and fascinating ones at that.

---

[1]As is well known, Freud began to also look at hysteria by visiting Charcot and coming into contact with Charcot, Janet, and what is called the "Nancy School." (See Freud's account [1885] or look at Jones [1953] or Gay [1988].) Charcot utilized hypnosis as a treatment method and Breuer and Freud did also up to about 1890 when Freud began to develop his own treatment methods. Their method was reasonably different from Charcot's technique.
[2]Although this is Bernfeld's idea, in our view only in the beginning of his career did Freud see himself primarily as a clinician, and the inventor of a new technique.

Freud as Therapist

The concepts of resistance, transference, and free association are basic to the psychoanalytic situation and begin to appear at this time in Freud's thought. Freud started in his pathway toward developing psychoanalytic technique by exploring the significance of hysteria and its childhood etiology.

The idea of making the unconscious conscious, one of the most famous Freudian phrases, could be used to characterize Breuer and Freud's stated goal when they published *Studies on Hysteria* (1893).[3] Not only did Breuer and Freud offer a new way of understanding hysteria, but Freud's last chapter in this volume presents a remarkable view of his early development as a psychotherapist. In this chapter, Freud presents a new technique for getting at *pathogenic memories* by making them conscious. Given today's emphasis in psychoanalysis on the role of transference, it is interesting to go back to a time when Freud was involved almost exclusively in the recovery of pathogenic memories. In *Studies on Hysteria*, we see the evolution of Freud as a therapist: in the first chapter co-authored with Breuer, he is a hypnotherapist; in the concluding chapter of the volume, Freud stands alone as a psychotherapist.

Before we begin our historical expedition, it is worth mentioning that, even when Freud was using hypnosis as a therapeutic tool, he distinguished the effects of hypnotic treatment from the effects of posthypnotic suggestion. It was his contention that when he unearthed memories under the influence of hypnosis, it was the process of remembering and abreacting that led to symptom reduction. In his view, symptom reduction did not occur as a result of a suggestion in the therapy that he and Breuer performed. In fact, in any of the treatments that he advocated, he maintained that suggestion was never the curative element in the treatment. Freud thought that suggestion had a role, but that role was always one that helped the patient enter and continue to participate in the treatment. While the distinction between suggestion and true therapeutic results is easy to outline, it is more elusive in actuality, and we will see that the issue of suggestion is not restricted to the earliest phase of Freud's career as a hypno- or psychotherapist.[4]

Hypno- and Psychotherapy

Freud tells us (1916) that "psycho-analysis started with researches into hysteria" (p. 207), and that hypnosis was his original therapeutic technique. The aim of his

---

[3]At this point in time, Freud's ideas about the unconscious were not fully developed. He equivocated on the status of what he called *the secondary group of ideas*. At times this concept seems equivalent to the unconscious; at other times he seems to be saying that the secondary group has ready access to consciousness. A few years later in *The Interpretation of Dreams* (1900), the term *unconscious* would begin to acquire its modern meaning.

[4]See Freud's review of and introduction to Bernheim's work on suggestion (1889).

hypnotic technique (Breuer and Freud 1893) was to bring about the "repro-duction of a memory which was of importance in bringing about the onset of the hysteria—the memory either of a single major trauma . . . or of a series of interconnected part-traumas" (p. 14). Underlying his therapeutic approach was the assumption that "hysterics suffer mainly from reminis-cences" (p. 7).

These memories or reminiscences are the result of psychical trauma "or more precisely the memory of the trauma . . . [which] acts like a foreign body which long after its entry must continue to be regarded as an agent that is still at work" (Breuer and Freud 1893, p. 6). Breuer and Freud also reported that to their surprise:

> Each individual hysterical symptom immediately and permanently disappeared when we had succeeded in bringing clearly to light the memory of the event by which it was provoked and in arousing its accompanying affect, and when the patient had described that event in the greatest possible detail and had put the effect into words. Recollection without effect almost invariably produces no result. [Breuer and Freud 1893, p. 6]

In this famous statement of theirs, in the initial chapter in *Studies on Hysteria*, they not only proposed a partial explanation for hysteria but also stated how to treat this disorder. Freud maintains that simply providing an intellectual understanding will not be curative. Patients must be allowed to abreact or have a full emotional reaction under hypnosis. Their cathartic method was thus dependent on the patient abreacting. While utilizing the hypnotic method, the patient's memories and verbalizations were "in accor-dance with the laws of association" (1893, p. 16). While the patient is hypno-tized it is possible to:

> [bring] to an end the operative force of the idea which was not abreacted in the first instance (in the person's normal life), by allowing its strangulated affect to find a way out through speech; and it subjects it to associative correction by introducing it into normal consciousness (under light hypnosis). [Breuer and Freud 1893, p. 17]

Thus in Freud's early conceptualizations about hysteria, he maintained that the symptoms associated with hysteria were related to painful, anxiety-provoking memories that were stored apart from the person's primary or conscious ideas about himself. These ideas, which were stored as a secondary group of ideas, were not accessible to consciousness. Normally, affect asso-ciated with disturbing experiences is worn away or discharged. When disturb-ing memories are not appropriately worn away or discharged, they must be handled in some other manner. Before we describe the alternative possibilities for these disturbing memories, we will look at Freud's ideas about how disturbing ideas or memories are handled normally:

The fading of a memory or the losing of its affect depends on various factors. The most important of these is whether there has been an energetic reaction to the event that provokes an affect. By "reaction" we here understand the whole class of voluntary and involuntary reflexes—from tears to acts of revenge—in which, as experience shows us, the affects are discharged. If this reaction takes place to a sufficient amount a large part of the effect disappears as a result. Linguistic usage bears witness to this fact of daily observation by such phrases as "to cry oneself out," and to "blow off steam" (literally "to rage oneself out"). If the reaction is suppressed, the affect remains attached to the memory. An injury that has been repaid, even if only in words, is recollected quite differently from one that has had to be accepted. [Breuer and Freud 1893, p. 8]

In this formulation, Freud maintained that under normal or optimal circumstances people are able to deal with, or wear away, distressing effects by fully experiencing them, thus being able to counteract an experience in thought or action. If, for instance, a situation stimulated an idea that brought up the affect of shame, people might be able to counteract this idea by reminding themselves of their positive attributes. By assuring themselves that the event that caused the affect of shame was a singular or infrequent occurrence in their lives, they could then wear away the affect of shame. Alternatively, they might do something in reality to counteract this experience. Thus, normal people are continually discharging affect or putting a memory of a disturbing or humiliating circumstance into an appropriate perspective "by considering (one's) own worth" (Breuer and Freud 1893, p. 9). A normal person can have either small abreactions (discharges of affect through thought or action) or deal with the personal insult or aversive effect more gradually "through the process of association." The fading or forgetting of memories takes place when the affect is "worn away." Freud believed that memories can be recaptured when the affect is reunited with the idea.

Breuer and Freud's technique to deal with hysterics is in effect an attempt to help the person do what normal people do continually: experience aversive situations, abreact, and then deal with the thoughts through the process of association (or rational thought). By the time *Studies on Hysteria* was published, Freud's position had changed and evolved into what can be considered the beginnings of psychoanalytic technique. Freud began to use a form of psychotherapy called the pressure technique (1893). In *Studies on Hysteria*, in a somewhat guarded manner, he states some of his reasons for abandoning the hypnotic method. He relates that a number of hysterical patients refused every attempt at hypnosis. For these and other reasons, Freud decided to bypass hypnosis and utilize the pressure technique. The aim of this new technique is still the recovery of pathogenic memories, but the recovery of memories is now accomplished without the aid of hypnosis:

When, at our first interview, I asked my patients if they remembered what had originally occasioned the symptom concerned, in some cases they said they knew nothing of it, while in others they brought forward something which they described as an obscure recollection and could not pursue further. If, following the example of Bernheim when he awoke in his patients impressions from their somnambulistic state which had ostensibly been forgotten, I now became insistent—if I assured them that they did know it, that it would occur to their minds— then, in the first cases, something did actually occur to them, and, in the others, their memory went a step further. After this I became still more insistent; I told the patients to lie down and deliberately close their eyes in order to "concentrate"—all of which had at least some resemblance to hypnosis. I then found that without any hypnosis new recollections emerged which went further back and which probably related to our topic. Experiences like this made me think that it would in fact be possible for the pathogenic groups of ideas, that were after all certainly present, to be brought to light by mere insistence; and since this insistence involved effort on my part and so suggested the idea that I had to overcome a resistance, the situation led me at once to the theory that by means of my psychical work I had to overcome a psychical force in the patients which was opposed to the pathogenic ideas becoming conscious (being remembered). A new understanding seemed to open before my eyes when it occurred to me that this must no doubt be the same psychical force that had played a part in the generating of the hysterical symptom and had at that time prevented the pathogenic idea from becoming conscious. . . . From all this there arose, as it were automatically, the thought of defense. [Breuer and Freud 1893, p. 268]

In these paragraphs Freud is not only telling us about his new technique, but also how he came upon the concept of defense. In a paper entitled "Neuro-Psychoses of Defense" (1894) he writes at greater length about his reasons for proposing the theory of defense. In this chapter on psychotherapy, he is writing about defense and a strongly related concept, *resistance*. What is resistance? Freud at times used the term synonymously with defense and gradually restricted the term so that resistance is thought of as anything that impedes the flow of the patient's associations. This distinction is more meaningful later in Freud's career when the concept of defense has been further developed. However, in 1894, Freud is already stating that when defenses are operative we see the patient *resist* attempts to recover the pathogenic ideas or memories.

How does Freud deal with resistance? To answer this question, he states another aspect of his new technique. Initially, he attempts to reassure the patients that if they try a little longer and harder they will think of something, but he acknowledges that this type of encouragement doesn't go very far. When the patient is resistant, Freud suggests:

a small technical device. . . . I inform the patient that, a moment later, I shall apply pressure to his forehead, and I assure him that, all the time the pressure lasts, he will see before him a recollection in the form of a picture or will have it in his thoughts in the form of an idea occurring to him; and I pledge him to communicate this picture or idea to me, whatever it may be. He is not to keep it to himself because he may happen to think it is not what is wanted, not the right thing, or because it would be too disagreeable for him to say it. There is to be no criticism of it, no reticence, either for emotional reasons or because it is judged unimportant. . . . I am of course aware that a pressure on the forehead like this could be replaced by any other signal or by some other exercise of physical influence on the patient; . . . the advantage of the procedure lies in the fact that by means of it I dissociate the patient's attention from his conscious searching and reflecting—from everything, in short, on which he can employ his will—in the same sort of way in which this is effected by staring into a crystal ball, and so on. [Breuer and Freud 1893, pp. 270-271]

We see that Freud deals with resistance by at once trying to convince, cajole, and help focus the patient on the task at hand. The task at hand is to associate freely. He assures a patient that he should communicate anything he thinks of, no matter how trivial; this as we will see is similar to instructions given to his patients in psychoanalysis. Of course, in psychoanalytic sessions Freud did not apply as much pressure to the patient's forehead or psyche as he does at this point in time. By using the pressure technique, Freud was trying to help patients put aside their more conscious critical facilities so that they could more easily relate their associations. What were the results of this technique?

The pathogenic idea which has ostensibly been forgotten is always lying ready close at hand and can be reached by associations that are easily accessible. It is merely a question of getting some obstacle out of the way. This obstacle seems once again to be the subject's will, and different people can learn with different degrees of ease to free themselves from their intentional thinking and to adopt an attitude of completely objective observation towards the psychical processes taking place in them. . . . What emerges under the pressure of my hand is not always a "forgotten" recollection; it is only in the rarest cases that the actual pathogenic recollections lie so easily . . . on the surface. It is much more frequent for an idea to emerge which is an intermediate link in the chain of associations between the idea from which we start and the pathogenic idea which we are in search of. [Breuer and Freud 1893, p. 271]

Freud relates later in the chapter that "it is quite hopeless to try to penetrate directly to the nucleus of the pathogenic organization" (p. 292).

These excerpts are rich in the ideas that have shaped decades of psychotherapeutic practice and stimulated a good deal of debate. At this point, we can highlight some of the questions that are raised by these paragraphs and by other similar issues that Freud begins to discuss in this chapter on psychotherapy.

Freud has here not only confirmed the central importance of defense in psychoanalytic theory, but he has begun to show how defense is manifested in a treatment situation. From this time forward, the idea of resistance will be an essential idea in psychoanalytic treatment. We have already stated that a patient's resistance in treatment is not thought to be perfectly synonymous with defense, but for the time being we will take it as a rough approximation of the way Freud conceived of defense in the treatment situation. Freud's idea is somewhat different from his later versions of defense. In this chapter and in the later paper ("The Neuro-Psychoses of Defense," 1894), Freud talks about defense as an act of will, meaning that the person has consciously intended to banish an idea from the primary group of ideas. Conversely, this means that, if a person can concentrate hard enough, then he can more easily get at (or will the return of) his pathogenic ideation. Since modern psychoanalysts are accustomed to thinking of defense as an unconscious process, this meaning of defense is not frequently used in modern psychoanalytic publications (Werman has written a chapter [Blum 1985] on suppression as a defense). Given that Freud thought of defense as an act of will, his handling of resistance becomes more understandable. The idea of a patient's displaying resistance connotes the patient's consciously disobeying the physician. Freud saw the patient's efforts as a resistance to remembering the pathogenic ideas or memories, as well as a reluctance or resistance to obeying instructions. Since Freud felt that this resistance is an act of will by the patient, he attempted to counter this act of will with a greater act of will. In more concrete terms, it is possible to pressure the patient into complying with the physician's instructions. Armed with this understanding of defense, Freud conceived of how the physician could use influence or suggestion to help the patient retrieve the memories that were causing conflict and pain.

This point, of course, is overstated. There are also indications that Freud had a more modern understanding of defense during this same period. His thinking did not fall into neat categories. Rather, at every phase of his theorizing, one can see elements from the past, present, and indeed even the future standing side by side. During this period, however, the idea of defense as a conscious act of will was a good deal more in keeping with his treatment methods. This point of view is present in the way he conceptualized not only resistance, but transference as well. In telling of occasions of the pressure technique failing, Freud relates:

> There are two possibilities: either, at the point at which we are investigating, there is really nothing more to be found—and this we can recognize from the complete calmness of the patient's facial expression; or we have come up against a resistance which can only be overcome later, we are faced by a new stratum into which we cannot yet penetrate—and this, once more, we can infer from the patient's facial expression, which is tense and gives evidence of mental effort. But there is yet a third possibility which bears witness equally to an obstacle, but an external obstacle, and not one inherent in the material. This happens when the patient's relation to the physician is disturbed, and it is the worst obstacle that we can come across. We can, however, reckon on meeting it in every comparatively serious analysis. I have already indicated the important part played by the figure of the physician in creating motives to defeat the psychical force of resistance. In not a few cases, especially with women and where it is a question of elucidating

erotic trains of thought, the patient's cooperation becomes a personal sacrifice, which must be compensated by some substitute for love. The trouble taken by the physician and his friendliness have to suffice for such a substitute. If, now, this relation of the patient to the physician is disturbed, her cooperativeness fails, too; when the physician tries to investigate the next pathological idea, the patient is held up by an intervening consciousness of the complaints against the physician that have been accumulating in her. In my experience, this obstacle arises in three principal cases:

(1) If there is a personal estrangement—if, for instance, the patient feels she has been neglected, has been too little appreciated or has been insulted, or if she has heard unfavourable comments on the physician or the method of treatment. This is the least serious case. . . .

(2) If the patient is seized by a dread of becoming too much accustomed to the physician personally, of losing her independence in relation to him, and even of perhaps becoming sexually dependent on him. This is a more important case, because its determinants are less individual. The cause of this obstacle lies in the solicitude inherent in the treatment. . . .

(3) If the patient is frightened at finding that she is transferring on to the figure of the physician the distressing ideas which arise from the content of the analysis. This is a frequent, and indeed in some analyses a regular, occurrence. Transference onto the physician takes place through a false connection.[5] . . . It is impossible to carry any analysis to a conclusion unless we know how to meet the resistance arising in these three ways. But we can find a way of doing so if we make up our minds that this new symptom that has been produced on the old model must be treated in the same way as the old symptoms. Our . . . task is to make the obstacle conscious to the patient. . . .

To begin with I was greatly annoyed at this increase in my psychological work, till I came to see that the whole process followed a law; and I then noticed, too, that transference of this kind brought about no great addition to what I had to do. For the patient the work remained the same: she had to overcome the distressing affect aroused by having been able to entertain such a wish even for a moment; and it seemed to make no difference to the success of the treatment whether she made this psychical repudiation the theme of her work in the historical instance or in the recent one connected with me. The patients, too, gradually learnt to realize that in these transferences on to the figure of the physician it was a question of a compulsion and an illusion which melted away with the conclusion of the analysis. [Breuer and Freud 1893, pp. 301-304]

It is interesting that Freud sees the idea of a disturbance in the patient's relation to the physician as an *external* obstacle, even though it is met with in every serious analysis. These three types of disturbances, including what Freud

[5]This is the first appearance of the use of transference in Freud's writings.

calls the transference, are not the main arena of the treatment, but rather are considered to be material to be mastered and gotten over as expeditiously as possible. He tells us that at first he was annoyed by the transference but now has dealt with his annoyance, since transference does not really add to his work.[6] Even in the few pages quoted, Freud vacillates in his view of transference. At times, he sees transference as an external obstacle or even as a nuisance deterring him from his main task of recovering pathogenic memories; at other times, he is surprisingly modern in his view of transference. Still, transference is restricted to distressing ideas arising from the content of the analysis, and they are ideas that are *false connections*.[7] These false connections, while important, are not the central issue for Freud's treatment to achieve success.

It is important to note one of the first, most famous and dramatic examples of transference that Freud witnessed. This example (Breuer's treatment of Anna O.) did not help Freud feel secure about the implications of transference in a treatment situation. When Anna professed her love for Breuer, Breuer's discomfort certainly was not lost on Freud. Freud commented that Breuer stopped his practice of hypnotherapy because of his experience with Anna O. (Freud 1914a, pp. 40–41). However one may interpret Breuer's reaction to his treatment of Anna O., there can be no question that this treatment raised quite intense feelings for Breuer and also for Freud. Freud must have been personally affected by this (and other) situations and was well aware of the criticisms that might be directed toward him, criticisms that he was inducing women to fall in love with him with this new technique. Even without this to deal with, there was no shortage of criticism of Freud's methods. Focusing only on these external historical factors leads us to overlook the difficulties any analyst encounters in dealing with transference. Freud could not have been an exception to these difficulties. In fact, we will see in his treatment of Dora (his first major case publication) that the issue of transference is pivotal for him.

Freud's distinctions among the three types of reactions are interesting in light of the discussion of the difficulties in dealing with transference in the analytic situation. He goes to great pains to say that if a patient feels neglected or feels frightened of becoming too dependent, this is not transference but a special form of resistance that is apart from transference. Perhaps one can say

---

[6]This is a different point of view than that taken by Freud later and, of course, is different from the views of many modern psychoanalytic authors who would consider the transference the main vehicle of analysis.

[7]Freud at this time considered obsessive symptomatology as essentially false connections. Thus if a person defended against one idea, and obsessed about another substitute (conscious) idea, the conscious idea was a false connection. He theorized that these super-valent conscious ideas were the result of energy transfers. The process of defense was involved with making a strong idea a weak one; when this happened there was now a new conscious strong idea, which was the false connection. Transference could be seen as just one type of false connection. Put in other terms, all false connections have a transfer of energy. For a look at Freud's views, see "The Neuro-Psychoses of Defense" (1894).

that if a patient hears something negative about this new form of treatment, it is understandable that the patient might have some reaction to these negative comments. But why would feelings of neglect or insult be considered apart from the content of a person's conflicts? Freud states that the sensitivity and suspiciousness of hysterical patients may occasionally attain surprising dimensions. This hardly seems to be a response that is situationally determined, or even necessarily the least serious conflict one might encounter. It is clear that today these two other types of reactions would usually be considered transference reactions and, indeed, transference reactions of some importance. Freud, however, saw these two types of reactions as factors to deal with expeditiously so that one can get back to the therapeutic work. He did not want to dwell on these reactions, but rather felt that while they may occur, they can be dealt with quickly, allowing the real work to proceed. As Freud says earlier in this same chapter, there are some "other patients [where] . . . their personal relation to him [the therapist] will force itself, for a time at least, unduly into the foreground" (Breuer and Freud 1893, p. 266). Thus, these personal reactions force themselves into the treatment and disrupt the treatment. By a disruption in the treatment, Freud meant that patients were no longer able to associate and produce material related to their pathogenic memories. The recovery of the pathogenic memories is the crucial element, while reaction of the patient to the physician was a disturbance not intrinsic to the material. To some extent, the hypnotic technique allowed one to bypass this difficulty; but, as Freud pointed out, the hypnotic technique had difficulties of its own. Moreover, based on Freud's experience and certainly Breuer's experience with Anna O., it was clearly possible for a patient to have intense reactions to the therapist even if one used hypnosis. It became Freud's destiny to deal with the intriguing issue of transference. It was a few years after writing the psychotherapy chapter that Freud treated a young woman who helped convince him that transference is a crucial and unavoidable element in the treatment situation.

DORA

Seven years after the publication of *Studies on Hysteria*, Freud wrote his first major psychoanalytic case report. During this time period, Freud's ideas had both developed and changed, particularly in terms of the etiology of neuroses. He had abandoned the seduction theory in 1896–1897 as a necessary or even a usual cause for neurotic conflict. He was on his way to developing his ideas about the universality of childhood or infantile sexuality. Moreover, he had just published what was perhaps his most significant psychoanalytic publication, *The Interpretation of Dreams* (1900). The case report of Dora consisted mainly of the analysis of two dreams. Although Freud stated that he was publishing the case in part to help more fully understand the etiology of hysteria, it is clear that these two dreams and their relation to his newly published "Dream Book" occupied center stage for Freud. In his postscript on the case, Freud developed yet another theme that significantly changed the practice of psychoanalysis. He relates that the failure of his treatment with Dora had to do with his handling of the transference. In this postscript, he states his views on transference.

Who was Dora and why did Freud want to publish a case that ended in such a frustrating manner? The first question is superficially easier to answer. Dora was a 16-year-old girl when Freud first interviewed her (at the behest of her father) and 18 years old when she entered analytic treatment with Freud. She stayed in treatment from October 1900 until December of the same year. She abandoned treatment at that time and informed Freud of her decision to leave treatment during their last session (on December 31, 1900). Dora was the daughter of an upper-middle-class Austrian family whose friendship with another family (Frau and Herr K.) occupied a place of special importance in her life. Dora's father was having an affair with Frau K., and Herr K. had been making advances to Dora from at least the time that she was 14 years old. Dora not only displayed a variety of symptoms, such as aphonia, chronic dyspnoea, unilateral headaches, attacks of nervous coughing, periodic depression, and at times suicidal ideation, but she was also obsessed with her father's relations with Frau K. to the extent that Freud called these thoughts *supervalent*. He used this term because it was his view that "no amount of conscious and voluntary effort of thought" on Dora's part was able to dissipate or remove these thoughts. She was not only obsessed with her father's sexual liaison, but clearly felt that many of her conflicts could be cleared up by changes in her father's behavior. She also desired her father's acceptance of the truth of her allegations concerning Herr K. Freud's view was that her "behavior went far beyond what would have been appropriate to filial concern. She felt and acted like a jealous wife" (1905, p. 56). Dora's father maintained that he didn't believe her allegations about Herr K. and that he considered these charges to be the fantasies of an adolescent girl. He also denied any sexual interest in Frau K. Dora's father was ostensibly turning to Freud for help in clearing up these fantasies and bringing Dora under control for her own good. Freud was suspicious of the father's motivations and realized that the father wanted Dora under control at least as much for his own benefit as for hers. Dora was upsetting the delicate balance of sexual liaisons between these two families.

Even though Freud evinced skepticism about the father's motivation, he agreed to see Dora in treatment. It is rare today for a modern commentator writing about this case not to join Freud in asserting that he did not perform as an ideal analyst with Dora. One can criticize Freud's performance from the very first consultation to the last meeting that he had with Dora. These criticisms have the benefit of ninety years of analytic or psychotherapeutic discussion and experience. Greenberg and Mitchell (1983), for instance, see the Dora case as a prime example of how Freud used what they call the drive-structural model. They take his understanding of Dora as an example of his final and more complete views "because it illustrates the way in which drives are construed as the sole determinants of an object relationship" (Greenberg and Mitchell 1983, p. 43). This interpretation shows that one can say virtually anything one wants about Freud's cases. Nearly every aspect of his theoretical understanding and the technique he applied in this case was to change over subsequent years. Even though analysts as eminent as Arlow have called for a moratorium in reinterpreting Freud's cases, they have been unsuccessful in halting other analysts from yet another exegesis of why Freud did what he did with Dora. The commentaries range from the sympathetic (Kanzer 1980b, Decker 1991) to the scornful (Langs 1980, Greenberg and Mitchell 1983); I would venture to say that we will continue to see them appear, since the attraction to reinterpreting Freud is so great.

Leaving aside modern renditions of Freud's motivations, what is clear is that he interprets early in the treatment and continues interpretations about Dora's repressed sexual wishes through the last day of treatment. For example, early in the case, Freud interprets that Dora's disgust at Herr K.'s kiss was really a reversal of affect and a displacement of sensations (Freud 1905b, pp. 28-29). Dora is viewed by Freud as presenting an admixture of adolescent love, incestuous fantasies, and, at rock bottom, conflicts over homosexual or lesbian relations (Freud 1905b, p. 120). This admixture is not unusual in an adolescent, but it is unusual to present this material to the adolescent without having gained some sense of her "cooperation" in the treatment. Here we can say that Freud's manner seems more that of a prosecuting attorney than an analyst. He treats Dora less as a confused and rebellious adolescent patient than as an adversary to be bested. It is, of course, a possibility that a rebellious adolescent might indeed break off a treatment even if things were handled reasonably well. But Freud did not handle the treatment well at all, and in hindsight it is easy to see that his treatment of her repeated the conflicts that she was going through with her father and Herr K.

Let us briefly go back to that last day of treatment. Freud in the previous two sessions has been analyzing the "second dream" of Dora. He has looked at this dream for most of the two sessions and he relates that on December 31,

> she opened the third session with these words: "Do you know that I am here for the last time today?" . . . "How can I know, as you have said nothing to me about it?" . . . "Yes, I made up my mind to put up with it till the New Year. But I shall wait no longer than that to be cured." . . . "You know that you are free to stop the treatment at any time. But for to-day we will go on with our work. When did you come to this decision?" . . . "A fortnight ago, I think." . . . "That sounds just like a maidservant or a governess—a fortnight's warning—" . . . "There was a governess who gave warning with the K.'s, when I was on my visit to them that time at L. (where she had a sexualized encounter with Herr K.), by the lake." . . . "Really? You never told me about her, tell me." [1905b, p. 107]

Dora then relates a story about the K.s' governess who told her that Herr
K. had made love to her and then abruptly ceased to pay attention to her. Herr
K. used virtually the same seduction language with this governess as he had
vith Dora. Freud interprets to Dora that she was not angry at Herr K.'s
·oposal to her, but that rather she was offended by him when she recognized
t the language he used with the governess was identical to the language he
zed in his entreaty to her. He goes on to further interpret that, like the
Dora wants Herr K. to leave his wife for her. In short, Freud continues
ne interpretations that have already proven to be less than completely
ʰul. He does not seriously consider her announcement that she is leaving
it, but continues with what he considers to be the analytic task; that is,
ɜ Dora's *true* thoughts and feelings. Whatever one's interpretation of
ₒ dynamics, one thing is certain: Freud aids Dora in acting out her
onflicts.[8] He repeatedly intrudes on her without seriously considering her
rience of the *analysis*. He attempts to defend his actions, but as one can see
ɔstscript, he develops serious misgivings about what transpired be-
ɹim and Dora. If we were going to pursue the case in greater detail, we
t wonder why Dora continued seeing Freud as long as she did, and why
ɛ answered so many of his questions. We might also want to explain why she
evisited Freud in April of 1902.

The question that we will speculate on is one that we asked before: Why
did Freud write up a case where the analysis was unsuccessful? Was it simply a
continuation of his Dream Book and an exposition of his views on hysteria or
was there something else that made it a special case? Apparently, Freud wrote
up this case quite quickly (Gay 1988) and yet he didn't publish the account of
the case until 1905. Gay indicates that Freud was "evidently disheartened by his
friend Oscar Rie's critical reception of the manuscript and also by the decay of
his most impassioned friendship" with Fliess (Gay 1988, p. 246). This no
doubt explains some delay in the publication, but it hardly seems to account for
the length of the delay, particularly since Freud was submitting other manuscripts during this period (e.g., *The Psychopathology of Everyday Life*, 1901).
Thus we may even be somewhat suspicious when Freud writes to Fliess that he
had withdrawn his work from the printer because "I (have) lost my last
audience in you" (Gay 1988, p. 246). There is evidence that Freud's relationship with Fliess was not the reason for the delay in the case being published.

The answer, if there is one, lies in part in Freud's postscript to the case.
We know that he must have written at least part of the postscript after April
1902 (since Dora saw him at this time and he included this visit in the
postscript). We also know that Freud was writing *The Psychopathology of
Everyday Life* (1901) during the same time period that he had written up the

---

[8]See Part II for a discussion of acting out, particularly Freud's paper, "Recollection, Repetition and
Working Through" (1914b).

Dora case. Freud wrote Fliess in 1897 (Letter 94) about issues that he covered in
The Psychopathology of Everyday Life. Why should he feel less encumbered in
terms of publishing this work as opposed to the case report? Fliess was as
much an audience for the issues covered in *The Psychopathology of Everyday
Life* as he would be for the case report. Moreover, Jones reports that Freud
attempted to publish the case report in June 1901, some time after the date of
the letter that Gay cites as the reason Freud withdrew the case report. On
June 9, 1901, Freud writes a letter to Fliess, one that Gay does not mention, in
which he tells Fliess that "'Dreams and Hysteria' has been sent off and will
probably not come to the attention of the astounded public until fall" (Masson
1985, p. 442). Jones reports (Jones 1955, p. 286) that the case was not accepted
for publication. An editor declined to publish the report maintaining that it
involved a breach of discretion. Thus, the issue of publication does not seem to
hinge on Freud's relationship to Fliess. One could say that Freud did not
immediately publish the case, since it was initially rejected, but why did he wait
another four years?

The editors of the Standard Edition state that "the internal evidence suggests . . . that he changed [the case report] very little during the four-year period.
The last section of the 'Postscript' was certainly added, as well as some passages
at least in the prefatory remarks . . ." (Freud 1905b, p. 5). They go on to note
that otherwise the paper seems to represent his views at the time. The issues in
which they are interested when they make this assertion are Freud's views on
sexuality and dreams. They point out that several of his letters written as early as
1897 have presaged his views on sexuality that do not appear in print until 1905
in "Three Essays on Sexuality." However, the postscript is a different matter.
There is a possibility that the section on Freud's last meeting with Dora was not
the only section added after 1902, but that several elements of his views on
transference were added as well. It is interesting in this context to note that Freud
published two papers between 1902 and 1904 on his new treatment, and does not
mention transference as an aspect of his treatment in either paper. In fact, the
term *transference* does not appear at all in these papers. This may be considered
indirect evidence that Freud wrote the passages on transference after those
papers were written. This is, of course, purely speculative, but what if the
speculation is correct? It would be one further piece of evidence that Freud's
realization of what had transpired with Dora came to him gradually, and
probably with a reasonable amount of psychological pain and conflict. Putting
aside this historical speculation, we can look at a curious mistake that Freud
makes three times in print. He mentions 1899, the wrong year, instead of the
correct year, 1900, when referring to his treatment of Dora. In his postscript, he
relates that he told Dora that the treatment would take approximately a year. By
his slip of dating the treatment 1899, Freud might have been expressing his wish
to rewrite history. If she had started in 1899, when she left Freud she would have
been in treatment for a little over a year. Perhaps things might have gone
differently, if only she had remained in treatment.

When Freud saw Dora for the last time in April 1902, he was still suspicious of her. He stated, "Dora came to see me again: to finish her story and to ask for help once more. One glance at her face, however, was enough to tell me that she was not in earnest over her request" (Freud 1905b, pp. 120–121). Even for Freud, one glance should not be pathognomonic. He is still feeling uneasy about her departure from analysis and obviously he felt he had been tricked by her. He saw her as viewing him as one of the *detestable men* on whom she wished to gain revenge; he was not going to be taken in again. His postscript on the importance of transference indicates that he wouldn't be fooled again, at least not in the same way. The measure of his genius and character is that he could eventually look at his failure and learn an important lesson that began to change the way he and generations of analysts after him conceived of patients' responses in analysis. Despite the fact that Freud was able to reassess his treatment of Dora, he was still tied strongly to his pathogenic memory model. Before we look again at his tie to the pathogenic memory model, let us go ahead to his views on transference.

Freud states in the postscript:

> During psycho-analytic treatment the formation of new symptoms is invariably stopped. But the productive powers of the neurosis are by no means extinguished; they are occupied in the creation of a special class of mental structures, for the most part unconscious, to which the name of 'transferences' may be given. [Freud 1905b, p. 116]

In the next paragraph, Freud presents a harbinger of his later views on the clinical significance of transference:

> What are the transferences? They are new editions or facsimiles of the impulses and phantasies which are aroused and made conscious during the progress of the analysis; but they have this peculiarity, which is characteristic for their species, that they replace some earlier person by the person of the physician. To put it another way: a whole series of psychological experiences are revived, not as belonging to the past, but as applying to the person of the physician at the present moment. Some of these transferences have a content which differs from that of their model in no respect whatever except for the substitution. These then—to keep to the same metaphor—are merely new impressions or reprints. Others are more ingeniously constructed; their content has been subjected to a moderating influence—to sublimation, as I call it—and they may even become conscious, by cleverly taking advantage of some real peculiarity in the physician's person or circumstances and attaching themselves to that. These, then, will no longer be new impressions, but revised editions. [Freud 1905b, p. 116]

In this cogent statement of transference, Freud presents a small model of the different varieties of transference. To be more precise, Freud is pointing out that what is transferred may appear largely uninfluenced or may be subject to change by conscious or preconscious influence. (That he calls this sublimation is a point worth considering if one were tracing the history of the concept of sublimation.) In the next paragraph, Freud addresses for the first time the significance of transference as a crucial process in analytic therapy:

> If the theory of analytic technique is gone into, it becomes evident that transference is an inevitable necessity. Practical experience, at all events, shows conclusively that there is no means of avoiding it, and that this latest creation of the disease must be combated like all the earlier ones. This happens, however, to be by far the hardest part of the whole task. It is easy to learn how to interpret dreams, to extract from the patient's associations his unconscious thoughts and memories, and to practise similar explanatory arts: for these the patient himself will always provide the text. Transference is the one thing the presence of which has to be detected almost without assistance and with only the slightest clues to go upon, while at the same time the risk of making arbitrary inferences has to be avoided. Nevertheless, transference cannot be evaded, since use is made of it in setting up all the obstacles that make the material inaccessible to treatment, and since it is only after the transference has been resolved that a patient arrives at a sense of conviction of the validity of the connections which have been constructed during the analysis. [Freud 1905b, pp. 116-117]

This marks a turning point; Freud is again considering transference to be an inevitable necessity but now there is a new sense of urgency. Approximately seven to nine years earlier his views on transference were similar, but he did not recognize the crucial role of transference for his new clinical work. Not only is transference essential, it is the vehicle that allows the patient the "conviction of the validity of the connections" made in an analysis. In *Studies on Hysteria*, Freud had already stated that "recollection without affect almost invariably produces no result." When he said this he was, of course, talking about the cathartic method, but this view remained unchanged: whatever the psychotherapeutic technique, the affect and the idea or mental representation must be experienced together in the treatment. In the developing analytic method, the idea and the affect and the conviction about the connections come via the transference. This is true even though Freud tells us it is "the hardest part of the whole (analytic) task" (Freud 1905b, p. 116).

We know that on the basis of his clinical experience with Dora he came to recognize that his failure in the case had to do with his lack of attention to Dora's repetitions of her conflicts in the treatment. Thus, Freud ignored the transference and concentrated on her sexual conflicts as he came to understand them through his analysis of her dreams, her associations to the dreams, and her history. He has stated that he wrote the case history of Dora as a continuation of his Dream Book (Freud 1905b); there are indications that Freud was disappointed to again come up against transference and thus find out about this new essential component of his evolving treatment method. It may be that his discovery and his reactions are a prototype for the analyst-in-training. It is quite common for an analyst to push away the transference and *regress* to the stance of psychotherapist, especially when the patient is manifesting signs of a transference reaction in which hostile wishes are expressed (negative transference). Most (perhaps all) beginning analysts have difficulty in dealing with transference manifestations of the treatment and find it easier to point out to the patient the unconscious meaning of a fantasy or to trace a patient's behavior or thoughts to their historical roots. In doing this, the transference is often avoided. In this interpretation, Freud's discovery of the analytic method is prototypic of the way most people come to know the analytic method. Freud was trying to avoid the implications of the transference by attempting to unravel Dora's pathogenic memories. Whether or not Freud's reactions can be considered prototypic, one can say that transference was the last major concept that Freud put forth in terms of his ideas on psychoanalytic technique. Even in the postscript he is not yet a welcoming creator to this new troublesome idea.

Freud calls transference an "inevitable necessity" (Freud 1905b, p. 116), hardly a receptive phrase. He also uses a military metaphor when he tells us that the latest creation (transference) must be combated like all the earlier ones. At times, when he uses a military metaphor, it appears that he is feeling less at ease with clinical material. When he tells us that "the physician's labours are not multiplied by transference" (Freud 1905b, p. 117), he is stating this in the same way in which he made this point in his psychotherapy chapter (Freud 1893–1895) several years earlier. He tells us on page 304 of that chapter that "transference . . . brought about no great addition to what I had to do." But these reassuring statements did not prove to be true. In the postscript, Freud, despite his uneasiness, is coming to terms with what was to become a revolutionary clinical concept.

Dora was the end of an era. After his experiences with her, Freud's conceptualization of the treatment situation would never be the same. We can say that the Dora case is a good example of a psychotherapy as Freud practiced it around 1899–1901. Although most of his fundamental concepts had been formed during these early years, all were to undergo some revision. Although his ideas about free association and resistance changed after Dora, he had already seen these as essential concepts for the therapeutic situation. It is only in the postscript of the Dora case that transference begins to be developed as an essential and curative component of psychoanalytic treatment. With the postscript to the Dora case and the later publication (seven years later) of "The Dynamics of Transference" (Freud 1912c), we see Freud stating why the handling of the transference is crucial in psychoanalysis. Even in the fully developed Freudian psychoanalytic technique, there is always a tension between analyzing the transference and attempting to recapture pathogenic memories. We follow this tension right up through the last of Freud's technique papers (Freud 1937b).

One might consider Freud's experiences with Dora an extension of the

Dream Book in a somewhat different way than Freud had considered this to be the case. In *The Interpretation of Dreams*, Freud provides a theoretical structure for the concept of transference (see Chapter 2 of this book). In his experiences with Dora he encounters transference in the clinical situation, and he is transformed into an analyst. This transformation was certainly not an immediate one (nor a fully lasting one), and I suspect it took Freud several years after he had seen Dora for the last time to come to terms with his new insights.[9] His delay in the publication of the case was symptomatic of the time he needed to address yet another upheaval in his conceptualization of the clinical situation.

[9]Bird (1972), an author we highlight in the transference section, has previously presented a similar view. He maintains that only as a result of Freud's "own self-analysis did he come to an understanding of the significance of transference." After he had understood transference via his relationship to Fliess, then he could apply to Dora "what he had learned in himself." Whether or not Freud learned about transference in his self-analysis, in my view it is likely that his delay in publication of the manuscript was because of his difficulties with the clinical implications of transference.

PART II

Transference as a Central Concept

2

The Evolution of the Concept of Transference

Freud's Early Theoretical Views

At this point in his career,[1] Freud had come to conceive of transference as a crucial aspect of the therapeutic process. One can only imagine that there were times when transference must have seemed, to the creator of psychoanalysis, like a living, breathing entity. Nevertheless the realization of the importance of transference was a painful one, given that it was conceived of amidst clinical difficulties and disappointments. It is no wonder that Freud's interest in the topic fluctuated throughout his career. As early as *Studies on Hysteria* and the Dora case, Freud was on his way toward recognizing the clinical importance of transference. In *The Interpretation of Dreams* (1900), written after *Studies on Hysteria*, Freud proposed a theoretical understanding of transference.

The concept of transference is explained as involving the unconscious system and preconscious system (two systems in what is called Freud's topographic model):

> An unconscious idea is as such quite incapable of entering the preconscious and can only exercise any effect there by establishing a connection with an idea which already belongs to the preconscious, by transferring its intensity on to it and by getting itself "covered" by it. Here we have the fact of "transference," which provides an explanation of so many striking phenomena in the mental life of neurotics. The preconscious idea, which thus acquires an undeserved degree of intensity (from the unconscious idea), may either be left unaltered by the

---

[1]One can specify "this point" as 1910–1911, the time of Freud's first transference paper. However, we know that Freud's recognition of the importance of transference comes sometime after the Dora case, and certainly by 1905 (the publication of the case).

transference, or it may have a modification forced upon it, derived from the content of the idea which effects the transference. [Freud 1900–1901, pp. 562–563]

Freud is telling us here that for an unconscious idea to have an effect on the preconscious, or eventually affect consciousness, it must transfer itself to an appropriate preconscious train of ideas or associations. In Chapter 7 of *The Interpretation of Dreams* he describes in detail the conditions for this type of transfer to take place. This theoretical statement is the converse of his ideas on defense or repression. Repression is, at this time, defined primarily as a withdrawal of cathexes[2] in the preconscious, from a given train of associations or ideas. When this withdrawal of cathexes takes place, the train of associations or ideas joins similar ideation already present in the unconscious. If the ideas of transference and defense are taken together, then we have a model for communication between the unconscious and preconscious systems. Repression is the manner in which ideas in the preconscious are rendered unconscious. Transference is the way unconscious ideas exert an influence in the preconscious. Freud intended this model to explain such divergent phenomena as dreams, slips of the tongue, and neurotic symptoms. In addition, the concept of the transference can obviously be used to explain why the analyst is the recipient of various unexpected feelings and thoughts during an analysis. Although Freud at the time possessed the intellectual framework to begin to understand transference, in the Dora case he did not yet understand that transference is important to the therapeutic situation. We see that even Freud's early theoretical understanding did not prepare him for the intensity of Dora's transference reactions.

A New Era

By the time (1907–1908) Freud was analyzing the Rat Man (Ernst Lanzer was his real name), his understanding of transference was considerably changed. In the published case, there were several detailed dreams and fantasies that Freud understood as manifestations of transference. Freud's daily notes for the beginning months of the case were found, and in the notes he relates a number of reactions of the patient that he considered to be transference manifestations. For example, in Freud's notes on November 21, he writes that only "after a fourty minutes' struggle" did Ernst see the implications of the transference. Analyzing the transference is now an important component of Freud's ideas about analytic treatment. During this session the Rat Man comes to a point (as was the case with Dora) where he wants to leave the treatment (in fact he wants Freud to put him out because he professes to be unworthy of warranting

---

[2]*Cathexis* is roughly translated as the amount of energy or interest in a given idea or mental representation.

Freud's time and attention). In this instance Freud does not (as he did with Dora) ignore the Rat Man's ideas about leaving the treatment. Rather he interprets to the patient that his refusal to talk and his wish to end the treatment are both elements of hostility directed at Freud. To quote from the notes:

> He came in a state of deep depression, and wanted to talk about indifferent subjects; but he soon admitted that he was in a crisis. The most frightful thing had occurred to his mind while he was in the tram yesterday. It was quite impossible to say it. His cure would not be worth such a sacrifice. I should turn him out, for it concerned the transference. Why should I put up with such a thing? None of the explanations I gave him about the transference . . . had any effect. It was only after a forty minutes' struggle—as it seemed to me—and after I had revealed the element of revenge against me and had shown him that by refusing to tell me and by giving up the treatment he would be taking a more outright revenge on me than by telling me—only after this did he give me to understand that it concerned my daughter. With this, the session came to an end. (Next day) It was still hard enough . . . he (then) surrendered the first of his ideas:
>
> (a) A naked female bottom, with nits (larvae of lice) in the hair.
>
> *Source*: A scene with his sister Julie which he had forgotten in his confession to me. After their romp she had thrown herself back on the bed in such a way that he saw those parts of her from in front . . . The themes are clear. Punishment for the pleasure he felt at the sight, asceticism making use of the technique of disgust, anger with me for forcing him to become aware of this; hence the transference thought, 'No doubt the same thing happens among your children.' (He has heard of a daughter of mine and knows I have a son.) . . . After quieting down and a short struggle he made a further difficult start on a whole series of ideas which, however, impressed him differently. He realized that he had no need to make use of the transference in their case, but the influence of the first case had made all the others go into the transference. [Freud 1909b, pp. 281-282]

The Rat Man had heard about Freud's daughter, and he knew that Freud also had a son. His transference reaction to Freud involved a fantasy about Freud's daughter. In contrast to the treatment of Dora, Freud is able to help the patient understand his reaction, and Ernst is able to continue in analysis. We can see that the concept of transference is no longer simply a theoretical tool, but rather an idea that directly affects Freud's clinical practice.

It is clear from this example that although Freud is now acknowledging the transference, his view of transference is still a limited one as is portrayed in his first paper on transference, "The Dynamics of Transference" (1912). There he sees transference primarily as a manifestation of resistance, and even in the example we can see that he is trying to help the patient *give up* his transference. It is interesting to see the evolution of his views from 1912 to 1914, and later in this chapter we trace this evolution.

Freud wrote about the Rat Man only three years before he published his first paper on technique. Jones and Gay indicate that as early as 1908 (Jones 1955b, Gay 1988), Freud was considering writing papers, or a book, that would be a general account of his psychoanalytic technique. Thus, during the time that Freud was seeing the Rat Man, he was contemplating the writing of the technique papers. We might say that Freud's treatment of the Rat Man is a reasonable indication of how he practiced psychoanalysis during the period of 1908–1912 (and beyond), just as we indicated that the Dora case is a good example of the psychotherapy Freud practiced at the turn of the century. Thus, the comparison of these two cases is in some ways a good indicator of the evolution of Freud's technique. (See Chapter 15 for a fuller comparison of these cases.)

Freud and Diagnostic Categories

Formal diagnosis was never a major concern for Freud. It was his belief that psychiatric nosology had little to offer psychoanalysis. Freud at times was involved with self-imposed diagnostic discriminations, and these are of importance if we are to understand some facets of Freud's thoughts about transference. In the 1890s, the concept of actual neurosis was an important diagnostic entity for Freud. When Freud saw patients who complained about anxiety reactions, a lack of energy (neurasthenia), or certain phobic reactions, etc., he assumed that the cause of these psychological difficulties had an actual physiological etiology. The physiological factor had to do with sexual practices and with appropriate orgasm. Thus, if one is a virgin and has not had sufficient sexual experiences, sexual libido (roughly, sexual tension or excitement) might accumulate and result in anxiety or even phobic reactions. Sexual practices of the time, such as coitus interruptus or reservatus, were interpreted by Freud as also leading to a tendency toward actual neurotic reactions. One must remember that, given the early stages of prophylactic devices, sexual practices such as coitus interruptus or reservatus were common at the time. Freud's remedies for symptoms that he diagnosed as a result of actual sexual practices involved straightforward counsel that advocated fuller sexuality. He thought that more sexual activity (with appropriate orgasm) would discharge the accumulating libido. Thus, the actual neurosis could be dealt with by sexual activities that would then dispel the symptoms.

Freud contrasted the actual neuroses with psychogenic neuroses, i.e., hysterical, obsessional, and some anxiety neuroses. He also believed that certain psychotic disorders were psychogenically derived. Psychogenic disorders, as we have seen, involved early trauma or at least difficulties in the person's early life. These difficulties, stored as memories, are stimulated at the time of the appearance of the person's symptoms. Before 1900, Freud had distinguished between actual and psychogenic neuroses and had developed ideas about hysteria, obsessional neuroses, and some beginning ideas about psychotic states (Freud 1894). He also believed that there were frequently mixed disorders, that is, disorders that were combinations of psychogenic and actual neuroses. In a series of papers from 1894 to 1900, Freud gradually spells out these concepts.

Freud explicitly puts forth the concept of fixation points (1911) in a paper about the now famous Dr. Schreber, "Psycho-Analytic Notes on an Autobiographical Account of a Case of Paranoia (Dementia Paranoides)." At this point, he has de-emphasized the concept of actual neurosis and has concentrated on psychogenic disorders. In section three of this work, Freud introduces the concept of narcissism. He tries to show that paranoia and schizophrenia have their roots in a person's early childhood during the narcissistic stage of development. The concept of narcissism is developed in several subsequent papers (Freud 1911, 1914c, 1915b, 1916/1917). In one of these papers, "On Narcissism: An Introduction" (1914c), he briefly reintroduces the concept of actual disorders. Here he maintains that not only are there actual neuroses but also actual narcissistic disorders. Hypochondriacal disorders are the actual narcissistic disorders that he cites. Thus, in some unspecified way, a person may actually focus narcissistic energy in a particular area of the body and develop later hypochondriacal symptoms. By 1917, Freud had specified fixation points for depression, paranoia, schizophrenia, and the transference neuroses (hysterical and obsessional neuroses). The transference neuroses involve fixation points that occur after the person has developed beyond the narcissistic stage. Freud called this point the stage of object love (Freud 1913a). He had an evolving diagnostic scheme that by 1917 included the psychogenic disorders and actual disorders. The psychogenic categories include the neuroses, depression, paranoia, and the schizophrenias. The actual disorders include neurotic symptoms and hypochondriacal symptoms.

One can tell even from this abbreviated summary of Freud's views that, as he developed as a clinician and theorist, he moved away from the importance of the actual neuroses in his conceptualizations (in fact, he rarely referred to this concept after 1900). Still, it is not until 1925a, in "Inhibitions, Symptoms and Anxiety," that he completely gives up the idea of actual disorders. Although the actual disorders were similar to ideas of the sexologists of his time, it is of some interest that Freud developed these ideas and continued to hold them for such a long period of time. It is my belief that the concept of transference can loosely be thought of as inversely related to the idea of actual neurosis. The concept of transference begins to put the focus on the relationship between the analyst and the patient. The actual neurosis takes the focus to the external world and the patient's real involvements. As Freud has shown, the transference relationship is frequently difficult for both patient and analyst to focus on; the analyst is brought into the patient's world and in direct touch with the patient's conflicts. It is at times hard to understand transference without taking into account the analyst's reactions to a patient's conflicts. The actual neurosis is a mechanical explanation, allowing the clinician to prescribe remedies that permit both analyst and patient to focus on the external world and away from their relationship. It is my view that Freud invoked the actual neurosis when the transference might prove to be a difficult one, or when for some reason he was not able to experience the patient's reactions to him. This could be the case with certain hypochondriacal patients who frequently have narcissistic difficulties. Freud's experience may have been that the patients were preoccupied with themselves and not concerned with him. Kohut and Bach (Kohut 1971, Bach 1985) write about the difficulties that such narcissistic patients pose for analytic clinicians. The analyst feels disregarded, at times bored, and is not engaged with this person, who seemingly completely absorbs himself in his bodily functions. It is often the case that these patients, at the beginning of treatment, will not be at all interested in what Freud considered the analytic task: free association. Thus it is my speculation that Freud may have used the diagnosis of an actual disorder (either neurosis or narcissistic), when he was unable to experience the patient reacting to him. This obviously was not his view, but it is my interpretation of why he utilized the diagnosis of actual disorder.

"Dynamics of Transference," "Recollection, Repetition and Working Through," and "Observations on Transference Love"

In most of the technique papers, transference is implicitly a central issue. In these three papers, Freud is explicitly setting out his views on transference. In the *Introductory Lectures* (1917), Freud summarizes these ideas, but not until "Beyond the Pleasure Principle" does Freud write again on the concept of transference (Freud 1920). If we compare "The Dynamics of Transference" with "Recollection, Repetition and Working Through" (Freud 1914b), we see a subtle, although decisive, shift in Freud's conceptualizations. In the "Dynamics" paper, Freud tells us that the concept of transference must be considered in three different ways. First, transference must be seen in terms of two different erotic types of transference. An erotic transference per se is a manifestation of defended or repressed *erotic impulses* or sexual fantasies. This transference represents some aspect of an early frustrated love (or sexualized) relationship. It is a representation of a relationship to some important person (love object), fantasized or real, in the patient's past. The transference relationship to the analyst is considered a displacement of this past relationship. The second type of erotic transference has been named the unobjectionable transference. "This type of transference is conscious, and brings about the successful result in psychoanalysis as in all other remedial methods" (Freud 1912c, p. 319).

The "negative transference" is the third type and, according to Freud, required a more thorough elucidation than was possible within the limits of that paper (Freud 1912c). In the curable forms of the neuroses "it is found alongside the affectionate transference," and Freud, following Beuler, calls this *ambivalence* (Freud 1912c). He briefly mentions the obsessional neuroses and points out, as he had previously done in the Rat Man and the Schreber cases, the relationship between obsessionals and paranoics. In obsessionals, there is an early separation of the positive and negative object representations (hence the ambivalence), but in paranoids Freud considers that there is not only a separation but the negative tendency to predominate over the positive representations. He considers the capacity for positive transference crucial in assessing the person's analyzability; he tells us that if the person's capacity for transference is limited to a negative one, there ceases to be any possibility of influence or cure. We hypothesize that if Freud was unable to sense relatively quickly the person's capacity for positive transference, then it was very difficult for him to treat the person, regardless of diagnosis. Patients who were labeled actual neurotics might very well have been those patients who did not display positive transference reactions toward Freud. These patients likely were not neurotics, but might have included a wide range of diagnostic types: in modern terms, hypochondriacal, narcissistic, borderline, and incapsulated psychotic patients.

Both the erotic positive and the negative transference are vehicles of resistance and as such must be interpreted quickly to the patient. For as soon as the patient comes under the influence of an extreme transference–resistance, "he then arrogates to himself the freedom to ignore the psychoanalytic rule (communicate without reserve whatever goes through his mind)" (Freud 1912c, p. 321). Although Freud has traveled a distance from his original ideas, the fundamental rule[3] is still (and always will be) the rule of free association. This rule must be respected so that one can fill in the gaps in terms of infantile or childhood memories. It is true that these gaps can only be filled in by allowing the patient to repeat her or his conflicts in the treatment. Freud, however, did not give up the essential idea of making pathogenic memories conscious. In this paper, his focus is mainly on regarding transference in terms of resistance. Thus, one can say that in "The Dynamics of Transference," he is demonstrating the continuity of the new technique with his past techniques (hypnosis, the pressure technique, and early psychotherapy or analysis). The continuity is based on the emphasis of the use of transference as a tool to recover memories.

Interestingly, he begins the "Recollection and Repetition" paper by comparing the hypnotic technique to the new psychoanalytic technique. After stating several differences he says that "the aim of these different techniques has, of course, remained the same throughout: descriptively, to recover the lost memories; dynamically, to *conquer* (italics mine) the resistances caused by

---

[3]The term *fundamental rule* is actually a term translated in the Standard Edition. In the present translation it is translated as the *psychoanalytic rule*. Since the term *fundamental rule* is so popular in English-speaking psychoanalytic circles, I have chosen to use it in this work.

repression" (p. 367). Although Freud begins the "Recollection" paper looking backward, the remainder of this short paper is remarkable in the number of new concepts that are presented.[4] This paper is considered notable in that in it Freud first mentions the compulsion to repeat and work through, yet it is of particular interest in this context because he makes his clearest statement about the importance of transference. The significance of transference is further highlighted when he introduces the concept of transference neurosis.

Transference neurosis is to have at least as long and extensive a history as the concept of the unobjectionable transference (London and Rosenblatt, 1987). A number of classical psychoanalysts have differed with both of these formulations. The term *transference neurosis* is one that has two somewhat overlapping meanings. When Freud used the term "transference neurotic," he was referring to a person with a particular diagnosis (Freud 1916/1917). Thus, hysterics and obsessional patients were called transference neurotics. The term transference neurosis or "transformed neurosis" (Freud 1916/1917) is used to note his view that, in his new analytic method, the original conflicts that caused the symptoms (or character traits) should be brought to the treatment situation via the transference. It was his thought that the formation of a full transference neurosis at some point during the treatment was essential for a completed analysis. Thus, at some point in the treatment, the patient should fully repeat his childhood conflicts via the transference. This perspective is one that has certainly been debated.

It was Freud's stance that only transference neurotics could be analyzed. This is stated in perhaps too restrictive a fashion, but it was certainly his thought that the more narcissism in a given person, the less the possibility of a successful analysis. Thus he stated: "We have good reason to recognize and to *dread* in the amount of his narcissism a barrier against the possibility of being influenced by even the best analytic technique . . . in general a man is only accessible . . . in so far as he is capable of a libidinal cathexis of objects" (Freud 1916/1917, p. 446). Patients capable of a libidinal cathexis were seen as capable of displacing this libidinal cathexis onto the person of the analyst. As importantly, they were capable of forming an unobjectionable positive transference relationship with the analyst. Without this, Freud saw the analytic task as difficult if not impossible. Freud took the paranoic as a prototype of narcissistic patients. He assumed that they had not formed stable-enough object relationships and were therefore not capable of forming a transference relationship with an analyst. Latter-day commentators have interpreted that Freud used the term *narcissistic* when he really meant *psychotic*. While this is certainly true at times, it is unlikely that he viewed all the hypochondriacal and neurasthenic patients he saw as psychotic. Yet all these patients were deemed unanalyzable. What is more likely is that Freud used these categories when he

---

[4]The paper was written about the time he was working on his most extensive case report (the Wolf Man).

was unable to experience any positive transference. We have interpreted his use of the diagnostic category of actual disorder to denote a case in which he was unable to experience a patient's psychological difficulties. He used the diagnostic category of narcissism when he recognized a patient's psychological difficulties, but was unable to detect a capacity for positive transference. In both instances, the patient is seen as unanalyzable.

Freud considered "Transference Love" (Freud 1915b) his finest technical paper; to some extent this is puzzling. In both "The Dynamics of Transference" and "Recollection, Repetition and Working Through," he introduced new concepts that influenced modern psychoanalytic theorizing. In the "Transference Love" paper, there are no such breakthroughs. Yet, obviously Freud greatly valued this paper. The paper consists of a discussion of the dangers of the transference overflowing the boundaries of the treatment situation. In this paper, Freud in effect warns the analyst to remember that transference love is simply another manifestation of transference and not to be acted on by patient or analyst. Here Freud is showing once again that he understands the concept of transference, not as an intellectual idea, but as something that he has intensely experienced in the analytic situation. Perhaps he most liked this paper because it is entirely clinical and stays with the analyst's experience of both the transference and potentially the countertransference. Although Freud did not write explicitly about countertransference (he mentioned the concept only four times in his career), one can view this paper as an essay about the dangers of countertransference reactions, particularly when the transference becomes intense and highly eroticized. As always with Freud, the paper touches on many more points, but it seems that Freud has taken this occasion to point out possible danger situations for the psychoanalyst.

Whatever Freud's reasons for his fondness of this paper, we can say that it is the culmination of his writing about transference. In my estimation, he begins to write about the importance of transference sometime after he sees Dora and he ends his exploration of the importance of transference with the "Transference Love" paper. During the writing of this series of papers, he no longer showed the elements of hesitancy that were characteristic of his writing in the Dora case and *Studies on Hysteria*. Rather, he had come to discover the importance of transference in a gradual and, I believe, prototypic manner. Thus the "Transference Love" and "Recollection" papers present us with an analyst who now firmly believes in the importance of transference in the clinical situation.

It has become fashionable to say that Freud did not practice what he advocated—that, for instance, he did not really analyze transference in the treatment situation. If we were to judge solely on the basis of the evolution of his thinking and the incisive way he eventually writes about transference, this seems quite unlikely. From his papers, it appears that uncovering the importance of transference was a slow and seemingly painful process. Still, Freud frequently reverted to what I have called the pathogenic memory model, where he would be content to analyze or reconstruct the patient's past while only minimally dealing with the transference.

The way he often dealt with transference would be considered fragmentary by today's standards. For example, what he calls a transference neurosis might today be considered the beginnings of a transference reaction. He certainly did not always focus on the transference in the way he suggested was necessary in a psychoanalytic treatment. But Freud must, at various times, have practiced what he wrote about. If this were not the case, the gradual and lawful development of his ideas is hard to explain. Moreover, these ideas fit in too well with the obvious clinical struggles that he partially chronicles for us with Dora. In "Recollection, Repetition and Working Through" and "Transference Love," he goes as far as he will travel away from the focus on pathogenic memories and toward the idea of analytic treatment being structured as a type of "playground, in which it (transference) is allowed to let itself go in almost complete freedom and is required to display before us all the pathogenic impulses hidden in the depths of the patient's mind" (Freud 1914b, p. 374). At this point, Freud is no longer viewing the transference as an *inevitable necessity* but is welcoming it into the arena of the analytic situation.

Freud's last significant writing about transference occurs in an unlikely place: "Beyond the Pleasure Principle," a major theoretical work in which his ideas about the nature of instincts or drives change. In this paper, written in 1920, he again asserts that a "patient cannot remember the whole of what is repressed in him, and what he cannot remember may be precisely the essential" aspect of his neurosis. Thus, if an analyst constructs the past for the patient:

> He acquires no sense of conviction of the correctness of the construction that has been communicated to him. He is obliged to repeat the repressed material as a contemporary experience instead of, as the physician would prefer to see, remembering it as something belonging to the past. When the person's infantile sexual life fully emerges in the transference, "It may be said that the earlier neurosis has now been replaced by a fresh 'transference neurosis.'" The analyst attempts "to keep this transference neurosis within the narrowest limits: to force as much as possible into the channel of memory and to allow as little as possible to emerge as repetition. The ratio between what is remembered and what is reproduced varies from case to case. . . . He (the analyst) must get him to re-experience some portion of his forgotten life, but must see to it, on the other hand, that the patient retains some degree of aloofness, which will enable him, in spite of everything, to recognize that what appears to be reality is in fact only a reflection of a forgotten past. [Freud 1920, p. 18]

In this historic paper Freud proposes the idea of the compulsion to repeat as an innate factor in all human beings (or in all organic life) and not only in neurotics. He introduces the concept of the ego as a structure (this was written two years before "The Ego and the Id") and points out that resistance does not spring from the unconscious but rather from the ego. In addition, in this paper and "The Ego and the Id," he clarifies the concept of defense as a fully unconscious process. In the quote above, Freud says that the analyst must help the patient to gain some degree of aloofness with respect to the analysis. Here he is pointing out that patients have to observe what is happening to them while the analysis is proceeding. Thus, Freud introduces the concept of the observing ego, where the patient can observe with the analyst what is going on and comprehend with the analyst what is being unleashed in the analytic process.

While the concept of the observing ego is important, what is of particular interest is the way in which Freud has here reaffirmed the concepts of transference and the transference neurosis. Since we know that his ideas are subject to change, it is significant that he has again highlighted these ideas in a major theoretical paper. His ideas on transference do not change or evolve after this publication.[5] The transference neurosis as a concept is not fully developed, nor does Freud give us clinical vignettes to illustrate what he means by transference neurosis. It is particularly significant to note that, while Freud reaffirmed the importance of transference, he never fully departs from the pathogenic memory model. He even leaves open the possibility that some patients may remember to a significant extent and therefore only have to repeat their conflicts minimally in analysis. In conclusion, we can see that Freud allows the idea of transference and his earlier ideas about pathogenic memories to linger side by side without his fully reconciling these concepts. He knows that the patient "is obliged to repeat the repressed material as a contemporary experience," but he still wishes that the patient would be able to remember these tendencies "as something belonging to the past" (Freud 1920, p. 18).

---

[5]He does state in *An Autobiographical Study*, written in 1925, that transference is a universal phenomenon of the mind and as such dominates the person's relation to his environment. This statement, while significant, does not in any way advance the concept of transference.

3

The Transference Papers

The Dynamics of the Transference[1]

(1912)

The almost inexhaustible subject of 'transference' has recently been dealt with in this Journal by W. Stekel in a descriptive manner.[2] I wish to add a few remarks in order to make clear how it happens that the transference inevitably arises during the analysis ■ 1 and comes to play its well-known part in the treatment.

Let us bear clearly in mind that every human being has acquired, by the combined operation of inherent disposition and of external influences in childhood, a special individuality in the exercise of his capacity to love—that is, in the conditions which he sets up for loving, in the impulses he gratifies by it, and in the aims he sets out to achieve in it.[3] This forms a *cliché* or stereotype in

■ 1
There are analysts who would not see transference as inevitably arising in the analytic situation. Freud himself maintained that patients with too much narcissism (narcissistic libido) would not be able to develop a transference relationship with an analyst. Kohut observes that narcissistic patients often have what he called strong nonspecific resistances to manifesting transference reactions in an analytic treatment. Transference is manifested only when these nonspecific resistances are analyzed.

[1]First published in the *Zentralblatt*, Bd. II., 1912; reprinted in *Sammlung*, Vierte Folge. [Translated by Joan Riviere.]
[2]*Zentralblatt*, Bd. II., Nr. II. S. 26.
[3]We will here provide against misconceptions and reproaches to the effect that we have denied the importance of the inborn (constitutional) factor because we have emphasized the importance of infantile impressions. Such an accusation arises

him, so to speak (or even several), which perpetually repeats and reproduces itself as life goes on, in so far as external circumstances and the nature of the accessible love-objects permit, and is indeed itself to some extent modifiable by later impressions. Now our experience has shown that of these feelings which determine the capacity to love only a part has undergone full psychical development; this part is directed towards reality, and can be made use of by the conscious personality, of which it forms part. The other part of these libidinal impulses has been held up in development, withheld from the conscious personality and from reality, and may either expend itself only in phantasy, or may remain completely buried in the unconscious so that the conscious personality is unaware of its existence. Expectant libidinal impulses will inevitably be roused, in anyone whose need for love is not being satisfactorily gratified in reality, by each new person coming upon the scene, and it is more than probable that both parts of the libido, the conscious and the unconscious, will participate in this attitude.

---

out of the narrowness with which mankind looks for causes, inasmuch as one single causal factor satisfies him, in spite of the many commonly underlying the face of reality. Psychoanalysis has said much about the 'accidental' component in ætiology and little about the constitutional, but only because it could throw new light upon the former, whereas of the latter it knows no more so far than is already known. We deprecate the assumption of an essential opposition between the two series of ætiological factors; we presume rather a perpetual interchange of both in producing the results observed. δαίμων καὶ τύχη determine the fate of man; seldom, perhaps never, one of these powers alone. The relative ætiological effectiveness of each is only to be measured individually and in single instances. In a series comprising varying degrees of both factors extreme cases will certainly also be found. According to the knowledge we possess we shall estimate the parts played by the forces of heredity and of environment differently in each case, and retain the right to modify our opinion in consequence of new knowledge. Further, we may venture to regard constitution itself as a residue from the effects of accidental influences on the endless procession of our forefathers. ■ 2

■ 2

Here Freud is defending himself from being accused of placing too much emphasis on environmental factors. Clearly, in his mind men of science emphasized heredity and physiological factors. He was frequently defensive about not being considered a man of science by physicians, even though he was differing with that same group on many, if not most, issues. Today, he has often been criticized for overly stressing factors of endowment. Not only is there something of a movement away from Freud's biologically oriented concepts, such as drive or instinct, but there are many analysts who advocate considering the analytic session as a literary text. Thus, Ricoeur and a variety of analysts with similar positions such as Spence and Schafer, would maintain that the analytic session should be viewed as such a text much the way the field of hermeneutics views any type of written text. If one accepts this premise, then there are various criteria for judging the adequacy of an interpretation, such as parsimony and completeness. For the analytic situation at least, this position moves the analyst some distance away from ideas of drive and perhaps even childhood sexuality.

It is therefore entirely normal and comprehensible that the libido-cathexes, expectant and in readiness as they are in those who have not adequate gratification, should be turned also towards the person of the physician. ■ 3 As we should expect, this accumulation of libido will be attached to prototypes, bound up with one of the *clichés* already established in the mind of the person concerned, or, to put it in another way, the patient will weave the figure of the physician into one of the 'series' already constructed in his mind. If the physician should be specially connected in this way with the father-imago (as Jung has happily named[4] it) it is quite in accordance with his actual relationship to the patient; ■ 4 but the transference is not bound to this prototype; it can also proceed from the mother- or brother-imago and so on. The peculiarity of the transference to the physician lies in its excess, in both character and degree, over

[4]*Symbole und Wandlungen der Libido.*

■ 3

Even in these two paragraphs Freud has managed to provide the beginnings of a theoretical position. He deals with environmental influence in a brief but definite statement. The environment can be a factor in change even relatively late in a person's life. He also states that both the conscious and unconscious portions of the libido (or sexuality) will have a share in forming the person's attitudes in love. His main interest, however, is in the portion of libidinal impulses that has been held up in the course of development and thus kept

■ 3 *continued*

away from the conscious personality and reality. Only a year before the present paper, Freud had developed his most complete model of fixation points in Chapter Three of the Schreber case. There he posited different fixation points for paranoia, schizophrenia, and the neuroses. In several other papers shortly after the present paper, he continued to develop this idea of fixation points and added specific points for the obsessive-compulsive and the melancholic or depressive. Although all fixation points lead to a derailment of libidinal development, analysis is not suitable (according to Freud) for all people that have such difficulties. From Freud's point of view, libidinal development must have progressed to conflicts that involved the object in terms of either object choice or as a love object (see disposition to obsession neurosis on the last pages of "Mourning and Melancholia"). If the person was not at the point of having such conflicts (and therefore had some type of narcissistic or psychotic disorder), then Freud believed that person was unable to be treated in analysis. They were also unable to display transference reactions, since for Freud the main form of transference literally was the turning of loving libidinal impulses "towards the person of the physician." We will see in this paper that Freud is primarily concerned with erotic transference states; this too is part of his ongoing concern with in-

fantile sexuality, the role of infantile sexuality in neurotic and psychotic development, and the influence of infantile sexuality in the choice of a love object.

Many analysts since Freud (and Abraham and others during Freud's lifetime) have defined transference more broadly and noted that patients with narcissistic disorders (Kohut) and borderline disorders (Winnicott, Kernberg) are able to develop stable transference relationships in analysis. Stone has written about the widening scope of psychoanalysis. Jacobson has written exquisite, although dense, descriptions of the nature of psychotic transference states. In addition, she has broadened the concept of transference. Freud's ideas on transference are based on the idea that the patient will displace or transfer unto the physician an existing fantasy of a person in the patient's past. Jacobson considers the projection of an aspect of the patient's ideas or fantasies about himself to be an important aspect of transference as well. Meissner has developed similar points in a series of papers.

■ 4

In this paragraph Freud states his view that if the patient sees the analyst in terms of a father-imago, that is quite in accordance with the analyst's "actual relationship to the patient." This implies that the analyst is, or should be, a paternal authority figure. Freud assumed that if the analyst was viewed in this light, his influence would help the analysis

■ *4 continued*

proceed. Other analysts such as Winnicott see the analyst as providing a more maternal atmosphere, one more akin to what Winnicott has called "good enough mothering or parenting." Still other analysts (Brenner, Kanzer) argue strongly that the analyst should provide an atmosphere of neutrality. Neither parental image is appropriate for the analyst to adopt. Patients, of course, should be free to see the analyst in any way that they choose, but in this conceptualization the analyst should avoid adopting a particular role. Of course, Freud would agree that patients should be free to see the analyst in any way that they choose, but implicitly here and explicitly elsewhere, Freud states that he does not think that the adoption of a particular stance by the analyst will affect the patient's ability to transfer unto the analyst. The issue of the neutrality of the analyst is one that is often popularly associated with Freud. As we can see here, Freud does not make a great effort to maintain neutrality. Rather, he accepts that the patient will view him in one or another manner because of some reality factors (how he acts, his office decor, etc.), some sociological factors (how the society at any point in time views analysts), and, most importantly, because of transference factors. From his point of view, the other factors will not seriously affect how the transference is manifested.

what is rational and justifiable—a peculiarity which becomes comprehensible when we consider that in this situation the transference is effected not merely by the conscious ideas and expectations of the patient, but also, by those that are under suppression, or unconscious.

Nothing more would need to be said or would perplex us concerning this characteristic of the transference, if it were not that two points which are of particular interest to psycho-analysts still remain unexplained by it. First, it is not clear why neurotic subjects under analysis develop the transference so much more intensely than those who are not being analysed; and secondly, it remains a mystery why in analysis the transference provides the *strongest resistance* to the cure, whereas in other forms of treatment we recognize it as the vehicle of the healing process, the necessary condition for success. Experience shows, and a test will always confirm it, that when the patient's free associations fail[5] the obstacle can be removed every time by an assurance that he is now possessed by a thought which concerns the person of the physician or something relating to him. No sooner is this explanation given than the obstacle is removed, or at least the absence of thoughts has been transformed into a refusal to speak. ■ 5

It appears at the first glance to be an enormous disadvantage in psycho-analysis as compared with other methods that in it the transference, elsewhere such a powerful instrument for success, should become here the most formidable ally of the resistance. On closer consideration, however, the first of these difficulties at least will disappear. It is not the fact that the transference in psycho-analysis develops more intensely and immoderately than outside it. Institutions and homes for the treatment of nervous patients by methods other than analysis provide instances of transference in its most excessive and unworthy forms, extending even to complete subjection, which also show its erotic character unmistakably. A sensitive observer, Gabriele Reuter, depicted these facts at a time when psycho-analysis hardly existed, in a remarkable book[6] which altogether reveals great insight into the nature and causes of the neuroses. This peculiarity of the transference is not, therefore, to be placed to the account of psycho-analysis but is to be ascribed to the neurosis itself. The second problem still remains unexplained.

This problem must now be tackled at close quarters: Why does the transference in analysis confront us as resistance? Let us call to mind the psychological situation in the treatment. One of

■ 5

When Freud talks about transference emerging "as the most powerful resistance to the treatment" and says that the "absence of thoughts is transformed into a refusal to speak," he is stating a view of his that was put forth in the psychotherapy chapter of *Studies on Hysteria*. In this paragraph, he writes as if the paramount goal of psychoanalytic treatment is the removal of obstacles to the patient's ability to free associate. This is in one sense the goal, but it is a matter of emphasis as to whether one sees the transference primarily as a powerful resistance to be cleared away, or as the main vehicle of the treatment. Thus, one might emphasize the resistance function of transference manifestations, or one might emphasize how, in the repetition that occurs in transference reactions, the patients are able to see the most complete and convincing manifestations of their conflicts. This issue is obviously colored by one's theoretical stance; if the recollection or reconstruction of childhood memories is viewed as the crucial aspect of psychoanalysis, then transference is more likely to be seen as a resistance to

[5]I mean here, when really nothing comes to his mind, and not when he keeps silence on account of some slight disagreeable feeling.
[6]*Aus guter Familie*, 1895.

■ 5 *continued*
recovering pathogenic memories. If one believes, as Gill does,
that transference is virtually the
only vehicle of the analytic situation, then recollection or reconstruction is not the main point;
all that is necessary is the analysis of the transference.

In this paragraph, Freud
is looking back toward his psychotherapeutic model (in terms
of the recovery of memories)
but is also building his argument, by chronicling how he
came upon the concept of
transference

the invariable and indispensable preliminary conditions in *every* case of psychoneurosis is the process which Jung has aptly named *introversion* of
the libido.[7] This means that the quantity of libido
which is capable of becoming conscious, and is
directed towards reality, has become diminished,
while the part which is unconscious and turned
away from reality (and, although it may still nour-
ish phantasies in the person concerned, belongs to
the unconscious) is by so much increased. The
libido (entirely or in part) has found its way back
into regression and has re-animated the infantile
imagos[8]; and thither we pursue it in the analytic
treatment, aiming always at unearthing it, making
it accessible to consciousness and at last service-
able to reality. Wherever in our analytic delving
we come upon one of the hiding-places of the

[7]Although many of Jung's utterances give the impression that
he sees introversion as something characteristic of dementia
præcox and not observable to the same extent in the other
neuroses.

[8]It would be easy to say: the libido has re-invested the infantile 'complexes'. But this would be erroneous; it would be
correct only if expressed thus: 'the unconscious part of these
complexes'. The exceptional intricacy of the theme dealt with
in this essay tempts one to discuss further a number of
adjunct problems, which require elucidation before one can
speak definitely enough about the psychical processes here
described. Such problems are: The definition of the boundary
between introversion and regression; the incorporation of the
complex-doctrine into the libido-theory; the relationship of
phantasy-creation to the conscious, the unconscious, and to
reality; etc. I need not apologize for having resisted these
temptations here.

withdrawn libido, there ensues a battle; all the forces which have brought about the regression of the libido will rise up as 'resistances' against our efforts in order to maintain the new condition. For if the introversion or regression of the libido had not been justified by some relation to the outer world (in the broadest terms, by a frustration of some desired gratification) ■ 6 and at the time been even expedient, it would never have taken place at all. Yet the resistances which have this origin are not the only ones, nor even the most powerful. The libido at the disposal of the personality had always been exposed to the attraction of unconscious complexes (strictly speaking, of that part of those complexes which belongs to the unconscious), and underwent regression because the attraction of reality had weakened. In order to free it, this attraction of the unconscious must now be overcome, ■ 7 that is, the repression of the unconscious impulses and their derivatives, which has subsequently developed in the mind of the person concerned, must be lifted. Here arises by far the greater part of the resistances, which so often succeed in upholding the illness, even though the original grounds for the recoil from reality have now disappeared. From both these sources come the resistances with which the analysis has to struggle. Every step of the treatment is accompanied by resistance; every single thought, every mental act of the patient's, must pay toll to the resistance, and represents a compromise between the forces urging towards the cure and those gathered to oppose it.

Now as we follow a pathogenic complex from its representative in consciousness (whether this be a conspicuous symptom or something apparently quite harmless) back to its root in the unconscious, we soon come to a place where the resistance makes itself felt so strongly that it affects the next association, which has to appear as a compromise between the demands of this resis-

■ 6

When Freud talks about the frustration of a desired gratification, he is including the possibility that the child has not received appropriate gratification during a given period of its life, as well as the possibility that the child has been overstimulated during this period. Either situation would lead to a fixation. There would be differences, of course, in the development of the child if one or the other path were the case.

Freud's use of the term gratification has a mechanistic ring when used in this fashion. By gratification he often referred to a wide range of human interactions rather than concentrating exclusively on eating or toilet training or sexual stimulation.

■ 7

When Freud maintains that "the attraction of the unconscious must now be overcome" he is writing before he had fully formulated the idea of unconscious defense, and before he had developed the structural model of ego, id, and superego. Within the topographic model (conscious and unconscious), it is difficult to talk about unconscious defense, since by definition anything in the unconscious is constantly striving for

■ 7 *continued*
release either through action, or through gaining access to consciousness. In this definition, defense is an activity seeking to stop the expression of impulses, so it cannot be part of the unconscious. In his later model, he can better explain what he is now beginning to observe: that defense is usually unconscious. In the new model, unconscious fantasy will be part of the id, while unconscious defense will be an ego function. There are parts of the ego that are unconscious, and it will be the id impulses or fantasies in the id that are always striving for release. In the new structural model, both defense (an aspect of the ego) and the entire id are seen as unconscious.

tance and those of the work of exploration. Experience shows that this is where the transference enters on the scene. When there is anything in the complex-material (the content of the complex) which can at all suitably be transferred on to the person of the physician such a transference will be effected, and from it will arise the next association; it will then manifest itself by the signs of resistance—for instance, a cessation in the flow of associations. We conclude from such experiences that this transferred idea is able to force itself through to consciousness in preference to all other possible associations, just *because* it also satisfies resistance. ■ 8 This type of incident is repeated innumerable times during an analysis. Over and over again, when one draws near to a pathogenic complex, that part of it which is first thrust forward into consciousness will be some aspect of it which can be transferred; having been so, it will then be defended with the utmost obstinacy by the patient.[9]

■ 8
Although transference may be the *preferred* form of resistance in that it has both a defensive and a gratifying aspect, several writers have maintained that with some types of patients, there are strong resistances to the expression of transference (Gedo, Kohut). Gill is quite explicit about how to interpret the patient's resistance to bringing the transference into the treatment situation.

[9]From which, however, one need not infer in general any very particular pathogenic importance in the point selected for resistance by transference. In warfare, when a bitter fight is raging over the possession of some little chapel or a single farmhouse, we do not necessarily assume that the church is a national monument, or that the barns contain the military funds. Their value may be merely tactical; in the next onslaught they will very likely be of no importance.

Once this point is won, the elements of that complex which are still unresolved cause little further difficulty. The longer the analysis lasts, and the more clearly the patient has recognized that distortions of the pathogenic material in themselves offer no protection against disclosure, the more consistently he makes use of that variety of distortion which obviously brings him the greatest advantage, the distortion by transference. These incidents all converge towards a situation in which eventually all the conflicts must be fought out on the field of transference.

Transference in analysis thus always seems at first to be only the strongest weapon of the resistance, and we are entitled to draw the inference that the intensity and duration of the transference are an effect and expression of the resistance. The mechanism of transference is indeed explained by the state of readiness in which the libido that has remained accumulated about the infantile imagos exists, but the part played by it in the process of cure is only intelligible in the light of its relation to the resistance.

How does it come about that the transference is so pre-eminently suitable as a weapon of resistance? One might think that this could easily be answered. It is surely clear enough that it must become peculiarly difficult to own up to any particular reprehended wish when the confession must be made to the very person with whom that feeling is most concerned. To proceed at all in such situations as this necessity produces would appear hardly possible in real life. This impossibility is precisely what the patient is aiming at when he merges the physician with the object of his emotions. Yet on closer consideration we see that this apparent gain cannot supply the answer to the riddle, for, on the contrary, an attitude of affectionate and devoted attachment can surmount any difficulty in confession; in analogous situations in real life we say: 'I don't feel ashamed with you; I can tell you everything'. The transference to the physician might quite as well relieve the difficulties of confession, and we still do not understand why it aggravates them.

The answer to this reiterated problem will not be found by pondering it any further, but must be sought in the experience gained by examination of individual instances of transference-resistance occurring in the course of an analysis. From these one perceives eventually that the use of the transference for resistance cannot be understood so long as one thinks simply of 'transference'. One is forced to distinguish 'positive' transference from 'negative' transference, the transference of affectionate feeling from that of hostile feeling, and to deal separately with the two varieties of the transference to the physician. Positive transference can then be divided further into such friendly or affectionate feelings as are capable of becoming conscious and the extensions of these in the unconscious. Of these last, analysis shows that they invariably rest ultimately on an erotic basis; so that we have to conclude that all the feelings of sympathy, friendship, trust and so forth which we expend in life are genetically connected with sexuality and have developed out of purely sexual desires by an enfeebling of their sexual aim, however pure and non-sensual they may appear in the forms they take on to our conscious self-perception. To begin with we knew none but sexual objects; psycho-analysis shows us that those persons whom in real life we merely respect or are fond of may be sexual objects to us in our unconscious minds still.

So the answer to the riddle is this, that the transference to the physician is only suited for resistance in so far as it consists in *negative* feeling ■ 9 or in the repressed *erotic* elements of positive feeling. As we 'raise' the transference by making it conscious we detach only these two components of the emotional relationship from

■ 9

The negative transference is a topic that Freud never really approached again. He touched

■ 9 *continued*
on the topic in "Beyond the
Pleasure Principle" (1920), but
in that paper his concerns were
quite different, and he did not
discuss the therapeutic aspects
of the negative transference.
The handling of the negative
transference is an issue that is
always a difficult one in psychoanalytic treatment. This is
particularly the case with patients that some therapists have
labeled nonclassical (Bach).
These patients may have a
greater tendency to put things
into action as opposed to

words, or take their negative
thoughts about the analyst as
real perceptions (Jacobson). In
addition, these patients also
seem to have a greater capacity
to elicit reactions from analysts
(Modell), making their negative
feelings and thoughts seem all
the more real. At different
points in his career, Freud
might have said that these patients were unanalyzable or not
able to endure analytic treatment. Freud, however, was
himself quite inconsistent about
applying his criteria of analyzability.

■ 10

Freud's division of transference
into three components is still
one contemporary understanding of the nature of transference. Brenner, following
another line of Freudian
thought, cautions against viewing a particular form of transference as either negative or
positive. Transference for
Brenner is a compromise formation and it is rare if ever
that one sees positive transference without negative components. Brenner maintains that
one should never assume that
transferences are simply positive or negative, reflecting only
sexual or aggressive wishes.
Rather, transference is always
ambivalent. Melanie Klein and
her followers introduced the
concept of splitting. Patients
who use splitting as a defense

the person of the physician; the conscious and
unobjectionable component of it remains, and
brings about the successful result in psycho-analysis as in all other remedial methods. ■ 10 In so far
we readily admit that the results of psycho-analysis rest upon a basis of suggestion; only by suggestion we must be understood to mean that which
we, with Ferenczi,[10] find that it consists of—influence on a person through and by means of the
transference-manifestations of which he is capable. The eventual independence of the patient is
our ultimate object when we use suggestion to
bring him to carry out a mental operation that will
necessarily result in a lasting improvement in his
mental condition. ■ 11

The next question is, Why do these manifestations of transference-resistance appear only in
psycho-analysis and not in other forms of treatment, in institutions, for example? The answer is
that they do appear there also, but they need to be
recognized for what they are. The outbreak of
negative transference is a very common occurrence in institutions; as soon as he is seized by it

[10]Ferenczi, *Introjection and Transference*.

■ 10 *continued*

may manifest one type of transference (positive), whereas the destructive or negative transference is consciously available but actively separated from the positive.

■ 11

The question of the unobjectionable positive transference has recently been an issue of some discussion. Stein and Brenner have put forth the view that the unobjectionable transference is an aspect of the transference to be analyzed as one would any manifestation of transference. For Freud, the positive, or erotic, transference is a source of resistance that should be interpreted as should any piece of resistance that is hindering the flow of free associations. However, the unobjectionable positive transference is admissible to consciousness and does not serve as a resistance, but rather is an aid to the treatment. Freud likened it to suggestion, which was utilized in both hypnosis and the pressure technique.

Modern theorists' ideas about the working alliance are an extension and modification of Freud's unobjectionable transference. A working alliance is formed when analyst and patient are united in the goal of exploring and observing the patient's conflicts. Zetzel, in writing about what she called the therapeutic alliance, sees its basis in an early maternal identification. Greenson defines the working alliance as a growing identification of the patient with the analyzing function of the analyst. The patient begins in effect to conduct aspects of the analysis himself. According to Greenson, this begins to happen in *classical* patients about the third to sixth month of analysis. Stone's ideas of the mature transference are similar to Greenson's working alliance. For Greenson, the working alliance is a crucial aspect of analytic treatment. Although at times it is difficult to distinguish transference reactions from the working alliance, the distinction is usually clear and important in order to conduct a successful analysis. Modell and Lampl-de Groot have recently reaffirmed the importance of these concepts for their work.

Brenner and others have stated that bonds occurring in analysis that might be conceptualized as a working or therapeutic alliance, as well as those that might be thought of in terms of the unobjectionable transference, are subjects to be analyzed in treatment as is any other material that arises in analysis. Brenner does not see much utility in either of these concepts. Both Stone and Brenner agree that the question of the importance of the therapeutic alliance turns on how much frustration versus gratification of the patient's wishes should occur in the analytic situation. If a patient has had a success or a failure, should the therapist acknowledge these occurrences in reality? Stone and Brenner differ on the extent to which the analyst realistically acknowledges the patient and the extent to which the analyst should stay

■ 11 *continued*
firmly within the boundaries of interpreting to patients the meaning of their conflicts. Brenner argues that the analyst can be of little help as anything but an analyst and must stay firmly within the limitations of the analytic situation. Stone thinks

that this is not beneficial to the patient in some cases. He argues that at times (and he is careful about these times) the analyst must go beyond the role of interpreting the patient's conflicts. Here again we see the issue of analytic neutrality as fundamental in analytic technique.

the patient leaves, uncured or worse. The erotic transference has not such an inhibitory effect in institutions, since there, as otherwise in life, it is decorously glossed over, instead of being exposed; nevertheless, it betrays itself unequivocally as resistance to the cure, not, indeed, by driving the patient out of the place—on the contrary, it binds him to the spot—but just as certainly by keeping him away from real life. Actually it is quite unimportant for his cure whether or not the patient can overcome this or that anxiety or inhibition in the institution; what is of importance, on the contrary, is whether or not he will be free from them in real life.

The negative transference requires a more thorough elucidation than is possible within the limits of this paper. It is found in the curable forms of the psychoneuroses alongside the affectionate transference, often both directed onto the same person at the same time, a condition for which Bleuler has coined the useful term ambivalence.[11] This ambivalence of the feelings appears to be normal up to a point, but a high degree of it is certainly a special peculiarity of neurotics. In the obsessional neurosis an early 'splitting of the pairs of opposites' seems to characterize the instinctual life and to form one of the constitutional conditions of this disease. The ability of neurotics to make the trans-

[11]E. Bleuler, *Dementia Praecox oder Gruppe der Schizophrenien*, in Aschaffenburg's *Handbuch der Psychiatrie*, 1911; also a Lecture on Ambivalence in Berne, 1910, abstracted in *Zentralblatt für Psychoanalyse*, Bd. 1., S. 266. W. Stekel had previously suggested the term *bipolarity* for the same phenomenon. ■ 12

■ 12

This is Freud's first use of the term *ambivalence*. At times, Freud uses the term to denote the co-instantaneous presence of active and passive impulses.

Freud has clearly observed that positive transference is often accompanied by negative or hostile transference reactions. Despite this observation, he still finds utility in differentiating positive and negative transference. Thus, for Freud, although patients may often be ambivalent, this is not always the case. This position is at variance with Brenner, who posits that there is always an ambivalent element in transference reactions. It must be that in most human reactions there are some elements of both positive and negative transference, but it is a different matter to state that in every transference reaction one should pay attention to the positive and negative. There may be times when the transference is overwhelmingly positive or negative.

ference a form of resistance is most easily accounted for by ambivalence in the flow of feelings. Where the capacity to transfer feeling has come to be of an essentially negative order, as with paranoids, the possibility of influence or cure ceases.

After all this investigation we have so far considered one aspect only of transference-phenomena; some attention must be given to another side of this question. Those who have formed a true impression of the effect of an extreme transference-resistance on the patient, of the way in which as soon as he comes under its influence he is hurled out of all reality in his relation to the physician— how he then arrogates to himself freedom to ignore the psycho-analytic rule (to communicate without reserve whatever goes through his mind), ■ 13 how all the resolutions with which he entered upon the analysis then become obliterated, and how the logical connections and conclusions which just before had impressed him deeply then become matters of indifference to him—will need some further explanation than that supplied by the factors mentioned above to account for this effect, and these other factors are, indeed, not far to seek; they lie again in the psychological situation in which the analysis has placed the patient.

■ 13

It is notable that even here, in a paper on transference, Freud is stating that free association is *the* psychoanalytic rule. In the Standard Edition, it is translated as the "fundamental" rule, and translated as "whatever comes into one's head must be reported without criticizing it." This is quite a different translation with a good deal more of a guilt-provoking ring

■ 13 *continued*
to it. This sentence appears in
the same way in his Clark University Lecture (1910). The
concept of free association has
its roots as early as Freud's
chapter, "On Psychotherapy,"
in *Studies on Hysteria*. The
fundamental rule is stated most
fully in his paper, "On Beginning the Treatment."

■ 14
The notion that transference is
the greatest difficulty for the
analyst was a challenging lesson for Freud to learn. Earlier
he had said that dealing with
the transference added no work
for the physician. Now that he
is writing as an analyst, he is
telling us what is closer to
modern experience, that
dealing with the transference is
an aspect of analysis that is
both hard and rewarding.

In following up the libido that is withdrawn
from consciousness we penetrate into the region
of the unconscious, and this provokes reactions
which bring with them to light many of the characteristics of unconscious processes as we have
learnt to know them from the study of dreams.
The unconscious feelings strive to avoid the recognition which the cure demands; they seek instead
for reproduction, with all the power of hallucination and the inappreciation of time characteristic
of the unconscious. The patient ascribes, just as in
dreams, currency and reality to what results from
the awakening of his unconscious feelings; he
seeks to discharge his emotions, regardless of the
reality of the situation. The physician requires of
him that he shall fit these emotions into their
place in the treatment and in his life-history, subject them to rational consideration, and appraise
them at their true psychical value. This struggle
between physician and patient, between intellect
and the forces of instinct, between recognition and
the striving for discharge, is fought out almost
entirely over the transference-manifestations. This
is the ground on which the victory must be won,
the final expression of which is lasting recovery
from the neurosis. It is undeniable that the subju-
gation of the transference-manifestations provides the greatest difficulties for the psycho-analyst; ■ 14 but it must not be forgotten that they, and
they only, render the invaluable service of making
the patient's buried and forgotten love-emotions
actual and manifest; for in the last resort no one
can be slain *in absentia* or *in effigie*.

Further Recommendations in the Technique of Psycho-Analysis[1]

RECOLLECTION, REPETITION AND WORKING THROUGH

(1914)

It seems to me not unnecessary constantly to remind students of the far-reaching changes which psycho-analytic technique has undergone since its first beginnings. Its first phase was that of Breuer's catharsis, direct concentration upon the events exciting symptom-formation and persistent efforts on this principle to obtain reproduction of the mental processes involved in that situation, in order to bring about a release of them through conscious operations. The aims pursued at that time, by the help of the hypnotic condition, were 'recollection' and 'abreaction'. Next, after hypnosis had been abandoned, the main task became that of divining from the patient's free associations what he failed to remember. Resistances were to be circumvented by the work of interpretation and by making its results known to the patient; concentration on the situations giving rise to symptom-

[1]First published in *Zeitschrift*, Bd. II., 1914; reprinted in *Sammlung*, Vierte Folge. [Translated by Joan Riviere.]

formation and on those which lay behind the outbreak of illness was retained, while abreaction
receded and seemed to be replaced by the work the
patient had to do in overcoming his critical objections to his associations, in accordance with
the fundamental psycho-analytic rule. Finally, the
present-day technique evolved itself, whereby the
analyst abandons concentration on any particular
element or problem, contents himself with studying whatever is occupying the patient's mind at
the moment, and employs the art of interpretation
mainly for the purpose of recognizing the resistances which come up in regard to this material
and making the patient aware of them. A rearrangement of the division of labour results from
this; the physician discovers the resistances which
are unknown to the patient; when these are removed the patient often relates the forgotten situations and connections without any difficulty.
The aim of these different procedures has of
course remained the same throughout: descriptively, to recover the lost memories; dynamically,
to conquer the resistances ▪ 16 caused by repression.

One is bound to be grateful still to the old
hypnotic technique for the way in which it un-
rolled before us certain of the mental processes of
analysis in an isolated and schematic form. Only
this could have given us the courage to create
complicated situations ourselves in the analytic
process and to keep them perspicuous.

Now in those days of hypnotic treatment 'recollection' took a very simple form. The patient put
himself back into an earlier situation, which he
seemed never to confound with the present, gave
an account of the mental processes belonging to it,
in so far as they were normal, and appended to
this whatever conclusions arose from making conscious what had before been unconscious.

I will here interpolate a few observations
which every analyst has found confirmed in his

▪ 16
The way Freud reviews his previous techniques reveals that
the concept of resistance has
led him to see transference as
the most important form of resistance. He says that the aim
of the different techniques has
remained the same: "to fill in
gaps in memory; dynamically
speaking, it is to overcome
resistances due to repression."
In telling how he conceives of
these similarities, Freud is combining elements of his psychotherapeutic approaches with his
newer ideas about psychoanalytic technique. The goal is still
remembering, although now
the question is what can be remembered, and how can this
remembering be accomplished?

■ 16 *continued*

The pathway to remembering is still by overcoming resistances, but the way to overcome resistances now occurs via the transference. Remembering does not necessarily or frequently occur directly, rather in analysis, through the transference, the patient repeats and the analyst's interpretations help the patient remember.

In the next paragraphs, Freud reports on an observation that indicates he has clearly been working as an analyst. He states that with the new procedure, by allowing the transference to unfold, patients often confuse the present with the past; this wasn't the case with the old techniques. This indicates that at this point, Freud was working analytically (via the transference) and in fact must have encountered at least moderately intense transference reactions for this type of confusion to be a notable one. A variety of modern analysts including Kohut, Bach, Kernberg, and Boesky have commented on how transference frequently feels quite real to patients who are called non-classical, narcissistic, or borderline patients. I would say that, in any analysis, there are times when the transference feels quite real.

experience. The forgetting of impressions, scenes, events, nearly always reduces itself to 'dissociation' of them. When the patient talks about these 'forgotten' matters he seldom fails to add: 'In a way I have always known that, only I never thought of it'. He often expresses himself as disappointed that not enough things come into his mind which he can hail as 'forgotten', which he has never thought of since they happened. Even this desire on his part is fulfilled, however, particularly in cases of conversion-hysteria. The 'forgotten' material is still further circumscribed when we estimate at their true value the screen-memories which are so generally present. In many cases I have had the impression that the familiar childhood-amnesia, which is theoretically so important to us, is entirely outweighed by the screen-memories. Not merely is much that is essential in childhood preserved in them, but actually all that is essential. Only one must understand how to extract it from them by analysis. They represent the forgotten years of childhood just as adequately as the manifest content represents the dream-thoughts. ■ 17

■ 17

Although beginning patients of analysis can't remember because of childhood amnesia or primal repression, the clues are there in terms of screen memories. Here screen memories are viewed in the same way that, many years later, he suggests that hallucinations be seen, that is, as containing important elements of childhood experiences.

The other group of mental processes, the purely internal mental activities, such as phantasies, relations between ideas, impulses, feelings, connections, may be contrasted with impressions and events experienced, and must be considered apart from them in its relation to forgetting and remembering. With these processes it particularly often happens that something is 'remembered' which never could have been 'forgotten', because it was never at any time noticed, never was conscious; as regards the fate of any such 'connection' in the mind, moreover, it seems to make no difference whatever whether it was conscious and then was forgotten or whether it never reached consciousness at all. The conviction which a patient obtains in the course of analysis is quite independent of remembering it in that way.

In the manifold forms of obsessional neurosis particularly, 'forgetting' consists mostly of a falling away of the links between various ideas, a failure to draw conclusions, an isolating of certain memories.

No memory of one special kind of highly important experience can usually be recovered: these are experiences which took place in very early childhood, before they could be comprehended, but which were *subsequently* interpreted and understood. One gains a knowledge of them from dreams, and is compelled to believe in them on irresistible evidence in the structure of the neurosis; moreover, one can convince oneself that after his resistances have been overcome the patient no longer invokes the absence of any memory of them (sensation of familiarity) as a ground for refusing to accept them. This matter, however, is one demanding so much critical caution and introducing so much that is novel and startling that I will reserve it for special discussion in connection with suitable material.[2] ■ 18

---

[2]Cf. Freud, 'From the History of an Infantile Neurosis', COLLECTED PAPERS, vol. iii.—Trans.

■ 18

Here Freud is referring to the
Wolf Man, who, as an adult, reported a dream from childhood
(the dream was thought to
have occurred when the patient
was four). Freud's interpretation of the dream was that the
actual event that stimulated the
dream occurred when the Wolf
Man was 1½ years old. Freud
was just completing this analysis when he wrote the present
paper. He discusses the issue of
childhood memories in the

Introductory Lectures. An interesting aspect of this paragraph
is that one can see that, although Freud has placed a
great emphasis on the role of
fantasy in childhood, he never
lost his interest in the role of
the environment and its impact
on the developing child. Thus,
in the case that he considered
his most significant, the Wolf
Man, one sees Freud helping
the patient understand a variety
of events that he thought traumatic for the Wolf Man.

To return to the comparison between the old
and the new techniques; in the latter there remains very little, often nothing, of this smooth
and pleasing course of events belonging to the
former. There are cases which, under the new
technique, conduct themselves up to a point like
those under the hypnotic technique and only later
abandon this behaviour; but others behave differently from the beginning. If we examine the latter
class in order to define this difference, we may say
that here the patient *remembers* nothing of what
is forgotten and repressed, but that he expresses it
in *action*. He reproduces it not in his memory but
in his behaviour; he *repeats* it, without of course
knowing that he is repeating it. ■ 19

For instance, the patient does not say that he
remembers how defiant and critical he used to be
in regard to the authority of his parents, but he
behaves in that way towards the physician. He
does not remember how he came to a helpless and
hopeless deadlock in his infantile searchings after
the truth of sexual matters, but he produces a mass
of confused dreams and associations, complains
that he never succeeds at anything, and describes it
as his fate never to be able to carry anything

■ 19

Although Freud used the term
acting out in the postscript of
the Dora case, this is his first
full discussion of this concept. It
is important to recognize that
Freud is talking about acting out
in terms of the patient's reactions in the transference. In the
next paragraph, he gives a series
of examples of how the patient
acts out the transference with

■ 19 *continued*

respect to the analyst. Today, the term *acting out* is frequently used to denote patients acting out their conflicts outside of the treatment situation. Thus Fenichel considers a behavior an acting out *if something has to be done regardless of towards whom*. In a recent article, Boesky emphasizes that what is crucial in acting out is the reality of the action or the actualization of the conflict. He quotes Bird in reminding analysts that there is always a possible unwitting congruence between the behavior of the analyst and pathogenic childhood object relations of the patient. Bird states, "*When that which has been actual in the past converges with that which . . . becomes actual by virtue of the analyst's complicity in the present, the potential for acting out is much increased.*"

that he never succeeds at anything, and describes it as his fate never to be able to carry anything through. He does not remember that he was intensely ashamed of certain sexual activities, but he makes it clear that he is ashamed of the treatment to which he has submitted himself, and does his utmost to keep it a secret; and so on.

Above all, the beginning of the treatment sets in with a repetition of this kind. When one announces the fundamental psycho-analytical rule to a patient with an eventful life-history and a long illness behind him, and then waits for him to pour forth a flood of information, the first thing that happens often is that he has nothing to say. He is silent and declares that nothing comes into his mind. That is of course nothing but the repetition of a homosexual attitude, which comes up as a resistance against remembering anything. As long as he is under treatment he never escapes from this compulsion to repeat; at last one understands that it is his way of remembering. ■ 20

■ 20

Freud's examples are not what most analysts today would call acting out, but rather a type of acting in the transference. The term *acting out* is normally reserved for those times when the patient is thought to put conflicts into action *outside* of

The relation between this compulsion to repeat and the transference and resistance is naturally what will interest us most of all. We soon perceive that the transference is itself only a bit of repetition, and that the repetition is the transference of the forgotten past not only on to the physician, but also on to all the other aspects of the current situation. We must be prepared to find, therefore, that the patient abandons himself to the compulsion to repeat, which is now replacing the impulse to remember, not only in his relation with the analyst but also in all other matters occupying and interesting him at the time, for instance, when he falls in love or sets about any project during the treatment. ■ 21 Moreover, the part played by resistance is easily recognized. The greater the resistance the more extensively will expressing in action (repetition) be substituted for recollecting. The ideal kind of recollection of the past which belongs to hypnosis is indeed a condition in which resistance is completely abrogated. If the treatment begins under the auspices of a mild and unpronounced positive transference, it makes an unearthing of memories like that in hypnosis possible to begin with, while the symptoms themselves are for the time quiescent; if then, as the analysis proceeds, this transference becomes hostile or unduly intense, consequently necessitating repression, remembering immediately gives way to expression in action. From then onward the resistances determine the succession of the various repetitions. The past is the patient's armoury out of which he fetches his weapons for defending himself against the progress of the analysis, weapons which we must wrest from him one by one.

The patient reproduces instead of remembering, and he reproduces according to the conditions of the resistance; we may now ask what it is exactly that he reproduces or expresses in action. The answer is that he reproduces everything in the reservoirs of repressed material that has already permeated his general character—his inhibitions and disadvantageous attitudes of mind, his pathological traits of character. He also repeats during the treatment all his symptoms. And now we can see that our special insistence upon the compulsion to repeat has not yielded any new fact, but is only a more comprehensive point of view.

■ 20 *continued*
the treatment situation. *Acting in* is conceived of as occurring when patients demonstrate their conflicts during the treatment instead of verbalizing the conflicts.

■ 21
Here, for the first time, Freud is using the concept of the repetition compulsion or the compulsion to repeat. We can see that Freud conceives of this compulsion as being in the service of resistance. The patient is compelled to repeat instead of remember and repeats according to the conditions of the resistance. The therapeutic task is twofold: to attempt to keep the repetition within the verbal sphere in the analytic situation and to accomplish the therapeutic task of translating this compulsion back into the terms of the past. During a period of positive transference (unobjectionable transference) the patient may remember without repeating, but once the first resistance appears, repetition begins. Steingart has pointed out that the need to keep repetitions in the verbal sphere in the psychoanalytic situation is overstated by Freud. Many times the analyst can use the patient's behavior as a type of association, much as language serves the associative process. Naturally there are likely to be risks involved when the patient puts his or her unconscious ideas into action.

We are only making it clear to ourselves that the patient's condition of illness does not cease when his analysis begins, that we have to treat his illness as an actual force, active at the moment, and not as an event in his past life. This condition of present illness is shifted bit by bit within the range and field of operation of the treatment, and while the patient lives it through as something real and actual, we have to accomplish the therapeutic task, which consists chiefly in translating it back again into terms of the past.

Causing memories to be revived under hypnosis gives the impression of an experiment in the laboratory. Allowing 'repetition' during analytic treatment, which is the latest form of technique, constitutes a conjuring into existence of a piece of real life, and can therefore not always be harmless and indifferent in its effects on all cases. The whole question of 'exacerbation of symptoms during treatment', so often unavoidable, is linked up with this.

The very beginning of the treatment above all brings about a change in the patient's conscious attitude towards his illness. He has contented himself usually with complaining of it, with regarding it as nonsense, and with underestimating its importance; for the rest, he has extended the ostrich-like conduct of repression which he adopted towards the sources of his illness on to its manifestations. Thus it happens that he does not rightly know what are the conditions under which his phobia breaks out, has not properly heard the actual words of his obsessive idea or not really grasped exactly what it is his obsessive impulse is impelling him to do. The treatment of course cannot allow this. He must find the courage to pay attention to the details of his illness. His illness itself must no longer seem to him contemptible, but must become an enemy worthy of his mettle, a part of his personality, kept up by good motives, out of which things of value for his future life have to be derived. The way to reconciliation with the repressed part of himself which is coming to expression in his symptoms is thus prepared from the beginning; yet a certain tolerance towards the illness itself is induced. Now if this new attitude towards the illness intensifies the conflicts and brings to the fore symptoms which till then had been indistinct, one can easily console the patient for this by pointing out that these are only necessary and temporary aggravations, and that one cannot overcome an enemy who is absent or not within range. The resistance, however, may try to exploit the situation to its own ends, and abuse the permission to be ill. It seems to say: 'See what happens when I really let myself go in these things! Haven't I been right to relegate them all to repression?' Young and childish persons in particular are inclined to make the necessity for paying attention to their illness a welcome excuse for luxuriating in their symptoms.

There is another danger, that in the course of the analysis, other, deeper-lying instinctual trends which had not yet become part of the personality may come to be 'reproduced'. Finally, it is possible that the patient's behaviour outside the transference may involve him in temporary disasters in life, or even be so designed as permanently to rob the health he is seeking of all its value.

The tactics adopted by the physician are easily justified. For him recollection in the old style, reproduction in the mind, remains the goal of his endeavours, even when he knows that it is not to be obtained by the newer method. He sets about a perpetual struggle with the patient to keep all the impulses which he would like to carry into action within the boundaries of his mind, and when it is possible to divert into the work of recollection any impulse which the patient wants to discharge in action, he celebrates it as a special triumph for the analysis. When the transference has developed to a sufficiently strong attachment, the treatment is in a position to prevent all the more important of the patient's repetition-actions and to make use of his intentions alone, *in statu nascendi*, as material for the therapeutic work. One best protects the patient from disasters brought about by carrying his impulses into action by making him promise to form no important decisions affecting his life during the course of the treatment, for instance, choice of a profession or of a permanent love-object, but to postpone all such projects until after recovery. ■ 22

■ 22

Given the possibilities of acting out, Freud issued his famous proclamation that, in order to protect patients, one must make them promise not to make any important decisions during the time of the treatment. This idea seems a bit quaint to us and it is unlikely today that many patients would agree to this condition. One might also remember that the length of contemporary analyses is approximately 5 to 7 years. Freud conducted analyses that lasted from 6 months to 3 years. The important question is the effect this type of instruction has on the patient's reaction to the analyst. However the restraint is presented, if the patient acquiesces, it is hard to see the analyst as a neutral figure after being granted so much authority.

Still, these paragraphs let us know that the transference situations Freud encountered were intense and that he considered the acting out of patients in the treatment, and outside of the treatment, as points along a continuum.

One important question that modern analysts might ask

At the same time one willingly accords the patient all the freedom that is compatible with these restrictions, nor does one hinder him from carrying out projects which, though foolish, are not of special significance; one remembers that it is only by dire experience that mankind ever learns sense. There are no doubt persons whom one cannot prevent from plunging into some quite undesirable project during the treatment and who become amenable and willing to submit the impulse to analysis only afterwards. Occasionally, too, it is bound to happen that the untamed instincts assert themselves before there is time for the curbing-rein of the transference to be placed on them, or that an act of reproduction causes the patient to break the bond that holds him to the treatment. As an extreme example of this, I might take the case of an elderly lady who had repeatedly fled from her house and her husband in a twilight state, and gone no one knew where, without having any idea of a motive for this 'elopement'. Her treatment with me began with a marked positive transference of affectionate feeling, which intensified itself with uncanny rapidity in the first few days, and by the end of a week she had 'eloped' again from me, before I had time to say anything to her which might have prevented this repetition.

The main instrument, however, for curbing the patient's compulsion to repeat and for turning it into a motive for remembering consists in the

■ 22 *continued*
concerning a patient's tendencies to act in or act out is their capacity to observe themselves and understand the illusory quality of the transference. If one thinks of the transference as analogous to play in children (as do Winnicott and Steingart), then one can ask to what extent the patient is able to experience the illusion, while at the same time recognizing that the *play* is not fully real. Still, when Freud points out that the newer technique is "conjuring up a piece of real life," he is describing what goes on in every intense analysis. That is, there are always at least some points in any analysis where the patient is experiencing the events as real and in the present, and at least for some time is not aware of the illusory quality of the transference. For some analysts, a crucial factor in determining the analyzability of a patient is the person's capacity to endure the regressive pulls in analysis without putting conflicts into action outside of the treatment situation. Other analysts, such as Winnicott or Bach, seem able to tolerate acting out and perhaps are more able to wait for patients to express their conflicts in the analysis.

handling of the transference. We render it harmless, and even make use of it, by according it the right to assert itself within certain limits. We admit it into the transference as to a playground, in which it is allowed to let itself go in almost complete freedom and is required to display before us all the pathogenic impulses hidden in the depths of the patient's mind. ■ 23 If the patient does but show compliance enough to respect the necessary conditions of the analysis we can regularly succeed in giving all the symptoms of the neurosis a new transference-colouring, and in replacing his whole ordinary neurosis by a 'transference-neurosis' of which he can be cured by the therapeutic work. ■ 24 The transference thus forms a kind of intermediary realm between illness and real life, through which the journey from the one to the other must be made. The new state of mind has absorbed all the features of the illness; it represents, however, an artificial illness which is at every point accessible to our interventions. It is at the same time a piece of real life, but adapted to our purposes by specially favourable conditions, and it is of a provisional character. From the repe-

■ 23
In these paragraphs, Freud is asserting that the person should be given as much freedom as possible to express transference tendencies. It is interesting that, while Freud frequently uses military metaphors to describe various aspects of analysis, here he uses the term *playground*, a term he also employs when he describes his views on fantasy. Freud is touching on transference as the type of illusory experience that various authors such as Winnicott have described. He comes close to saying this when he states that "the transference creates an intermediate region between ill-

■ 23 *continued*
ness and real life." Winnicott
uses the term *illusion* with respect to the transference field;
in these passages Winnicott
and Freud sound quite similar.
Steingart, in explaining transference as an illusion, has been
able to show the relevance of
both Winnicott's and Piaget's
ideas to the concept of transference. Steingart relates transference to both illusion and play.

■ 24
The term *transference-neurosis*
is one that has two overlapping
meanings. Freud uses this term
to denote the two neuroses
(hysteria and obsessive-
compulsive neuroses) that he
thought appropriate for analytic treatment. It was his assumption that only people with

these types of disorders could
form full analyzable transference relationships. The term
transference-neurosis in this
context conveys the idea that
there is special point in an
analysis where one fully reproduces the original conflictual
relationships that are central to
a person's neurotic condition.
This full-blown manifestation
of the person's conflicts then
allows the analyst to interpret
how the conflicts are manifested in the present and to reconstruct the person's infantile
conflicts. Contemporary analysts such as Brenner do not accept the concept of transference
neurosis and view all transference as involving neurotic formation. Other analysts, such as
Kanzer, have found continued
utility in the concept.

tition-reactions which are exhibited in the transference the familiar paths lead back to the awakening of the memories, which yield themselves without difficulty after the resistances have been
overcome.

I might break off at this point but for the title
of this paper, which requires me to discuss a further point in analytic technique. The first step in
overcoming the resistance is made, as we know, by
the analyst's discovering the resistance, which is
never recognized by the patient, and acquainting
him with it. Now it seems that beginners in analytic practice are inclined to look upon this as the
end of the work. I have often been asked to advise
upon cases in which the physician complained that
he had pointed out his resistance to the patient
and that all the same no change had set in; in fact,
the resistance had only then become really pro-
nounced and the whole situation had become more

obscure than ever. The treatment seemed to make no progress. This gloomy foreboding always proved mistaken. The treatment was as a rule progressing quite satisfactorily; only the analyst had forgotten that naming the resistance could not result in its immediate suspension. One must allow the patient time to get to know this resistance of which he is ignorant, to 'work through' ■ 25 it, to overcome it, by continuing the work according to the analytic rule in defiance of it. Only when it has come to its height can one, with the patient's co-operation, discover the repressed instinctual trends which are feeding the resistance; and only by living them through in this way will the patient be convinced of their existence and their power. The physician has nothing more to do than to wait and let things take their course, a course which cannot be avoided nor always be hastened. If he holds fast to this principle, he will often be spared the disappointment of failure in cases where all the time he has conducted the treatment quite correctly.

This 'working through' of the resistances may in practice amount to an arduous task for the patient and a trial of patience for the analyst. Nevertheless, it is the part of the work that effects the greatest changes in the patient and that distinguishes analytic treatment from every kind of suggestive treatment. Theoretically one may correlate it with the 'abreaction' of quantities of affect pent-up by repression, without which the hypnotic treatment remained ineffective.

■ 25
In these last two paragraphs, Freud seems to have had several things in mind. One was similar to the modern-day meaning of working through, which one might roughly state as the process of following and continuing to analyze the various manifestations of a conflict after the core conflict has been analyzed. Thus, it may be that a patient understands the meaning of a particular action, and, in working through a conflict, may come to understand how other actions or thoughts are manifestations of the same conflict. This, however, does not seem to be Freud's main meaning. Rather, as stated above, he seems to be saying that one must work on, or through, the conflict when the conflict is most intense. The conflict(s) should be worked on *in defiance of* the conflict. It is only at this point that patients will be convinced of the power of the conflict that has dominated their lives. This meaning of working through is a type of reminder to analysts that one cannot simply voice an interpretation and expect it to have a curative effect. In fact, Freud seems to be saying that the curative effects of analysis happen

■ 25 *continued*

only when the resistance is at
its height (ostensibly during
the transference-neurosis). In
this way, both the patient and
the analyst go through a trial
by fire—a distinguishing mark
of psychoanalysis. The early
therapies attempted to evade
the transference and resistance,
but psychoanalysis allows both
to reach their heights before a
full interpretative effort is put
forth. Some contemporary analysts, such as Pine, advocate
that, with nonclassical patients,
one should strike when the
iron is cold—that is, only when
the patient is not intensely experiencing a conflict. Bach
would state that patients can
only reach the type of experience Freud is describing when
they feel alive and whole; this
may take a good deal of time in
the analysis.

Further Recommendations in the Technique of Psycho-Analysis[1]

OBSERVATIONS ON TRANSFERENCE-LOVE

(1915)

Every beginner in psycho-analysis probably feels alarmed at first at the difficulties in store for him when he comes to interpret the patient's associations and deal with the reproduction of repressed material. When the time comes, however, he soon learns to look upon these difficulties as insignificant and instead becomes convinced that the only serious difficulties are encountered in handling the transference.

Among the situations to which the transference gives rise, one is very sharply outlined, and I will select this, partly because it occurs so often and is so important in reality and partly because of its theoretical interest. The case I mean is that in which a woman or girl patient shows by unmistakable allusions or openly avows that she has fallen in love, like any other mortal woman, with the physician who is analysing her. This situation has its distressing and its comical aspects as well as its

[1]First published in *Zeitschrift*, Bd. III., 1915; reprinted in *Sammlung*, Vierte Folge. [Translated by Joan Riviere.]

serious ones; it is so complicated, and conditioned by so many factors, so unavoidable and so difficult to dissolve, that discussion of it has long been a pressing need of analytic technique. But since those who mock at the failings of others are not always themselves free from them, we have hardly been inclined to rush in to the fulfilment of this task. The obligation of professional discretion, which cannot be disregarded in life but which is useless in our science, makes itself felt here again and again. In so far as psycho-analytical publications are a part of life, we have here an insoluble conflict. I have recently disregarded this matter of discretion for once[2] and shown how this same transference situation at first retarded the development of psycho-analytic therapy for ten years.

To a cultivated layman—and in their relation to psycho-analysis the attitude of such men is the best we encounter—matters concerned with love cannot be measured by the same standards as other things: it is as though they were written on a page by themselves which would not take any other script. If a patient falls in love with her doctor, then, such a man will think only two outcomes are possible—one comparatively rare, in which all the circumstances allow of a permanent legal union between them, ■ 25 and the other much commoner, in which physician and patient part, and abandon the work begun which should have led to her recovery, as though it had been prevented by some elemental phenomenon. There is certainly a third conceivable way out, which even appears compatible with continuing the treatment, and that is a love-relationship between them of an illicit character, not intended to last permanently; but both conventional morality and professional dignity surely make this impossible. In any event our layman would beg the analyst to

■ 25
In Freud's time these issues were being newly encountered in psychoanalysis. Today, because there has been more experience, there is greater agreement that marriage between an analyst and a patient would be under the powerful influence of both transference and counter-transference.

[2]'On the History of the Psycho-Analytic Movement', 1914, COLLECTED PAPERS, vol. 1.

reassure him as unambiguously as possible that this third alternative is out of the question.

It is clear that the analyst's point of view must be different from this.

Let us take the case of the second possible alternative. After the patient has fallen in love with the physician, they part; the treatment is given up. But very soon the patient's condition necessitates her making another attempt at cure with another physician; the next thing that happens is that she feels she has fallen in love with the second physician, and just the same again when she had broken off and begun again with a third, and so on. ■ 26 This phenomenon, which occurs with such regularity and is one of the foundations of psycho-analytical theory, may be regarded from two points of view, that of the physician analysing and that of the patient in need of analysis.

To the physician it represents an invaluable explanation and a useful warning against any tendency to counter-transference which may be lurking in his own mind. He must recognize that the patient's falling in love is induced by the analytic situation and is not to be ascribed to the charms of his person, that he has no reason whatever therefore to be proud of such a 'conquest', as it would be called outside analysis. And it is always well to be reminded of this. For the patient, however, there are two alternatives: either she must abandon her analytic treatment or she must make up her mind to being in love with physicians as to an inevitable destiny.[3]

I have no doubt that the patient's relatives and friends would decide as emphatically in favour of the first of the two alternatives as the analyst would for the second. In my opinion, however, this

[3]We know that the transference can express itself by other less tender feelings, but I do not propose to go into that side of the matter here.

■ 26

It is interesting that here Freud does not consider the idea of the patient, a woman in this example, going to see a female analyst rather than continuing to see a male analyst. By raising this, we are not suggesting that this would be an answer to the situation that Freud is presenting. It is of interest that Freud does not discuss this obvious possibility. To avoid anachronistic interpretations, we must remember the role of women in early twentieth-century society.

At this time in the history of psychoanalysis, Freud is detailing what he considers a clear and present danger. He recognizes how easy it might be for an analyst to mistake a transference reaction for real affection. Moreover, he recognizes the power of the transference where both the patient and the analyst are susceptible to manipulation. The responsibility in the analytic situation rests with the analyst; Freud is reminding analysts of this. This

■ 26 continued
issue has been a persistent one
in psychoanalysis, and the editors of the Standard Edition
point out a letter of Freud's to
Ferenczi that deals with this
issue. A recent publication of
*The Clinical Diary of Sándor
Ferenczi* gives a different version of this letter.

is a case in which the decision cannot be left to the
tender—or rather, the jealous egoistic—mercies of
the relatives and friends. The patient's welfare
alone should decide. The love of her relatives cannot cure her neurosis. It is not necessary for the
psycho-analyst to force himself upon anyone, but
he may take up the stand that for certain purposes
he is indispensable. Anyone who takes up Tol-
stoy's attitude to this problem can remain in undisputed possession of his wife or daughter, but
must try to put up with her retaining her neurosis
and with the disturbance it involves in her capacity
for love. After all, it is the same situation as that of
a gynecological treatment. Incidentally, the jealous
father or husband makes a great mistake if he
thinks the patient will escape falling in love with
the physician if he hands her over to some other
kind of treatment than that of analysis in order to
get rid of her neurosis. The difference will be, on
the contrary, that her falling in love in a way
which is bound to remain unexpressed and unana-
lysed can never render that aid to her recovery
which analysis would have extracted from it.

It has come to my knowledge that certain
physicians who practise analysis frequently prepare their patients for the advent of a love-transference or even instruct them to 'go ahead and fall
in love with the analyst so that the treatment may
make progress'. I can hardly imagine a more nonsensical proceeding. It robs the phenomenon itself
of the element of spontaneity which is so convincing and it lays up obstacles ahead which are extremely difficult to overcome. ■ 27

■ 27

From Freud's point of view, the
idea of warning a patient of a
reaction does little to help and
a great deal to hinder. One can
only speculate on the future obstacles to which Freud alludes.
It is possible that a patient will
fall into a pattern of wanting a
preview of the entire analysis if

At the first glance it certainly does not look as
if any advantage to the treatment could result
from the patient's falling in love in the transference. No matter how amenable she has been up
till then, she now suddenly loses all understanding
of and interest in the treatment, and will not hear
or speak of anything but her love, the return of
which she demands; she has either given up her

■ 27 *continued*

the analyst predicts the patient's reactions. More significantly, the patient will utilize this type of intervention in the service of resistance. There will be a significant difference in this resistance to other aspects of the resistance, for here the analyst has done something in reality to collaborate with the patient. Thus, if a patient tends to idealize the analyst, a prediction will be taken as evidence of the analyst's omnipotence. Similarly, if the patient needs to denigrate the analyst, "incorrect" predictions will show how out of tune or incorrect the analyst can be.

symptoms or else she ignores them: she even declares herself well. A complete transformation ensues in the scene—it is as though some make-believe had been interrupted by a real emergency, just as when the cry of fire is raised in a theatre. Any physician experiencing this for the first time will not find it easy to keep a grasp of the analytic situation and not to succumb to the illusion that the treatment is really at an end. ■ 28

On reflection one realizes the true state of things. One remembers above all the suspicion that everything impeding the progress of the treatment may be an expression of resistance. It certainly plays a great part in the outbreak of passionate demands for love. One has long noticed in the patient the signs of an affectionate transference on to the physician and could with certainty ascribe to this attitude her docility, her acceptance of the analytic explanations, her remarkable comprehension and the high degree of intelligence which she displayed during this period. This is now all swept away; she has become completely lacking in understanding and seems to be swallowed up in her love; and this change always came over her just as one had to bring her to the point of confessing or remembering one of the particularly painful or heavily repressed vicissitudes in her life-history. She had been in love, that is to say, for a long time; but now the resistance is beginning to make use of it in order to hinder the

■ 28

In this next paragraph, Freud shows how easily the transference becomes a reality for the patient and the analyst alike, when the transference becomes particularly intense. Although he was reluctant to write technique papers, it is easy to understand in reading a passage like this one why he decided to undertake these papers: Who better than Freud could write about the experience of an analyst encountering transference for the first time? In the Dora case, it is clear that he felt the intensity of Dora's reactions and that, at least to some extent, he came to understand the intensity of his own reactions. With the aid of the present paper, analysts have at least some markers to help them chart

■ 28 *continued*
the way during stormy transference–countertransference
sequences.

■ 29
In this paragraph Freud shows
how even the most intense
transference response is to be
considered in the service of resistance. It is of note that at
times, Freud is still taking an
accusatory tone toward the patient. He is writing as if the
patient actually puts the analyst
in a "painful and embarrassing
position." It is as if the analyst
is the victim of the patient's resistance.

progress of the treatment, to distract her interest
from the work and to put the analyst into a painful
and embarrassing position. ■ 29

If one looks into the situation more closely
one can recognize that more complicated motives
are also at work, of which some are connected
with the falling in love, and others are particular
expressions of resistance. To the first belong the
patient's efforts to re-assure herself of her irresis-
tibility, to destroy the physician's authority by
bringing him down to the level of a lover, and to
gain all the other advantages which she forsees as
incidental to gratification of her love. With regard
to the resistance, one may presume that at times it
uses the declarations of love as a test for the strait-
laced analyst, so that compliance on his part would
call down on him a reprimand. But above all one
obtains the impression that the resistance acts as
an *agent provocateur*, intensifying the love of the
patient and exaggerating her readiness for the
sexual surrender, in order thereby to vindicate
the action of her repression more emphatically by
pointing to the dangers of such licentiousness. All
this by-play, which in less complicated cases may
not be present at all, has as we know been regarded by A. Adler as the essential element in the
whole process.

But how is the analyst to behave in this situation if he is not to come to grief and yet believes
that the treatment should be continued through
this love-transference and in spite of it?

It would be very simple for me now, on the
score of conventional morality, emphatically to
insist that the analyst must never in any circumstances accept or return the tender passion prof-
fered him—that instead he must watch for his

chance to urge the infatuated woman to take the moral path and see the necessity of renunciation, and induce her to overcome the animal side of her nature and subdue her passion, so as to continue the analytic work.

I shall not fulfil these expectations, however—neither the first nor the second. Not the first, because I am writing not for patients, but for physicians who have serious difficulties to contend with, and also because in this instance I can go behind moral prescriptions to the source of them, namely, to utility. I am on this occasion in the happy position of being able to put the requirements of analytic technique in the place of a moral decree without any alteration in the results.

Even more emphatically, however, do I decline to fulfil the second of the expectations suggested above. To urge the patient to suppress, to renounce and to sublimate the promptings of her instincts, as soon as she has confessed her love-transference, would be not an analytic way of dealing with them, but a senseless way. It would be the same thing as to conjure up a spirit from the underworld by means of a crafty spell and then to dispatch him back again without a question. One would have brought the repressed impulses out into consciousness only in terror to send them back into repression once more. Nor should one deceive oneself about the success of any such proceeding. When levelled at the passions, lofty language achieves very little, as we all know. The patient will only feel the humiliation, and will not fail to revenge herself for it.

Just as little can I advocate a middle course which would recommend itself to some as especially ingenious; this would consist in averring one's response to the patient's feelings of affection, but in refraining from all the physical accompaniments of these tender feelings, until one could guide the situation along calmer channels and raise it on to a higher level. Against this expedient

I have to object that the psycho-analytic treatment is founded on truthfulness. A great part of its educative effect and its ethical value lies in this very fact. It is dangerous to depart from this sure foundation. When a man's life has become bound up with the analytic technique, he finds himself at a loss altogether for the lies and the guile which are otherwise so indispensable to a physician, and if for once with the best intentions he attempts to use them he is likely to betray himself. Since we demand strict truthfulness from our patients, we jeopardize our whole authority if we let ourselves be caught by them in a departure from the truth. And besides, this experimental adoption of tender feeling for the patient is by no means without danger. One cannot keep such complete control of oneself as not one day suddenly to go further than was intended. In my opinion, therefore, it is not permissible to disavow the indifference one has developed by keeping the counter-transference in check.

I have already let it be seen that the analytic technique requires the physician to deny the patient who is longing for love the satisfaction she craves. The treatment must be carried through in a state of abstinence; I do not mean merely corporal abstinence, nor yet deprivation of everything desired, for this could perhaps not be tolerated by any sick person. But I would state as a fundamental principle that the patient's desire and longing are to be allowed to remain, to serve as driving forces for the work and for the changes to be wrought, and that one must beware of granting this source of strength some discharge by surrogates. Indeed, one could not offer the patient anything but surrogates, for until the repressions are lifted her condition makes her incapable of true satisfaction. ■ 30

Let us admit that this principle—of carrying through the analytic treatment in a state of renunciation—extends far beyond the case we are dis-

■ 30

Here Freud is stating that the analyst should not fool himself into thinking that

■ 30 *continued*

he can offer the patient something in reality that can permanently alleviate a patient's
suffering. Some analysts have
taken this type of passage to
show that Freud advocated neutrality in psychoanalysis, and
that in every aspect of their

behavior, analysts should be
careful not to gratify a patient's
wishes. Other analysts have
strongly disagreed, maintaining
that Freud was referring to the
analyst's acting out with the
patient, not to the analyst's
everyday behavior.

cussing, and that it needs close consideration in
order to define the limits of its possible application. But we will refrain from going into this
question now and will keep as closely as possible
to the situation we started from. What would
happen if the physician were to behave differently,
and avail himself of a freedom perhaps available to
them both to return the love of the patient and to
appease her longing for tenderness from him?

If he had been guided in his decision by the
argument that compliance on his part would
strengthen his power over the patient so that he
could influence her to perform the tasks required
by the treatment, that is, could achieve a permanent cure of her neurosis by this means, experience would teach him that he had miscalculated.
The patient would achieve her aim, but he would
never achieve his. There is an amusing story about
a pastor and an insurance agent which describes
what would happen. An ungodly insurance agent
lay at the point of death and his relatives fetched
the holy man to convert him before he died. The
interview lasted so long that those outside began
to have some hope. At last the door of the sick
chamber opened. The free-thinker had not been
converted—but the pastor went away insured.

If her advances were returned, it would be a
great triumph for the patient, but a complete
overthrow for the cure. She would have succeeded
in what all patients struggle for, in expressing in
action, in reproducing in real life, what she ought

only to remember, to reproduce as the content of
her mind and to retain within the mental sphere.[4]
In the further course of the love-relationship all
the inhibitions and pathological reactions of her
love-development would come out, yet there
would be no possibility of correcting them, and the
painful episode would end in remorse and a
strengthening of her tendency to repression. The
love-relationship actually destroys the influence of
the analytic treatment on the patient; a combination of the two would be an inconceivable thing.

It is therefore just as disastrous for the analysis if the patient's craving for love prevails as if it
is suppressed. The way the analyst must take is
neither of these; it is one for which there is no
prototype in real life. He must guard against ig-
noring the transference-love, scaring it away or
making the patient disgusted with it; and just as
resolutely must he withhold any response to it. He
must face the transference-love boldly but treat it
like something unreal, as a condition which must
be gone through during the treatment and traced
back to its unconscious origins, so that it shall
assist in bringing to light all that is most hidden in
the development of the patient's erotic life, and
help her to learn to control it. The more plainly
the analyst lets it be seen that he is proof against
every temptation, the sooner will the advantage
from the situation accrue to the analysis. The patient, whose sexual repressions are of course not
yet removed but merely pushed into the background, will then feel safe enough to allow all her
conditions for loving, all the phantasies of her
sexual desires, all the individual details of her way
of being in love to come to light, and then will
herself open up the way back from them to the
infantile roots of her love.

With one type of woman, to be sure, this
attempt to preserve the love-transference for the

[4]Cf. pp. 49 and 55 *et seq.* [in this volume].

purposes of analytic work without gratifying it will not succeed. These are women of an elemental passionateness; they tolerate no surrogates; they are children of nature who refuse to accept the spiritual instead of the material; to use the poet's words, they are amenable only to the 'logic of gruel and the argument of dumplings'. ▪ 31 With such people one has the choice: either to return their love or else to bring down upon oneself the full force of the mortified woman's fury. In neither event can one safeguard the interests of the treatment. One must acknowledge failure and withdraw; and may at leisure study the problem of how the capacity for neurosis can be combined with such an intractable craving for love.

Many analysts must have discovered the way in which other women, less violent in their love, can be brought round gradually to the analytic point of view. Above all, the unmistakable element of resistance in their 'love' must be insisted upon. Genuine love would make the patient docile and intensify her readiness to solve the problems of her case, simply because the man she loved expected it. A woman who was really in love would gladly choose the road to completion of the cure, in order to give herself a value in the physician's eyes and to prepare herself for real life where her feelings of love could find their proper outlet. Instead of this, she is showing a stubborn and rebellious spirit, has thrown up all interest in her treatment, and clearly too all respect for the physician's well-founded judgement. She is bringing out a resistance, therefore, under the guise of being in love; and in addition to this, she has no compunction about trying to lead him into a cleft stick. For if he refuses her love, as duty and his understanding compel him to do, she can take up the attitude that she has been humiliated and, out of revenge and resentment, make herself inaccessible to cure by him, just as she is now doing ostensibly out of love.

▪ 31
This is perhaps one of the more unfortunate quotes that Freud uses, and one is attempted to be apologetic about his use of it. However, he is talking about people who, at some points in treatment, are unable to understand the symbolic nature of transference. Freud's view of the choices that are available is different from the views of a number of contemporary analysts. Modell, following Winnicott, writes convincingly about the need for a holding environment for patients who feel as if they need to have their love returned in reality.

As a second argument against the genuineness of this love one advances the fact that it shows not a single new feature connecting it with the present situation, but is entirely composed of repetitions and 'rechauffés' of earlier reactions, including childish ones. One then sets about proving this by detailed analysis of the patient's behaviour in love.

When the necessary amount of patience is added to these arguments it is usually possible to overcome the difficult situation and to continue the work, the patient having either moderated her love or transformed it; the aim of the work then becomes the discovery of the infantile object-choice and of the phantasies woven around it. I will now, however, examine these arguments critically and put the question whether they really represent the truth or whether by employing them we are not in our desperation resorting to prevarication and misrepresentation. In other words: can the love which is manifested in analytic treatment not truly be called real?

I think that we have told the patient the truth, but not the whole truth without regard for consequences. Of our two arguments the first is the stronger. The part taken by resistance in the transference-love is unquestionable and very considerable. But this love was not created by the resistance; the latter finds it ready to hand, exploits it and aggravates the manifestations of it. Nor is its genuineness impugned by the resistance. The second argument is far weaker; it is true that the love consists of new editions of old traces and that it repeats infantile reactions. But this is the essential character of every love. There is no love that does not reproduce infantile prototypes. The infantile conditioning factor in it is just what gives it its compulsive character which verges on the pathological. The transference-love has perhaps a degree less of freedom than the love which appears in ordinary life and is called normal; it displays its dependence on the infantile pattern more clearly, is less adaptable and capable of modification, but that is all and that is nothing essential.

By what other signs can the genuineness of a love be recognized? By its power to achieve results, its capacity to accomplish its aim? In this respect the transference-love seems to give place to none; one has the impression that one could achieve anything by its means.

Let us resume, therefore: One has no right to dispute the 'genuine' nature of the love which makes its appearance in the course of analytic treatment. However lacking in normality it may seem to be, this quality is sufficiently explained when we remember that the condition of being in love in ordinary life outside analysis is also more like abnormal than normal mental phenomena. The transference-love is characterized, nevertheless, by certain features which ensure it a special position. In the first place, it is provoked by the analytic situation; secondly, it is greatly intensified by the resistance which dominates this situation; and thirdly, it is to a high degree lacking in regard for reality, is less sensible, less concerned about consequences, more blind in its estimation of the person loved, than we are willing to admit of normal love. We should not forget, however, that it is precisely these departures from the norm that make up the essential element in the condition of being in love.

The first of these three characteristics of the transference-love is what determines the physician's course of action. He has evoked this love by undertaking analytic treatment in order to cure the neurosis; for him it is an unavoidable consequence of the medical situation, as inevitable as the exposure of a patient's body or being told some life-and-death secret. It is therefore plain to him that he is not to derive any personal advantage from it. The patient's willingness makes no difference whatever; it merely throws the whole responsibility on him. Indeed, as he must know, the patient had from the beginning entertained hopes of this way of being cured. After all the difficulties are overcome she will often confess to a phantasy, an expectation that she had had as she began the treatment—'if she behaved well, she would be rewarded in the end by the doctor's love for her'.

For the physician there are ethical motives which combine with the technical reasons to hinder him from according the patient his love. The aim that he has to keep in view is that this woman, whose capacity for love is disabled by infantile fixations, should attain complete access over this function which is so inestimably important for her in life, not that she should fritter it away in the treatment, but preserve it for real life, if so be that after her cure life makes that demand on her. He must not let the scene of the race between the dogs be enacted, in which the prize was a chaplet of sausages and which a funny fellow spoilt by throwing one sausage on to the course; the dogs fell upon it and forgot about the race and the chaplet in the distance luring them on to win. I do not mean to say that it is always easy for the physician to keep within the bounds prescribed by technique and ethics. Younger men especially, who are not yet bound by a permanent tie, may find it a hard task. The love between the sexes is undoubtedly one of the first things in life, and the combination of mental and bodily satisfaction attained in the enjoyment of love is literally one of life's culminations. Apart from a few perverse fanatics, all the world knows this and conducts life accordingly; only science is too refined to confess it. Again, when a woman sues for love, to reject and refuse is a painful part for a man to play; and in spite of neurosis and resistance there is an incomparable fascination about a noble woman who confesses her passion. It is not the grossly sensual desires of the patient that constitute the temptation. These are more likely to repel and to demand the exercise of toleration in order to regard them as a natural phenomenon. It is perhaps the finer impulses, those 'inhibited in their aim', which lead a man into the danger of forgetting the rules of technique and the physician's task for the sake of a wonderful experience.

And yet the analyst is absolutely debarred from giving way. However highly he may prize love, he must prize even more highly the opportunity to help his patient over a decisive moment in her life. She has to learn from him to overcome the pleasure-principle, to give up a gratification which lies to hand but is not sanctioned by the world she lives in, in favour of a distant and perhaps altogether doubtful one, which is, however, socially and psychologically unimpeachable. To achieve this mastery of herself she must be taken through the primordial era of her mental development and in this way reach that greater freedom within the mind which distinguishes conscious mental activity—in the systematic sense—from unconscious.

The analytic psychotherapist thus has a three-fold battle to wage—in his own mind against the forces which would draw him down below the level of analysis; outside analysis against the opponents who dispute the importance he attaches to the sexual instinctual forces and hinder him from making use of them in his scientific method; and in the analysis against his patients, who at first behave like his critics but later on disclose the over-estimation of sexual life which has them in thrall, and who try to take him captive in the net of their socially ungovernable passions.

The lay public, of whose attitude to psycho-analysis I spoke at the outset, will certainly seize the opportunity given it by this discussion of the transference-love to direct the attention of the world to the dangers of this therapeutic method. The psycho-analyst knows that the forces he works with are of the most explosive kind and that he needs as much caution and conscientiousness as a chemist. But when has it ever been forbidden to a chemist, on account of its danger, to occupy himself with the explosives which, just because of their effectiveness, are so indispensable? It is remarkable that psycho-analysis has to win for itself afresh all the liberties which have long been accorded to other medical work. I certainly do not advocate that the harmless methods of treatment should be abandoned. For many cases they suffice, and when all is said, the *furor sanandi* is no more use to human society than any other kind of fanaticism. But it is grossly to undervalue both the origins and the practical significance of the psychoneuroses to suppose that these disorders are to be removed by pottering about with a few harmless remedies. No; in medical practice there will always be room for the '*ferrum*' and the '*ignis*' as well as for the '*medicina*', and there a strictly regular, unmodified psycho-analysis, which is not afraid to handle the most dangerous forces in the mind and set them to work for the benefit of the patient, will be found indispensable.

4

Contemporary Perspectives

We can see that Freud was able to state his views on transference not only in clinical terms but also within two different theoretical contexts (Freud 1900, 1920). First, he gave a theoretical definition of the relationship of transference in terms of the system unconscious and its relationship to the preconscious/conscious (Freud 1900). Twenty years later he extended the concept of the "compulsion to repeat" to the status of a universal tendency (present in all humans), and thus logically extended the concept of transference to a universal tendency (Freud 1920). He placed this vision in his new structural model of the ego, superego, and id. Freud did not explore the implications of his new postulate and its ramifications for the concept of transference. The paragraph that we have previously quoted from "Beyond the Pleasure Principle" (1920) is his most significant statement of the relationship of transference to the compulsion to repeat.

Brian Bird

No contemporary writer has dealt with the subject of transference as powerfully as Brian Bird (1972, 1973). His views on Freud and the role of transference in the analytic situation are both refreshing and, in his words, "admittedly extreme."

Bird sees transference as a "universal mental function which may well be the basis of all human relationships" (Bird 1972, p. 267).[1] Bird not only

[1] It is interesting that Bird sees the idea of transference as universal tendency as a new idea. Bird does not refer to Freud's quote in "Beyond the Pleasure Principle" in the way that we have and does

conceives of transference as a universal tendency, but as assuming "characteristics of a major ego function" (Bird 1972, p. 267).[2] Not surprisingly, Bird's view
is that in the analytic situation the

> resolution of a transference neurosis is the only avenue to the farthest reaches of
> the mind. It is also my belief that transference, in one form or another, is always
> present, active, and significant in the analytic situation. . . . I would also be
> inclined to agree with those, perhaps few in number, who harbor the idea that
> analysts themselves regularly develop transference reactions to their patients,
> including periods of transference neurosis, and that these transference reactions
> play an essential role in the analytic process.[3] [Bird 1972, p. 267]

From these illustrations of Bird's thoughts, we can see that transference has
achieved a centrality for him that is only implied in Freud's conceptualizations. In
talking about transference, Bird maintains that, historically, its introduction
"brought about an entire change in the nature of analysis. The introduction of
free association . . . a much lesser change, received and still receives much more
recognition." Freud, from Bird's perspective, was clearest about the importance of
transference when writing his postscript to the Dora case: "These remarkable
observations, written in declarative style, with no hint of vacillation, vagueness,
or ambivalence, convey a sense of deep conviction that could arise, one feels, only
from Freud's own hard-won inner experience" (1972, p. 273).

While I am not in agreement with Bird's historical accounting, his general
point of view is of great interest.[4] To follow his narrative a step further, he sees
Freud after the Dora case pulling back from his hard-won victory and becoming less specific and even interpersonal in his orientation toward transference.

---

not therefore comment on this statement of Freud's that implies that transference is a universal
tendency. In any case, this is merely an academic oversight, for, as we have indicated, Freud did not
develop this idea in subsequent writings.

[2]Here Bird is differing from Freud's conceptualizations for he is conceptualizing transference as a
structural concept. In Freud's model, transference is a result of the interaction of different
structures. Again, it seems to me this is more of an academic difference, for Bird does not spell out
the theoretical implications of what he means in talking about transference as an ego function (like
speech or perception, etc.).

[3]Today (19 years later) many analysts would agree that they regularly develop transference
reactions to their patients. The idea of analysts developing a transference neurosis is an interesting
and as yet not fully explored theoretical concept.

[4]While I think Bird is incorrect historically, I view this as a minor matter. To document the
historical consideration, we have seen Freud in "Recollection, Repetition and Working Through"
quite specific in his views on the importance of transference. We have also seen that the views that
Freud stated in the Dora case are at least in part echoes of the psychotherapy chapter in *Studies on
Hysteria*. Thus, they are not as revolutionary as Bird has stated. It is my thought that Freud
oscillated in his point of view about transference, depending on his current clinical experience and
the theoretical issue that was of interest to him at the moment. At times, his insight was
penetrating; occasionally, he backed away from his insights.

Bird's words help to focus us on Freud's difficulty in continuing to develop the concept of transference. Bird relates that Freud was consistently "on-and-off" in his tendency to regard transference as a merely technical matter. He notes Freud's frequent references to transference as an asset only when positive—and a liability when negative.

We can summarize two of Bird's central points in the following manner: (1) Freud, in a remarkable insight, was able to conceptualize transference in the Dora case, but he was not able to develop the implications of this crucial theoretical–clinical concept. (2) Freud was particularly unable to understand the implications of negative transference, and, because of this, he degraded the general importance of transference.

For Bird, the negative transference at its core (as a universal tendency) is involved with destructive wishes. Wishes to annihilate and do away with are fundamental tendencies that are not a response to unempathic parenting but rather innate tendencies that have not been brought under control of the ego. It may very well be that this lack of ego control may have occurred because of lack of parental empathy, but not as *response* to a parental failing.[5] Although the importance of destructive tendencies is highlighted in Freud's theoretical writings, Bird correctly points out that in his clinical papers Freud seems to eschew analyzing destructive tendencies and, I would add, most aspects of negative transference. Bird's view is that missing this aspect of a person's inner world of necessity means that the person is undergoing an incomplete analysis at best. To be sure, he does not underestimate the difficulty of analyzing negative transference, but he does see it as crucial if the analysis is to have the liberating effects that he thinks are possible.

I will end this brief review by alluding to what Bird considers perhaps the most important issue of transference, the transference neurosis. I believe it is fair to say that Bird is even more correct now (as compared with 1972), when he says that "most analysts only work with transference feelings. They either ignore the transference neurosis or believe, as anyone has a right to, that there are no significant differences between a transference neurosis and other transference reactions, that transference is simply transference" (Bird 1972, p. 278).

Bird distinguishes three types of relationships in the analysis: the transference neurosis, ordinary transference, and a relationship based on reality considerations. He says that a transference neurosis "is merely a new edition of the patient's original neurosis, but with me (the analyst) in it" (p. 281). Bird postulates that transference reactions are displacements "from early memories" (of one's father, for example) onto the analyst. Transference then is a displacement of one person to another, and a repeating of the past in the present. In Bird's framework, if a patient sees me as her father, the identities of

---

[5] I am emphasizing this here so that Bird's difference with Kohut will be highlighted for the reader later, when Kohut's views are discussed.

the father and myself are merged, but the "patient's own identity and my identity remain clear and separate" (Bird 1972, p. 281). In the transference neurosis, however, the patient

> includes me somehow in the structure, or part structure of his neurosis. As a result of this process, the identity difference between him and me is lost, and at the moment and for the particular area affected by the transference neurosis, I come to represent the *patient himself*. More specifically, I come to represent some complex of the patient's neurosis or some element of his ego, superego, drives, defense, etc. which has become part of his neurosis. I do not represent . . . actual persons from the past, except in the form in which they have been incorporated into the patient's neurotic organization. [1972, pp. 281–282]

Here, Bird is distinguishing between what he regards as the patient repeating a past memory (transference) and the patient symbolizing the analyst as an aspect of his, the patient's, neurotic organization (transference neurosis). In this distinction, I believe that Bird is attempting to capture something clinically important. I also believe that the manner in which he conceives of the difference between transference and transference neurosis raises as many questions as it resolves. Is a person's neurotic organization encoded in memory in a different form from the other transference memories that Bird alludes to? This seems to be the case, but Bird has not accounted for this or provided an explanation in his theoretical formulations. Why does the representation of neurotic organization in the transference neurosis imply a breakdown (even if temporary) between the representation of the analyst and the patient? One can think of several reasons, but it is my sense that these questions (and others) have not been fully addressed in Bird's work. Perhaps the clinical examples he alludes to might be better explained by a concept like projective identification,[6] where one would expect self-object differentiation to be impaired. There are several alternative formulations for this aspect of Bird's work, but for our purposes it is exciting to go back and summarize, however briefly, some of the issues that this interesting and provocative writer-clinician has brought forth.

Bird has stated clearly and without vacillation or ambiguity the importance of transference. He has provided the beginnings of a more complete theoretical understanding of transference. To my mind, he correctly emphasizes the importance of analyzing the negative transference. In his clinical vignettes, he provides illustrations of how it is possible to analyze the negative transference in an empathic manner that can allow the bond between patient and analyst to remain intact, even while they are talking about what are often especially difficult issues. Bird in stating his positions has done so in a way that I think will prove conducive to further elaboration of his efforts.

---

[6]This is a concept put forth by Klein (1957) and Bion (1954) in which, as one ramification of the process, the boundaries between analyst and patient are obscured or at times obliterated.

Charles Brenner

Brenner is considered by many analysts to be a principal spokesman for the classical position. He is a synthesizer and advocate of Freud's later theoretical writings. Arlow and Brenner's book on the structural theory (1964) is one of the major works that inform classical or ego psychoanalysts. Brenner's more recent works (1976, 1982) are our primary sources for his positions on technique, and these books have also been well received in the analytic community. The term *classical analyst* connotes close contact with Freudian thought, and classical analysts are considered by many to be the inheritors of Freudian tradition. In this context, if is of note that Brenner does not adhere to many of Freud's suggestions and distinctions. As we will see later, he holds to even fewer of Freud's actual practices. He has developed, however, one aspect of Freud's theoretical position,[7] and in this respect he certainly is an inheritor and developer of the implications of Freudian thought.

One of the important aspects of Brenner's work is the way in which he is able to apply certain aspects of Freudian theory to psychoanalytic technique. He is frequently able to do this in a more consistent manner than Freud. Before we go into a discussion of Brenner's specific views on transference, I will try to give a brief indication of some of Brenner's theoretical leanings. When I mentioned that Brenner was a classical analyst, even this designation is not specific enough to indicate his theoretical predilections. His work with Arlow established in classical theory both the primacy of the structural model and the importance of the oedipal period of development. It was only in the final phases of his theorizing that Freud saw the oedipal period as the crucible of all psychogenic conflicts. Even at that late point Freud evinced some doubts or tentativeness about his formulation (Freud 1925a). Arlow and Brenner evince no such tentativeness, and the primacy of the oedipal stage is established by them without hesitation. Thus, there may be a myriad of diagnostic outcomes based on oedipal conflicts, but the content of the conflicts may look remarkably similar. What will differ is the intensity or quantitative aspect of the conflict. A schizophrenic patient will thus have more intense oedipal conflicts than a neurotic patient will in this theoretical matrix. In addition, what will be affected are different ego functions. A schizophrenic's reality testing, and the ego functions that are subsumed under reality testing (perception, thought, etc.), are impoverished by their conflicts, whereas different ego functions are

---

[7]I am making two distinctions here: First, that Brenner may agree with Freudian theory and not with Freud's suggestions about technique. Second, that although Brenner agrees with and has significantly developed Freudian theory, he has developed one aspect of Freudian theory and left out certain aspects of Freud's thought that others find quite valuable. I believe that the aspect of Freud's thought that Brenner has developed is Freud's dominant position in the later stages of his career. Still there are those of us who may feel that Freud made more significant and richer contributions in the early and middle parts of his career. I have included this long, convoluted footnote to indicate to the reader my belief that there are many analysts who consider themselves Freudian who are *not* classical analysts in the way the term is typically used in psychoanalysis.

modified in a neurotic disorder.[8] In this parsimonious explanation of the content of conflicts, there are, of course, other differences as well. Superego structure in different disorders will look quite different according to this theory, and the nature and consistency of superego control will be indicative of the disorder. In a similar vein, classical theory in the hands of Anna Freud explicated and extended Freud's ideas on defense (A. Freud 1936). Primarily under the initial impetus of Anna Freud, classical theory solidified the idea of defense as an ego function that is unconscious. Hartmann (1939) and then Arlow and Brenner continued and expanded upon Anna Freud's contribution.

As one can see from this brief review, Brenner is an analyst who has attempted to clarify and expand Freudian thought. One important aspect of Freud's theorizing that Brenner has utilized and extended is the idea of compromise formation. Freud, as early as *The Interpretation of Dreams*, put forth the idea of the dream as a compromise formation.[9] Dreams are a compromise in that the manifest dream contains both elements of defense and the unconscious fantasy or wish.[10] Freud used this formulation to explain not only dream formation but a variety of other phenomena as well (including symptom formation). Freud, however, did not take this central concept and systematically apply it to the concept of transference. Freud mentions in "The Dynamics of Transference" that all transference is an admixture of positive and negative transference, but he never realizes the full implications of this thought. Rather, according to Bird, Freud regarded positive transference as an asset to analysis and negative transference as a liability to it. Brenner, unlike Freud, has systematically applied the concept of compromise formation to his ideas on transference. Thus, he sees transference formations as ambivalent admixtures of sexual and aggressive fantasies. Accordingly, the distinction between positive and negative transference is for him a spurious one that does not capture the complexity of transference reactions. He does not attempt to nurture any type of positive transference. Rather, he sees the manifestation of all transference reactions as material to be understood and interpreted to the patient. Brenner has extended the concept of transference to all avenues of a person's life. Transference is to be encountered not only in an analyst's office but in virtually every human transaction. While it is again true that Freud gives hints of this position, it remains for writers like Bird and Brenner to more systematically and convincingly detail the universal importance of transference.

[8]Even if the same ego functions are modified, the extent of the modification will vary considerably.
[9]The idea of compromise formation pervades a good deal of Freud's theorizing about mental events. Thus, not only are dreams compromise formations, but symptoms, slips of the tongue, momentary forgetting, and a variety of other mental phenomena are conceived of in this way.
[10]This is, of course, an overly simplified way of stating the formation of a dream. Freud's ideas about dream formation are a good deal more complex (see chapter on dreams) but in his formulation he does state that dreams are a compromise between the underlying wish (that has been stimulated by the day residue) and the censorship. The censorship is a preconscious agency that was part of Freud's theory at the time of the onset of the topographic model (1900). I am using it as roughly equivalent to the concept of defense, and certainly Freud thought of the censorship as initiating defensive functions.

We have seen that Freud talked about three types of transference—two types of positive and one type of negative transference. Brenner has stated that it is a mistake to separate the positive and negative transference, but what about the form of positive transference that Freud labels the unobjectionable transference? Brenner tells us that what is called the unobjectionable transference is also an ambivalent admixture, as is any transference. Thus, Brenner is in agreement with Stein (Stein 1981) when he maintains that the unobjectionable transference should be analyzed just as one should analyze any aspect of transference. Here we see Brenner trying to eliminate even this form of influence that Freud considered unobjectionable. Freud thought that this form of transference is necessary for the success of the treatment and enabled the patient to persevere even when difficult topics were emerging in the analysis. Freud in effect used this concept to explain why the patient continued in treatment during periods of intense resistance (particularly during periods of negative transference).

My view is that contemporary analysts have used terms like *working* or *therapeutic alliance*[11] as ways of explaining the same issues that Freud was attempting to elucidate. Brenner also sees these concepts as unnecessary theoretical tools. In what I consider to be a careful review of the clinical evidence that has been put forth supporting the concept of working alliance,[12] Brenner maintains that concepts such as the working or therapeutic alliance can be better explained as transference manifestations (Brenner 1979). He sees nothing unique about the clinical evidence that is presented and indeed considers that what is being presented as evidence of a therapeutic alliance should have been interpreted as transference. Brenner's position is that the appropriate analysis or interpretation of a patient's conflicts is what is necessary and perhaps sufficient for a successful analytic treatment. In my opinion, he views these constructs (working and therapeutic alliance) as at best superfluous, and, at worst, attempts to evade the analytic process. The only unique role for the analyst is to offer the patient, at the appropriate time, help in understanding the conflicts he is experiencing in the transference.[13]

Many analysts have argued that patients who have been deemed classical patients may be able to withstand Brenner's version of analytic technique, but other types of patients are not appropriate for this type of rigorous treatment (Bach 1985). Some have said that there is a large group of modern patients that analysts from Greenson (1967) to Bach (1985) have called nonclassical patients, who would be unable to tolerate Brenner's form of analysis. This type of discussion calls into question not only the type of patient one is discussing, but also a definition of what one means by psychoanalytic treatment. From

---

[11]Although there is some difference in the way analysts have used these two terms, for the present purposes I will use them synonymously.

[12]The evidence that has been presented by Zetzel (1965, 1966), Greenson (1967), and Stone (1967).

[13]Brenner would admit, though, that there are occasions for extratransference interpretations.

Brenner's perspective it is possible to do classical analysis with some people who are diagnosed as borderline. In fact a recent Kris Study Group volume by Abend, Porter, and Willick (1983)[14] presents evidence that offers some support for this claim,[15] perhaps giving indications of a widening scope in classical treatment.

Brenner eschews the idea of transference neurosis and wonders what meaning one can place on such a concept. All transference is a compromise formation, and so all transference within his framework contains the elements of neurotic formation. There may be more or less intense transference reactions, but from Brenner's perspective no aspect of the transference warrants being designated as the *transference neurosis*. Brenner obviously differs from Freud in his view of the transference neurosis, how he categorizes transference reactions, as well as how he conceptualizes what Freud called the unobjectionable transference (or what modern analysts call the therapeutic or working alliance).[16] As is true with many contemporary analysts, Brenner places more emphasis on transference in the treatment situation than Freud did. Although it may seem as if Brenner has moved a considerable distance from Freud's positions, this is at least somewhat illusory, since his views on the meaning of patients' communications are derived from Freud's structural theory.

Merton Gill

If one had the idea that he or she could, in a concise manner, summarize Gill's theoretical positions after reading through his pioneering, innovative work, we will dispel that illusion here. Gill has written interesting, provocative, and illuminating treatises from a variety of theoretical viewpoints. It was Rapaport and Gill (1959) who proposed the criteria for what should be considered a complete metapsychological statement in psychoanalysis. It was Pribram and Gill (1976) who drew our attention to the fascinating aspects of Freud's early attempt to create a neurophysiological model in *The Project*. Gill has written sophisticated statements comparing models of psychoanalysis (1984) and has been involved in a variety of research, as well as a myriad of theoretical, discussions. It does not come as a complete surprise that Gill over the last ten

[14]Brenner was the analyst who initially presented a case to this group and who I would say was one of the guiding lights of this enterprise.

[15]In my opinion, the support that is offered by this volume is difficult to assess. The authors are not able to provide much of a rationale as to why some patients are successful and others are not. One could say that this type of rationale is not present anywhere in the literature, but I would argue that a number of authors have at least provided some theoretical context for an explanation of variable therapeutic results for patients who have been diagnosed as borderline—Kernberg (1975), Kohut (1971), and Stolorow, Brandchaft, and Atwood (1987), to name a few.

[16]Brenner also differs with Freud in terms of the timing of interpretations. Freud advocated interpreting (or cropping away) the transference as it is manifested as a resistance. Brenner favors interpreting as the transference becomes "significant" in the treatment.

to fourteen years has presented an interesting and extreme position on the role of transference in the psychoanalytic situation.

Gill in numerous publications maintains that Freud, as well as contemporary analysts, have overlooked the central importance of transference reactions. Gill's position is that "the analysis of transference should play a greater and more central role in analytic technique than I believe it does in prevailing practice" (1982a, p. 177).

Gill implies that this shortcoming of prevailing practice derives in part from analysts' efforts to emulate Freud. Moreover, Gill maintains that the analysis of transference never became as "central" as it should have been for Freud. In Gill's account, "Freud remained of the view that the analysis of transference is *ancillary* to the analysis of the neurosis rather than contending that the analysis of the neurosis should take place essentially by way of the analysis of the transference" (1982a, p. 177).

Gill defines transference as "an analysis" of past and present, by a patient who responds to the analytic situation, as *plausibly* as is possible. In his view, transference results from the interaction between patient and analyst, rather than merely from a distortion of the present on the patient's part.[17] The patient then is seen as consistently and idiosyncratically reacting to the analyst's actions. The analyst in turn is a participant-observer in Sullivan's sense of the term. The analyst should see how he is contributing to the patient's experience, while helping the patient understand how he is giving meaning to the analytic situation in his/her own idiosyncratic way.

Gill maintains that the transference is "ubiquitously" present from the beginning of treatment and should be interpreted as such from the beginning. Thus, he disagrees with Freud's recommendation that the analyst should not interpret the transference until it becomes a source of resistance.

In his view, transference interpretations involve two types: (1) interpretations of resistance to the awareness of transference and (2) interpretations intended to resolve the transference. Ideally, they should be delivered in progressive sequence, leading to transference resolution. Gill argues that patients are always talking about their transference experiences, even when they are not directly referring to them. Gill asserts that they *allude* to the transference in their associations, attitudes, feelings, and wishes. Gill advocates that the analyst make explicit these allusions to the transference so that analytic explanation can focus on how the patient is experiencing the analyst and the analytic situation. These interpretations represent interpretations of the patient's resistance to the awareness of transference. Once the patient has become aware of his transference experience, the analyst can shift to helping the patient understand how he came to construct this transference experience.

[17]We can remember that Freud's view in the Dora postscript was that patients sometimes sublimate their transference reactions, and sometimes repeat directly in terms of their transference reactions. Gill's view, in terms of this distinction, is that the patient always sublimates.

These interpretations of resistance to the resolution of the transference begin with identifying what has actually occurred in the analytic situation to stimulate the patient's reaction and go on to clarify how the patient came to understand the occurrence in his particular way. The patient then must recognize his idiosyncratic contribution to this experience, the contribution from the past.

Gill theorizes that this collaborative exploration leads to transference resolution in two ways: (1) The patient achieves a better understanding of how and what he contributes to his transference experience. (2) The patient has an interpersonal experience with the analyst that is more beneficent than the transference experience, constituting a "corrective emotional experience" as a byproduct of the work. Gill stresses interpretations of the transference in the here-and-now, de-emphasizing other types of interpretation, including genetic interpretations. Gill then gives reconstruction of the past a minor role at best in analytic technique.

Gill's approach[18] is a radical focusing on the patient's implicit and explicit reactions to the analyst. Everything the patient brings to the session is seen as a manifestation of transference reaction. If a patient dresses in an unusual manner, Gill might make this the subject of an interpretation whether or not the patient has mentioned it in the session. Moreover, it is possible that Gill will focus on the patient's dress and question the patient about it. In a session, he asks a female patient, "What is the writing on your tee shirt?" This is done before the patient has had a chance to say almost anything in the session. This line of inquiry arises from Gill's view that virtually everything in a session is a manifestation of transference. It is also his view that the position of neutrality of the analyst is an illusion.

From his purview, the analyst enters the treatment situation with various preconceived theoretical notions. It is better to acknowledge these theoretical biases and work within them than to attempt to reach an impossible goal of analytic neutrality. Thus, he is quite accepting of Freud's idea of the unobjectionable transference and of Freud's personal approach to his patients. He agrees with Freud's division of the transference into three types of transference but feels that Freud did not analyze the implications of any of the transferences sufficiently. From Gill's perspective, Freud's offering and providing the Rat Man a meal is not a technical difficulty; rather, it is Freud's failure to subsequently attend to the transference implications of this gift that creates a difficulty.[19] Gill is in agreement with Brenner in not distinguishing between the transference and the transference neurosis. He states that analysts have viewed transference phenomena as a transference neurosis because they have not systematically analyzed the transference during the entire analysis. Thus, when the transference is not analyzed and it then intensifies, it begins to look

---

[18]Gill has not only written about transference; he has also provided audiotapes of his sessions. Thus, I have some primary data on which to base my comments.
[19]See Chapter 14 and Lipton's views for a similar position.

more like what one would call a transference neurosis. Systematic analysis of the transference would prevent this intensification.

Given this array of agreements and disagreements with Freud's ideas on technique, one may wonder why some characterize Gill as employing a radical version of psychoanalysis as compared with Freud. It is radical to the extent that he focuses on and interprets what he considers to be manifestations of transference. Moreover, there is little attention paid to the patient's history and little focus on reconstructing the patient's past. This, at times, makes Gill's position difficult to distinguish from those of certain interpersonal therapists (neo-Sullivanian therapists) who focus exclusively on patient–therapist interaction. We might say that Gill's position is a 180-degree turn from Freud's psychotherapy technique, in which the goal was the recovery of pathogenic memories.

Heinz Kohut

Kohut's writing about the diagnosis, treatment, and theoretical understanding of narcissism can be divided into two phases in relationship to Freudian theory: Up to 1972 he stated that his contributions were attempts to elaborate and clarify Freudian thought (1966, 1968, 1971, 1972); and after his publication of *The Restoration of the Self* (Kohut 1977), he clearly rejected basic tenets of Freudian thought.[20] In my view, *The Analysis of the Self* (1971) did clarify aspects of Freud's theory of narcissism[21] and certainly pointed out logical inconsistencies in Freud's ideas about the treatment of people with narcissistic difficulties. Freud's conclusions, when writing about treatment, posit that there is a linear relationship between narcissistic development and object relations,[22] such that the more narcissism the less the capacity for object relations and vice

[20]It certainly is possible to see aspects of Kohutian thought before 1977 that seemed to presage his moving in non-Freudian directions. For purposes of exposition, however, I will continue to write using this dichotomous classification.

[21]Kohut's papers during this period also should be included in these comments. His paper on narcissistic rage (1972) is well worth reading for its poignant clinical descriptions, if for nothing else.

[22]This is his famous U-tube analogy, in which he relies (a rare event in his writings) on his energy model for an explanation of narcissistic development and narcissistic phenomena. Essentially, he says that there is a fixed amount of energy available to an individual; if this energy is rooted in narcissistic fixations or energy it is unavailable for object relations. What Freud means by object relations is then the key to this theoretical matrix. He proposes a sophisticated view (even by modern standards) of the development of narcissism (1911, 1914c, 1915b) and of the capacity of the child for object choice (1913a) and the development of object love (1914c). His love papers add to this model, but Freud rarely referred to these ideas after 1923 and his writing of "The Ego and the Id." What is left for most analysts of Freud's statements is his prohibition about treating narcissistic patients. In my view, this prohibition is incompatible with some of his assumptions about narcissistic development. I should state that my view on this matter is not a generally accepted one and for me to document my reasons for this interpretation is not possible in this context.

versa.[23] It is Freud's view that if the person does not have sufficient capacity for object relations (or sufficient object libido), then they are not able to be analyzed. This is the case because people with narcissistic fixations will not be able to form a transference relationship with the analyst. Analytic transference relationships are difficult because they will not be able to displace, or transfer to, the analyst derivatives of object-related[24] unconscious conflicts or fantasies. Without a transference relationship, Freud maintains there can be no analytic treatment.

Even when Kohut is writing within (or elaborating on) Freud's assumptions about narcissistic development, there is a disagreement about the implications of these ideas for the treatment of people with narcissistic difficulties. Kohut asserts that Freud (and a good part of the analytic community) draws a false dichotomy in opposing narcissism and object relations. He assumes that narcissism implies an obstacle to the development of mature love (object love), as opposed to an obstacle to other types of object relations. In my view this is implied in Freud's own writings about narcissism, but whether or not this is the case, Kohut explicitly makes this important theoretical–clinical statement. This initial statement about the possibility of narcissistic transference relationships sets the stage for Kohut to describe narcissistic transference(s). He begins this description by relating that there are nonspecific[25] resistances to developing narcissistic transferences. The goal of analytic treatment is to provide a facilitating atmosphere, in which the person can allow the transference(s) to emerge. Kohut is, then, attempting to set the analytic stage as a place that is welcoming of the manifestation of transference reactions. Interestingly, he does not advocate interpreting the meaning of transference states to the patient; rather, his approach is one that is quite different from Freud's, Brenner's, or Gill's in handling the manifestations of transference. Before approaching this difference, let us look at Kohut's view of narcissistic transference states and then briefly relate how he has developed the beginnings of a more general theoretical point of view.

There are a number of areas in which Kohut and Freud converge in terms of therapeutic technique. Kohut, like Freud, considers the transference to be best characterized in terms of positive or negative transference. Kohut considers that the positive transference may take two different forms: the patient may enter into an idealizing or mirroring transference, or some combination of the two. The mirroring transference has three different forms that vary in terms of the extent of self-object differentiation and developmental significance. Although negative transference can have different manifestations, the

---

[23]That is, the more the capacity for object relations, the less one's narcissistic tendencies. This formulation of Freud's, which is his best-known concept in this area, does not fit in with several of his other conclusions.
[24]From Freud's point of view because they had not developed object-related fantasies or conflicts.
[25]By nonspecific he means resistances that do not relate to specific content but rather to a general vulnerability of the person.

negative transference that Kohut has written about most definitively is what he calls narcissistic rage (1972). Negative transference occurs when the patient perceives there to be a lack of empathy on the part of the analyst. This can occur in a variety of ways, from the analyst leaving on vacation, to an analytic interpretation that the patient perceives as irritating or irrelevant to their present concerns. Kohut sees negative transference as a reaction to the analytic environment, that is, a repetition for the patient of an aspect of their childhood. Typically, the significance of negative transference reactions lies in a repetition of early empathic failures that the patient has experienced. During periods of negative transference (perceived breaks in empathy) the analyst, if possible, should reconstruct these experiences. Here again is a similarity to Freud's position; Kohut sees helping the patient understand their past as an important component of analytic treatment. Through the interpretation of negative transference, the analyst helps the patient understand the types of early empathic failures that they have weathered during childhood. Here we can bring together some of the similarities between Kohut and Freud; both interpret the negative transference rapidly and tend to provide reconstructions for the patient. And both, as mentioned earlier, tend to see the transference as divided into three aspects: two forms of positive and one form of negative transference. Both allow certain types of positive transference to proceed without providing an interpretation to the analysand.

We have seen that Freud does not interpret the unobjectionable positive transference, and Kohut advocates not interpreting positive transference states.[26] These two points are by no means completely overlapping, for, while Freud does not interpret one form of positive transference, he advocates full interpretation whenever one sees manifestations of the eroticized or sexual transference. In fact, if this transference is not interpreted, Freud perceives that there will be adverse consequences to the analysis. This is a major point of difference; Kohut maintains that allowing the positive transferences to continue or unfold is therapeutic for the patient[27] whereas Freud contends that allowing the continuation of a positive transference is counterproductive. Is there any simple way of reconciling these positions? Perhaps Kohut's focus upon narcissistic patients accounts for the disagreement? This is a possibility; it may be that what Freud calls the unobjectionable positive transference is really a form of idealizing or mirroring transference. Thus, neither Freud nor Kohut interprets this type of transference, but their understanding of the role

[26]This is a point that is easily misunderstood and needs to be underscored. Kohut advocates not interpreting transference unless it becomes some form of negative transference. From his perspective, this means that the patient is therefore perceiving a break in empathy in the analytic situation. Kohut advocates, when this happens, interpretation, so that the patient may be restored to a state of positive transference. He sees the positive transferences as vehicles that aid in structure-building or helping the patient to "transmute internalizations" in a way that will be beneficial.

[27]Freud would maintain that either one will see an induced regression or the patient will become hopelessly addicted to the treatment in a way that will not provide him analytic benefits.

and the importance of this type of transference is quite different. This speculation gains slight credibility when we see that Freud rarely (if ever) interpreted a transference that might be considered an idealizing transference. When we compare Brenner and Kohut, it is easier to see a clear and decisive difference. Brenner would state that one should interpret any aspect of the transference, and that systematically excluding one form of transference guarantees an incomplete analysis at best.

To turn our attention more fully to the unobjectionable transference, we see that Kohut does not use the term; however, his ideas on the importance of the working alliance in the analytic situation are close to Zetzel's (1966) and Greenson's (1967). Kohut states that it is important in an analysis to develop an alliance and indeed one can say that he has developed significant ideas on how to develop such an alliance.[28] In fact, we can say that a good deal of his ideas on technique are designed (or may be interpreted this way) to promote what I would call analytic trust. To enter into a full critique of Kohut is beyond the scope of this chapter, but I have maintained (1985b) that there are various difficulties in interpreting the ongoing transference in the manner that Kohut advocates.

It is of note that Kohut's final analytic positions reject important aspects of Freudian drive theory (psychosexuality and aggression or destructive tendencies) and replaces these concepts with concerns about the maintenance of self-esteem and self-cohesion. In other terms, he is moving from Freud's metaphor of "guilty man" to the Kohutian idea of "tragic man." Freud's idea of guilty man is based on a person having guilty reactions about impulses and fantasies that are felt or thought to be wrong or prohibited by the person's internal conscience (superego).[29] Kohut thinks that shame and the regulation of self-esteem are more crucial issues than guilt and the conflicts among the ego, superego, and id that Freud depicts. Thus, the tragic man is that person who experiences shame and sees himself (or herself) as defective, rather than viewing a particular action as wrong or inappropriate ("guilty man"). Clearly,

---

[28]Kohut tells us that early in the treatment one should attempt to create a situation in which the patient is able to be reflected or understood in terms of his or her experiences and vulnerabilities. Bach (1985) has described being attuned to narcissistic states in perhaps the most complete and convincing manner that I have encountered. From my perspective this type of attunement, reflection, or synthesizing brings the patient to start to trust in the analytic situation. This analytic trust is not equivalent to transference, but rather an experience that the patient acquires in an analysis that provides a facilitating environment.

[29]Freud's concept of the superego is a good deal more complex than the present characterization. Freud saw the superego as providing the person with appropriate ideals and standards to help guide the person's realistic ambitions. A guilt-provoking conscience is another aspect of the superego, but one would say that if a person feels frequently guilty, superego development hasn't been complete. We could loosely say that the superego (in mature form) involves a blend of ideals, prohibitions, and punishments. Insofar as the superego is not in conflict with the ego, we can say that it is providing standards for the person to live by that are ego syntonic (or acceptable) to the person.

Kohut has focused us on issues of self-esteem in a way that is powerful and I believe clinically relevant. Whether he is correct in assuming that his theoretical writings involve an important paradigm shift is another question. In my opinion, Freud's writings on narcissism contain a good deal of what Kohut focuses (or perhaps refocuses) our attention on. This is not to diminish Kohut's clinical emphasis; it does raise the question of the paradigm or theory that is best able to contain the myriad of human experiences that we already have encountered. Put in other terms, is there a theory that accommodates both the tragic and guilty person and points to the differences, connections, and similarities between guilt and shame?

PART III

Dream Interpretation

5

The Exceptional Position of the Dream in Freudian Thought

In this chapter, we briefly review some of Freud's major theoretical writings. This is necessary since the two papers on dreams in Chapter 6 were written twelve years apart, and during that time there were major shifts in Freud's theoretical position. Nevertheless, it is surprising how Freud's position on dream analysis does not seem to change dramatically over this decade when so many aspects of the theory are undergoing transformation. The implications are important when one attempts to summarize Freud's mature or final position on psychoanalytic technique.

The Early Importance of Dream Formation

Freud had already mentioned the significance of dreams by 1893. While writing *Studies on Hysteria*, Freud conceived of the dream as symbolically representing certain aspects of every normal person's waking life. In talking about the nature of symptoms, Freud tells us that at times the relationship between the precipitating cause and the final expression of the symptom "consists only in what might be called a 'symbolic' relation . . . a relation such as healthy people form in dreams" (Breuer and Freud 1893, p. 5).

Here already, Freud sees the dream as providing symbolic relationships for normal people, while at the same time he recognizes a continuity between symptom formation and dream formation. This may then be seen as heralding his idea that dreams occur every night and that all dreams are instigated by a wish. We know that for Freud, not only are dreams universal phenomena, but they also provide a model for the formation of symptoms and the ordinary events of everyday life (momentary forgetting and parapraxes, for example). One might ask, how is it that Freud had the idea of dreams as symbolically expressing conflict so early in his career? Perhaps an indirect attempt at this question might be the best way of capturing an aspect of Freud's early career that bears some relation to his interest in dreams.

It is difficult for some of us to keep in mind the dramatic and ubiquitous nature of hysteria in Europe in the 1880s and 1890s. In Vienna, and in his important fourteen weeks with Charcot in France, Freud witnessed patients who at least appeared to be in altered states of consciousness. Hence, writers like Janet saw hysteria as a degenerative disease that eventually resulted in a person's sense of self remaining in a permanently disassociated state. Patients in this state certainly seemed to have a diminished capacity for self-awareness, and it was not unusual for Freud to witness *hysterics* go into states of delirium. In searching for an analogue, Freud hit upon dreams. He somehow realized that they are normally occurring events in which we hallucinate and experience a diminished sense of self-awareness. At times during this state, there is a bizarre, uncanny quality to dreams (Ellman and Weinstein 1991). In retrospect, we can see Freud's logic in choosing the dream state as providing a model for a wide variety of phenomena. To take this analogy a step further, we can say that the treatments that Freud saw around him frequently involved inducing a change in the patient's state of consciousness. Hypnosis, the treatment he witnessed at Charcot's clinic, is a prime example of attempting to induce an altered state of consciousness. Charcot and other hypnotists of Freud's era used hypnosis primarily as a method of suggestion to provide symptom relief. Although Breuer and Freud used hypnosis to facilitate remembering, they still induced the patient to enter an altered state of consciousness.

Freud's use of the pressure technique also attempted to put the patient in an altered state; Freud asked the patients to close their eyes and allow themselves to travel a pathway that was certainly an unusual one for that era. He instructed patients to put aside normal feelings of discomfort or embarrassment and concentrate solely on what entered their minds, with particular emphasis on their memories and thoughts about their symptoms. His use of the couch began then. It is exciting to imagine what it must have been like to have this physician asking you to recline and attempt to recover memories. It is hard to believe that most patients did not enter into a state that was distinctively different from most of their previous experiences. Certainly Freud was attempting to put patients in a frame of mind that would help them leave their everyday modes of thinking and enter into this new method of reminiscing. Thus, not only did Freud see hysteria as a disassociative state, but he put patients in an altered state to help them recover memories. Dreams came to be viewed as prototypic of symptom formation, and some observers have thought of Chapter 7 in *The Interpretation of Dreams* (Freud 1900) as providing a model of free association during therapy. While it is true that Freud was beginning to conceive of all these relationships between dreaming and other phenomena (slightly later this list included ordinary forgetting, slips of the tongue, etc.), a prime reason for his views on the importance of dreams had to do with his own therapy experience.

What has been termed Freud's self-analysis began in 1897 and ended in 1902 (if we can take seriously such beginning and ending dates) (Gay 1988). An important part of his analysis is expressed in his letters to Fliess. His letters and his published work also reveal that he was actively analyzing his own dreams during this period. Some commentators have concluded that analysis of his dreams was the principal component of his treatment. Freud confirms this idea when he writes in "Remarks upon the Theory and Practice of Dream-Interpretation" (1923) that the best way to conduct a self-analysis is through dream interpretation. Many of his own dreams are used as illustrations in *The Interpretation of Dreams* (1900). *The Interpretation of Dreams* was not only an important turning point for Freud in some ways, but he also considered it a singular achievement. Gay quotes Freud as stating in 1910 that *The Interpretation of Dreams* was his "most significant work . . . (if) it should find recognition, normal psychology too would have to be put on a new basis" (Gay 1988, p. 96). In 1931 Freud writes that the work "contains, even according to my present-day judgement, the most valuable of all the discoveries it has been my good fortune to make. Insight such as this falls to one's lot but once in a lifetime. Whenever I began to have doubts of the correctness of my wavering conclusions, the successful transformation of a senseless and muddled dream into a logical and intelligible mental process in the dreamer would renew my confidence of being on the right track" (Freud 1933, p. 7). Not only did Freud value his intellectual achievement in writing *The Interpretation of Dreams*, but the work itself also bears witness to Freud's self-analysis. As Freud said about the pain of publishing the work, it was a matter of separating from his emotional rather than his intellectual property. Gay maintains that "we know that he regarded *The Interpretation of Dreams* as part of his self-analysis, and his letters to Fliess abound with references to progress, and to impediments, in his continuous, pitiless self-probing" (Gay 1988, p. 96). Certainly we know that Freud included many of his own dreams in this work and that his analysis of his own dreams extended far beyond the various analyses that he presented to the public.

Altered states of consciousness, particularly the dreaming state, were of great interest to Freud many years before he published his technique papers. He was interested in dreams and altered states as points of reference in his model of the mind. We can also say that his psychotherapeutic methods seek to induce an altered state to help facilitate his therapeutic mission. Since *The Interpretation of Dreams* embodied both a model of the mind and a view of the therapeutic process, it is understandable that it became the work he most cherished.

"The Employment of Dream-Interpretation in Psycho-Analysis"

This paper is one more instance of the significant shift in Freud's position since the Dora case. Its significance partially arises from the exceptional position of the dream in Freudian thought. As I have stated, dreams were important, if not central, to his self-analysis. Freud's attachment to dream analysis cannot be underestimated, and yet it was the strength of his vision and the value he attached to his clinical experience that won out over even this favored pathway to the unconscious, the dream. Of course, it was not just Freud's self-analysis that elevated the status of the dream for him at this time. We must remember that Freud's idea that dreams are the "royal road to the unconscious" opened the possibility of a new psychotherapy in which the patients could tell the therapist their dreams, and these dreams would lead them back to their pathogenic memories. Thus dream analysis could be the heir to hypnosis and to the pressure technique. One wouldn't have to pressure patients to recall past events; this recall would flow from the dream.

The recognition that analytic treatment could not proceed in this manner came in stages. The Dora case is an example of Freud's attempt to reconstruct a patient's conflicts through the analysis of two dreams. Freud's therapeutic stance in this case was markedly different from his present recommendations. In this "analysis" Freud violates almost all of the tenets he puts forth in the present paper (see Chapter 1). This is perhaps not surprising, since Freud had both just completed *The Interpretation of Dreams* and was involved in his self-analysis as he began his treatment with Dora. One can imagine that Freud believed that Dora might be helped in the same way that he himself had been, if he could just show her the hidden meanings of her dreams. Yet Freud must have had more than her benefit in mind when he relentlessly pursued the details of her dreams. He tells us that in publishing the case he had two objects in view:

> In the first place, I wished to supplement my book on the interpretation of dreams by showing how an art, which would otherwise be useless, can be turned to account for the discovery of the hidden and repressed parts of mental life. (Incidentally, in the process of analyzing the two dreams dealt with in the paper, the technique of dream-interpretation, which is similar to that of psycho-analysis, has come under consideration.) In the second place, I wished to stimulate interest in a whole group of phenomena of which science is still in complete ignorance to-day because they can only be brought to light by the use of this particular method. No one, I believe, can have had any true conception of the complexity of the psychological events in a case of hysteria. [Freud 1905, p. 114]

In the statement of both these reasons, Freud is concerned with emphasizing the technique of psychoanalysis. This must have been part of the reason that Freud was publishing this case. One must assume that Freud had other patients whose dreams were at least of some interest, yet he chose to publish a case in which the patient ended the treatment and in which one can say that he was not completely successful in helping the patient. We have speculated that one of the reasons Freud published this particular case was a reminder to himself and other analysts that the way he proceeded in this treatment was a mistake.[1] At the very least, it can be said that, in the present paper, Freud opposes virtually everything he did in the Dora case. He tells us clearly that nothing should supersede the importance of the analysis itself. He takes up this theme more forcefully in his paper "On Beginning the Treatment" (1913b), but here he is clear on this point as well.

When one realizes the tenacity with which most authors cling to the importance of their discoveries or theoretical positions, it is a matter of some amazement that Freud was able to tolerate the diminished importance of the dream in the psychoanalytic situation. This again speaks to the point that Freud's technical suggestions neither sprang from his head nor were purely theoretical, but rather he is telling the analytic community about his insights that were derived from clinical experience. It is hard to imagine that Freud would have wanted to remove the dream from the position as the royal road to the unconscious, and yet in this paper he is doing exactly that. It is one more step in moving from a model that would directly recover pathogenic memories, to a treatment model that starts from the surface (from the patient's experience) and moves deeper to understand the patient's unconscious fantasies via the transference.

"Remarks upon the Theory and Practice of Dream-Interpretation"

Here Freud is writing about the clinical use of dreams while occasionally considering the revision of his theoretical ideas of dream formation. He published this paper twelve years after his first paper on dream interpretation appeared, and while his theoretical ideas underwent a significant alteration between 1911 and 1923, his ideas about the handling of dreams in analysis and the significance of dreams did not change appreciably. The significant shift in Freud's position on dream interpretation had already taken place in 1911, and one might wonder why Freud wrote the present paper. To answer this question in a meaningful manner, we will briefly review some of the ground that Freud traveled in considering the issue of dream formation and the importance of the dream in analytic practice.

In *The Interpretation of Dreams* (1900), Freud gave expression not only

---

[1]It must also be added that he learned a good deal about Dora through her dreams, and this also must have been a large part of the initial impetus to publish this case.

to his ideas about dreams but also to the importance of the unconscious ideation in human motivation. The secret of dreams was revealed to him through the concept of unconscious motivation and primary process. He assumed that unconscious processes were governed by primary process thinking and that in early development, primary process cognitions tended to predominate over the more realistic second process mode of thinking. Freud's discovery or theoretical understanding in the Dream Book is that the ultimate meaning of all dreams resides in the understanding of unconscious fantasies or wishes. In this model, dreams are stimulated by an event during the preceding day that in one way or another links up with an unresolved or frustrated unconscious wish. How the wish is distorted or defended against is part of the model that Freud labels the dream work. This distortion is accomplished in different ways during sleep and continues to take place during waking in a process that Freud calls secondary revision. Freud was under no illusions that the dream the patient brought to the session was the uncontaminated dream of the previous night. Rather, he assumed that something akin to a defensive process could influence the report of the dream at any point in the formation of the dream.

Despite this sophisticated understanding of dreaming (for a fuller review of dreams and modern sleep and dream research, see Ellman and Antrobus 1991), Freud behaved as though he could understand every aspect of the dream when he was analyzing Dora. He acted in this case as if there was no aspect of her dreams that could evade his scrutiny and understanding. The distinction of dreams that are stimulated from above (from conscious waking material) and dreams that are stimulated from below (from unconscious, or id, sources) was not one that he could fully appreciate in the early 1900s. Rather, he was attempting to understand the dream in terms of the "capital" that fueled it, or as he said:

> A daytime thought may very well play the part of entrepreneur for a dream but the entrepreneur, who . . . has the idea and the initiative to carry it out, can do nothing without capital; he needs a capitalist who can afford the outlay, and the capitalist who provides the psychical outlay for the dream is invariably and indisputably, whatever may be the thoughts of the previous day, *a wish from the unconscious.* [Freud 1900, p. 561]

Daytime events or the day residue could stimulate dreaming, but the capital came from below, the unconscious. The aim of interpretation was to uncover the capital that remained hidden in the structure of the dream. Freud's assumption that dreams occurred every night implies that in all humans there is enough capital in the unconscious to energize a nightly dream effort regardless of the person's psychological well-being. Thus, dreaming and psychological conflict are universals for Freud after 1900, and the role of the unconscious was seen as influencing many functions that were not clearly understood in that way before Freud wrote *The Interpretation of Dreams* and *The Psycho-pathology of Everyday Life* in the early 1900s.

In the Dream Book, in addition to theorizing about the role of the unconscious, primary and secondary processes, the role of censorship in dreams, regression, and other important topics in psychoanalysis, Freud also put forth the beginnings of what has been called the topographic model (Stewart 1967). The topographic model layers the mind in terms of states of consciousness. Freud's tri-layering of the mind involved accompanying structures with each state of consciousness. Thus, the conscious and preconscious levels of awareness tended toward one type of thought process (secondary process), while the unconscious utilized only primary process thinking. Optimally, the preconscious and conscious organizations work together in a secondary process mode. Derivatives from the unconscious that entered into the preconscious are either sublimated, defended against, stimulate symptom formation, enter into the formation of perversions, or influence thought processes in the preconscious-conscious. In this model, the process of defense occurs at the juncture of the unconscious-preconscious. Logically, this model implies that people can be aware of their defensive processes. Freud, in fact, acted as if patients were either aware of their attempts to defend, or could become aware of various internal events, if they could just try a little harder. We have seen (1895-1902) how Freud initially attempted to pressure patients into associating or understanding the significance of a symptom or dream. He did so, since it was his belief that they were able to consciously observe and then overcome their defensive processes. This type of thinking implied that defensive processes are conscious; this view stood side by side with Freud's new views at the time that he was writing most of his technique papers.

During this period (1911-1917), there were many indications that Freud was aware that defensive processes should be conceived of as occurring mostly outside of consciousness. He noted that patients were usually unaware of their defensive attempts; it is a reasonable inference to assume that defenses are unconscious. This, however, collided with Freud's systematic definition of the unconscious as a structure that was involved with discharge or with the primary process. The difficulty can be stated in the following manner: if everything in the unconscious is involved in wishful attempts or striving for discharge, how can there be unconscious defenses that are attempting to inhibit or block primary process derivatives from being discharged by the preconscious-conscious system? Freud could have answered this question in a variety of ways; the theoretical paradigm that he devised is the now-familiar structural model in which he envisioned the mind as being divided into three systems: the ego, id, and superego.

In the structural model, the unconscious is no longer a system but a level of awareness. In this formulation, defenses are unconscious and part of the ego, whereas the id is the structure that contains the drives and operates according to the primary process. Thus, in this model, aspects of any structure can be unconscious, but only aspects of the ego and superego are conscious. The id is totally unconscious, and only derivatives of the id can achieve consciousness. Freud's new formulation allowed him to resolve various contradictory elements in his theoretical formulations. For purposes of our discussion, he was able to conceive of defense as an unconscious process, and, as seen in the present paper, his ideas about treatment began to shift to new areas. These new areas were never fully explored by Freud, and in fact it is Anna Freud (1936) and Heinz Hartmann (1939) who more fully spell out the implications of the structural theory.

In the present paper, Freud begins by listing four different ways to proceed when interpreting a dream in analysis. The first three procedures[2] all harken back to Freud's interest in the dream and the experience of the dream, since he believed it to be the original psychoanalytic decoder of dream symbols. He reminds us of the vivid sensory nature of dreams and the fact that there is often spoken material in dreams that recreates speech from waking life. He brings us back to the way he associated dreams and the idea of the day residue. Finally he tells us, as the last of the four methods, "If the dreamer is already familiar with the technique of interpretation, avoid giving him any instructions and leave it to him to decide with which associations to the dream he shall begin" (Freud 1923b, pp. 136–137). This last suggestion is what some modern analysts strongly advocate, but Freud tells us that he "cannot lay it down that one or the other of these techniques is preferable or in general yields better results" (1923b, p. 137). If we look at his first three ideas of dream interpretation, we see that all of these ideas are from the Dream Book. The last of the four alternatives is the only one that would allow the analyst to avoid showing interest (or fascination) with the dream. We can say that the first three suggestions would all fit in the pathogenic memory model of technique, whereas only the last one would find comfort with the newer transference model of technique. Put in this context, it is striking that in 1923 Freud could not choose which of the suggestions was preferable to him. It indicates his continued tie to the *classical view of the dream* and the pathogenic memory model, even after he presents the structural model. A question to ask in this context is whether Freud's tie is simply an historical circumstance in which the creator of the Dream Book and the pathogenic memory model is unable to break completely from his former creations, or whether there are good clinical reasons not to turn completely away from some of Freud's earlier conceptualizations.

[2]Freud tells us that one can (a) proceed chronologically and get the dreamer to bring up his associations to the elements of the dream in the order in which those elements occurred in his account of the dream. Or one can (b) start the work of interpretation from some particular element of the dream which one picks out from the middle of it. . . . For instance, one can choose the most striking piece of it, or the piece which shows the greatest clarity or sensory intensity. . . . Or one can (c) begin by entirely disregarding the manifest content and instead ask the dreamer what events of the previous day are associated in his mind with the dream.

I have chosen to highlight one of Freud's mixed messages that appear early in this essay. There are several of these messages occurring in the paper. Freud mentions here that the dream theory should be updated but does not indicate how this is to be done, nor is it something that he ever seriously undertakes. One might say that this paper is an interesting amalgam of old and new views that are occasioned by his new creation, the structural model. It can also be said that Freud's first paper on dream interpretation presents a more unified view than does his later paper. It is more unified in the sense that, in this paper, Freud says unequivocally that, when a patient presents a dream, the analyst must remember not to become absorbed in the dream to the exclusion of the transference. The analyst must remember that the dream may be uninterpretable in the context in which it is told. In the present paper, he takes a slight step back from this position and is more concerned with the *correct* interpretation of the dream as opposed to being concerned about the continuation of the analytic process.

6

Freud's Dream Papers

The Employment of Dream-Interpretation in Psycho-Analysis[1]

(1912)

The *Zentralblatt für Psychoanalyse* was not designed solely to keep its readers informed of the advances made in psychoanalytical knowledge, and itself to publish lesser contributions to the subject; but it aims also at presenting to the student a clear outline of what is already known, so that by means of suitable directions the beginner in analytical practice should be saved waste of time and effort. Henceforward, therefore, articles of a didactic nature and a technical content, not necessarily containing new matter, will appear in this Journal.

The question with which I now intend to deal is not that of the technique of dream-interpretation; neither the methods by which dreams may be interpreted nor the use of such interpretations when made will be considered, but merely the way in which the analyst should employ the art of dream-interpretation in the psychoanalytic treat-

[1]First published in the *Zentralblatt*, Bd. II., 1912; reprinted in *Sammlung*, Vierte Folge. [Translated by Joan Riviere.]

ment of patients. There are undoubtedly different ways of going to work in the matter, but then the answer to questions of technique in analysis is never a matter of course. Although there may perhaps be more than one good road to follow, still there are very many bad ones, and a comparison of the various methods can only be illuminating, even if it should not lead to a decision in favour of any particular one.

Anyone coming from the study of dream-interpretation to analytic practice will retain his interest in the content of dreams, and his inclination will be to interpret as fully as possible every dream related by the patient. But he will soon remark that he is now working under very different conditions, and that in attempting to carry out such an intention he will come into conflict with the most immediate aims of the treatment. ■ 1 Even if a patient's first dream proves to be admirably suited for the introduction of the first explanations to be given, other dreams will straightway appear, so long and so obscure that the full meaning cannot be extracted from them in the limited hour of one day's work. If the physician pursues the work of interpretation throughout the next few days, fresh dreams which have been produced in the meantime will have to be put aside until he can regard the first dream as finally resolved. The supply of dreams is at times so copious, and the patient's progress towards comprehension of them so slow, that a suspicion will force itself upon the analyst that the appearance of the material in this form may be simply a manifestation of the patient's resistance perceiving and taking advantage of the inability of the method to master adequately what is so presented. Moreover, the treatment will meanwhile have fallen some way behind the present and quite lost touch with actuality. In opposition to this method stands the rule that it is of the greatest importance for the cure that the analyst should always be aware of what is

■ 1

This statement immediately signals that Freud has substantially changed his ideas on the issue of dream interpretation. In the Dora case (which he conducted at the end of 1900), Freud dealt with the patient's two dreams by going over each and every aspect of the dream, and then he offered several related interpretations for each dream. In this paper, he reveals that this is no longer the way he deals with dreams in the analytic situation. This is a historic change, for if the dream can be displaced from what had been a preeminent position, one can see that Freud is quite serious about his new ideas on technique. It is of interest to note that he makes a sharp distinction between someone who is "coming from dream interpretation" and someone involved in analytic practice. Clearly, Freud no longer sees chiefly occupying the surface of the patient's mind at the moment, that he should know just what complexes and resistances are active and what conscious reaction to them will govern the patient's behaviour. It is seldom if ever advisable to sacrifice this therapeutic aim to an interest in dream-interpretation. ▪ 2

Then if we take account of this rule how are we to proceed with interpreting dreams in analysis? More or less as follows: The interpretation which can be obtained in an hour should be taken as sufficient and it is not to be counted a loss if the content of a dream is not fully revealed. On the following day, the thread of the dream is not to be taken up again as a matter of course, unless it is first evident that nothing has happened meanwhile to come more into the foreground of the patient's thoughts. Therefore no exception in favour of uninterrupted dream-interpretation is to be made to the rule that what first comes to the patient's mind is first to be dealt with. If fresh dreams occur before the others are disposed of, they must be attended to, and no uneasiness need be felt about neglecting the others. If the dreams become altogether too diffuse and voluminous, all hope of completely unravelling them should tacitly be given up at the start. ▪ 3 One must generally guard against displaying special interest in the meaning of dreams, or arousing the idea that the work would come to a standstill if no dreams were forthcoming; otherwise there is a danger of resistance being directed against the production of dreams and a risk of bringing about a cessation of them. The patient must be brought to believe, on the contrary, that material is always at hand for analysis, regardless of whether or no he has dreams to report or what measure of attention is bestowed upon them.

It will now be asked: If dreams are in practice only to be interpreted in this restricted way, will not too much valuable material which might

▪ 1 *continued*
himself as a dream interpreter, although he has certainly traveled this pathway.

▪ 2
In this paragraph one can see how far he has traveled from his earlier views. He relates that "it is of greatest importance for the treatment that the analyst should be aware of the surface of the patient's mind." In voicing this concern, he begins to move from a psychology that is involved with only the unearthing process, into one that emphasizes the relating of the patient's experience to unconscious processes. Thus, continuing to unearth, in several sessions, the meanings of a given dream may leave the analyst far behind the patient's present issues and resistances. In fact, the analyst who unfailingly analyzes the patient's dreams regardless of circumstance may well be colluding with the patient in her or his resistance. If we return to the Dora case, we see that Freud not only completely analyzed Dora's dreams, but continued this analysis over several sessions. In that case, he violates most of the ideas he presents in this paper.

▪ 3
Freud is pointing out that a patient who has a large number of dreams, or exceedingly long ones, may be moving away from issues that are particularly important to him or her at a particular phase in the treat-

■ 3 *continued*

ment. Freud also has become sensitive to his interest in dreams being communicated to the patient and thus directing the patient to produce a large number of dreams. We can see that, when an analyst expresses an extraordinary interest in any aspect of the patient's functioning, this interest can affect the manifestations of the transference. An interest of the analyst can become a resistance that is particularly difficult to look at, since the patient can view his

activities as attempts to do only what the analyst has asked. This would be something that Freud as well as many modern analysts would have difficulty with (Freud because he did not want to obstruct the patient's free associations). Many modern analysts believe that, to the extent one attempts to influence the patient in any manner, then to that extent one gives up certain aspects of an analysis, particularly the analyst's ability to analyze the transference.

■ 4

Freud tells us that it may be possible many months later to understand the meaning of a dream that is told to us earlier in the treatment. At times dur-

throw light on the unconscious be lost? The answer to this is as follows: The loss is by no means so great as might appear from a superficial view of the matter. To begin with, the analyst should recognize that in cases of severe neurosis any elaborate dream-productions are to be regarded as, theoretically and in the nature of the case, incapable of complete solution. A dream of this kind is often based on the entire pathogenic material of the case, as yet unknown to both analyst and patient (so-called descriptive and biographical dreams, etc.), and is sometimes equivalent to a translation into dream-language of the whole content of the neurosis. In the attempt to find the meaning of such a dream all the latent, as yet untouched resistances will be roused to activity and soon make it impossible to penetrate very far. The full interpretation of such a dream will coincide with the completion of the whole analysis; if a note is made of it at the beginning, it may be possible to understand it at the end, after many months. ■ 4 In the same way as with the elucidation of a single symptom (the main symptom, perhaps), the explanation will depend upon the whole analysis, during which one must endeavour to lay hold of first this, then that, fragment of its

■ 4 *continued*
ing treatment patients will return several years later to an earlier dream, and understand some element of the dream that is now relevant to some experience in the analysis. It is interesting that, at times, seemingly forgotten dreams will reappear for the patient when

he or she is experiencing something that stimulates the memory of the dream. Of course, for the dream to be remembered, certain aspects of resistance usually have been understood (through the transference). It may be interesting for the reader to read Freud's ideas on déjà vu.

meaning, one after another, until one can finally piece them all together. Similarly, no more can be expected of a dream in the early stages of the analysis; one must be content with bringing a single pathogenic wish-motive to light in the attempt at interpretation.

Thus nothing that could have been attained is abandoned by relinquishing the idea of a perfect dream-interpretation; neither is anything lost, as a rule, by breaking off from one dream to another more recent one. We have found from fine examples of fully analysed dreams that the several successive scenes of one dream may contain the same idea running through them all, perhaps with gathering distinctness, and likewise we have learnt that several dreams occurring on the same night are generally nothing more than attempts, expressed in various forms, to represent one meaning. ■ 5 In general, we can rest assured that every wish-impulse which creates a dream to-day will reappear in other dreams as long as it has not been understood and withdrawn from the control of the unconscious. It often happens, therefore, that the best way to complete the interpretation of a dream is to dismiss it and to devote attention to a new dream, which may contain the same material in perhaps a more accessible form. I know that it is making a great demand, not only on the patient but also on the physician, to expect them both to put aside all thought of the conscious aim of the treatment, and to abandon themselves to prompt-

■ 5

First of all it is intriguing that somehow Freud assumed or knew that there were several dreams in a single night. Modern sleep and dream research has confirmed this view. His main point that several dreams occurring in the same night are attempts at expressing one particular meaning is also an idea that finds some support in terms of modern dream research. This finding is in dispute, but the present author believes there is more support for the idea than evidence against it.

ings which, in spite of all, still seem to us so accidental. But I can answer for it that one is rewarded every time that one resolves to have faith in one's theoretical principles, and prevails upon oneself not to compete with the guidance of the unconscious towards the establishment of the connection.

I submit, therefore, that dream-interpretation should not be pursued in analytic treatment as an art for its own sake, but that its use should be subject to those technical rules that govern the conduct of the analysis throughout. Naturally, one can at times adopt the other course and give way a little to theoretical interest; but one should always be well aware of what one is doing. Another situation to be considered is that which has arisen since we have acquired more confidence in our understanding of dream-symbolism, and in this way know ourselves to be more independent of the patient's associations. An unusually skilful interpreter will sometimes be able to see through every dream a patient brings without requiring him to go through the tedious and time-absorbing process of dissection. Such an analyst does not experience these conflicts between the demands of the cure and those of dream-interpretation. And then he will be tempted to make full use every time of his interpretations, by telling the patient all that he has seen in the dream. In so doing, however, he will be conducting the analysis in a way which departs considerably from the established method, as I shall point out in another connection. Beginners in analytic practice, at any rate, are urged against taking this exceptional case as a model. ■ 6

Every analyst will be in the position of this supposed expert of ours in regard to the first dreams that his patients bring on beginning the treatment, before they have learnt anything of the process of dream-interpretation. These initial dreams are, so to speak, naïve; they betray a great

■ 6

Freud is stating the same views he later presented in "On Beginning the Treatment." In that paper he is quite adamant about analysts not interpreting *until patients are no more than a step away from the in-*

■ 6 *continued*

terpretation." In this paper he
is not as firm, even though he
indicates that if one interpreted
without patients' associations,
"*he will have adopted a
method . . . which departs considerably from the established
one.*" He says in this context

that beginners are advised not
to follow this model. This is
quite a muted statement and is
probably muted because the
dream occupied an exceptional
position for Freud. Of course,
this paper was also written before "On Beginning the Treatment."

deal to the auditor, like the dreams of so-called
healthy people. The question then arises whether
the analyst is promptly to translate and communicate to the patient all that he himself sees in them.
However, this question will not be answered here,
for it obviously forms part of the wider question:
at what stage in the treatment and how rapidly
should the analyst guide him to the knowledge of
that which lies veiled in the patient's mind? The
more the patient has learnt of the method of
dream-interpretation the more obscure do his
later dreams become, as a rule. All the acquired
knowledge about dreams serves also as a warning
to the dream-work. ■ 7

In the 'scientific' works about dreams, which
in spite of their repudiation of dream-interpretation have received a new stimulus from psycho-
analysis, one repeatedly finds a very superfluous
care exercised about the accurate preservation of
the text of the dream. This is thought necessary in
order to guard it against the distortions and accre-
tions supervening in the hours immediately after
waking. Even many psycho-analysts, in giving the
patient instructions to write down the dream
immediately upon waking, seem not to rely consistently enough upon their knowledge of the conditions of dream-making. This direction is superfluous in the treatment; and the patients are glad
enough to make use of it to disturb their slumbers
and to display eager obedience where it cannot
serve any useful purpose. Even if the substance of
a dream is in this way laboriously rescued from

■ 7

Freud is again addressing the
problem of when one should
interpret to the patient. That
he is still considering the question indicates that the old psychotherapy model certainly has
not disappeared from view.
This view is substantiated when
one realizes that Freud still
writes as if he believed that one
could accurately interpret a first
dream from a patient. This
view will never completely
change, and it is understandable
that the first person to systematically grasp the importance of
unconscious motivation could
believe that the secrets of the
unconscious might at times be
instantaneously revealed to
him. One must also realize that

■ 7 *continued*
often first dreams in analysis
do form a type of road map for
at least parts of the analysis. It
is rare today that analysts believe they can decipher these
maps without allowing the
transference to unfold in the
treatment situation.

■ 8
Freud is referring to issues
dealt with in both "On Beginning the Treatment" and "Recollection, Repetition and Working Through."

■ 9
Here Freud is already telling
analysts that even in so-called
confirmatory dreams there are
hints of what has previously
been hidden. This is certainly a
different position from the one
Freud appeared to take that an
analyst can decipher a patient's
conflicts by interpreting his
first dream. It is obvious that
Freud has, by this time, mostly
left that position, and when he
writes the subsequent technique
papers he more clearly leaves
the pathogenic memories position behind him.

oblivion, it is easy enough to convince oneself that
nothing has thereby been achieved for the patient.
The associations will not come to the text, and the
result is the same as if the dream had not been
preserved. The physician certainly has acquired
some knowledge which he would not have done
otherwise. But it is by no means the same thing
whether the analyst knows something or the patient knows it; later on the importance of this
distinction in the technique of psycho-analysis will
be more fully considered. ■ 8

In conclusion, I will mention a particular type
of dream which, in the nature of the case, occurs
only in the course of psycho-analytic treatment,
and may bewilder or deceive beginners in practice.
These are the corroborating dreams which follow,
as one may say, like 'hangers-on'; they are easily
translated, and contain merely what has been arrived at by analysis of the previous few days' material. It looks as though the patient had had the
amiability to reproduce for us in dream-form exactly what we had been 'suggesting' to him immediately beforehand in the treatment. The more
experienced analyst will certainly have some difficulty in attributing any such graciousness to the
patient; he accepts such dreams as hoped-for confirmations, and recognizes that they are only to be
observed under certain conditions brought about
under the influence of the treatment. ■ 9 The great
majority of the dreams forge ahead of the analysis,
so that, after subtraction of all that in them which
is already known and understood, there still remains a more or less clear indication of something
hitherto deeply hidden.

Remarks upon the Theory and Practice of Dream-Interpretation[1]

(1923)

The accidental circumstance that the last editions of my *Interpretation of Dreams* (1900) have been printed from stereotype plates has led me to issue the following remarks in an independent form, instead of introducing them into the text as modifications or additions.

I

In interpreting a dream during an analysis a choice lies open to one between several technical procedures.

One can (*a*) proceed chronologically and get the dreamer to bring up his associations to the elements of the dream in the order in which those elements occurred in his account of the dream. This is the original, classical method, which I still regard as the best if one is analysing one's own dreams. ■ 10

[1]'Bemerkungen zur Theorie und Praxis der Traumdeutung.' First published *Int. Z. Psychoanal.*, 9, I; reprinted *Ges. Schr.*, 3, 305, and *Ges. W.*, 13, 301. [Translation, reprinted from *Int. J. Psycho-Anal.*, 24 (1943), 66, by James Strachey.]

■ 10

Here is indirect verification that Freud both modeled the early analytic method after his own self-analysis and heavily utilized dreams in his self-analysis.

Or one can (*b*) start the work of interpretation from some one particular element of the dream which one picks out from the middle of it. For instance, one can choose the most striking piece of it, or the piece which shows the greatest clarity or sensory intensity; or, again, one can start off from some spoken words in the dream, in the expectation that they will lead to the recollection of some spoken words in waking life.

Or one can (*c*) begin by entirely disregarding the manifest content and instead ask the dreamer what events of the previous day are associated in his mind with the dream he has just described.

Finally, one can (*d*) ▪ 11 if the dreamer is already familiar with the technique of interpretation, avoid giving him any instructions and leave it to him to decide with which associations to the dream he shall begin.

I cannot lay it down that one or the other of these techniques is preferable or in general yields better results. ▪ 12

II

What is of far greater importance is the question of whether the work of interpretation proceeds under a pressure of resistance which is high or low—a point upon which the analyst never remains long in doubt. If the pressure is high, one may perhaps succeed in discovering what the things are with which the dream is concerned, but one cannot make out what it says about these things. It is as though one were trying to listen to a conversation taking place at a distance or in a very low voice. In that case, one can feel confident that there is not much prospect of collaborating with the dreamer, one decides not to bother too much about it and not to give him much help, and one is content to put before him a few translations of symbols that seem probable.

▪ 11

All of these alternatives are directing the analysand to deal with the dream in a manner the analyst determines. Of necessity, if one proceeds in any one of these ways, it is a limitation to the patient's free associations. Gill would not focus the patient in this manner but rather would look for a transferential element that he would be able to interpret. This element could appear in any of the patient's verbalizations and, if it happened right after the patient presented a dream, it is possible that the dream would not be analyzed. The focus is thus shifted from the understanding of the dream to the understanding of the here and now transference as superseding all other contents in the treatment. For different reasons, other analysts considered to be more allied with Freudian tradition have also reduced the exceptional place of the dream even in terms of Freud's later positions.

■ 12

Here then we can discern something akin to Freud's mature technique: if the patient is resistant—which must be translated as either in an intense and not easily interpreted state of eroticized transference, or, more likely, in a state of negative transference—then it is difficult to ascertain the true meaning of the dream. During a state of *high* resistance, the patient's associations broaden across topics rather than deepen within an area. By *deepen*, Freud means that the patient is able to understand more of her infantile unconscious fantasy life. This concept is a residue of the topographic model in which the mind is understood in terms of layers of consciousness. *Broaden* is meant to refer to the type of associations that spread over a range of topics but that, from Freud's point of view, do not lead to the unconscious material that is involved in conflict. We see here that even the concepts of broadening and deepening relate to the pathogenic memory ideas and that Freud sees the patient as resistant unless he is moving toward unconscious material. There are other possibilities; there may be certain points in a treatment when a patient may want to share with the analyst conscious secrets that have never

been told to anyone else. It may be that this does not lead the person immediately closer to unconscious material, but it might begin to establish in the patient a sense of trust. It is unlikely that Freud would disagree that there are times when the analysand's associations may not lead toward unconscious material and still the analysis progresses. Nevertheless, the manner in which he states his views consistently leads the analyst to look for deepening of associations. Today there are various analysts (Kohut, Bach, Winnicott, Zetzel, and Greenson) who have pointed out that there may be a long period of time in the initial phases of treatment in which looking for the unconscious meaning of the patient's associations is not of primary importance.

This distinction of broadening rather than deepening is used today by Bach to talk about the diagnosis of patients with narcissistic and borderline disorders. One can say that this type of patient is resistant to exploring unconscious meaning for a good period of time in psychoanalytic treatment. Of course, the question of whether one can treat narcissistic patients psychoanalytically is one that has been debated in the past and to some extent is still a subject of debate.

The majority of dreams in a difficult analysis are of this kind; so that one cannot learn much from them about the nature and mechanism of dream-formation. Least of all can one learn anything from them upon the recurring question of where the dream's wish-fulfilment may lie hidden. When the pressure of resistance is quite extremely high, one meets with the phenomenon of the dreamer's associations broadening instead of deepening. In place of the desired associations to the dream that has already been narrated, there appear a constant succession of new fragments of dream, which in their turn remain without associations.

It is only when the resistance is kept within moderate limits that the familiar picture of the work of interpretation comes into view: the dreamer's associations begin by *diverging* widely from the manifest elements, so that a great number of subjects and ranges of ideas are touched upon, after which, a second series of associations suddenly *converge* from these on to the dream-thoughts that are being looked for. When this is so, collaboration between the analyst and the dreamer becomes possible; whereas under a high pressure of resistance it would not even be of any advantage.

A number of dreams which occur during analyses are untranslatable even though they do not actually make much show of the resistance that is there. They exhibit free renderings of the latent dream-thoughts behind them and are comparable to successful creative writings which have been artistically worked over and in which the basic themes are still recognizable though they have been subjected to any amount of rearrangement and transformation. Dreams of this kind serve in the treatment as an introduction to thoughts and memories of the dreamer without their own actual content coming into account.

III

It is possible to distinguish between dreams *from above* and dreams *from below*, provided the distinction is not made too sharply. Dreams from below are those which are provoked by the strength of an unconscious (repressed) wish which has found a means of being represented in some of the day's residues. They may be regarded as inroads of the repressed into waking life. Dreams from above correspond to thoughts or intentions of the day before which have contrived during the night to obtain reinforcement from repressed material which is debarred from the ego. ■ 13 When this is so, analysis as a rule disregards this unconscious ally and succeeds in inserting the latent dream-thoughts into the complex of waking thought. This distinction calls for no modification in the theory of dreams.

IV

In some analyses, or in some periods of an analysis, a divorce may become apparent between dream-life and waking life, like the divorce between the activity of phantasy and waking life which is found in the 'continued story' (a novel in day-dreams). In that case one dream leads off from another, taking as its central point some element which was lightly touched upon in its predecessor, and so on. But we find far more frequently that dreams are not attached to one another but are interpolated into a successive series of fragments of waking thought.

V

The interpretation of a dream falls into two phases: the phase in which it is translated and the phase in which it is judged or has its value assessed. During the first phase one must not allow oneself to be influenced by any consideration whatever for the second phase. It is as though one had before one a chapter from some work in a foreign language—by Livy, for instance. The first thing one wants to know is what Livy says in the

■ 13

This is also a famous distinction that today is used in a number of contexts. The question of interpretation from above or below is one that is important and has different implications given the particular theorist. To follow the consideration in the previous footnote, a narcissistic patient from Bach's point of view should at least at the beginning of a psychoanalytic treatment receive many more interpretations from above (on conscious aspects of the ego). Kernberg, on the other hand, with borderline patients is much more prone to interpret from below (to interpret defended-against ideas and emotions).

Freud's use of the term *ego* is now in the context of the structural model, where the term has a new meaning as a central psychological structure. In a letter to Maxime Leroy he comments on dreams from above in terms of some dreams of Descartes. Freud had noted such dreams as early as *The Interpretation of Dreams* (p. 560).

chapter; and it is only after this that the discussion arises of whether what one has read is an historical narrative or a legend or a digression on the part of the author.

What conclusions can one draw from a correctly translated dream? I have an impression that analytic practice has not always avoided errors and over-estimates on this point, partly owing to an exaggerated respect for the 'mysterious unconscious'. It is only too easy to forget that a dream is as a rule merely a thought like any other, made possible by an easing-up of the censorship and by unconscious intensification, and distorted by the operation of the censorship and by unconscious elaboration. ■ 14

■ 14
Freud again is cautioning the analytic community (and probably himself) not to overestimate the importance of dreams in the analytic situation. He had commented before that dreams are only a form of thinking; he also makes this point in the first paper in this chapter. Still, even though dreams are *only* a form of thinking, it is clear that even at this point Freud is still looking at the dream as the prototype for many forms of thinking that have interested him for almost his whole analytic career. Obviously, Freud never truly gives up the exceptional position of the dream.

Let us take as an example the so-called dreams of recovery. If a patient has had a dream of this kind, in which he seems to abandon the restrictions of his neurosis—if, for instance, he overcomes some phobia or gives up some emotional attachment—we are inclined to think that he has made a great step forward, that he is ready to take his place in a new condition of life, that he has begun to reckon upon his recovery, etc. This may often be true, but quite as often such dreams of recovery only have the value of dreams of convenience: they signify a wish to be well at last, in order to avoid another portion of the work of analysis which is felt to lie ahead. In this sense, dreams of recovery very frequently occur, for instance, when the patient is about to enter upon a new and disagreeable phase of the transference. He is behaving just like some neurotics who after a few hours of analysis declare they have been cured—because they want to escape all the unpleasantness that is bound to come up for discussion in the analysis. Sufferers from war neuroses, too, who gave up their symptoms because the therapy adopted by the army doctors succeeded in making being ill even more uncomfortable than serving at the front—these sufferers, too, were following the same economic laws, and in both cases alike the cures have proved to be only temporary.

VI

It is by no means easy to arrive at general conclusions upon the value of correctly translated dreams. If a conflict of ambivalence is taking place in a patient, then the emergence in him of a hostile thought certainly does not imply a permanent overcoming of his affectionate impulse, that is to say, a resolution of the conflict: neither does any such implication follow from a *dream* with a similarly hostile content. During a conflict of ambivalence such as this, there are often two dreams every night, each of them representing an opposite attitude. In that case the progress lies in the fact that a complete isolation of the two contrasted impulses has been achieved and that each of them, with the help of its unconscious intensifications, can be followed and understood to its extreme limits. And if it sometimes happens that one of the two ambivalent dreams has been forgotten, one must not be deceived into assuming that a decision has been made in favour of the one side. ■ 15 The fact that one of the dreams has been forgotten shows, it is true, that for the moment one tendency is in the ascendant, but that is true only of the one day, and may be changed. The next night may perhaps bring the opposite expression into the foreground. The true state of the conflict can only be determined by taking into account all the other indications, including those of waking life.

VII

The question of the value to be assigned to dreams is intimately related to the other question of their susceptibility to influence from 'suggestion' by the physician. Analysts may at first be

■ 15
The idea of ambivalent patients having two different types of dreams during the night is an interesting and testable idea. There are patients who have undergone analysis while their dreams have been recorded in a sleep laboratory. It would be interesting to attempt to look at patients during states of ambivalence and see if there were more occasions in which there were contrasting dreams during the same night.

alarmed at the mention of this possibility. But on further reflection this alarm will give place to the realization that the influencing of the patient's dreams is no more a blunder on the part of the analyst or disgrace to him than the guiding of the patient's conscious thoughts.

The fact that the manifest content of dreams is influenced by the analytic treatment stands in no need of proof. It follows from our knowledge that dreams are dependent upon waking life and work over material derived from it. Occurrences during analytic treatment are of course among the impressions of waking life and soon become some of the most powerful of these. So it is not to be wondered at that patients should dream of things which the analyst has discussed with them and of which he has aroused expectations in them. At least it is no more to be wondered at than what is implied in the familiar fact of 'experimental' dreams. ■ 16

And, from here, our interest proceeds to the question whether the latent dream-thoughts that have to be arrived at by interpretation can also be influenced or suggested by the analyst. And to this the answer must once more be that they obviously can be. For a portion of these latent dream-thoughts correspond to preconscious thought-formations, perfectly capable of being conscious, with which the dreamer might quite well have reacted to the physician's remarks in his waking state too—whether the patient's reactions were favourable to those remarks or in opposition to them. In fact, if we replace the dream by the dream-thoughts which it contains, the question of how far one can suggest dreams coincides with the more general question of how far a patient in analysis is accessible to suggestion.

On the mechanism of dream-formation itself, on the dream-work in the strict sense of the word, one never exercises any influence: of that one may be quite sure.

■ 16

Freud is still concerned about the issue of suggestion, but, as he tells us, we needn't be worried about suggesting an influence over the unconscious, only the form in which derivatives from the unconscious are manifested. Modern commentators outside of the analytic community at times argue that Freudian analysts get Freudian dreams. Interpersonalist analysts get interpersonalist dreams, etc. Freud is maintaining that is not the case if one knows how to interpret dream formation. He is much less concerned about the analyst's influence, since the analyst's role is still the interpretation of the unconscious and the recovery of memories. Today, many analysts are more concerned about the influence of the analyst on the content of any of the patient's associations.

Besides that portion of the dream which we have already discussed—the preconscious dream-thoughts—every true dream contains indications of the repressed wishful impulses to which it owes the possibility of its formation. The doubter will reply that they appear in the dream because the dreamer knows that he ought to produce them—that they are expected by the analyst. The analyst himself will rightly think otherwise.

If a dream brings up situations that can be interpreted as referring to scenes from the dreamer's past, it seems especially important to ask whether the physician's influence can also play a part in such elements as those. And this question is most urgent of all in the case of what are called 'confirmatory' dreams, dreams which, as it were, lag after the analysis. With some patients these are the only dreams that one obtains. Such patients reproduce the forgotten experiences of their childhood only after one has constructed them from their symptoms, associations and other signs and has propounded these constructions to them. Then follow the confirmatory dreams, concerning which, however, the doubt arises whether they may not be entirely without evidential value, since they may have been imagined in compliance with the physician's words instead of having been brought to light from the dreamer's unconscious. This ambiguous position cannot be escaped in the analysis, since with these patients unless one interprets, constructs and propounds, one never obtains access to what is repressed in them.

The situation takes a favourable turn if the analysis of a confirmatory, lagging dream of this sort is immediately followed by feelings of remembering what has hitherto been forgotten. But even then the sceptic can fall back upon an assertion that the recollections are illusory. Moreover, such feelings are for the most part absent. The repressed material is only allowed through bit by bit; and every lack of completeness inhibits or delays the forming of a sense of conviction. Furthermore, what we are dealing with may not be the reproduction of a real or forgotten event but the emergence of an unconscious phantasy, about which no feeling of memory is ever to be expected, though the possibility may sometimes remain of a sense of subjective conviction.

Is it possible, then, that confirmatory dreams are really the result of suggestion, that they are compliant dreams? The patients who produce only confirmatory dreams are the same patients in whom doubt plays the principal part in resistance. One makes no attempt at shouting down this doubt by means of one's authority or at reducing it by arguments. It must persist until it is brought to an end in the further course of the analysis. The analyst, too, may himself retain a doubt of the same kind in some particular instances. What makes him certain in the end is precisely the complication of the problem before him, which is like the solution of a jigsaw puzzle. A coloured picture, pasted upon a thin sheet of wood and fitting exactly into a wooden frame, is cut into a large number of pieces of the most irregular and crooked shapes. If one succeeds in arranging the confused heap of fragments, each of which bears upon it an unintelligible piece of drawing, so that the picture acquires a meaning, so that there is no gap anywhere in the design and so that the whole fits into the frame—if all these conditions are fulfilled, then one knows that one has solved the puzzle and that there is no alternative solution.

An analogy of this kind can of course have no meaning for a patient while the work of analysis is still uncompleted. At this point I recall a discussion which I was led into with a patient whose exceptionally ambivalent attitude was expressed in the most intense compulsive doubt. He did not dispute my interpretations of his dreams and was very much struck by their agreement with the hypotheses which I put forward. But he asked whether these confirmatory dreams might not be an expression of his compliance towards me. I pointed out that the dreams had also brought up a quantity of details of which I could have had no suspicion and that his behaviour in the treatment apart from this had not been precisely characterized by compliance. Whereupon he switched over to another theory and asked whether his narcissistic wish to be cured might not have caused him to produce these dreams, since, after all, I had held out to him a prospect of recovery if he were able to accept my constructions. I could only reply that I had not yet come across any such mechanism of dream-formation. But a decision was reached by another road. He recollected some dreams which he had had before starting analysis and indeed before he had known anything about it; and the analysis of these dreams, which were free from all suspicion of suggestion, led to the same interpretations as the later ones. It is true that his obsession for contradiction once more found a way out in the idea that the earlier dreams had been less clear than those that occurred during the treatment; but I was satisfied with their similarity. I think that in general it is a good plan occasionally to bear in mind the fact that people were in the habit of dreaming before there was such a thing as psycho-analysis.

VIII

It may well be that dreams during psycho-analysis succeed in bringing to light what is repressed to a greater extent than dreams outside that situation. But it cannot be proved, since the two situations are not comparable; the employment of dreams in analysis is something very remote from their original purpose. On the other hand, it cannot be doubted that within an analysis far more of the repressed is brought to light in connection with dreams than by any other

■ 17

Here Freud is stating the new exceptional position of the dream; it should be handled in a manner that does not make it too much of a point of interest for the analyst and patient, but it is still the vehicle through which more of the repressed is brought to light than any other vehicle or method. Like transference, the dream is not subject to suggestion in that a meaning can be suggested. Here again, Freud is pointing out the importance of the unobjectionable positive transference in inducing the patient to allow an alliance in analysis to take place. He is maintaining that the patient will not be willing to repeat his conflicts in treatment without such an alliance. Brenner argues cogently against conceiving of a therapeutic alliance in the analytic situation. Other modern authors have attempted to deepen Freud's ideas, and the concept of therapeutic alliance at this point has a long and distinguished history. Interestingly, while on one hand Freud argues that meanings cannot be suggested, he does not exclude the possibility that meanings can be suppressed. When Freud talks about the compulsion to repeat returning not merely in the form of dream-pictures, he is talking about the patient repeating outside the treatment in action (acting out). This, of course, is not a desired result, but it is present in most treatments to some extent. The extent to which this type of *acting out* is present is an important issue in determining the analyzability of a patient.

method. ■ 17 In order to account for this, there must be some motive power, some unconscious force, which is better able to lend support to the purposes of analysis during the state of sleep than at other times. What is here in question cannot well be any factor other than the patient's compliance towards the analyst which is derived from his parental complex—in other words, the positive portion of what we call the transference; and in fact, in many dreams which recall what has been forgotten and repressed, it is impossible to discover any other unconscious wish to which the motive force for the formation of the dream can be attributed. So that if anyone wishes to maintain that most of the dreams that can be made use of in analysis are compliant dreams and owe their origin to suggestion, nothing can be said against that opinion from the point of view of analytical theory. I need only add a reference to what I have said in my *Introductory Lectures* [(1916–17) Lecture XXVIII], where I have dealt with the relation between transference and suggestion and shown how little the trustworthiness of our results is affected by a recognition of the operation of suggestion in our sense of the word.

In *Beyond the Pleasure Principle* [(1920), trans., 1922, 17ff.; new trans., 1950, 18ff.] I have dealt with the economic problem of how what are in every respect distressing experiences of the early infantile sexual period can succeed in forcing their way through to any kind of reproduction. I was obliged to ascribe to them an extraordinarily strong upward drive in the shape of the 'compulsion to repeat'—a force able to overcome the repression which, in the service of the pleasure principle, weighs down upon them—though not until 'the work of the treatment, operating in the same direction, has loosened the repression'. Here we may add that it is the positive transference that gives this assistance to the compulsion to repeat. Thus an alliance has been made between the treatment and the compulsion to repeat, an alliance which is directed in the first instance against the pleasure principle but of which the ultimate purpose is the establishment of the dominion of the reality principle. As I have shown in the passage to which I am referring, it happens only too often that the compulsion to repeat throws over its obligations under this alliance and is not content with the return of the repressed merely in the form of dream-pictures.

IX

So far as I can at present see, dreams that occur in a traumatic neurosis are the only *genuine* exceptions, and punishment dreams are the only *apparent* exceptions, to the rule that dreams are directed to wards wish-fulfilment. ■ 18 In the latter class of dreams we are met by the remarkable fact that actually nothing belonging to the latent dream-thoughts is taken up into the manifest content of the dream. Something quite different appears instead, which must be described as a reaction-formation against the dream-thoughts, a rejection and complete contradiction of them. Such offensive action as this against the dream can only be ascribed to the critical function of the ego and it must therefore be assumed that the latter, provoked by the unconscious wish-fulfilment, has been temporarily re-established even during the sleeping state. It might have reacted to the undesirable content of the dream by waking up; but it has found a means, by the construction of the punishment dream, of avoiding an interruption of sleep.

For instance, in the case of the well-known dreams of the poet Rosegger which I have mentioned in *The Interpretation of Dreams* [English translation, revised ed. (1932), 438–440], we must suspect the existence of a suppressed version with an arrogant and boastful text, whereas the actual dream said to him: 'You are an incompetent

■ 18
Punishment dreams according to Freud fit into his ideas of wish fulfillment that he proposed in *The Interpretation of Dreams*. Punishment dreams are simply manifestations of the dreamer being punished for exhibiting his wishes, even in disguised form. Dreams that occur as a result of trauma (dreams that a concentration camp victim might have, for example) are a genuine exception to the idea of wish fulfillment. These dreams are not motivated by a wish, but are under the influence of Thanatos (the death instinct) and represent a more basic compulsion to repeat. This compulsion to repeat is part of the death instinct. For present purposes, we might state again that this formulation of Freud's was not accepted by many analysts even during Freud's lifetime. Freud was aware of this and com-

■ 18 *continued*
mented on this lack of acceptance of his new instinct theory
in "Analysis Terminable and
Interminable."

journeyman-tailor.' It would, of course, be useless
to look for a repressed wishful impulse as the
motive power for a manifest dream such as this;
one must be content with the fulfilment of the
wish for self-criticism.

A dream-structure of this kind will excite less
astonishment if one considers how frequently
dream-distortion, acting in the service of the censorship, replaces a particular element by something that is in some sense or other its opposite or
contrary. It is only a short step from there to the
replacement of a characteristic portion of the content of the dream by a defensive denial, and one
further step will lead to the whole objectionable
dream-content being replaced by the punishment
dream. I should like to give a couple of characteristic examples of the intermediate phase in the
falsification of the manifest content.

Here is an extract from the dream of a girl
with a strong fixation to her father, who had
difficulty in talking during the analysis. She was
sitting in a room with a girl friend, and dressed
only in a kimono. A gentleman came in and she
felt embarrassed. But the gentleman said: 'Why,
this is the girl we once saw dressed so nicely!'—
The gentleman stood for me, and, further back, for
her father. But we can make nothing of the dream
unless we make up our mind to replace the most
important element in the gentleman's speech by
its contrary: 'This is the girl I once saw *undressed*
and who looked so nice then!' When she was a
child of three or four she had for some time slept
in the same room as her father and everything
goes to suggest that she used then to throw back
her clothes in her sleep in order to look pleasing
to her father. The subsequent repression of her
pleasure in exhibiting herself was the motive for
her secretiveness in the treatment, her dislike of
showing herself openly.

And here is another scene from the same
dream. She was reading her own case history, which

she had before her in print. In it was a statement
that a young man murdered his *fiancée*—cocoa—
that comes under anal erotism. This last phrase
was a thought that she had in the dream at the
mention of cocoa.—The interpretation of this
piece of the dream was even more difficult than
the former one. It emerged at last that before
going to sleep she had been reading my 'History of
an Infantile Neurosis' [(1918) *Collected Papers, 3,*
473], the central point of which is the real or
imagined observation by a patient of his parents
copulating. She had already once before related
this case history to her own, and this was not the
only indication that in her case as well there was a
question of an observation of the same kind. The
young man murdering his *fiancée* was a clear reference to a sadistic view of the scene of copulation.
But the next element, the cocoa, was very remote
from it. Her only association to cocoa was that her
mother used to say that cocoa gave one a headache,
and she maintained that she had heard the same
thing from other women. Moreover she had at
one time identified herself with her mother by
means of headaches like hers. Now I could find no
link between the two elements of the dream except by supposing that she wanted to make a
diversion from the consequences of the observation of coitus. No, she was saying, coitus had
nothing to do with the procreation of children;
children came from something one ate (as they do
in fairy tales); and the mention of anal erotism,
which looks like an attempt in the dream at interpretation, supplemented the infantile theory
which she had called to her help, by adding anal
birth to it.

X

Astonishment is sometimes expressed at the fact
that the dreamer's ego can appear two or more
times in the manifest dream, once as himself and

again disguised behind the figures of other people. During the course of the construction of the dream, the secondary elaboration has evidently sought to obliterate this multiplicity of the ego, which cannot fit in with any possible scenic situation; but it is re-established by the work of interpretation. In itself this multiplicity is no more remarkable than the multiple appearance of the ego in a waking thought, especially when the ego divides itself into subject and object, puts one part of itself as an observing and critical agency in contrast to the other, or compares its present nature with its recollected past, which was also ego once; for instance, in such sentences as 'When *I* think what *I*'ve done to this man' or 'When *I* think that *I* too was a child once'. But I should reject as a meaningless and unjustifiable piece of speculation the notion that *all* figures that appear in a dream are to be regarded as fragmentations and representatives of the dreamer's own ego. It is enough that we should keep firmly to the fact that the separation of the ego from an observing, critical, punishing agency (an ego-ideal) must be taken into account in the interpretation of dreams.

7

Contemporary Perspectives

It is surprising that, after Freud, dreams received relatively little attention in psychoanalytic literature, in terms of either the theory of dream formation or the role of dreams in psychoanalytic treatment. There were, of course, dreams used in many clinical illustrations, but it remained for modern sleep research[1] to bring a resurgence of interest in the dream. Freudian thought immediately occupied a central focus with various researchers maintaining that modern research was in some ways confirmatory of Freudian positions, whereas others attempted to demonstrate that Freud's theories had for once and for all been disproven. One of the more radical attempts (Hobson and McCarley 1977, Crick and Mitchison 1986) to disprove psychoanalytic notions has been to maintain that dreams in and of themselves are meaningless events having no intrinsic meaning. Vogel (1978) and Ellman and Weinstein (1991) have at least shown that there is enough experimental evidence to cast aside these claims. The discovery of rapid eye movement (REM) sleep has not as yet led to evidence that would confirm any one of several theories (Ellman and Weinstein, 1991) of dream formation or the salience of the dream. Perhaps it is because so many analysts have been active in sleep and dream research that REM sleep research renewed contemporary interest in the dream. (That interest has at this time partly waned.)

The Kris Study Group's monograph twenty-four years ago (Kris Study Group 1967) on the position of the dream in psychoanalysis is still a good example of a type of bifurcation that exists in the field. This is directly

---

[1]With the discovery of rapid eye movement (REM) sleep and the reports of dreaming occurring during this period of sleep, a great deal of interest was restored to the process of dreaming.

traceable to Freud's alternating views of the dream in the psychoanalytic situation. We have seen that in his earlier paper on dream interpretation (Freud 1912) Freud placed the dream on a more equal footing with other associations in the psychoanalytic situation. Later on he vacillated, and the dream took on some of the special features that Freud had ascribed to it in *The Interpretation of Dreams* (1900) and the Dora case. Freud's difficulty in reconciling the importance of the dream is mirrored by modern analysts' alternate views of the place of the dream in psychoanalytic treatment. In the 1967 monograph by the Kris Study Group we can witness a debate (by two groups of analysts) on the role of the dream in the analytic situation. One group of analysts maintains that:

> The dream is a definably unique product of mental functioning, being formed in an altered ego state, during sleep, which is unlike altered ego states to be observed in other conditions which favor regression. The interplay of forces between what is to be repressed and what accomplishes the repression, theoretically resembles the compromises which result in symptom formation, acting out, character disorders, and the whole spectrum of neurotic disorder, but there is a qualitatively different situation in the dream. . . .
>
> In addition to the dream's capacity to register the impression and experience of recent and current events in a particularly sensitive way, the dream also seems to have a special capacity for the recollection of experiences of childhood no longer available to ordinary memory. "There is one special class of experiences of the utmost importance for which no memory can, as a rule, be recovered. These are experiences which occurred very early in childhood and were not understood at the time but which were subsequently understood and interpreted. One gains a knowledge of them through dreams and one is obliged to believe in them on the compelling evidence provided by the fabric of the neurosis" (Freud 1914). [Kris Study Group 1967, pp. 97–98]

This perspective is a continuation of one aspect of Freudian thought that is present in the second paper included in the previous chapter. This statement (written by Altman) clearly enunciates the group's view of the exceptional position of the dream in psychoanalytic treatment. Freud is quoted on how primal repression can be overcome through no other avenue except the dream state. These contemporary analysts present clinical examples of why certain experiences are best understood, perhaps can only be comprehended, through dream analysis. Even the style of the Altman group's statement indicates the distinctive status of the dream.[2] In any case, this group argues that the "predominantly somatovisceral responses of the preverbal child and the infant are without word representations for future reference. . . . Such vegetative-

---

[2]When they write "in addition to the dream's capacity, etc.," it sounds as if the dream has a life of its own, its own capacity, that stands apart from the dreamer. Indeed, at times, this is the view of the dreamer, that the dream is being produced by another person or power.

affective recollections not infrequently come to light in the dream as special sensory impressions" (Kris Study Group 1967, p. 98).

Here, they are arguing not only for the special status of the dream but also implicitly asserting the therapeutic importance of capturing early memories. It is a matter of consequence to unearth early memories even if the memories are laid down during the preverbal era and come to light through sensory impressions[3]. So that this case is not overstated, we must remember that the quote from Freud came in a work in which he was reaffirming and extending the importance of transference in analysis. In addition, all of the analysts who came to this view emphasized that appropriate dream interpretation must take place in the context of a treatment that emphasizes the understanding of the transference.

What is the alternative to the status of the dream in analytic treatment? Waldhorn of the Kris Study Group advanced the thesis that the dream was

> clinically speaking, a communication in the course of the analysis similar to all others with which we, as analysts, work. One obvious proposition implicit in such an understanding is that "we analyze the patient, not the dream." The manifest dream reported is, after all, the patient's first set of associations to the dream experience, and, as such, can be treated as any other set of associations. . . . Only those aspects of a dream should be interpreted which can throw light on or prepare the way for dealing with aspects of the analysis which are considered timely and necessary for the progress of the analytic work. . . . For example, one would not analyze a dream offered by a patient in his first hour, which deals with sleeping with his mother or being stabbed by the analyst, except, perhaps to deal with the resistance aspect of such communications if that seems necessary at the outset. . . . This regression (involved in dreaming) in the direction of infantile (primary process) mental functioning with its reliance on visual imagery is not unique for sleep. It appears as well in other temporary regressions (daydreams, reverie, fatigue, inattention, excitement, etc.) including those related to jokes, art and other "regressions in the service of the ego." [Kris Study Group 1967, pp. 100-101]

After reading the previous two quotes, the bifurcation is obvious. Not only does the second group advocate treating the dream as one other association, but they also deny the dream an ontological status afforded to it by at least some investigators and analysts (Altman 1969, Ellman and Weinstein 1991, Vogel 1978). They make an intriguing empirical statement when they indicate

---

[3]It is my view that a type of reconstruction can be accomplished through the understanding of such sensory impressions. This is, of course, a matter in dispute; see Spence on narrative truth (Spence 1982). It is a question of whether reconstruction is even possible, and whether it is useful therapeutically. Clearly, this type of memory would ordinarily be produced before the child had reached the oedipal stage. One can deduce from this that there may be some correlation between analysts who view the dream as having distinctive, perhaps even unique, status in the analytic situation, and those analysts who see pre-oedipal factors as having substantial importance.

that there is nothing unique about the regressive aspects of the dream[4]. On the other hand, the first group's assertion that early memories are available in the dream, and not through other avenues of expression, is also an empirical statement that is buttressed only by a quotation from Freud. (The type of questions that are being raised by these two points of view are ones that can be investigated by analysts studying analytic transcripts, hopefully using sophisticated ways of looking at regression and the reporting of early memories.) The hope that empirical methods will reconcile these views is naive, for the overriding difference between these two groups is probably dependent on the amount of extratransference interpretations that a given analyst deems appropriate to an analytic treatment.

It is clear that the second group's stance is easily reconciled with Brenner's position. Undoubtedly, this group would be at home with Brenner's idea that the emphasis on dream interpretation is a residue of the earlier topographic model. Brenner contends that Freud's movement to the structural model pointed away from dream interpretation, as Freud understood it in prestructural terms. Thus, for Brenner the dream is to be considered as one more association of the patient; showing increased interest in the dream or any other aspect of the patient's functioning would for Brenner be a technical mistake. We must again make the historical point that Freud's paper on dreams written in 1923[5] is more in line with what Brenner calls a residue of the topographic model than is his earlier paper on dream interpretation.[6] It is difficult to use Freud to bolster one's point of view on this issue of technique.[7]

Are there ways to reconcile these two positions? Perhaps, but there is at least one irreconcilable element present and potentially other points of disagreement implicit in these positions. That the dream is seen by one group as unique in the analytic situation, conveying experiences that are unavailable in other forms of communication, is obviously a point of difference that cannot be reconciled. It is clearly at odds with the idea that the dream is simply one form of association and that the same feeling and transference states, as well as remembrances, can be achieved through alternative forms of communication or associations. It is a difference that I believe can be argued to some extent

[4]In their statement (the quote referred to), they contend that the "regression (involved in dreaming) . . . with its reliance on visual imagery" is not unique to dreaming; that the same regression appears in daydreaming, fatigue, etc. Here I would say that there is at least some evidence that this is not the case; we have been able to distinguish fantasies from REM dreams. Moreover, the underlying neurophysiology in REM sleep and fatigue is quite different, and I would predict that more and more psychological differences will be found between these two states. It seems to me that the REM state may in fact be unique and offer a different type of regressive experience than is the case with other states of consciousness. This, of course, should be an empirical question.

[5]This is at a point when a good deal of the structural model had been presented.

[6]This paper was written before any aspect of the structural model had been presented.

[7]Freud's ideas about technique are not easily reconciled with Brenner's point of view. This, while irrelevant substantively, is unfortunately important for other reasons (socio-historical ones).

through empirical methodology.[8] Implicitly, it seems to me that the first group is arguing that the recovering of early memories is an important aspect of analytic treatment. Alternatively, I would say that the second group is less interested in the attempt to recover early memories. This hypothesized difference would tend to lead to a difference in the way the transference is handled. Here, of course, the differences are easy to reconcile. It is possible to see the dream as extremely important without necessarily communicating this to the patient. The analyst might at times display her interest in dreams, or the associations to dreams, and this might involve the patient in attempting to remember or not remember dreams in reaction to the analyst's implicit or explicit show of interest. This is a rough statement about the type of difficulty that many contemporary analysts (e.g., Brenner 1976, Greenson 1958, 1967, Kris Study Group 1967) highlight when the issue of the special status of the dream is discussed. In fact, this difficulty can be generalized to the analyst focusing on any one type of association that the patient might introduce. The argument is that the analyst is determining the patient's selection of topic by selectively focusing on an issue. Thus, the question of technique is possible to reconcile as long as the first group does not indicate to the patient their interest in the dream. If they do not think this is necessary, then there is again an irreconcilable difference between the two groups. Here again we can see the interrelated aspects of a theory of technique. How much one can focus on the dream is to some extent determined by one's view of neutrality, the importance of transference, and the extent that one sees the recovery (or construction) of early events (or memories) as important to the treatment situation. It also depends on the extent to which one thinks that transference will be affected by what an analyst like Lipton (1977b) might call the more inconsequential aspects of analytic treatment.

If one accepts the view that the analyst functioning perfectly does not allow himself to focus selectively on patients' associations, then clearly the analyst cannot focus on the dream or any particular content. One can question the assumption that this type of neutrality is a possibility. One might say that all analysts of necessity focus selectively when they make interpretive comments, and that the selectivity implicit in interpretative comments is no different from the selectivity in communicating to patients that you are interested in their dream life.[9] Freud accepted the fact that he would be

[8]I am really grouping two questions together: The first involves the status of the dream; the second involves the necessity of using the dream in analytic treatment. One could agree that the dream offers a unique type of experience and still maintain that to afford it special status in the treatment situation is a mistake because too much is given up in terms of analytic neutrality.
[9]One might ask why lying on the couch is an analytic condition that is communicated to the patient as a requirement of treatment, but this is not viewed as an abridgement of neutrality. Clearly, the patient knows the analyst is not neutral with respect to his lying on the couch. The analyst believes that the couch will facilitate the treatment and is willing to say so. Is this different from the analyst saying that he is interested in a particular type of content?

influencing a patient's associations, but for him this was relatively unimportant, since he believed that the patient's conflicts would surface under most of what he (Freud) considered to be normal analytic circumstances.[10] His aim was to be able to recapture memories either directly (early in his career) or through constructions (later in his career); transference for him was never the central issue that it is for most modern analysts. He was therefore not overly concerned about influencing the manifestations of transference. If transference is the central and perhaps exclusive pathway of your treatment model, then the issue of selective attention is one that has to be attended to with greater care. This is particularly the case if your theoretical assumptions maintain the analyst in a neutral position. To complicate the issue, let me point out that one can view transference as the main vehicle of the treatment and not see the analyst as maintaining neutrality in Brenner's sense of the term.

To restate the issue, it is my view that every interpretation is a selective focusing on associations that the patient brings up in the treatment. We may develop some rules about how and why we make these interpretations, but these rules of necessity focus us on one type of communication or experience and redirect other communications to the background of the treatment. As a variety of analysts have maintained and even begun to demonstrate (Wallerstein and Sampson 1971, Weiss et al. 1986), the setting of the analysis and the manner in which the analyst handles many aspects of interactions with the analysand greatly affect the communications in the analysis. Whether an analyst is old or young, tall or short, has good or bad taste (from the patient's point of view), all affect how the treatment will progress. Some of these factors are irreversible, and as such they simply have to be accepted by the analyst as conditions of treatment. What some analysts would maintain is that through this myriad of factors, the transference will be manifested in similar ways if the analyst can maintain neutrality. From this perspective, focusing on the dream is giving up an aspect of neutrality. If, however, your position is that neutrality is an impossibility, then this argument against focusing on the dream loses its power. The question then becomes not whether one influences the patient but rather how much and in what ways? In other terms, one might ask what type of influence is facilitatory and with what patients. These types of questions imply a different model than is inherent in seeing the analyst as neutral observer;[11] they lead to thinking of the analyst at least as participant-observer.

---

[10]Freud did not see that analytic circumstances needed to be examined to the extent that many contemporary analysts have examined these conditions. He was also content to say that he didn't like to treat certain types of patients, and was seemingly at home with this statement. It seems to me that Freud was by today's standards cavalier in his disregard for the conditions of analytic treatment. On the other hand, at times the focus of analysts on some details may be equally extreme. This issue is taken up again when we discuss the case of the Rat Man.

[11]The question of neutrality is also separate from the issue of objectivity. It is possible to retain objectivity and not be neutral with respect to a number of issues. What these issues are, of course, is the complicated question. Grunes (1984) has written an interesting paper distinguishing objectivity and neutrality, cogently untangling two concepts that are often linked. The way we

I will not try to go further in posing these questions in this section of the book, but rather I will merely state again that how one views dreams in analysis depends on (a) one's view of the importance of dreams, and (b) one's overall conception of analytic neutrality in particular, and, of course, one's more general notions about technique.

Brenner, Kohut, and Gill on Dreams

We can make this section a short one, since Brenner's and Gill's positions on the dream have already implicitly, and to some degree explicitly, been demarcated. It is clear that neither Gill nor Brenner would have us focus the patient on attempting to remember dreams, nor would they question patients about their dreams to any greater extent than they would about any other aspect of their associations or verbalizations. None of these authors focus their attention on the dream to any great extent, but Kohut probably reports more dreams from his patients than I have encountered in either Gill's or Brenner's writings. Whether or not this is the case, Kohut clearly has no difficulty in providing the patient with constructions in some of his dream interpretations. He, of course, sees the dream in terms of self psychology—self-state dreams— as opposed to the expression of unconscious wishes. Thus, if we are to look at a difference between Brenner and Kohut, we have to say that it may be that Kohut focuses more on the patient's dream life than Brenner does, although this is a matter of conjecture. The main difference, however, would be how they interpreted the content of the dream. Neither analyst would accord the dream special status in his analytic technique.

---

have been stating the question is again in dichotomous fashion; it may be better to think of the analyst as neutral to a degree with certain patients and around certain issues. It is unlikely that an analyst will be neutral with respect to severely self-destructive behavior on the part of the analysand. Some would argue that if the analyst can't maintain his neutrality then the patient is not analyzable. This, it seems to me, leaves open a more interesting question: To what extent can neutrality be forsaken while one is maintaining an analytic process? To answer this question we would, of course, need an independent definition of the term *analytic process*. I think that this is possible.

PART IV

Clinical Practice

8

Freud's Practical Suggestions

Calling the content of Freud's recommendations papers his "practical suggestions" is somewhat misleading. In all of his papers Freud transcends the
practical and presents part of his theoretical vision. The issue of psychoanalytic
technique is hardly an exception to this generalization. Freud probably did not
want to state hard-and-fast rules of technique because he did not want to rule
out the possibility of exploration of new technical innovations and partly
because he believed that to some extent all analysts have to develop their own
methods. These considerations were balanced by his concern that "wild analysis"[1] would be practiced in the name of psychoanalysis. Given all these different factors, we can say that all of the technique papers are a type of compromise formation that delicately balances these concerns. This is particularly the
case with the following two papers, which deal more explicitly with practical
issues. Freud is at times quite circumspect in writing about technique, and one
has to be able to read between the lines to fully ferret out his meaning. He
states most of his warnings in tones that are balanced, at times even mild. He
rarely makes mention of his own clinical experience, even though it is clear
that, if one traces the evolution of his thought, many of the points he makes in
his technique papers are designed to rewrite earlier views that he has presented in case studies or in previous papers. One can say that these two

---

[1]Freud's first technique paper was his paper on wild analysis. In this paper he distinguishes
psychoanalysis as a treatment technique from psychoanalytically "informed" observations. Freud
had heard of physicians without psychoanalytic training making quasi-analytic interpretations to
patients. He wanted to make clear that this was not equivalent to psychoanalytic treatment in any
way. I have not included this paper, since it is more a warning of what *not* to do rather than a paper
on technique.

"practical papers" are a combination of practical advice, carefully scripted warnings, and at times important theoretical statements. These papers form an intriguing blend that in some ways gives insight into the manner in which Freud went back and forth between practical issues and issues of clinical relevance, while continuously attempting to place his observations into a theoretical framework.

In many ways it is a wonder that Freud published these practical papers. Clearly he was ambivalent about writing technique papers, particularly ones with practical suggestions. He was concerned about letting the general public know the secrets of psychoanalysis. It was his view that patients should not read about psychoanalysis, since he thought that intellectual knowledge would serve as a resistance in analysis. In some small measure, we have the danger of wild analysis to thank for these papers, for Freud clearly wanted to differentiate the psychoanalytic method from the practice of wild analysis.

Beginning Considerations

We can consider these papers as a continuation of other papers that Freud had written previously. In 1903–1904 he wrote two papers that were quite similar in content and that described in schematic form "Freud's psycho-analytic procedure" (Freud 1904). Neither of these papers mentioned the concept of transference, even though they were ostensibly written (see Chapter 1) after the Dora case in which Freud discusses the importance of transference. Freud does discuss several points in these early papers that he only alludes to or references in the present papers. Therefore, we might review some issues that he brings up only in the early papers. Going over these issues will enable us to bring together Freud's suggestions on how to set up adequate conditions for an analytic treatment. For example, patient selection is one such condition. In the present papers, when he discusses the issue of patient selection he comments only that he has previously dealt with this issue. When we look back we can see that Freud had clear ideas about patient selection even at a relatively early point in his psychoanalytic career.

Patient Selection and Early Thoughts on Analyzability

Patients should possess a "reasonable degree of education" and should be driven to the treatment "by their own sufferings." As we can see in the Dora case and in a later case,[2] Freud was suspicious of patients who entered treatment as a result of being pressured by friends or family members. Freud goes on to say:

[2]"The Psychogenesis of a Case of Female Homosexuality," *Standard Edition* 18 (1920), pp. 145–172.

One should limit one's choice of patients to those who possess a normal mental condition, since in the psycho-analytic method this is used as a foothold from which to obtain control of the morbid manifestations. Psychoses, states of confusion and deeply-rooted (I might say toxic) depression are therefore not suitable for psycho-analysis; at least not for the method as it has been practised up to the present. We may succeed in overcoming this contraindication—and so be able to initiate a psychotherapy of the psychoses. [1905a, p. 264]

Freud adds that "psychoanalysis should not be attempted when the speedy removal of dangerous symptoms is required, as, for example, in a case of hysterical anorexia" (1905a, p. 264). His views on patient pathology became more delineated ten years later when he maintained (Freud 1916/1917) that there was an inverse correlation between the person's narcissism and his or her suitability for analysis (i.e., the more narcissistic, the less suitable for analysis). Age is also a condition for one's suitability, and Freud tells us that the person should be under the age of 50 since "old people are no longer educable" (Freud 1905a, p. 264). Freud felt that older people no longer had the *flexibility* to change and that psychoanalytic treatment would not be successful without this flexibility. Interestingly, many analytic institutes have continued this policy and have limited the age of both analysands and analytic candidates.

Although Freud placed a variety of restrictions on the people who were analyzable he was not disturbed by these restrictions; rather, he stated that "it is gratifying that precisely the most valuable and most highly developed persons are best suited for this procedure; and one may also safely claim that in cases where analytic psycho-therapy has been able to achieve but little, any other therapy would certainly not have been able to effect anything at all" (1905a, pp. 264–265). This issue is viewed quite differently today. Given Freud's views on analyzability, it is easy to understand that, if one were considered unanalyzable, there would be many negative connotations that would accompany such a designation. Certainly, for people in the analytic community, that type of statement is virtually a death knell for one's analytic career. This, of course, can be placed in understandable historical terms, but nevertheless Freud's statement about the most highly developed persons being those who can benefit from analysis is extremely value laden. This statement, and others like it, have in many ways set the tone for much of the discussion of analyzability in analytic publications.

There is an issue in many of the technique papers that Freud only briefly alludes to: the issue of suggestion. After writing the chapter on psychotherapy in *Studies on Hysteria*, Freud took great pains to demonstrate that his technique does not operate on the basis of suggestion. Moreover, one of the benefits of his technique over hypnosis is that it does not depend on whether the patient can be hypnotized. One might raise the question whether or not Freud admits only those patients who are open to suggestion. If a patient is not willing to restrict her or his decisions for the duration of an analysis, that person is deemed unanalyzable. What about the patient who has doubts about the method and is not willing to fully commit him- or herself to this new method? Or if one puts this in contemporary terms, what about those patients who are thinking about alternative treatment modalities? Are we to consider only those patients who hold no mental reservations and are willing to accept our initial conditions without withholding anything, as good analytic patients? It might be reasonable to assume that these patients are ones who are reasonably suggestible and tend to be somewhat compliant. This type of patient population, or the selection criteria for this patient population, tends toward the type of person who may enter analysis with a positive transference state (see Part II). What is being hypothesized is that Freud's selection criteria are in part geared to choosing patients who will tend to enter analysis in a positive transference state and who tend to be compliant. The implication is that, although Freud wanted to do away with suggestion in the analytic situation, he inadvertently introduced suggestion because of his need to see patients who were compliant in terms of some aspects of analytic technique. It should be noted that the amount and type of suggestion that Freud introduced in his technique was minimal when compared to the hypnotic technique, and indeed when compared to many other psychotherapeutic techniques that are practiced today.

As we will see, Freud did not always follow his own suggestions in the selection of patients. In fact, he tells us it is not always so easy to assess analyzability in the first few sessions (consultations). He suggests that analysts institute a *trial analysis* and that the results of the trial analysis determine the patient's analyzability. Even at the time Freud was writing, analysts were somewhat unreceptive to this idea. The idea of a trial analysis has been replaced by the analytic consultation, in which a consulting analyst attempts to determine a patient's suitability for analysis. Very often during consultations, an analyst will offer small interpretations in order to assess a patient's responsiveness to analytic conditions. Although this is not considered a trial analysis, in many ways it has the same function. A brief consultation may be an adequate substitute for the idea of a trial analysis if one has quite definite ideas about who is analyzable and the nature of analytic treatment. Since both of these issues are under a great deal of discussion today, the whole question of analyzability is one that is often determined by analysts' predilections for both theory and technique. In terms of patient selection, it is safe to say that a variety of analysts (including Freud) have gone beyond the analytic boundaries that Freud erected in these technique papers.

Beginning Questions and the Analytic Setting

Freud relates that, at the beginning of treatment, patients will frequently ask how long a given treatment will go on. Freud's answer that it is impossible to know the length of a person's stride in the journey through analysis is a telling and apt metaphor. In previous (and subsequent) papers, Freud relates that an analysis usually has a duration of six months to three years. Freud saw patients six times a week; at times with resistant patients, he might see them more than once a day or for longer sessions (his typical session lasted fifty minutes). The average length of an analysis today is approximately five to seven years. It is clear from his reaction to the Wolf Man and his comments in "Analysis Terminable and Interminable" (1937b) that Freud had difficulty with analyses that were relatively long (at least those that were longer than three years). One has to wonder what factors led Freud to consider that an analysis was appropriately terminated in less than half the time it takes in contemporary treatments.[3] Shorter analyses were one condition that allowed Freud to impose some of the restrictions that seem, to modern readers, archaic.

Freud advocated telling patients that they should make no significant decisions in their lives during analysis. Marriage, changing jobs, or any similar decisions were ruled out. The rationale for this was that the regressive pull of analysis might severely affect the analysand's ability to make a balanced decision. Freud also advocated restricting the patient's freedom to read about psychoanalysis. Clearly, it was his view that if patients read about analysis they would use this knowledge as a resistance in treatment. Freud doesn't discuss the implications of these policies, but we know that at times he seriously enforced his policies (Freud 1918). It would be virtually impossible today to prevent an analysand from obtaining information about psychoanalysis. (It might almost be preferable to have patients read about analysis to counteract the stereotypical information that is promulgated by the media.) It would still be possible to tell a patient that he shouldn't read technical papers about analysis, but this is rarely done today. In a parallel vein, it is rare that an analyst will attempt to categorically forbid patients from making decisions during their analysis. Despite the fact that these particular policies are no longer practiced, Freud's attitude raises the question of the position of analyst as authority figure in the analytic setting. In other terms, if the analyst tries to set up some prohibitions during an analysis, what effect does this have on the development of the transference? In a similar vein, since many analyses are training analyses, one might ask what effect the authority of the training institute has on an analysis. There is, of course, a wide literature spanning both these questions (Calef 1954, Calef and Weinshel 1973, Ekstein 1955).

---

[3]One is tempted to say that Freud's treatments were shorter because he saw patients six times a week, compared to most contemporary psychotherapists who see their patients only once or twice weekly. While this is a factor even when we compare analytic treatments that are conducted on a five-times-a-week basis, we see that Freud's analyses were relatively brief.

The Fundamental Rule

By the time Freud wrote the psychotherapy papers, he no longer required patients to close their eyes during sessions. This change occurred between 1900 and 1905. His fundamental rule, of course, remained (although in different form), and we can see that its importance had in no way diminished for Freud: he wanted patients to attempt to say everything that they thought, even though he recognized that at some point they would not adhere to this instruction. Freud reported that, under certain conditions, when a patient refused to talk about some issues, he terminated the treatment. Freud warned about patients who have mental reservations concerning the fundamental rule and questioned whether or not they would be analyzable, despite the fact that he knew that resistance (most often in the form of transference) will prevent a patient from complying with the fundamental rule. Clearly, he views a resistance that is not within the patient's conscious control as occupying a different position than a resistance that is seemingly within the patient's control. This is an arbitrary division, since, as Freud taught us, the extent of our conscious control over decisions is often quite illusory. Freud's observation may be interpreted to mean that frequently patients with strong reservations about the fundamental rule will be more likely to begin the treatment in a state of negative transference. Secretly deciding to withhold material may be a sign of certain paranoid trends, or simply an indication of a patient who will display various negativistic traits in the treatment situation. Freud's lack of tolerance with such patients was not his strongest asset. Today, one might say that certain patients find the whole analytic situation a humiliation and need some period of time to acclimate to it. This is an area of intense concern to many contemporary analysts.

Pausing for a moment, we can see that we have briefly reviewed many aspects of the conditions that Freud established for the beginning of the treatment. He gave criteria for selecting patients, told how to answer various questions that typically arise at the beginning of treatment, and advised how often to see a patient and how to present and consider the fundamental rule. He assumed that all analysts knew that patients are to lie on a couch, but he spent little time on the rationale for this assumption. In fact, his rationale is much more convincing than the one he presents in the present papers. However, here he honestly states a personal reason for his advocating the use of the couch; that is, he prefers not having face-to-face contact for 8–10 hours a day.[4]

---

[4]It is clear from Freud's interest in altered states (dreaming, fantasies, etc.), that he thought the use of the couch induced them. From this point of view, it is easier to facilitate regressions and to elicit feelings and thoughts that are closer to unconscious fantasies.

Some Considerations about the Role of Interpretation

The question now presents itself as to what happens once the patient has begun the treatment. Freud has several suggestions for the analyst, even in the present papers. Before we present these suggestions, it is important to remember a basic tenet of Freud's: that analysis is considered to be mainly (once it is underway) a vehicle that is furthered by the use of interpretation. Interpretation, then,

> takes on the task of, as it were, extracting the pure metal of the repressed thoughts from the ore of unintentional ideas. This work of interpretation is applied not only to the patient's ideas but also to his dreams, which open up the most direct approach to a knowledge of the unconscious. . . . The details of this technique of interpretation or translation have not yet been published by Freud. According to indications he has given, they comprise a number of rules, reached empirically, of how the unconscious material may be reconstructed from the associations, directions on how to know what it means when the patient's ideas cease to flow, and experiences of the most important typical resistances that arise in the course of such treatments. A bulky volume called *The Interpretation of Dreams*, published by Freud in 1900, may be regarded as the forerunner of an initiation into his technique. [Freud 1904, p. 252]

The role of interpretation will always be crucially important in Freud's technique, but in his recommendations papers (in Chapter 9) we can see a change in his attitude in terms of the context of the analyst's interpretative efforts. Freud advises that one should not attempt interpretative efforts until an effective rapport has been developed with the patient. He indicates that "the first aim of the treatment consists in attaching him [the patient] *to the person of the physician*" (Freud 1913b, p. 342). To paraphrase, one must exhibit a serious interest in the patient, carefully clear away the resistances that crop up, avoid making certain serious mistakes, and the patient will, in the course of treatment, attach himself to the analyst. They will then transfer to the analyst one or another fantasy image from their past. To quote more directly, Freud states:

> It is certainly possible to forfeit . . . success if from the start one takes up any standpoint other than one of sympathetic understanding, such as a moralizing one, or if one behaves like a representative or advocate of some contending party—of the other member of a married couple, for instance. . . .
>
> It is not difficult for a skilled analyst to read the patient's hidden wishes plainly between the lines of his complaints and the story of his illness; but what a measure of self-complacency and thoughtlessness must exist in one who can, upon the shortest acquaintance, inform a stranger who is entirely ignorant of analytic doctrines that he is bound by an incestuous love for his mother, that he harbors wishes for the death of his wife . . . and so forth. . . . Even in the later

stages of analysis one must be careful not to communicate the meaning of a symptom or the interpretation of a wish until the patient is already so close upon it that he has only a short step more to take in order to grasp the explanation for himself. In former years I often found that premature communication of interpretations brought the treatment to an untimely end, both on account not only of the resistances suddenly aroused thereby but also because of the relief resulting from the insight so obtained. [Freud 1913b, pp. 360-361]

Here Freud speaks clearly and eloquently about the need for analytic tact. He advocates the analyst adopting a sympathetic attitude, or, as he points out, it will be difficult if not impossible to obtain positive therapeutic results. He not only advises against premature interpretations (particularly early in the treatment) but also points out that the interpretive efforts should always stay closely linked to the patient's state of mind or experience. All of this is a very different attitude from that which Freud demonstrated in the Dora case. Interestingly, he tells us at the end that he has reached his conclusions because of the untimely end of various treatments he has conducted. He must have Dora in mind, but evidently he has other patients in mind as well. This and other passages make it clear that Freud believed that one must be able to convey a caring attitude if the analysis is to succeed. As importantly, it shows how Freud has moved from "the earliest days of analytic technique (where) we took an intellectualist view of the situation" (Freud 1913b, p. 362). At this point the patient's experience is crucial, and Freud warns that analysts should remember to make a distinction between their own knowledge and the patient's knowledge of the patient's unconscious fantasy life. He sees it as a mistake to interpret to the patient too early, since this would imply that all one had to do was make the patient intellectually aware of certain unconscious wishes to effect a cure. This was Freud's understanding in the early days of analysis, but experience has since corrected this view. There is, however, little doubt in these papers as to whether the analyst can understand the patient's unconscious life. This part of the equation is almost taken for granted. Freud assumes that it is frequently possible to understand dreams from their manifest content, and the meaning of symptoms from a relatively brief history of the patient's life. This certainty, or seeming certainty, implies an analytic attitude that is under frequent discussion today. Leaving aside the analyst's attitude, this position raises the larger question of what one means by an adequate analytic explanation. Is the *correct* translation of the patient's unconscious wishes what we mean when we say that we know or understand the patient's conflicts? What are our criteria for determining that we have reached a correct level of understanding of a dream, a symptom, or a transference state of the analysand? Freud does not really tackle this question until we reach the paper, "Constructions in Analysis." Even if we could agree on what constituted a correct interpretation, many analysts would maintain that the question of understanding involves factors that go beyond the present discussion of explicating unconscious wishes and fantasies (Bach 1985, Greenson 1967, Stone 1961, Winnicott 1971). Differences in conceptualizing the analytic process may well lead to differences in how one thinks of analytic knowledge. In fact, there is tension in Freud's own conceptualization of what might be considered an adequate analytic explanation. Ultimately, however, he maintains that analytic understanding involves a translation of the unconscious into terms that will eventually lead us to grasp the significance of the person's childhood experiences and original conflicts.

The Analyst

We have talked about how Freud suggested the analyst set up the conditions for analysis, but we have left out some of his ideas about the analyst's state during analysis. His analytical corollary to the rule that the patient should engage in free association is that the analyst be in a state of evenly suspended attention. His picture of the analyst as a receptor for the patient's unconscious derivatives is one that has been highly evocative. Some analysts have challenged this idea and suggested that evenly suspended attention is a type of platonic ideal to be thought about, but never reached, and, thus should be abandoned. They maintain that analysts are better off recognizing their inclinations and proceeding according to the theoretical biases that would govern their attitudes in any case. While it must be true that the state of evenly suspended attention is an ideal, one must question whether a principle should be thrown out *because* it will never be fully realized. This could be considered akin to abandoning the republic because we know that it never works in the way it was intended to by the framers of the constitution. The question should be whether the model of evenly suspended attention is useful as a guide in conducting an analysis. Even though our view of the therapeutic process is in part dictated by our theories, the ideal of remaining open to the unconscious derivatives of both parties in the analysis is still an important one to consider.[5] It may be that while we should acknowledge our predilections, we should also strive to see experiences that run contrary to our concepts. Leaving theory aside, the idea of remaining open to our own associations seems like an important ideal whatever one's theoretical orientation.

Freud (1916) and Abraham (1953) both recommend against an analyst taking notes during a session. The reason given is that it will disrupt the analyst's evenly suspended attention. For Freud, notetaking during a session would disrupt the analyst's access to his own associations. The model that Freud is proposing is one in which the analyst can be seen as both a sensitive tuning fork that can be activated easily by the patient's unconscious derivatives,

[5]Warren Poland's work describes how this concept is useful in alerting the analyst to unconscious fantasies (1984, 1991).

and then be able to formulate the meaning of these derivatives in terms that will help the analysand deepen and continue the analytic process. In this model, Freud felt that taking notes would disrupt his receptivity. It is possible to imagine that, for other analysts, writing notes either continuously or occasionally might not disrupt this process. This question can only be answered by individual analysts if they are particularly sensitive to the flow of unconscious derivatives. Thus Freud assumed that analysts would understand their own unconscious conflicts and strivings quite well. For Freud, the idea of a training analysis or for repeated analyses for the analyst was not an academic suggestion but one that is essential to his model of the receptive and, if you will, well-tuned analyst.

As a last point, we will only note that our recurrent theme appears once again in the present papers. When Freud advocates that there are times when patients should be seen for longer than a fifty-minute session or twice a day to overcome resistances, he is at least implicitly returning to the pathogenic memory model. There is again the suggestion that if one can facilitate or pressure the person to free associate by overcoming resistances, then one can reach the appropriate material. With this type of suggestion, the idea of allowing the treatment situation to be the playground for transference is placed in the background. Instead, the patient must come up with the appropriate associations. Even Freud's stress on the idea of free association is an example of the influence of the pathogenic memory model. His instructions to the patient about free association are pedantic and, to my mind, somewhat severe. It is one thing to have an ideal of free association and to help the patients understand and work through their difficulties in achieving this ideal. It is another matter, however, to pressure the patient. In attempting to help the patient free associate, Freud was harkening back to his ideas of encouraging the patient to associate in order to get at the pathogenic ideas or memories. Although this tendency is still present in Freud's writings partly because he has not fully developed his concept of defense (that is, defense as an unconscious process), this tension between analysis as conducted via the transference and the recovery of pathogenic memories continues throughout Freud's writings.

9

Freud's Recommendations Papers

Recommendations for Physicians on the Psycho-Analytic Method of Treatment[1]

(1912)

The technical rules which I bring forward here have been evolved out of my own experience in the course of many years, after I had renounced other methods which had cost me dear. It will easily be seen that they may be summed up, or at least many of them, in one single injunction. My hope is that compliance with them will spare physicians practising analysis much unavailing effort and warn them of various possibilities which they might otherwise overlook. I must, however, expressly state that this technique has proved to be the only method suited to my individuality; I do not venture to deny that a physician quite differently constituted might feel impelled to adopt a different attitude to his patients and to the task before him. ■ 1

(*a*) To the analyst who is treating more than one patient in the day, the first necessity with

[1] First published in *Zentralblatt*, Bd. II., 1912; reprinted in *Sammlung*. Vierte Folge. [Translated by Joan Riviere.]

■ 1

Although Freud is quite correct about the individuality of technique, a number of analysts have taken his statements at less than face value. Clearly he

■ 1 *continued*
is talking about individuality
within certain accepted analytic
guidelines. Nevertheless, there
is nothing to indicate that
Freud is anything less than sincere in this statement, at least
when talking about his own behavior. In fact, judging by his
individuality, one might say
that he was quite tolerant of at
least his own experimentation.
The history of psychoanalysis,
however, is dotted with conflicts that involve analysts de-
parting from Freud's ideas of
both theory and technique.
Rank, for example, was an analyst who hoped to shorten analytic treatment by focusing on
only one issue (birth anxiety).
Freud dispatched Rank's ideas
with an incisive and forceful
critique. Ferenczi also attempted far-reaching changes
in psychoanalytic technique,
which were not easily tolerated
in the psychoanalytic movement. Ferenczi's conflicts with
Freud were not simply intellectual differences but involved
personal feelings of the deepest
nature. In contemporary analysis, it remains to be seen
whether followers of Kohut, as
an example, will continue to be
part of the same analytic community alongside classical
analysts.

which he is faced will seem the hardest. It is, of
course, that of keeping in mind all the innumerable names, dates, detailed reminiscences, associations, and effects of the disease which each patient
communicates during the treatment in the course
of months or years, and not confounding them
with similar material proceeding from other patients treated simultaneously or previously. When
one is required to analyse six, eight, or even more
patients daily, the effort of memory necessary to
achieve this evokes incredulity, astonishment, or
even pity in the uninformed. Curiosity is inevitably
aroused about the technique which makes it possible to deal with such abundance of material, and
the expectation is that some special means are
required for the purpose.

The technique, however, is a very simple one.
It disclaims the use of any special aids, even of
notetaking, as we shall see, and simply consists in
making no effort to concentrate the attention on
anything in particular, and in maintaining in regard to all that one hears the same measure of
calm, quiet attentiveness—of 'evenly-hovering attention', as I once before described it. In this way a
strain which could not be kept up for several hours
daily and a danger inseparable from deliberate
attentiveness are avoided. For as soon as attention
is deliberately concentrated in a certain degree,
one begins to select from the material before one;
one point will be fixed in the mind with particular
clearness and some other consequently disregarded, and in this selection one's expectations or
one's inclinations will be followed. This is just
what must not be done, however; if one's expectations are followed in this selection there is the
danger of never finding anything but what is already known, and if one follows one's inclinations
anything which is to be perceived will most certainly be falsified. It must not be forgotten that the
meaning of the things one hears is, at all events
for the most part, only recognizable later on.

It will be seen, therefore, that the principle of evenly-distributed attention ■ 2 is the necessary corollary to the demand on the patient to communicate everything that occurs to him without criticism or selection. If the physician behaves otherwise he is throwing aside most of the advantage to be gained by the patient's obedience to the 'fundamental rule of psychoanalysis'. For the physician the rule may be expressed thus: All conscious exertion is to be withheld from the capacity for attention, and one's 'unconscious memory' is to be given full play; or to express it in terms of technique, pure and simple: One has simply to listen and not to trouble to keep in mind anything in particular.

What one achieves in this way will be sufficient for all requirements during the treatment. Those elements of the material which have a connection with one another will be at the conscious disposal of the physician; the rest, as yet unconnected, chaotic and indistinguishable, seems at first to disappear, but rises readily into recollection as soon as the patient brings something further to which it is related, and by which it can be developed. The undeserved compliment of a 'remarkably good memory' which the patient pays when one reproduces some detail after a year and a day is then accepted with a smile, whereas a conscious effort to retain a recollection of the point would probably have resulted in nothing.

Mistakes in recollection occur only at times and in places where some personal consideration has intervened (see below); that is, where there is a notable failure to reach the ideal set up for the analyst. Confusion with the communications of other patients arises very rarely. In a disagreement with the patient whether he said some particular thing, or how he said it, the physician is usually right.[2]

(*b*) I do not recommend that during the sitting, in the patient's presence, full notes should be

■ 2
The idea of evenly suspended attention is analogous to the patient's task of free association. It puts the analyst in the position of being sensitized to her or his own unconscious impulses or fantasies. This is Freud's way of getting into the topic of the analyst's reactions to the patient's transference (often called countertransference). The issue of countertransference is today widely discussed and written about. In Freud's time, it was rarely written about and, by today's standards, infrequently discussed. Thus, it remained for modern times to have books such as Racker's *Transference and Countertransference* (1968).

■ 3

This is a recommendation that
is still viable today, although
certain prominent analysts do
not necessarily adhere to it.
Winnicott suggests that it is
difficult to keep silent through
a number of sessions, and that
he has found it useful to write
down formulations during sessions. Sometimes, he will write
down interpretations that he
deems premature or speculative. Thus, in lieu of delivering
these interpretations to the patient, he writes them down and
evaluates them himself. Other
analysts at times tell analytic
candidates to take notes. Freud
and Abraham, however, both
felt that notetaking deflected
the analyst from the analytic
task—that is, the task of allowing oneself to resonate to the
patient's associations. It is interesting to speculate in this
era of recorded analyses what
effect taping an analysis (audio
or video) will have on the analyst's evenly suspended attention. Perhaps H. Dahl's research involving extended
recordings of analytic sessions
will soon provide some answers
to this speculation.

■ 4

The whole question of tape-
recording analyses for training
is a tangentially related point.
Some supervisors, and more
often supervisees, have argued
that it is useful for the super-
vision process to have the actual session recorded. Then the
supervisor will know what is
"really" going on in the treat-

made or a shorthand record kept, and so on. ■ 3
Apart from the unfavourable impression which
this makes on many patients, the same considerations as have been advanced in regard to attention
also apply here. A prejudicial selection will of
necessity be made in taking down notes or shorthand, and part of one's own mental activity is
occupied in this way which would be better employed in interpreting what one hears. Exceptions
may be made to this rule without reproach in the
case of dates, the text of dreams, or single incidents of a noteworthy kind which can easily be
detached from their context to serve an independent purpose as examples. I am not in the habit of
doing this either, however. I write down examples
from memory in the evening after work is over;
the text of a dream in which I find something
useful I ask the patient to write down for me after
he has related it.

(c) Note-taking during the sitting with the
patient might be supported on the ground of an
intention to publish a scientific study of the case.
■ 4 In theory this can hardly be denied. But in
practice it must not be forgotten that exact reports
of an analytic history of a case are less valuable
than might be expected. Strictly speaking, they
only convey that appearance of exactness which
'modern' psychiatry presents in many conspicuous
instances. They are wearisome to the reader as a
rule, and yet they do not go far enough as a
substitute for actual presence at the analysis. Altogether, experience shows that a reader who is

---

[2]The patient often asserts that he has previously mentioned
some particular thing, while one can assure him with calm
authority that he has now mentioned it for the first time. It
then turns out that the patient had previously had the intention to mention it, but had been hindered in so doing by a
resistance which had not yet been overcome. The memory of
his intention is indistinguishable in his mind from the memory of the act itself.

willing to believe an analyst at all will give him credit for the touch of revision to which he has subjected his material; but if the reader is unwilling to take analysis or the analyst seriously, the most faithful shorthand reports of the treatment of cases will not influence him. This does not seem to be the way to make up for the deficiency in evidence found in psycho-analytical descriptions of cases.

(*d*) It is indeed one of the distinctions of psychoanalysis that research and treatment proceed hand in hand, but still the technique required for the one begins at a certain point to diverge from that of the other. It is not a good thing to formulate a case scientifically while treatment is proceeding, to reconstruct its development, anticipate its progress, and take notes from time to time of the condition at the moment, as scientific interests would require. Cases which are thus destined at the start to scientific purposes and treated accordingly suffer in consequence; ■ 5 while the most successful cases are those in which one proceeds, as it were, aimlessly, and allows oneself to be overtaken by any surprises, always presenting to them an open mind, free from any expectations. ■ 6 To swing over as required from one mental attitude to another, to avoid speculation or brooding over cases while the analysis proceeds, and to submit the material gained to the synthetic process only after the analysis is concluded, is the right course for the analyst. The distinction here drawn between the two different attitudes would have no significance if we already possessed all the knowledge (or even the essential knowledge) about the unconscious and the structure of the neuroses which is obtained by means of the analytic work. At the present time we are still far from this goal and must not cut ourselves off from the means by which we can test what we already know and learn more.

■ 4 *continued*

ment. This procedure mitigates against the supervisee attempting to understand why he or she has forgotten certain material, or why she or he is reluctant to present certain material to the supervisor. These matters are frequently crucial in dealing with an analysis.

■ 5

Of course Freud might have been thinking of Dora; he was initially motivated to write about her as a continuation of the Dream Book (*The Interpretation of Dreams*). He may have felt that his difficulties in the case stemmed in part from his desire to "use" her to prove his case concerning the importance of dreams.

■ 6

Even in so-called "ordinary analysis," if the analysis is going well, there will be a sense of discovery as if one had uncovered something for the first time. This may have to do with the sense of release and creativity that analyst and analysand may experience during a successful analysis. This sense of discovery is so strong that,

■ 6 *continued*
in a recent publication, an
analyst (Bergmann) maintained
that all analyses involved the

■ 7
This is a much-quoted passage
of Freud's and is in a sense
contradicted by other things
that he has said and certainly
by his recorded behavior with
various patients. One can reconcile these contradictions by
simply accepting that Freud at
times was not totally consistent. One can also say that his
powerful metaphor is used here
to help the analyst with rescue
fantasies that are frequently
present as countertransference
tendencies. Freud is attempting
to counteract therapists' tendencies to do something dramatic and "meaningful" to help
the patient. Here, Freud seems
to be reminding the analyst
that the patient is not under
one's command and that there
are other factors beyond the
analyst's powers that will determine the outcome of the analysis. While this type of dispas-
sionate reserve may at times be
desirable, it is nonetheless difficult to achieve.

use of creativity by the analyst.
One can understand this feeling
while objecting to this use of
the concept of creativity.

(*e*) I cannot recommend my colleagues emphatically enough to take as a model in psychoanalytic treatment the surgeon who puts aside all
his own feelings, including that of human sympathy, and concentrates his mind on one single
purpose, that of performing the operation as skil-
fully as possible. ■ 7 Under present conditions the
affective impulse of greatest danger to the psycho-
analyst will be the therapeutic ambition to achieve
by this novel and disputed method something
which will impress and convince others. This will
not only cause a state of mind unfavourable for the
work in him personally, but he will find himself in
consequence helpless against certain of the patient's resistances, upon the struggle with which
the cure primarily depends. The justification for
this coldness in feeling in the analyst is that it is
the condition which brings the greatest advantage
to both persons involved, ensuring a needful protection for the physician's emotional life and the
greatest measure of aid for the patient that is
possible at the present time. An old surgeon once
took for his motto the words: *Je le pansai, Dieu le
guérit*. The analyst should content himself with a
similar thought.

(*f*) All these rules which I have brought forward coincide at one point which is easily discern-
ible. They all aim at creating for the physician a
complement to the 'fundamental rule of psycho-
analysis' for the patient. Just as the patient must
relate all that self-observation can detect, and
must restrain all the logical and affective objections which would urge him to select, so the physician must put himself in a position to use all that
is told him for the purposes of interpretation and
recognition of what is hidden in the unconscious,

without substituting a censorship of his own for the selection which the patient forgoes. Expressed in a formula, he must bend his own unconscious like a receptive organ towards the emerging unconscious of the patient, be as the receiver of the telephone to the disc. As the receiver transmutes the electric vibrations induced by the sound-waves back again into sound-waves, so is the physician's unconscious mind able to reconstruct the patient's unconscious, which has directed his associations, from the communications derived from it.

But if the physician is to be able to use his own unconscious in this way as an instrument in the analysis, he must himself fulfil one psychological condition in a high degree. He may tolerate no resistances in himself which withhold from his consciousness what is perceived by his unconscious, otherwise he would introduce into the analysis a new form of selection and distortion which would be far more injurious than that resulting from the concentration of conscious attention. It does not suffice for this that the physician should be of approximate normality himself; it is a justifiable requisition that he should further submit himself to a psycho-analytic purification and become aware of those complexes in himself which would be apt to affect his comprehension of the patient's disclosures. There can be no reasonable doubt about the disqualifying effect of such personal defects; every unresolved repression in the physician constitutes what W. Stekel has well named a 'blind spot' in his capacity for analytic perception. ■ 8

Years ago I replied to the question how one becomes an analyst with the answer: By the analysis of one's own dreams. This training certainly suffices for many people, but not for all those who wish to learn to analyse. Moreover, not everyone is able to interpret his own dreams without the help of another. I count it one of the valuable services of the Zürich school of analysis that they have

■ 8

Here one can see the beginnings of Freud's arguing for the need of training analyses. Despite the fact that one might be "normal," even "normal" people have defended against something in their past, and thus need an analysis if they want to be an analyst. More

■ **8** *continued*

importantly, in these passages one can see the logical conclusion of the idea of evenly suspended attention. Freud is maintaining that the analyst should be acting as an antenna for the patient's unconscious communications. Since it was Freud's view that the main locus was in the analyst's unconscious, obviously the analyst should know his or her unconscious tendencies quite well. Sections like this were interpreted by the analytic world as implicit warnings about the danger of countertransference, particularly if one were not well analyzed. As we have noted, in today's analytic world, the topic of countertransference is proportionately a much larger topic than it was in Freud's time. Freud was quite sensitive to outsiders criticizing psychoanalysis and psychoanalysts. He did not want the world to see analysts as suffering from the same afflictions as the patients whom they treated. It is understandable that Freud would be sensitive to this type of criticism; he was trying to establish a new field in the world of health care. Nevertheless, it is ironic that this type of sensitivity exists even today, since all of Freud's writings point to the universality of neurotic afflictions.

emphasized this necessity and laid it down as a requisition that anyone who wishes to practise analysis of others should first submit to be analysed himself by a competent person. Anyone taking up the work seriously should choose this course, which offers more than one advantage; the sacrifice involved in laying oneself bare to a stranger without the necessity incurred by illness is amply rewarded. Not only is the purpose of learning to know what is hidden in one's own mind far more quickly attained and with less expense of affect, but impressions and convictions are received in one's own person which may be sought in vain by studying books and attending lectures. In addition, the gain resulting from the lasting personal relationship which usually springs up between the learner and his guide is not to be estimated lightly.

Such analysis of a person who is for all practical purposes healthy will naturally remain uncompleted. Whoever knows how to appreciate the high value of the self-knowledge and increase in self-control so acquired will afterwards continue the analytic examination of his own personality by a self-analysis, and willingly recognize that, in himself as in others, he must always expect to find something new. That analyst, however, who has despised the provision of analysis for himself will be penalized, not merely by an incapacity to learn more than a certain amount from his patient, but by risking a more serious danger, one which may become a danger for others. He will easily yield to the temptation of projecting as a scientific theory of general applicability some of the peculiarities of his own personality which he has dimly perceived; he will bring the psycho-analytic method into discredit, and lead the inexperienced astray. ■ 9

(g) I will now add a few other rules which will make a transition from the attitude of the physician to the treatment of the patient.

The young and eager psycho-analyst will certainly be tempted to bring his own individuality freely into the discussion, in order to draw out the patient and help him over the confines of his narrow personality. One would expect it to be entirely permissible, and even desirable, for the overcoming of the patient's resistances, that the physician should afford him a glimpse into his own mental defects and conflicts and lead him to form comparisons by making intimate disclosures from his own life. One confidence repays another, and anyone demanding intimate revelations from another must be prepared to make them himself.

But the psycho-analytic relationship is a thing apart; much of it takes a different course from that which the psychology of consciousness would lead us to expect. Experience does not bear witness to the excellence of an affective technique of this kind. Further, it is not difficult to see that it involves a departure from psycho-analytic principles and verges upon treatment by suggestion. It will induce the patient to bring forward sooner and

■ 9

Freud is now talking about the value of an analysis for everyone and certainly the necessity of analysis for someone who wants to be an analyst. It is, of course, commonplace to point out that Freud himself did not have an analysis. At various points in his career, Freud thought of himself (and some of his family and friends) as exceptions to the normal practices of psychoanalysis. Thus, he could analyze friends and family with impunity.

with less difficulty what he already knows and
would otherwise have kept back for a time on
account of conventional objections. But this technique achieves nothing towards the discovery of
the patient's unconscious; it makes him less able
than ever to overcome the deeper resistances, and
in the more severe cases it invariably fails on
account of the insatiability it rouses in the patient,
who then tries to reverse the situation, finding the
analysis of the physician more interesting than his
own. The loosening of the transference, too—one
of the main tasks of the cure—is made more difficult by too intimate an attitude on the part of the
doctor, so that a doubtful gain in the beginning is
more than cancelled in the end. Therefore I do not
hesitate to condemn this kind of technique as
incorrect. The physician should be impenetrable
to the patient, and, like a mirror, reflect nothing
but what is shown to him. In practice, it is true,
one cannot object to a psycho-therapeutist combining a certain amount of analysis with some
suggestive treatment in order to achieve a percep-
tible result in a shorter time—as is necessary, for
instance, in institutions; but one may demand that
he himself should be in no doubt about what he is
doing and should know that his method is not that
of true psycho-analysis. ▪ 10

(*h*) Another temptation arises out of the educative function which in a psycho-analytic treatment falls to the physician without any special
intention on his part. As the inhibitions in development are undone it inevitably happens that the
physician finds himself in a position to point out
new aims for the impulses which have been set
free. It is but a natural ambition for him then to
endeavour to make something specially excellent
out of the person whose neurosis has cost so much
labour, and to set up high aims for these impulses.
But here again the physician should restrain himself and take the patient's capacities rather than
his own wishes as his standard. Talent for a high

▪ 10
Freud touches on what is today
a type of technique for some
forms of therapy. He stresses
that what might be momentary
intimacy, and momentarily facilitating for a treatment, would
in the long run be a resistance
to the successful analysis of the
transference.

degree of sublimation is not found in all neurotics; of many of them one can believe that they would never have fallen ill had they possessed the art of sublimating their impulses. In pressing them unduly towards sublimation, and cutting them off from the easier and simpler gratifications, life may often be made even harder for them than they feel it otherwise. A physician must always be tolerant of a patient's weakness, and must be content to win back a part of the capacity for work and enjoyment even for a person of but moderate worth. Ambitiousness in the educative direction is as undesirable as in the therapeutic. Moreover, it must not be forgotten that many people succumb to illness in the very effort towards sublimation beyond the limit of their capacity, and that in those who are capable of it the process usually takes place from within as soon as their inhibitions have been removed by the analysis. In my opinion, therefore, efforts to bring about sublimations of the impulses in the course of psycho-analytic treatment are no doubt always praiseworthy but most certainly not in all cases advisable. ■ 11

(i) To what extent should the intellectual co-operation of the patient be called for in the treatment? It is difficult to say anything of general applicability on this point; the personality of the patient is here the principal deciding factor. In any case caution and self-restraint are to be observed in this matter. It is incorrect to set the patient tasks, such as collecting his memories, thinking over a certain period of his life, and so on. On the contrary, the patient has above all to learn, what never comes easily to anyone, that such mental activities as thinking over a matter, or concentrating the will and attention, avail nothing in solving the riddles of the neurosis; but that this can only be done by patiently adhering to the psycho-analytic rule demanding the exclusion of all criticism of the unconscious or of its derivatives. One must especially insist upon the following of the

■ 11

Freud is recommending that the analyst not try to make the patient into her or his own image, that the analyst allow patients to lead their own lives. It is seemingly an obvious recommendation, but not so easily accomplished either by Freud or, at times, by contemporary analysts. It is also an interesting note on sublimation, since it leads to a view of the patient as weak and incapacitated. His view of sublimation is based on his idea of a fixed amount of psychic energy. Thus, if one has a certain amount of energy expended in neurotic conflict, one must of necessity not have enough energy to sublimate to other activities. This view does

■ 11 *continued*
not seem to fit many workahol-
ics who find themselves patients in psychoanalysis. One
could say that many of today's
analysands have sublimated too
extensively, and there is little
energy left for intimacy and
closeness in their personal

lives. It might be better to leave
this idea completely and conceive of people having conflicts
in various areas of their lives;
these conflicts may or may not
affect other areas of their lives
depending on the nature and
intensity of the conflict.

rule most rigidly with those patients whose habitual manœuvre it is to shirk analysis by sheering
off into the intellectual, and who speculate much
and often with great wisdom over their condition,
thereby sparing themselves from taking steps to
overcome it. For this reason I dislike resorting to
analytical writings as an aid to patients; I require
them to learn by personal experience, and I assure
them that in this way they will acquire wider and
more valuable knowledge than the whole literature of psycho-analysis could afford them. I recognize, however, that under the conditions of institution treatment it may be very advantageous to
employ reading as a preparation for patients in
analysis and as a means of creating an atmosphere
favourable to influence. ■ 12

The most urgent warning I have to express is
against any attempt to engage the confidence or
support of parents or relatives by giving them
psycho-analytical books to read—either of an introductory or of an advanced kind. This well-
meant step usually has the effect of evoking prematurely the natural and inevitable opposition of
the relatives to the treatment, which in consequence is never even begun.

I will here express the hope that advances in
the experience of psycho-analysts will soon lead to
agreement upon the most expedient technique for
the treatment of neurotic persons. As for treatment of the 'relatives', I must confess myself ut-
terly at a loss, and I have altogether little faith in
any individual treatment of them.

■ 12
At times, analysts have forbidden their patients to read analytic works. One can only say
that such rules for analytic patients are counterproductive. In
any case, Freud's admonition
against the use of influence is a
good one. Patients will lead
their lives, and the analyst can
only help them to lead a less
conflicted life; hopefully, this
will help the patient find more
fulfilling alternatives for himself.

Further Recommendations in the Technique of Psycho-Analysis[1]

ON BEGINNING THE TREATMENT. THE QUESTION OF THE FIRST COMMUNICATIONS. THE DYNAMICS OF THE CURE.

(1913)

He who hopes to learn the fine art of the game of chess from books will soon discover that only the opening and closing moves of the game admit of exhaustive systematic description, and that the endless variety of the moves which develop from the opening defies description; the gap left in the instructions can only be filled in by the zealous study of games fought out by master-hands. The rules which can be laid down for the practical application of psycho-analysis in treatment are subject to similar limitations. ■ 13

I intend now to try to collect together for the use of practising analysts some of the rules for the opening of the treatment. Among them there are some which may seem to be mere details, as indeed they are. Their justification is that they are simply rules of the game, acquiring their importance by their connection with the whole plan of

■ 13
In chess, of course, there are voluminous writings on beginning the game, but in contemporary psychoanalysis, interestingly enough, the beginning of treatment has received relatively little attention.

[1]First published in *Zeitschrift*, Bd. I., 1913; reprinted in *Sammlung*, Vierte Folge. [Translated by Joan Riviere.]

■ 14

It is understandable that Freud should be ambivalent about whether to consider his writing recommendations or rules. On one hand, he wanted to stem the spread of what he considered to be "wild analysis," while, on the other hand, he did not want to stifle all new attempts at technical innovation.

■ 15

The trial analysis has largely been replaced by the preparatory analysis. The issue of diagnosis and analyzability is, however, still a topic that is quite current. Stone was one of the first of contemporary analysts to advocate and suggest how the scope of analysis could be widened. His criteria for analyzability differed from Freud's stated positions. In his writings on borderline patients, Kernberg has spoken most directly to ways in which one can conduct a diagnostic interview to determine the patient's analyzability.

the game. I do well, however, to bring them forward as 'recommendations' without claiming any unconditional acceptance for them. ■ 14 The exceptional diversity in the mental constellations concerned, the plasticity of all mental processes, and the great number of the determining factors involved prevent the formulation of a stereotyped technique, and also bring it about that a course of action, ordinarily legitimate, may be at times ineffective, while one which is usually erroneous may occasionally lead to the desired end. These circumstances do not prevent us from establishing a procedure for the physician which will be found most generally efficient.

Some years ago I set forth the considerations of chief importance in the selection of patients, which I shall therefore not repeat here,[2] since that time other psycho-analysts have confirmed their validity. I will add, though, that since then, when I know little of a case, I have formed the practice of first undertaking it only provisionally for one or two weeks. ■ 15 If one breaks off within this period the patient is spared the distress of an unsuccessful attempt at cure; it was only 'taking a sounding' in order to learn more about the case and to decide whether it was a suitable one for psycho-analysis. No other kind of preliminary examination is possible; the most lengthy discussions and questionings in ordinary consultation are no substitute. This experiment, however, is in itself the beginning of an analysis, and must conform to its rules; there may perhaps be this difference in that on the whole one lets the patient talk, and explains nothing more than is absolutely necessary to keep him talking.

For the purposes of diagnosis, also, it is an advantage to begin with a period of a few weeks designed as an experiment. Often enough, when one sees a case of neurosis with hysterical or ob-

[2]'On Psychotherapy', COLLECTED PAPERS, vol. i.

sessional symptoms, mild in character and of short duration (just the type of case, that is, which one would regard as suitable for the treatment), a doubt which must not be overlooked arises whether the case may not be one of incipient dementia præcox, so called (schizophrenia, according to Bleuler; paraphrenia, as I prefer to call it), and may not sooner or later develop well-marked signs of this disease. I do not agree that it is always possible to effect the distinction so easily. I know that there are psychiatrists who hesitate less often in their differential diagnosis, but I have been convinced that they are just as often mistaken. For the psycho-analyst, however, the mistake is more serious than for so-called clinical psychiatrists. The latter has little of value to offer either to the one type of case or to the other; he merely runs the risk of a theoretical mistake, and his diagnosis has but an academic interest. In an unsuitable case, however, the psycho-analyst has committed a practical error; he has occasioned useless expense and discredited his method of treatment; he cannot fulfill his promise of cure if the patient is suffering from paraphrenia instead of from hysteria or obsessional neurosis, and therefore he has particularly strong motives for avoiding mistakes in diagnosis. In an experimental course of a few weeks suspicious signs will often be observed which will decide him not to pursue the attempt further. Unfortunately I cannot assert that an attempt of this kind will invariably ensure certainty; it is but one more useful precaution.[3]

---

[3]There is much to be said on the subject of this uncertainty in diagnosis, on the prospects of analysis in the milder forms of paraphrenia, and on the explanation of the similarity between the two diseases, which I cannot bring forward in this connection. I should be willing to contrast hysteria and the obsessional neurosis, under the name of 'transference neuroses', with the paraphrenic group, under the name of 'introversion neuroses', in accordance with Jung's formula, if the term 'introversion' (of the libido) were not alienated by such usage from its only legitimate meaning.

■ 16
In many analytic centers, it is
difficult to have a practice if
one doesn't see patients who
have been in other forms of
treatment or in other analyses.
It is surprising how accurate
Freud is when he reports that
past transference reactions will
endure in the present treatment. It is difficult to imagine
that in 1911–1912 he saw many
patients who had previously
been to another analyst. Clearly
some patients who came to see
him had been in other treatment methods, and Freud could
experience himself as a recipient of these continuing transference reactions. Here is
another indication of how
firmly the concept of transference is established in Freud's
attempts at explaining clinical
phenomena (see Part II).

■ 17
Mistrusting patients who want
to delay the beginning of treatment is probably good advice
statistically. I had always been
impressed by this advice. Then
a patient referred to me suddenly had the opportunity to

Lengthy preliminary discussions before the
beginning of the treatment, previous treatment by
another method, and also previous acquaintance
between physician and patient, have certain disadvantageous consequences for which one must be
prepared. They result in the patient entering upon
the analysis with a transference already effected,
which must then be slowly uncovered by the physician; whereas otherwise he is in a position to
observe the growth and development of it from
the outset. By this means the patient gains a start
upon us which we do not willingly grant him in
the treatment. ■ 16

One must distrust all those who wish to put
off beginning the treatment. Experience shows
that at the appointed time they fail to return, even
though their motive for the delay (that is, their
rationalization of the intention) appears to the
novice to be above suspicion. ■ 17

Special difficulties arise when friendship or
acquaintance already exists between the physician
and the patient, or their families. The psycho-
analyst who is asked to undertake treatment of the
wife or child of a friend must be prepared for it to
cost him the friendship, no matter what the outcome of the treatment; nevertheless he must make
the sacrifice unless he can propose a trustworthy
substitute. ■ 18

Both the general public and medical men—
still fain to confound psycho-analytic with suggestive treatment—are inclined to attribute great importance to the expectations which the patient
brings to the new treatment. They often believe
that one patient will not give much trouble because he has a great belief in psycho-analysis and
is fully convinced of its truth and curative power;
and that another patient will doubtless prove
more difficult because he is of a sceptical nature
and will not believe until he has experienced good
results in his own person. Actually, however, this
attitude on the part of the patient has very little

■ 17 *continued*
direct a play and had to delay
the beginning of his treatment.
A year later, I was surprised
when this patient called and
subsequently began treatment.
The patient had felt he didn't
want to begin when he couldn't
give his treatment sufficient attention. This person proved to
be someone who was quite dedicated to his treatment and for
whom analysis has been beneficial. This is an example of how,
even though Freud's observations are generally correct, one
must remember the difference
between clinical inference and
statistical generalizations.

■ 18
This is an interesting comment

given Freud's performing various analyses of people who became his friends and supporters. We also know that Freud
analyzed his own daughter,
Anna Freud. We must assume
that he rationalized this undertaking by maintaining that he
could not find a trustworthy
substitute. It is my interpretation that Freud felt he could
somehow be an exception to
the workings of the unconscious. Despite Freud's actions,
he has presented good advice,
and his later experiences with
Ferenczi attest to the difficulties of mixing friendship with
an analytic relationship. Ferenczi presents his side of the
analysis in his *Clinical Diary*
(1988).

importance; his preliminary belief or disbelief is
almost negligible compared with the inner resistances which hold the neurosis fast. A blissful
trustfulness on the patient's part makes the relationship at first a very pleasant one; one thanks
him for it, but warns him that this favourable
prepossession will be shattered by the first difficulty arising in the analysis. To the sceptic one says
that the analysis requires no faith; that he may be
as critical and suspicious as he pleases; that one
does not regard this attitude as the effect of his
judgement at all, for he is not in a position to form
a reliable judgement on the matter; his distrust is
but a symptom like his other symptoms and will
not interfere if he conscientiously carries out what
the rule of the treatment requires of him. ■ 19

Whoever is familiar with the nature of neurosis will not be astonished to hear that even a man
who is very well able to carry out analysis upon
others can behave like any other mortal and be
capable of producing violent resistances as soon as

■ 19
Freud is warning analysts not
to be overly impressed with a
patient's conscious attitude toward analysis. He maintains
that a person's initial confidence in analysis is of little im-

■ 19 *continued*

portance in the course of his or her analysis. What are more crucial are the patient's internal resistances, which once encountered will shatter (or at least disrupt) the patient's initial confidence in analysis. The thinking involved in this formulation assumes that the analyst, to some extent, will confront the patient when a resistance is met. Freud's meaning of resistance in this context is anything that the patient utilizes to inhibit the flow of associative process. Counterbalancing the patient's reactions will be the confidence they will require if they carry out *what the rule of the treatment requires of* them, that is, continuing to free associate. This type of thinking leaves as

unanalyzable the resistant patient who is unwilling or unable to conscientiously carry out what is "required" of him. Many patients cannot trust the analyst until the analysis has been going on for a long period of time. Some analysts have advocated changes in the analytic situation to enable these patients (whom Freud might have considered unanalyzable) to have successful analytic treatments. One can consider some of Greenson's, Stone's, Bach's, or Kohut's suggestions as ways of allowing certain patients to establish trust in the analyst and in the analytic process. Bach details the experiences of nonclassical patients in a manner that is useful for any practitioner who wants to gain a sense of the inner world of this type of patient.

he himself becomes the object of analytic investigation. When this happens it serves to remind us again of the dimensions which the mind has in regard to its depth, and it does not surprise us to find that a neurosis is rooted in mental strata that were never penetrated by an intellectual study of analysis.

Points of importance for the beginning of the treatment are the arrangements about time and money. In regard to time, I adhere rigidly to the principle of leasing a definite hour. A certain hour of my available working day is appointed to each patient; it is his, and he is liable for it, even if he does not make use of it. This arrangement, which is regarded as a matter of course for teachers of music or language among our upper classes, perhaps seems too rigorous for a medical man, or even unworthy of the profession. All the many accidents which may prevent the patient from attending every day at the same hour will be referred to, and some allowance will be expected for the numerous intercurrent ailments which may arise in the course of a lengthy analytic treatment. My only answer is: No other way is practicable. ■ 20 Under a less stringent régime the 'occasional' non-attendances accumulate so greatly that the physician's material existence is threatened; whereas strict adherence to the arrangement has the effect that accidental hindrances do not arise at all and intercurrent illnesses but seldom. One is hardly ever put in the position of enjoying a leisure hour which one is paid for and would be ashamed of; the work continues without interruptions, and one is spared the disheartening and bewildering experience that an unexpected pause in the work always occurs just when it promises to be especially important and productive. Nothing brings home to one with such overwhelming conviction the significance of the psychogenic factor in the daily life of mankind, the frequency of fictitious 'indispositions', and the non-existence of chance as the practice of psycho-analysis for some years strictly on the principle of hire by the hour. In cases of indubitable organic illness, the occurrence of which cannot be excluded in spite of interest in the psychical work, I break off the treatment, regard myself as entitled to dispose otherwise of the hour which becomes free, and take the patient back again when he has recovered and I again have a free hour.

I work with my patients every day, except Sundays and public holidays, that is, usually six days a week. For slight cases, or the continuation of a treatment already well advanced, three days a week will suffice. Otherwise, restriction of the time expended brings no advantage to physician or patient; it is not to be thought of at the beginning. Even short interruptions have a disconcerting effect on the work; we used to speak jokingly of the 'Monday-crust' ■ 21 when we began work again after the rest on Sunday; with more frequent intervals the risk arises that one will not be able to

■ 20

In today's psychotherapeutic world, there are many other practices concerning missed hours. Very few therapists today see patients six times a week as Freud did. In fact, most psychotherapy is probably conducted on a once- or twice-a-week basis. This, of course, constitutes a much smaller percentage of one's income than is the case if one sees a patient four to six times a week. Thus it is easier for a therapist not to charge for missed sessions. Many analysts think that other policies concerning missed sessions put the analyst in a position of judging the patient's reasons for missing sessions, and this is the main reason for the policy that Freud is advocating.

■ 21

The Monday crust is a famous passage, and given today's ten-

■ 21 *continued*
dency toward less frequent sessions, one wonders how thick
the crust often is in some treatments in which the sessions are
once or twice a week.

■ 22
Here Freud is showing a type
of flexibility that is rare in today's analytic world. Generally
patients are now seen for extended sessions only if there is
some type of emergency. Freud,
of course, assumed that the
length of an analysis would be
much shorter, and that it was
important to have a patient
"open out." Today one would
assume that this altering of the
normal schedule would introduce some elements into an
analysis that would need to be
analyzed and perhaps be undesirable. In today's analytic
world, treatments almost always go on for a longer time
than in Freud's era, and so analysts may wait a longer time
for a patient to begin to communicate. Since the fundamental rule is so central to Freud, it
is, of course, crucial to get the
analysand to begin to free associate.

■ 23
The question of length of treatment is still frequently asked
despite the well-publicized
length of psychoanalytic treat-
ment(s). There are people who
advocate telling the patient the
average length of treatment,
but this procedure has its drawbacks. The question would undoubtedly arise as to the length
of one's stride as Freud has put
it. The length of stride or one's

keep pace with the patient's real life, that the
analysis will lose contact with the present and be
forced into by-paths. Occasionally one meets with
patients to whom one must give more than the
average time of one hour a day, because the best
part of an hour is gone before they begin to open
out and to communicate anything at all. ■ 22

An unwelcome question which the patient
asks the physician at the outset is: How long will
the treatment last? What length of time will you
require to relieve me of my trouble? ■ 23 If one has
proposed an experimental course of a few weeks
one can avoid a direct reply to this question by
undertaking to give a more trustworthy answer
later on. The answer is like that of Aesop in the
fable of the Wanderer; on being asked the length
of the journey he answered 'Go', and gave the
explanation that he must know the pilgrim's pace
before he could tell the time his journey would
take him. This explanation helps one over the
difficulty at the start, but the comparison is not a
good one, for the neurotic can easily alter his pace
and at times make but very slow progress. The
question of the probable duration of the treatment
is hardly to be answered at all, in fact.

As a result of the lack of insight on the part of
patients combined with the lack of straightfor-
wardness on the part of physicians, analysis is
expected to realize the most boundless claims in
the shortest time. As an example I will give some
details from a letter which I received a few days
ago from a lady in Russia. Her age is fifty-three;
her illness began twenty-three years ago; for the
last ten years she has been incapable of continued
work; 'various cures in homes' have not succeeded
in making an 'active life' possible for her. She
hopes to be completely cured by psycho-analysis,
of which she has read, but her illness has already
cost her family so much that she cannot undertake
a visit of more than six weeks or two months to
Vienna. In addition to this there is another diffi-

culty: she wishes to 'explain herself' from the beginning in writing, since any discussion of her complexes would excite an attack or render her 'temporarily dumb'. No one would expect a man to lift a heavy table with two fingers as if it were a little stool, or to build a large house in the time it would take to put up a wooden hut, but as soon as it becomes a question of the neuroses (which mankind seems not yet to have fitted into the general scheme of his ideas) even intelligent people forget the necessity for proportion between work, time and success—a comprehensible result, too, of the deep ignorance which prevails concerning the ætiology of neuroses. Thanks to this ignorance a neurosis is generally regarded as a sort of 'maiden from afar'; the world knows not whence it comes, and therefore expects it to vanish away some day.

Medical men support this happy belief; even the experienced among them often fail to estimate properly the severity of nervous disorders. A friend and colleague of mine, to whose credit I account it that after several decades of scientific work on other principles he has betaken himself to the recognition of psycho-analysis, once wrote to me: What we need is a short, convenient form of treatment for out-patients suffering from obsessional neurosis. I could not supply him with it, and felt ashamed; so I tried to excuse myself with the remark that probably physicians would also be very glad of a treatment for consumption or cancer which combined these advantages.

To speak more plainly, psycho-analysis is always a matter of long periods of time, of six months or a year, or more—a longer time than the patient expects. It is therefore a duty to explain this fact to the patient before he finally resolves upon the treatment. I hold it to be altogether more honourable, and also more expedient, to draw his attention, without alarming him unduly but from the very beginning, to the difficulties and sacri-

■ 23 *continued*
propensity for analytic work is naturally not the only factor that will determine the length of an analysis. Frequently, accidental factors such as the death of a parent or spouse, or any of the exigencies of life, will have a decisive impact on the course of a treatment. Analysis is, in addition, such a personal unfolding of one's life experiences that it is hard, if not impossible, to talk with any degree of accuracy about the length of stride or propensity for analytic work.

fices involved by analytic treatment; thereby depriving him of the right to assert later on that he had been inveigled into a treatment the implications and extent of which he did not realize. The patient who lets himself be dissuaded by these considerations would later on have shown himself unsuitable; it is a good thing to institute a selection in this way before the beginning of the treatment. With the progress of understanding among patients the number of those who stand this first test increases.

I do not bind patients to continue the treatment for a certain length of time; I permit each one to break off whenever he likes, though I do not conceal from him that no success will result from a treatment broken off after only a small amount of work, and that it may easily, like an unfinished operation, leave him in an unsatisfactory condition. In the early years of my practice of psycho-analysis I had the greatest difficulty in prevailing upon patients to continue; this difficulty has long since altered; I must now anxiously exert myself to induce them to give it up.

The shortening of the analytic treatment remains a reasonable wish, the realization of which, as we shall hear, is being sought after in various ways. Unfortunately, it is opposed by a very important element in the situation—namely, the slowness with which profound changes in the mind bring themselves about, fundamentally the same thing as the 'inappreciation of time' characteristic of our unconscious processes. ■ 24 When the patients are confronted with the great expenditure of time required for the analysis they often bethink themselves of suggesting a makeshift way out of the difficulty. They divide up their complaints and describe some as unendurable and others as secondary, saying, 'If only you will relieve me of this (for instance, a headache or a particular fear) I will manage by myself to endure life with the other troubles'. They exaggerate the selective capacity of the analysis in this. The analyst is

■ 24
Freud's views on shortening the treatment show that he recognized various obstacles to speeding the natural processes of analysis. In the case of the Wolf Man, we will see he felt that he had to attempt to shorten the process, so a time limit was set. Freud discusses this in "Analysis Terminable and Interminable."

certainly able to do a great deal, but he cannot determine beforehand exactly what results he will effect. He sets in operation a certain process, the 'loosening' of the existing repressions: he can watch over it, further it, remove difficulties in the way of it, and certainly do much also to vitiate it; but on the whole, once begun, the process goes its own way and does not admit of prescribed direction, either in the course it pursues or in the order in which the various stages to be gone through are taken. The power of the analyst over the symptoms of disease is comparable in a way to sexual potency; the strongest man can beget a whole child, it is true, but he cannot effect the production of a head alone, or an arm, or a leg in the female organ, he cannot even prescribe the sex of the child. He, too, only sets in operation a highly complicated process, determined by foregone events, and ending with the severance of the child from the mother. Again, a neurosis has the character of an organism; its component manifestations are not independent of one another, they each condition and mutually support the others; a man can only suffer from one neurosis, never from several accidentally combined in his person. Suppose one had freed the patient, according to his wish, from the one unendurable symptom, he might then have discovered that a symptom which was previously negligible had increased until it in turn had become intolerable. In general, the analyst who wishes the results to be as independent as possible of the influence of suggestion from himself (that is, of transference) will do best to refrain from using even the fraction of selective influence upon the results of the cure which is perhaps open to him. The patients who are most welcome to the psycho-analyst will be those who desire complete health so far as they are capable of it, and who will place as much time at his disposal for the cure as the process requires. Naturally, such favourable conditions are to be met with only in the minority of cases.

The next point to be decided on beginning the treatment is the money question, the physician's fee. The analyst does not dispute that money is to be regarded first and foremost as the means by which life is supported and power is obtained, but he maintains that, besides this, powerful sexual factors are involved in the value set upon it; he may expect, therefore, that money questions will be treated by cultured people in the same manner as sexual matters, with the same inconsistency, prudishness and hypocrisy. He is therefore determined beforehand not to concur in this attitude, and in his dealings with patients to treat of money matters with the same matter-of-course frankness that he wishes to induce in them towards matters relating to sexual life. By voluntarily introducing the subject of fees and stating the price for which he gives his time, he shows the patient that he himself has cast aside false shame in these matters. Ordinary prudence then demands that the sums to be paid should not be allowed to accumulate until they are very large, but that payment should be made at fairly short regular intervals (every month or so). (It is well known that the value of the treatment is not enhanced in the patient's eyes if a very low fee is asked.) This is of course not the usual practice of neurologists or other physicians in our European cities. But the psycho-analyst may put himself in the position of surgeons, who are both honest and expensive because they deal in measures which can be of aid. In my opinion it is more dignified and ethically less open to objection to acknowledge one's actual claims and needs rather than, as the practice is now among medical men, to act the part of the disinterested philanthropist, while that enviable situation is denied to one and one grumbles in secret, or animadverts loudly, over the lack of consideration or the miserliness shown by patients. In estimating his fee the analyst must allow for the fact that, in spite of strenuous work, he can never earn as much as other medical specialists.

For the same reasons he may refrain from giving treatment gratuitously, making no exceptions to this in favour of his colleagues or their relatives. This last requisition seems to conflict with the claims of professional fellow-feeling; one must consider, however, that gratuitous treatment means much more to a psycho-analyst than to other medical men—namely, the dedication of a considerable portion (an eighth or a seventh part, perhaps) of the time available for his livelihood over a period of several months. Another treatment conducted gratuitously at the same time would rob him of a quarter or a third of his earning capacity, which would be comparable to the effects of some serious accident. ■ 25

Then the question arises whether the advantage to the patient would not outweigh the physician's sacrifice. I may rely on my own judgement in this matter, since I have given an hour daily, and sometimes two, for ten years to gratuitous treatment, because I wished, for the purpose of studying the neuroses, to work with the fewest possible hindrances. The advantages which I sought in this way were not forthcoming. Gratuitous treatment enormously increases many neurotic resistances, such as the temptations of the transference-relationship for young women, or the opposition to the obligatory gratitude in young men arising from the father-complex, which is one of the most troublesome obstacles to the treatment. The absence of the corrective influence in payment of the professional fee is felt as a serious handicap; the whole relationship recedes into an unreal world; and the patient is deprived of a useful incentive to exert himself to bring the cure to an end. ■ 26

One may stand quite aloof from the ascetic view of money as a curse and yet regret that analytic therapy is almost unattainable for the

■ 25
Freud must have been concerned with the prospect of analysis being a profession whose practitioners make a decent living. He was maintaining that analysts have a right to charge for their time, for their services are valuable. The question of allowing for professional courtesy is important, since many (or most) members of the analytic community are or have been patients at one time or another. It is hard to imagine what would have happened to analytic practices if Freud had insisted that one always show professional courtesy.

■ 26

The whole question of fee must have been difficult and highly conflictual for Freud. As he

states, he had been much more
flexible than he advises others
to be. This flexibility did not
disappear with the writing of
this article, and as we know, at
times he assisted a patient who
no longer had any monetary resources (for example, the Wolf
Man).

poor, both for external and for internal reasons.
Little can be done to remedy this. Perhaps there is
some truth in the widespread belief that those
who are forced by necessity to a life of heavy
labour succumb less easily to neurosis. But at all
events experience shows without a doubt that, in
this class, a neurosis once acquired is only with
very great difficulty eradicated. It renders the sufferer too good service in the struggle for existence;
the accompanying secondary 'epinosic gain' has
here too much importance. The pity which the
world has refused to his material distress the sufferer now claims by right of his neurosis and
absolves himself from the obligation of combating
his poverty by work. Any one who tries to deal by
psychotherapeutic means with a neurosis in a poor
person usually makes the discovery that what is
really required of him in such a case is a very
different, material kind of therapy—the sort of
healing which, according to tradition, Emperor
Joseph II. used to dispense. Naturally, one does
occasionally meet with people of worth who are
helpless from no fault of their own, in whom
unpaid treatment leads to excellent results without exciting any of the difficulties mentioned.

For the middle classes the necessary expense
of psycho-analysis is only apparently excessive.
Quite apart from the fact that restored health and
capacity for life on the one hand, and a moderate
outlay in money on the other, cannot be measured
in the same category; if one contrasts a computa-
tion of the never-ceasing costs of nursing homes
and medical treatment with the increase of capacity to live well and earn well after a successful
analytic treatment, one may say that the patient
has made a good bargain. Nothing in life is so
expensive as illness—and foolishness.

Before I conclude these remarks on beginning
the analytic treatment a word must be said about a
certain ceremonial observance regarding the position in which the treatment is carried out. I adhere

firmly to the plan of requiring the patient to recline upon a sofa, while one sits behind him out of his sight. ■ 27 This arrangement has an historic meaning; it is the last vestige of the hypnotic method out of which psycho-analysis was evolved; but for many reasons it deserves to be retained. The first is a personal motive, one that others may share with me, however. I cannot bear to be gazed at for eight hours a day (or more). Since, while I listen, I resign myself to the control of my unconscious thoughts I do not wish my expression to give the patient indications which he may interpret or which may influence him in his communications. The patient usually regards being required to take up this position as a hardship and objects to it, especially when scoptophilia plays an important part in the neurosis. I persist in the measure, however, for the intention and result of it are that all imperceptible influence on the patient's associations by the transference may be avoided, so that the transference may be isolated and clearly outlined when it appears as a resistance. I know that many analysts work in a different way, though I do not know whether the main motive of their departure is the ambition to work in a different way or an advantage which they gain thereby.

The conditions of the treatment being now regulated in this manner, the question arises at what point and with what material it shall begin.

What subject-matter the treatment begins with is on the whole immaterial, whether with the patient's life-story, with a history of the illness or with recollections of childhood; but in any case the patient must be left to talk, and the choice of subject left to him. One says to him, therefore, 'Before I can say anything to you, I must know a great deal about you; please tell me what you know about yourself'.

The only exception to this concerns the fundamental rule of the psycho-analytic technique which the patient must observe. This must be

■ 27
The whole question of the couch is one in which the deviations to which Freud alludes have continued to this day. Interestingly, some analysts who have rejected a good deal of what Freud has said, use the couch while some avowed "Freudians" eschew the use of the couch. The reasons that Freud states here seem more idiosyncratic than the ones he put forth in other places. To call the couch a remnant of the hypnotic method is true historically but allows for certain misunderstandings of the theoretical rationale for the use of the couch. The same might be said of Freud's "personal motive." If the only reason that one gave for the use of the couch was that it was difficult for the analyst to endure patient's gazes, then I suspect the use of the couch might have died an early death. Freud also allows that the use of the couch facilitates regressive tendencies and is useful as well to clearly spell out and isolate tranference tendencies, particularly as they manifest themselves in the resistance. It is all too frequently stated that Freud's use of the couch was dictated by his aversion to looking at patients. While this may have been a contributing factor to his instituting the couch, its importance in the analytic situation goes beyond this accidental circumstance.

imparted to him at the very beginning: 'One thing
more, before you begin. Your talk with me must
differ in one respect from an ordinary conversation. Whereas usually you rightly try to keep the
threads of your story together and to exclude all
intruding associations and side-issues, so as not to
wander too far from the point, here you must
proceed differently. You will notice that as you
relate things various ideas will occur to you which
you feel inclined to put aside with certain criticisms and objections. You will be tempted to say to
yourself: "This or that has no connection here, or
it is quite unimportant, or it is nonsensical, so it
cannot be necessary to mention it". Never give in
to these objections, but mention it even if you feel
a disinclination against it, or indeed just because of
this. Later on you will perceive and learn to understand the reason for this injunction, which is really
the only one that you have to follow. So say whatever goes through your mind. Act as if you were
sitting at the window of a railway train and describing to some one behind you the changing
views you see outside. Finally, never forget that
you have promised absolute honesty, and never
leave anything unsaid because for any reason it is
unpleasant to say it.'[4] ■ 28

■ 28

Here is the rule of free association stated in two distinctly different forms. When one says to
a patient that they are free to
choose at what point to begin,
this is a communication that
starts to give the treatment to
the patient. However, Freud
states that the patient must observe the fundamental rule.
When Freud intones that the
patient "must proceed differently" than they ordinarily do,
he is invoking the authority of
the analyst and putting his instructions in a form that can be
potentially highly critical or

[4]Much might be said about our experience with the fundamental rule of psycho-analysis. One meets occasionally with
people who behave as if they had instituted this rule for
themselves; others offend against it from the beginning. It is
indispensable, and also advantageous, to mention it at the
first stage of the treatment; later, under the influence of
resistances, obedience to it weakens and there comes a time in
every analysis when the patient disregards it. One must remember how irresistible was the temptation in one's self-
analysis to yield to those cavilling pretexts for rejecting certain thoughts. The feeble effect of the patient's agreement to
the bargain made with him about the 'fundamental rule' is
regularly demonstrated when something of an intimate nature about a third person rises to his mind for the first time;
the patient knows that he must say everything, but he makes
a new obstacle out of the discretion required on behalf of
others. 'Must I really say everything? I thought that only

■ 28 *continued*
judgmental. When he says,"You must never give in to these criticisms," he is again intoning that the patient should fight against what he knows will eventually take place; transference–resistance will at some point negate even the most motivated patient's attempt to follow the "fundamental rule" of psychoanalysis. But one might ask why adherence to the fundamental rule is so crucial to the success of an analysis, particularly if we know that at some point an analysand will fail or break the rule? One could say to the patient that it is important that you say whatever goes through your mind, although at times you may

find it difficult to do so. Included in this preamble might be an illustration of how side thoughts occasionally intrude, and that these thoughts may be as important as the main theme that a patient has begun to talk about. This type of instruction would still encourage the patient to verbalize thoughts, but at the same time would acknowledge to the patient that at times he might not be able to follow the instruction. For Freud, however, the failure to free associate is to be combatted so that one can reach pathogenic memories. This is the case even if the analyst must pressure the patient to associate.

At this point in time, Freud was somewhat concerned about the secrecy of his method of treatment. It is unlikely that he wanted to tell the patient too much about what might follow in the course of treatment. Interestingly, once having said this, we can see that Freud often seemed to give little lectures to his patients about the nature of mental functioning, as well as the process of psychoanalytic technique. The resolution of these paradoxical trends awaits yet another analysis of Freud, which, of course, will never be accomplished satisfactorily. One can only state that, while he set down these principles and frequently expressed concern about the secrecy of the psychoanalytic method, once he was engaged in a treatment he did not feel bound to follow these principles.

applied to what concerns myself.' It is naturally impossible to carry out an analysis if the patient's relations with other people and his thoughts about them are excluded. *Pour faire une omelette il faut casser des œufs.* An honourable man readily forgets such of the private affairs of strangers as do not seem important for him to know. Names, too, cannot be excepted from communication; otherwise the patient's narratives become rather shadowy, like the scenes of Goethe's *Natural Daughter*, and do not remain in the physician's memory; moreover, the names withheld cover the approach to all kinds of important connections. One may perhaps leave names until the patient has become more familiar with the physician and the process of analysis. It is a most remarkable thing that the whole undertaking becomes lost labour if a single concession is made to secrecy. If at any one spot in a town the right of sanctuary existed, one can well imagine that it would not be long before all the riff-raff of the town would gather there. I once treated a high official who was bound by oath not to communicate certain State secrets, and the analysis came to grief as a consequence of this restriction. The psycho-analytic treatment must override everything which comes in its way, because the neurosis and the resistances are equally relentless.

Patients who date their illness from a particular time usually concentrate upon the events leading up to it; others who themselves recognize the
connection of their neurosis with their childhood
often begin with an account of their whole life-
story. A consecutive narrative should never be expected and nothing should be done to encourage it.
Every detail of the story will later have to be
related afresh, and only with this repetition will
additional matter appear enabling the significant
connections which are unknown to the patient to
be traced.

There are patients who from the first hour
carefully prepare their communications, ostensibly
so as to make better use of the time given to
treatment. This appears to be eagerness on their
part, but it is resistance. One must disallow this
preparation; it is employed to guard against the
appearance of unwelcome thoughts;[5] the patient
may believe ever so honestly in his praise-worthy
intention, but resistance will play its part in this
kind of considered preparation and will see to it
that in this way the most valuable part of the
communication escapes. One will soon find that
the patient invents yet other methods by which
the required material may be withheld from analysis. He will perhaps talk over the treatment every
day with some intimate friend, and in this discussion bring out all the thoughts which should occur
to him in the presence of the physician. The treatment then suffers from a leak which lets through
just what is most valuable. It will then soon be
time to recommend the patient to treat the analysis as a matter between himself and his physician,
and to exclude everyone else from sharing in it, no
matter how closely bound to him or how inquisi-
tive they may be. In later stages of the treatment
the patient is not usually tempted in this way.

[5]Exceptions may be made only of such data as the family
relationships, visits, operations, and so on.

Certain patients wish their treatment kept secret, often because they have kept their neurosis secret, and I put no obstacle in the way of this. That in consequence the world hears nothing of some of the most brilliantly successful cures is of course a consideration not to be taken into account. Obviously the patient's decision in favour of secrecy at once reveals one feature of his inner history.

In advising at the beginning of treatment that as few persons as possible shall be informed of it, one protects patients to some extent from the many hostile influences seeking to detach them from the analysis. Such influences may be very mischievous at the outset of the cure; later they are usually immaterial, or even useful in bringing into prominence resistances which are attempting concealment.

If during the course of the analysis the patient requires temporarily some other medical or special treatment, it is far wiser to call in some colleague outside analytic work than to administer this treatment oneself. Analysis combined with other treatment, for neurotic maladies with a strong organic connection, is nearly always impracticable; the patients withdraw their interest from the analysis when there is more than one way leading them to health. Preferably one postpones the organic treatment until after the conclusion of the mental; if the former were tried first, in most cases it would do no good. ■ 29

To return to the beginning of the treatment. Patients are occasionally met with who begin the treatment with an absolute disclaimer of the existence of any thoughts in their minds which they could utter, although the whole field of their life-history and their neurosis lies before them untrodden. One must accede this first time as little as at any other to their request that one should propose something for them to speak of. One must bear in mind what it is that confronts one in these cases.

■ 29
Here Freud is presaging some of the views that he will later express in his ideas on lay analysis. It is his view that the analyst should not engage in medical or organic treatment; he uses this later as one argument to demonstrate that there is no necessary benefit in being a medical doctor in the practice of psychoanalysis.

A formidable resistance has come out into the
open in order to defend the neurosis; one takes up
its challenge then and there, and grips it by the
throat. Emphatic and repeated assurance that the
absence of all ideas at the beginning is an impossibility, and that there is some resistance against the
analysis, soon brings the expected confessions
from the patient or else leads to the first discovery
of some part of his complexes. It is ominous if he
has to confess that while listening to the rule of
the analysis he formed a determination in spite of
it not to communicate this or that; not quite so bad
if he only has to declare the distrust he has of the
treatment or the appalling things he has heard
about it. If he denies these and similar possibilities
when they are suggested to him, further pressure
will constrain him to acknowledge that he has
neglected certain thoughts which are occupying
his mind. He was thinking of the treatment itself
but not in a definite way, or else the appearance of
the room he is in occupied him, or he found
himself thinking of the objects round him in the
consulting-room, or of the fact that he is lying on a
sofa; for all of which thoughts he has substituted
'nothing'. These indications are surely intelligible;
everything connected with the situation of the
moment represents a transference to the physician which proves suitable for use as resistance. It
is necessary then to begin by uncovering this
transference; thence the way leads rapidly to pene-
tration of the pathogenic material in the case.
Women who are prepared by events in their past
lives for a sexual overture, or men with unusually
strong, repressed homosexuality, are the most
prone to exhibit this denial of all ideas at the
outset of the analysis.

The first symptoms or chance actions of the
patient, like the first resistance, have a special
interest and will betray one of the governing complexes of the neurosis. A clever young philoso-
pher, with leanings towards æsthetic exquisite-

ness, hastens to twitch the crease in his trousers into place before lying down for the first sitting; he reveals himself as an erstwhile coprophiliac of the highest refinement, as was to be expected of the developed æsthete. A young girl on the same occasion hurriedly pulls the hem of her skirt over her exposed ankle; she has betrayed the kernel of what analysis will discover later, her bodily beauty and her tendencies to exhibitionism.

Very many patients object especially to the arrangement of reclining in a position where the physician sits out of sight behind them; they beg to be allowed to undergo analysis in some other position, mostly because they do not wish to be deprived of a view of the physician. Permission is invariably refused; one cannot prevent them, however, from contriving to say a few words before the beginning of the 'sitting itself', and after one has signified its termination and they have risen from the sofa. In this way they make in their own minds a division of the treatment into an official part, in which they behave in a very inhibited manner, and an informal 'friendly' part, in which they really speak freely and say a good deal that they do not themselves regard as belonging to the treatment. The physician does not fall in for long with this division of the time, he makes a note of what is said before or after the sitting, and in bringing it up at the next opportunity he tears down the partition which the patient has tried to erect. It again is a structure formed from the material of a transference-resistance.

So long as the patient continues to utter without obstruction the thoughts and ideas rising to his mind, the theme of the transference should be left untouched. One must wait until the transference, which is the most delicate matter of all to deal with, comes to be employed as resistance.

The next question with which we are confronted is a main one. It runs: When shall we begin our disclosures to the patient? When is it time to unfold to him the hidden meaning of his thoughts and associations, to initiate him into the postulates of analysis and its technical devices?

The answer to this can only be: Not until a dependable transference, a well-developed *rapport*, is established in the patient. The first aim of the treatment consists in attaching him to the treatment and to the person of the physician. To ensure this one need do nothing but allow him time. If one devotes serious interest to him, clears away carefully the first resistances that arise and avoids certain mistakes, such an attachment develops in the patient of itself, and the physician becomes linked up with one of the imagos of those persons from whom he was used to receive kindness. It is certainly possible to forfeit this primary success if one takes up from the start any standpoint other than that of understanding, such as a moralizing attitude, perhaps, or if one behaves as the representative or advocate of some third person, maybe the husband or wife, and so on.

This answer of course involves a condemnation of that mode or procedure which consists in communicating to the patient the interpretation of the symptoms as soon as one perceives it oneself, or of that attitude which would account it a special triumph to hurl these 'solutions' in his face at the first interview. It is not difficult for a skilled analyst to read the patient's hidden wishes plainly between the lines of his complaints and the story of his illness; but what a measure of self-complacency and thoughtlessness must exist in one who can upon the shortest acquaintance inform a stranger, who is entirely ignorant of analytical doctrines, that he is bound by an incestuous love for his mother, that he harbours wishes for the death of the wife he appears to love, that he conceals within himself the intention to deceive his chief, and so forth! I have heard that analysts exist who plume themselves upon these kinds of lightning-diagnoses and 'express'-treatments, but

I warn everyone against following such examples. Such conduct brings both the man and the treatment into discredit and arouses the most violent opposition, whether the interpretations be correct or not; yes, and the truer they are actually the more violent is the resistance they arouse. Usually the therapeutic effect at the moment is nothing; the resulting horror of analysis, however, is ineradicable. Even in later stages of the analysis one must be careful not to communicate the meaning of a symptom or the interpretation of a wish until the patient is already close upon it, so that he has only a short step to take in order to grasp the explanation himself. In former years I often found that premature communication of interpretations brought the treatment to an untimely end, both on account of the resistances suddenly aroused thereby and also because of the relief resulting from the insight so obtained. ■ 30

The following objection will be raised here: Is it then our task to lengthen the treatment, and not rather to bring it to an end as rapidly as possible? Are not the patient's sufferings due to his lack of knowledge and understanding, and is it not a duty to enlighten him as soon as possible, that is, as soon as the physician himself knows the explanations? The answer to this question requires a short digression concerning the significance of knowledge and the mechanism of the cure in psychoanalysis.

In the early days of analytic technique it is true that we regarded the matter intellectually and set a high value on the patient's knowledge of that which had been forgotten, so that we hardly made a distinction between our knowledge and his in these matters. We accounted it specially fortunate if it were possible to obtain information of the forgotten traumas of childhood from external sources, from parents or nurses, for instance, or from the seducer himself, as occurred occasionally; and we hastened to convey the information and

■ 30

When are we to make our communications? When Freud says that we should wait until there has been an effective transference or a proper rapport, he is telling us something that is extremely important and that has been a subject of discussion up through the present time. Various analysts have used the concept of therapeutic alliance to capture and elaborate on what Freud called a proper rapport. It is interesting that Freud sees the analytic process as literally unfolding naturally if one gives the patient time and follows his other suggestions. He expressly warns even the skilled analyst to avoid the tendency "to fling (the analyst's) 'solutions'" in the face of the patient in the first interview. Freud then extends this idea and points out that it is thoughtless to presume that

■ 30 *continued*
anyone could or would be willing to hear intimate observations about his conflicts from
someone who doesn't even
know him well. The question
of when to interpret, of course,
is a subject still under much
discussion. At this point in
time, Freud had clearly moved
from what he called an intellectualist position to one that
firmly considered the patient's
readiness to hear the analyst's
observations. Unfortunately, he
frequently did not follow his
own advice.

■ 31

Freud's views on the importance
of intellectual knowledge have
obviously undergone a dramatic
shift from his views as presented in *Studies on Hysteria* and
his implicit views in the Dora
case. Shortly after he wrote the
technique papers, he was quite
concerned with conceptualizing

proofs of its correctness to the patient, in the
certain expectation of bringing the neurosis and
the treatment to a rapid end by this means. It was
a bitter disappointment when the expected success
was not forthcoming. How could it happen that
the patient, who now had the knowledge of his
traumatic experience, still behaved in spite of it as
if he knew no more than before? Not even would
the recollection of the repressed trauma come to
mind after it had been told and described to him.

In one particular case the mother of an hysterical girl had confided to me the homosexual
experience which had greatly influenced the fixation of the attacks. The mother herself had come
suddenly upon the scene and had been a witness of
it; the girl, however, had totally forgotten it, although it had occurred not long before puberty.
Thereupon I made a most instructive observation.
Every time that I repeated the mother's story to
the girl she reacted to it with an hysterical attack,
after which the story was again forgotten. There
was no doubt that the patient was expressing a
violent resistance against the knowledge which was
being forced upon her; at last she simulated imbecil-
ity and total loss of memory in order to defend
herself against what I told her. After this, there was
no alternative but to abandon the previous attribu-
tion of importance to knowledge in itself, and to lay
the stress upon the resistances which had originally
induced the condition of ignorance and were still
now prepared to defend it. Conscious knowledge,
even if it were not again expelled, was powerless
against these resistances. ■ 31

This disconcerting ability in patients to combine conscious knowledge with ignorance remains
unexplained by what is called normal psychology.
By reason of the recognition of the unconscious,
psycho-analysis finds no difficulty in it; the
phenomenon described is, however, one of the
best confirmations of the conception by which
mental processes are approached as being differ-

■ 31 *continued*
(or reconceptualizing) questions
that concern the status of repression or defense. This had
previously been a concern to
him in Chapter 7 of *The Interpretation of Dreams* ("Little
Hans, Two Principles of Mental Functioning"), as well as his
paper on wild analysis. The
question of intellectual knowledge (and of what he will call
double representation) will be
taken up explicitly in his papers on the unconscious and repression. Thus, in the next
page, he gives what he might
have called a *metapsychological
analysis* of the processes that
he had just been discussing.
One might state parenthetically
that all the points that he summarizes in energetic language
had been made previously by
him without the aid of this language. It is also of interest to
note that, in the course of this
summary, he gives a working
definition of the concept of
what will later be called *transference cure* and mentions the
concept of secondary gain,
which he had begun to formulate in the Dora case.

Freud states that the pa-
tient may be able to get better
simply under the influence of
the transference, but, once that
influence is gone or diminished,
the cure will leave as well. Implicitly then, he is suggesting
that there are other criteria
than symptom removal that
one must employ to evaluate
the efficacy of a treatment.

entiated topographically. The patients are aware,
in thought, of the repressed experience, but the
connection between the thought and the point
where the repressed recollection is in some way
imprisoned is lacking. No change is possible until
the conscious thought-process has penetrated to
this point and has overcome the resistances of the
repression there. It is just as if a decree were
promulgated by the Ministry of Justice to the effect that juvenile misdemeanours should be dealt
with by certain lenient methods. As long as this
concession has not come to the knowledge of the
individual magistrates, or in the event of their not
choosing to make use of it but preferring to deal
justice according to their own lights, nothing will
be changed in the treatment accorded to youthful
delinquents. For the sake of complete accuracy,
though, it may be added that communicating to
the patient's consciousness information about
what is repressed does not entirely fail of any

effect at all. It does not produce the hoped-for
result of abolishing the symptoms, but it has other
consequences. It first arouses resistances, but
when these are overcome it sets a mental process
in action, in the course of which the desired influence upon the unconscious memory is eventually
effected.

At this point we should review the play of
forces brought into action by the treatment. The
primary motive-power used in therapy is the patient's suffering and the wish to be cured which
arises from it. The volume of this motive-force is
diminished in various ways, discoverable only in
the course of the analysis, above all by what we call
the 'epinosic gain'; the motive-power itself must
be maintained until the end of the treatment;
every improvement effects a diminution of it.
Alone, however, the force of this motive is insufficient to overcome the illness; two things are lacking in it, the knowledge of the paths by which the
desired end may be reached, and the amount of
energy needed to oppose the resistances. The analytic treatment helps to supply both these defi-
ciencies. The accumulation of energy necessary to
overcome the resistances is supplied by analytic
utilization of the energies which are always ready
to be 'transferred'; and by timely communications
to the patient at the right moment analysis points
out the direction in which these energies should be
employed. The transference alone frequently suffices to bring about a disappearance of the symptoms of the disease, but this is merely temporary
and lasts only as long as the transference itself is
maintained. The treatment is then nothing more
than suggestion, not a psycho-analysis. It deserves
the latter name only when the intensity of the
transference has been utilized to overcome the
resistances; only then does illness become impossible, even though the transference is again dis-
solved as its function in the treatment requires.

In the course of the treatment another helpful

agency is roused—the patient's intellectual interest and understanding. But this alone is hardly
worth consideration by the side of the other forces
engaged in the struggle, for it is always in danger
of succumbing to the clouding of reasoning power
under the influence of resistances. Hence it follows that the new sources of strength for which
the sufferer is indebted to the analyst resolve
themselves into transference, and instruction (by
explanation). The patient only makes use of the
instruction, however, in so far as he is induced to
do so by the transference; and therefore until a
powerful transference is established the first explanation should be withheld; and likewise, we
may add, with each subsequent one, we must wait
until each disturbance of the transference by the
transference-resistances arising in succession has
been removed.

10

Contemporary Perspectives

Heinz Kohut

There is much in what we have gone over in this section of Freud's writings that Kohut has departed from in his ideas of analytic practice. The most obvious example is patient selection. When he began to write articles about patients with "narcissistic" difficulties, Kohut pointed out some of the problems with psychoanalytic views of narcissism. Kohut's new emphasis is important to understand in order to appreciate his thoughts about analyzability. It is Kohut's contention that analysts tended to follow the altruistic value system of Western societies and see all aspects of narcissism as negative. This limited view both puts the analyst in a normative position and more importantly is a misleading theory of human development. In Freud's theoretical writings, there is a stipulated tension between narcissism and object relations (see Chapter 4) such that the more an individual is narcissistic, the less object-related that individual can be. This necessary link between object relations and narcissism is questioned by Kohut,[1] and this questioning leads him to view narcissism as having its own line of development. In his theoretical understanding there is an important interplay between the development of internalized object relations and the development of the self as a cohesive structure. Kohut's conceiving of the self as a psychological structure, having a separate line of development, allows him to see the possibility of people with narcissistic difficulties being object-related. Freud concluded that, insofar as one had narcissistic difficulties, object relations were canceled out, and Kohut corrects that conclusion.

[1] As I said in Part II, it is my view that Kohut's questioning of Freud's position leads one to see that Freud was logically inconsistent in his view of analyzability based on his own theory of narcissism.

Kohut's latter views departed from Freud in more central ways, and he envisioned what he called his concept of "tragic man" replacing Freud's view of "guilty man." Kohut initially thought of early development as involving two separate lines that included what he called the grandiose self and the idealized object. The development of the grandiose self eventuates into a person's sense of self imbued with healthy ambition. The idealized object is gradually internalized as an aspect of the superego in this conceptual scheme. In Kohut's later ideas he saw these two lines of development as related aspects of the person's emerging sense of self—hence the title *bipolar self*, which tries to do justice to these two forces contributing to the development of the self-organization. His idea of the bipolar self became central in his developmental concepts. Self-esteem and self-cohesion become theoretical linchpins, while childhood sexuality and aggression retreat in importance and are seen as appearing as principal issues in childhood only when there is a lack of parental empathy.

If we look at the range of Kohut's work, it is clear that even when he placed his theoretical ideas within a Freudian framework his concern with empathy in the analytic situation is his dominant clinical interest. How the analyst initially approached the patient was exceedingly important for Kohut. Patients with narcissistic vulnerabilities (Kohut 1972) could easily be stimulated into periods of disaffection and even rage within the analytic process. In Kohut's version of the widening scope of psychoanalysis, narcissistic patients can be treated, but one must recognize how easily disruptions can occur in the initial stages of therapy. One must be particularly sensitive to how the patient will view the analyst in an idealized manner or will need to utilize the analyst as a mirroring figure. The patient does not want to see the analyst as a totally separate person who will *merely* provide insight that has previously eluded the analysand. In fact, Kohut maintains that attempts at providing insight early in the treatment will serve as a method of inducing anger or even narcissistic rage (Kohut 1972). If there are to be interpretations, it is not transference that is interpreted, but rather the patient's resistance to, or difficulties in, establishing a consistent transference relationship. In Kohut's examples of such interpretations (Kohut 1968, 1971), it is not clear that Brenner or Gill would even consider these interventions to be interpretations. Kohut at times calls his interventions attempts at empathic reflections or mirroring. I would say that his interventions are usually clarifications, or a synthesis of comments that the patient has already put forward. In meaningfully bringing together divergent comments from the patient, the analyst's ability to empathize is established. At times, this type of intervention may put the patient more in touch with an emotion or vividly depict a feeling or thought. It may be that these clarifying statements also provide insight, but the important aspect is that these comments begin to give the patient a sense of being understood and allow the analyst to be placed in a transference relationship.[2]

---

[2]I have commented that I would consider this process as the establishment of analytic trust.

Although Freud told us that we shouldn't fling interpretations at a patient, in Kohut's view a good deal of Freud's technique involved early interpretation, which tended to upset the patient's equilibrium and did not create an appropriate analytic atmosphere. We are tempted to say that, since Kohut maintained that narcissistic patients can be seen in analysis, his ideas about the conduct of analysis shifted. Thus, his ideas about the beginning of analysis, while appropriate for narcissistic patients, might be unnecessary for neurotic patients. What appeared to be differences with Freud or Brenner are really only differences in the patient population they commented on. At one time, this account of Kohut's views might have been reasonable (perhaps up to 1972), but after his 1977 book, *Restoration of the Self*, one could no longer hold this opinion. Then, Kohut is clearly no longer restricting his ideas about development or treatment to patients with narcissistic difficulties; rather he is suggesting that his concepts are universally relevant—that, indeed, these issues are at the center of human existence for all or at least most people. After 1977 we can say that he widened the scope of analysis, and that the technical ideas he put forth were in his view relevant to most if not all analysands. Thus, insight at the beginning of treatment—and, one could argue, throughout it—is replaced by the empathic analyst, who is able to allow the patient to use him as a mirroring object. In other terms, the analyst for large parts of the analysis becomes part of the patient's bipolar self. In Kohut's terms, a self-object transference is formed.

Throughout his writings on narcissism, Kohut talks about what he regards as the typical type of countertransference reactions the analyst may experience. He cites an example in which the patient early in treatment assumes her analyst is Catholic. In the interests of *objectivity*, the analyst corrects the patient and relates that he is not Catholic.[3] Kohut maintains that what is going on in this seemingly inconsequential encounter is the analyst rejecting the patient's attempts to establish one form of a mirroring transference or self-object bond. The analyst's need to establish himself as a realistic figure in the treatment demonstrates his inability (at this point in time) to be utilized in a narcissistic transference. Kohut, of course, provides more dramatic and complete examples of countertransference, but we have cited this example to illustrate the ubiquitous nature of countertransference possibilities.

Clearly Kohut wouldn't subscribe to Freud's metaphor of the implacable surgeon, but rather Freud's suggestion that the analyst should take care to establish a relationship with the patient, before attempting interpretations. In fact, as we have seen, Kohut takes this last point quite seriously and warns the analyst not to intrude with interpretations. We have commented that Kohut has helped to widen the scope of psychoanalysis in terms of the type of patient he would classify as analyzable. Let us look at this point at how Kohut views

---

[3]Of course, if the patient wanted to see only a Catholic in analysis, I assume the analyst would answer the question at the beginning of treatment. In this case, however, the patient was only reflecting on her impressions of the analyst.

the limits of this widening scope. In the following quote, he is stating the conditions that are necessary for his form of analysis to be effective. One of the conditions is the patient's ability to maintain certain boundaries.

> The pathognomonically specific, transferencelike, therapeutically salutary conditions, however, on which I am focusing, are based on the activation of psychologically elaborated, cohesive configurations which enter into stable amalgamations with the narcissistically perceived psychic representation of the analyst. The relative stability of this narcissistic transference-amalgamation, however, is the prerequisite for the performance of the analytic task in the pathogenic narcissistic areas of the personality. [Kohut 1968, p. 87]

In this quote, the important aspect for Kohut is the cohesion of the self when entering into a perceived amalgamation (self-object transference[4]) with the analyst. The analysand must be able to continue a stable relationship with the analyst and not display rapid oscillations or regressions. In short, the analysand should be able to continue to experience a stable sense of self, even during intense periods of transference.[5] Kohut is excluding from analytic treatment patients whom other analysts (Kernberg) call borderline characters or personality disorders. Some Kohutians tend to deny that there are borderline characters but argue rather that certain people enter into borderline states during periods of perceived breaks in empathy (Stolorow et al. 1987). It is their view that the empathic analyst will prevent continuous borderline states. They state that "the borderline state . . . indeed treatable . . . (is) a product . . . of a specific intersubjective situation" (p. 113). The specific intersubjective situation is in the unempathic analyst. This seems to be an extension of Kohut's perspective and one that is certainly not accepted by all clinicians who work with borderline patients.[6] Although Kohut's widening scope may be narrower than that of other clinicians, analysts who have followed in his tradi-

---

[4]By using the term "self-object," Kohut is trying to account for the type of narcissistic transference that occurs when the analysand thinks of the analyst as part of himself. It may be that the analyst is seen as one or another type of mirroring person or object, or it may be that the analyst is idealized and seen as the omnipotent or omniscient figure that will be there for the analysand if any threatening circumstance occurs. In any case, the analyst is seen as a parental figure who is an aspect of the self, or an object that is tied to oneself and responsive to one's wishes.

[5]Obviously, during any given session, the patient may experience intense swings, but Kohut is talking about a sense of cohesion between most sessions. He is also talking about the ability of a person to regroup following an intense analytic session (Kohut 1968, 1971).

[6]Kernberg (1975) sees the borderline personality as "a discrete, stable, pathological character structure rooted in internal instinctual conflicts and primitive defenses." This is obviously quite a different view, and Stolorow, Brandchaft, and Atwood are arguing that there is a histrogenic element in Kernberg's approach to borderline personalities (or people called this) that is producing the syndrome that he is describing. This is a difficult argument for most clinicians to fully accept but intriguing nevertheless. The full implication of their arguments seems to be a denial of stable, enduring personality characteristics. They might deny that this is the case, but as of yet it still seems to me that this is the implication of their position.

tion (Stolorow et al. 1987) are obviously attempting to widen the scope of self-psychology.

It is again of interest that Kohut sounds quite similar to Freud when he discusses the question of psychiatric diagnosis. He tells us that it is only when we see the type of transference reactions that the patient displays that we know how to answer the question of diagnosis. This is quite similar to Freud when he evinces skepticism about diagnosis until he notes the patient's responses in a trial analysis.

Even when he is attempting to establish his theoretical stance as an alternative to Freudian thought, Kohut remains within the analytic tradition in terms of the practical questions of missed sessions and issues such as the use of the couch. It would have been interesting to ask Kohut his rationale for the continued use of the couch. Freud's rationale is bound up in his ideas about the unconscious (or id) striving for release. Freud sees the couch and the relative absence of other stimuli as facilitating the expression of free association and increasing the probability of primary process ideation becoming conscious. Is this Kohut's rationale or does he have an alternative explanation? Does Kohut continue to emphasize the importance of unconscious fantasy, or is this pillar of Freudian thought somewhat weakened in Kohut's theoretical structure? The answers to these and other questions will both directly and indirectly determine the extent to which Kohut's thought will lead some analysts to diverge from Freud's positions. One thing is clear: Freud's central ideas of drive and the importance of childhood sexuality have been displaced in Kohutian thought, and this already signifies a major gap between Freud's thought and future theories that are based on Kohut's ideas.

Merton Gill

Gill's position is an interesting one, for unlike Brenner, and certainly Kohut, he is not presenting an overarching theory along with his ideas about technique. He might maintain that he is taking an empirical approach; that he is using the couch or other analytic devices because he has found them to be effective. Given his experience as a researcher and commentator on psychoanalysis, his thoughts are usually at the least stimulating and informative. He has taken positions on almost all the issues that Freud has raised, and he is quite specific about the question of early interpretation. He advocates interpretation of the here-and-now transference from the beginning of the treatment:

> The technique of interpreting fairly obvious, albeit disguised transference expressions, in the here-and-now, from the beginning, will more quickly lead to a more observable, detailed and readily demonstrable transference than prevailing practice would allow. The current practice of delaying the analysis of the transference

because of the failure to realize that it is a resistance from the beginning may play a role in the common phenomenon of a rapid amelioration of symptoms. Only later when the transference as resistance can no longer be ignored is it interpreted with a recrudescence of symptoms. [Gill 1984, p. 169]

Gill's approach is partly in response to his perception that analysts have underestimated the extent to which there are transference manifestations in the treatment situation. If we put this consideration in the context of the present work, we can say that in his view many psychoanalytic clinicians are still influenced by Freud's pathogenic memory model. The extent to which this is the case is, of course, a question that is difficult if not impossible to answer. It seems hard to disagree with Gill's argument that the role of transference in the treatment situation is misunderstood, and often major transference themes are overlooked or left uninterpreted. One can say that Bird has a congruent perception and sees the role of transference being diminished in analytic treatment by modern analysts.[7] Gill clearly is advocating that transference phenomena be in the forefront of the analytic situation from very early on in the treatment as well as throughout the course of therapy.

We might ask Gill two related questions: What are the criteria for what he calls "fairly obvious expressions of transference"? Having listened to a tape of Gill's actual sessions, as well as having read his work, I am not sure that Gill would find easy agreement among other analysts about what are fairly obvious manifestations of transference. Let us leave this question and assume that we can arrive at an operational definition of transference.[8] Should these transference reactions be interpreted in the manner that Gill is advocating?

Let us posit that a patient has developed an eroticized transference and has been behaving seductively toward the analyst. If a patient wears a certain type of clothing to a session, should the clothing be considered a manifestation of transference? To go to an example of Gill's, a woman analysand wore a tee shirt to a session. The shirt had an inscription on the front. Gill in the beginning of the session inquired about the inscription, asking the patient what was written on the front of her shirt. During the session she did not mention the shirt or what she was wearing. Toward the end of the session, Gill interpreted the transference reasons for the patient wearing this clothing; his formulation was that the wearing of the shirt was an attempt at being sexually provocative. What also might seem provocative is Gill inquiring about the inscription on the front of her shirt.

Let us assume that Gill is correct and that the patient's behavior was an attempt at being seductive. Is the wearing of this clothing something that could be or should be interpreted as transference? One could then say that whatever a

---

[7]Bird, of course, did not advocate that transference be interpreted as soon as it became fairly obvious.
[8]I believe that Gill has done this to a reasonable extent.

patient wears to the treatment situation is a manifestation of transference. This expanded conceptualization allows the analyst a much broader range of behavior to interpret; however, it also does not take into account a variety of other influences that might be determining the patient's behavior. It may also introduce a type of self-consciousness that is not conducive to free expression in the analytic situation. It also puts the analyst in a position of constantly interpreting on the basis of what has to be partial information. All these considerations, of course, may be irrelevant if analysis proceeds in the way that Gill maintains it does via his method. At this point, I would say that Gill, more than most analysts, is striving to make his results public and open to scrutiny. We can only commend this approach and try to ask other questions that might help stimulate inquiry. In the example cited, I took what I regarded as an extreme example to attempt to give some sense of the expanded scope of Gill's definition of transference.

How do patients experience Gill's methods? How might they react to his interpretations? Would they be surprised or even offended by the analyst always interpreting the patient's remarks in terms of the transference? Is it possible that some of the patients that Kohut describes (narcissistic or nonclassical patients)[9] would become angry or even enraged at this type of technique? Can we talk about patients in general or do we have to talk about different types of patients and how they might differentially respond to Gill's approach? Fortunately, Gill provides some of his own answers to these questions.

In terms of the analytic setting (use of the couch, frequency of sessions) as well as transference analysis, with nonclassical patients, he tells us that:

> It follows that no universal prescription can be given for this or that type of case. One may generalize that analytic work is better with healthier patients lying down, sicker patients sitting up and frequency of sessions for both levels of patients, but a particular patient may not conform to the rule. The meaning of the setting must be analyzed in each instance. Nor is degree of pathology the only variable which determines a patient's response to the analysis of transference. Apart from pathology some take to it like a duck to water and can work despite infrequent sessions, while others never seem to find it congenial. [Gill 1984, p. 174]

Gill is telling us clearly here that he understands that his principles may have to undergo modification in many individual cases. Still, he would argue that the analysis of the here-and-now transference at the beginning of treatment is important if not crucial in most analytic treatments. Gill reminds us that Freud's views of transference and when to interpret transference are clearly quite different than his formulations. Freud interpreted transference

---

[9]Clearly, Kohutians should predict that a reasonable number of narcissistically vulnerable patients will not be able to or want to endure Gill's psychoanalytic techniques.

when he thought that transference was hindering the patient's ability to free associate. For Freud, the fundamental rule embodied his fundamental concern, the recovery of early memories. Freud learned that free association will be interrupted by manifestations of transference (and other things), but we should always keep the ideal of free association as a goal in the analysis. Gill, on the other hand, tells us that "I understand the rule of the free association to mean that the therapist establishes the general condition that the patient is invited, even urged to express his thoughts freely even if he feels reluctant to do so, and that after intermittently intervening *the therapist is alert to the consequences of his interventions upon the patient's flow of ideas*" (Gill 1984, p. 171).

Gill is telling us here that the way we instruct the patient will, of course, affect the patient's reactions in manifestations of transference. Moreover, we have to be sensitive to the analyst's part, in inducing reactions in the treatment situation. In this respect Gill is emphasizing an aspect of the treatment situation that Langs (1974, 1975) has emphatically stressed. Freud is generally less concerned with the impact of the analyst than is the case with almost any contemporary analyst. Freud's lack of concern has probably affected analysts up to the present time so that Gill and others do well to remind us that the analyst of necessity affects the responses of the patient.

Although Gill seems to be only adding to Freud's thoughts when he talks about free association, when he talks about Freud's idea of the analyst maintaining evenly suspended attention, he is more critical. For Gill this ideal is a type of mythology, and analysts would do well to disregard the mythology. Gill's thought is that this type of evenly suspended attention is an impossibility, since all analysts' observations will be guided by their theoretical predilections. While it is hard to deny this is the case, it appears that Gill is confounding two issues that are raised in Freud's concept. The first is the idea that somehow the analyst can be a perfect receiving station without any theoretical bias. It is possible that we can excuse Freud for maintaining this type of mythology. However, it was not even possible for the first analyst to be free of theoretical bias. Of course, Gill is correct in his belief that it is impossible for any subsequent analyst to be this type of tabula rasa. The second aspect of Freud's idea is, I believe, the more important one and perhaps the main reason that Freud proposed this view of the analyst's role. He saw the analyst as receiving information from her or his own fantasy life rather than only from patients' associations. This information can be considered to be crucial to the analytic process, and it seems to me Freud in a muted way is drawing attention to this possibility. Moreover, even if one agrees with Gill's stance concerning theoretical predispositions, it is possible that one can at times put theory aside. We might hypothesize that, to the extent that we can be open to experiences not predicted by our own theory, it is possible to have interesting new theories. Gill may be interpreted as challenging a number of analysts to put aside their theoretical predispositions in the clinical situation.

Charles Brenner

In approaching any of Brenner's ideas, one must keep in mind that Brenner maintains that most manifestations of the patient's attitudes reflect compromise formations. This conceptualization dominates Brenner's position. In considering the question of early interpretation of transference, Brenner says that

> it seems that neither analytic practice nor the theories on which it is based support the precept that manifestations of transference are to be analyzed only when they are clearly in the service of resistance.[10] On the contrary, transference should be dealt with and interpreted like anything else in the analytic material: that it is as it appears and in accordance with its importance at the moment relative to other material. [Brenner 1969, p. 337]

In this quote, Brenner is certainly changing analytic theory as Freud had stated it. Putting this historical issue aside, let us turn to some of the reasons that Brenner provides for his new perspective:

> A common reason for transference behavior that is analytically unmanageable is undue delay in interpreting to a patient his transference wishes and conflicts. . . . There is not just a single right moment for presenting an interpretation to a patient. Correct timing means only *not long before a patient is ready nor very long after he was first ready*. If the analyst is confronted by transference manifestations that are analytically unmanageable . . . one of the questions he should ask himself is whether he has failed to interpret an important aspect of the transference to his patient in good time.[11] [Brenner 1976, pp. 124–125]

Brenner tells us here that if the transference is not analyzed in good time it may become unmanageable. How might that occur? The intensity of the transference might become too great for the analyst to rely solely on interpretation as an intervention. One might see a rapid regression on the part of the patient, and the analyst might have to intervene in a manner that jeopardizes the analysis. This type of dramatic response may occur if the transference is not analyzed in due time. Here again we can note that Gill makes a similar point, whereas Freud and Kohut both take different positions from the one that Brenner has articulated.

Although Freud thought that only transference neurotics could be analyzed, he also maintained that the best diagnostic test was a trial analysis. One can say that Brenner has an updated view of this position:

> When one applies what has just been said about the goals of analysis to the situation of evaluating a patient's suitability for analysis, it is evident that a part of

---

[10]It is interesting how similar some parts of this quote are to Gill's position.
[11]Here again we see Brenner and Gill pointing to the same issues and considerations concerning analysts not interpreting the transference and it then becoming unmanageable.

any such evaluation is an attempt to decide what the likelihood is that the patient's conflicts can be understood and beneficially altered by analysis. . . . When the task of evaluation is viewed in this way, such questions as the prognostic significance of one or another symptom, the relative importance of this or that character trait, whether a patient has a "symptom neurosis" or a "character neurosis" and the like, appear in a better perspective. All such questions are seen to be subordinate to the more general one raised here concerning a patient's conflicts. [1976, pp. 176-177]

For Brenner, the crucial issue in determining analyzability is an empirical test—that is, whether the transference is understandable and manageable by analytic means in an analytic situation (1976, p. 124). This can be seen as a modern version of a trial analysis. Essentially using Brenner's criteria for analyzability, Abend, Porter, and Willick (1983) discuss how at least some patients who are diagnosed as borderline personalities are analyzable. This view of analyzability is new[12] in that non-neurotic patients are deemed analyzable. A natural question arises (as it does with Freud) as to whether we can meaningfully talk about the essential characteristics of non-neurotic patients who are analyzable. Can we specify the traits of these patients that allow analysis to be effective? We can, in fact, ask the same question of neurotic patients, since I believe that no one would argue that all neurotic patients are equally analyzable.

It might be the case that if one makes analyzability a question of how the patient responds to the analytic situation, then how the analyst defines the situation is a crucial factor in determining analyzability. In my view, the question of analyzability is intimately bound up with how one begins the treatment. Thus, the question of interpreting early in the treatment may mean that some patients are unanalyzable because they cannot tolerate this version of the analytic situation. The extreme version of this argument is presented by Stolorow, Brandchaft, and Atwood (1987) who maintain that even the concept of borderline personality is "histrogenic" to given analytic methods. In their intersubjective approach they contend that other analytic approaches (like Brenner's) produce borderline states in patients. Kohut posits that with patients who are narcissistically vulnerable, interpreting transference will be seen as a humiliation at the hands of the analyst. One might state that these patients who cannot tolerate early interpretation are not analyzable but that they could become so as they progress in treatment. This is certainly one way of reconciling the disagreements, but it begs the question of the patient's experience in the beginning of treatment when transference interpretations are made. Clearly, Gill and Brenner are making empirical–clinical observations quite different from Kohut's. It would seem important to more fully understand the

---

[12]It isn't, of course, really a new view; many analysts from Ferenczi and Abraham to Winnicott, Bion, Bach, and Kernberg have maintained that non-neurotic or non-classical patients can be analyzed. What is somewhat new is that view coming from the American wing of classical analysts.

experience of all patients at the beginning of treatment, or to more fully make a comparison of the experience of patients who begin treatment in these different ways.

In talking about Freud's fundamental rule (free association), Brenner accepts the rule with the understanding that "a patient's thought, his associations, are never free of the influence of ego and super-ego functioning. . . . They are always compromise formations, as much so at the end of a successful analysis as they are at the beginning" (Brenner 1976, p. 192).

This amendment focuses us on a point that logically follows from Freud's own theories.[13] Thus the rule of free association is the fundamental rule for Freud but receives a diminished status not only for Brenner but for Gill and Bird as well. The instruction can be given to the patient, but the patient can never fully adhere to the instruction. For Brenner, the idea of attempting to influence the patient to associate is a futile one at best. This does not mean that Brenner does not want to provide conditions for the patient to speak as freely as possible, but he understands there are limits to the conditions that the analyst can provide. He sees the use of the couch as quite important in this regard:

> If a patient is to be in analysis, it is to his advantage to use the couch and face away from his analyst. For him to do so substantially facilitates his saying freely whatever comes to his mind with as little interference as possible from external stimuli. For this reason then, it is of real, practical advantage for an analytic patient to use the couch. If he will not use it despite his analyst's suggestion that he do so, his inability or unwillingness is essentially a symptom of his psychic conflicts. In other words, one can do some analyzing face to face, but one cannot carry on an analysis in that way beyond a certain point. In that sense, then, one cannot analyze a patient face to face. [Brenner 1976, pp. 183–184]

Clearly, Brenner is emphasizing the importance of the couch in analytic treatment. An implication of this quote, however, is that if a patient does not agree to use the couch, he is unanalyzable. Brenner seems to be suggesting that the patient is unanalyzable because he is not agreeing with the analyst's suggestion. He does not tell us what is crucial about the couch that makes it a necessary condition for analytic treatment. Is it the case that, if the patient refuses any of the conditions that the analyst thinks are reasonable, the patient is unanalyzable?[14] Or is lying on the couch different from a variety of other analytic conditions?

[13]Again we can say that Freud never fully accepted the implications of this theorizing in his ideas about psychoanalytic technique.
[14]To consider an extreme example, if the patient said that he couldn't pay the fee the analyst set, would that mean the patient was unanalyzable? Our first response to this question might entail an inquiry about the patient's finances. It could say nothing about the patient's analyzability, if financially unable to pay an analytic fee. Let us imagine for a moment that the analyst is certain that the patient is able to pay the fee and that the analysand is refusing for reasons that are related

Both Brenner and Freud are obviously implying that a patient's being able to talk while reclining, facing away from the analyst, tells us something meaningful about the patient. Brenner tells us that it *substantially* facilitates a patient's saying freely whatever comes to his mind. This occurs primarily because there is as little interference as possible from external stimuli while lying on a couch. Does the facilitation occur because of an absence of external stimuli? As a patient of mine once asked me, "Why not let me turn my chair away from you?" Do all patients require the same freedom from external stimuli? If the couch is simply freedom from external stimuli does this mean that, if one can achieve this freedom in another way, the couch can be dispensed with? It seems to me that while Brenner is correct that lying on a couch provides few external distractions, this is not a satisfactory analytic rationale; it fails to provide what this absence of stimuli is thought to induce in the analysand. I suspect that Brenner is attempting to provide a more empirical rationale, by pointing to an obvious effect of having the patient lie on the couch.

From my perspective, the important question is whether or not lying on the couch more easily induces a state that is difficult to replicate while sitting up or being in any other position in an analytic office. One might then ask what state does lying on a couch induce? The answer to this question is crucial, if one maintains that lying on a couch is a necessary condition for an analysis. The alternative to this position would profess that complying with the analyst's conditions is a necessary condition for analyzability. This is an untenable position if one also wants to provide a condition in which the patient is able to freely say what is on his mind.[15]

To conclude this section on Brenner, we might go over two of his positions on some other practical aspects of the treatment situation. "A patient's consent and cooperation are necessary with respect to all the practical arrangements, but it is just as necessary, if a patient objects to any reasonable and conventional arrangements, to discover why he does so; insofar as his objections derive from his conflicts, it is important to deal with them analytically" (1976, p. 186).

---

to his conflicts. In that case the patient is not going along with a condition of analysis, and it is possible that the analyst might conclude that the person is unanalyzable. Let us presuppose that the patient goes to see another analyst who charges a lower fee and decides to go into analysis at this lower fee. In this imaginary case, let us suppose that the patient not only goes into analysis but is successful in the analysis. In this illustration, we would conclude that either the analyst was wrong, or that at the very least the analyst could only say this patient was unanalyzable under the conditions that had been set by him. In this instance, one can conclude that the patient's ability to pay a particular analytic fee is not an ability that is needed to be a successful analysand.

[15] If we really were to go into the issue of the couch, we would have to also talk about the way the analyst introduces the issue. It seems to me that the optimal analytic approach is to be able to talk about why the couch would be useful for a particular patient, rather than stating that the couch is a necessary condition for an analysis. This issue could lead us to a number of others and how they are presented in the analytic situation.

Here we see that Brenner is not only concerned with the patient's cooperation but with continuing to maintain an analytic attitude regardless of the issue that is present in the analysis. All topics should be subject to analytic investigation and experienced in this context. The question arises, however, if we can easily agree on what are reasonable and conventional arrangements. To illustrate, we can turn to Brenner's views on why analysts should charge for missed sessions:

> Both from my own experience and from discussions with colleagues it seems to me that any other arrangement is motivated by an analyst's unconscious desire to deny his competitive and sadistic wishes . . . an arrangement that presents an analyst as being careful to avoid an appearance of profiting from his patient's misfortune, i.e., as being free from any desire to do so. To say to a patient, "you need not pay if it was really your bad luck that kept you from keeping your appointment," is to present oneself in just such a light. [Brenner 1976, p. 188]

It is hard to discount the experience of an analyst as sensitive and thoughtful as Brenner. It is also difficult to say that any other arrangement but the one that is being advocated by Brenner is necessarily motivated by the analyst's unconscious desire to deny his competitive and sadistic wishes. Isn't it possible that the analyst might undertake a deviation in this policy to gratify unconscious grandiose fantasies? Isn't it possible that a variety of compromises might be established with respect to this policy or any other aspect of analysis? More to the point, are there any reasons that are not *primarily* generated by unconscious conflicts that might lead to a deviation from this rule? It is perhaps more the form of the reasoning, as opposed to the conclusion, that I am addressing, but the conclusion is also open to some question. It is important to note that the conclusion is again (as with regard to lying on the couch) stated in dichotomous terms. If the analyst does not institute this rule, this can be construed as an attempt at denial. As importantly, there is an implication that there cannot be a real analysis if the rule is not adhered to. Implied in this statement is the assertion that you are not well analyzed if you don't adhere to this suggestion. It may be that empirically all of this is the case, but it seems unlikely to me that even Brenner has had enough experience to make this type of statement in a form that would be definitive for the whole discipline. Here we can touch on another perceived difficulty in analysis and analytic training: the questioning of principles is often taken to mean that one is not well analyzed. While this often may be true, it is hardly an adequate answer. Here again I must state it is not Brenner's conclusion that I would challenge, but I would question the reasoning that leads to this aspect of his position. I would also restate that if Brenner has observed this trend, then it seems to me that it is an observation well worth paying attention to, whether or not one agrees with his form of stating the observation.

It is interesting (at least in my experience) that charging for missed sessions is a policy that is difficult for many patients to genuinely accept. Most patients will grudgingly go along with the policy, but many harbor both conscious and unconscious hostility toward the analyst for this policy. It seems to me that it is a difficult analytic task with some patients to get to a point where they are truly cooperative with respect to this analytic condition. I believe that this is a reasonable policy, but I also believe that there are other ways to conduct an analysis. I think it must be acknowledged that charging for missed sessions is done for the analyst's benefit as well as being an attempt to create an appropriate analytic atmosphere.

PART V

Freud's Final Views

11

Freud on Analyzability, Termination, and Recovery of Pathogenic Memories

At first glance, the two papers discussed in the following pages are quite different in both style and intent. "Analysis Terminable and Interminable" is a long, dense paper filled with palpably different mood swings. Its length makes it necessary to reprint only a small portion, but the paper is discussed extensively in this chapter. "Constructions in Analysis," on the other hand, is a short paper that brings up several interesting issues and ends on an exploratory note. In discussing these last two technique papers, we will look at each of them separately because they show remarkably different aspects of Freud's views on analytic treatment.

"Analysis Terminable and Interminable"

HISTORICAL SOURCES

It is important to read this paper in the context of Freud's life and his surroundings. The following brief look at Freud's life is enhanced by Gay's recent biography of Freud (1988) as well as Schur's book *Freud: Living and Dying* (1972). In addition, a recent book by Mahony (1989) examines "Analysis Terminable and Interminable" (Freud 1937b) and attempts to explain aspects of content and writing style in terms of a variety of factors in Freud's surroundings. This work, *On Defining Freud's Discourse*, makes interesting reading because Mahony is both informative and extreme in the conclusions he draws.

A BRIEF LOOK AT FREUD'S LIFE AND TIMES

The period in which Freud wrote "Analysis Terminable and Interminable" was rich in historical and personal significance and somewhat less obscure than some other periods in Freud's life. Still, there are undoubtedly manuscripts that remain to be released that will contain new information about Freud and the psychoanalytic movement of this time.

Max Schur (1972) and a recent work by Clark (1980) tell us that Freud underwent an operation in 1936. By July of that year, laboratory tests documented a recurrence of his cancer. Freud had gone thirteen years without an operable recurrence of his original cancer. Now, shortly before undertaking the present work,[1] he was diagnosed as having another bout with the dreaded disease—what would turn out to be the beginning of his final bout. Various authors (Schur 1972, Mahony 1989) have suggested that the tone of this work was strongly influenced by this diagnosis. It is hard to imagine how they could be wrong. In addition, Freud was to encounter a friend of deep significance from the past. Undoubtedly Freud was shocked to learn of the discovery of his long-forgotten letters to Fliess. Mahony describes his view of the significance of this discovery to Freud: "I should like to bring this chronology into a most astounding relation that has hitherto been neglected by critics—the return of the suppressed and perhaps even partially repressed Fliess connection" (Mahony 1989, p. 61).

To paraphrase Mahony, on December 30, 1936, Marie Bonaparte, a long-time supporter, friend, and patient of Freud's, wrote that she had discovered his correspondence with Fliess and was about to purchase it from a dealer. Freud wrote back to her that his correspondence with Fliess had been of the most intimate nature, and that it would be highly embarrassing to have it fall into the hands of strangers. He also makes it clear that he does not "want any of them [the letters] to become known to so-called posterity" (Mahony 1989, p. 62. The letter is in Masson 1985, p. 7).

In addition to this discovery, Freud's beloved dog died twelve days before the date that Mahony gives as the day "Freud drew up the final version of 'Analysis Terminable and Interminable'" (Mahony 1989, p. 63). And finally, in my opinion, one should not fail to mention the dreaded specter of the Nazis to the east, as well as what Mahony calls "a drumroll of less public factors":

> The ravaging debilitation of terminal disease amplified by numerological super-
> stitions about the amount of life remaining to him, the death of his comforting
> dog, and the sudden reemergence of his intimate letters to Fliess. Freud was
> experiencing a certain disaffection with his lifelong wife, while around him he
> saw psychoanalysis increasingly beset with difficulties: defections of close col-

---

[1]Mahony dates Freud's writing of the present manuscript to early January 1937.

laborators multiplied, and Freud even felt deserted by Felix and Helene Deutsch and many others who left to practice in America, the land he had so long disdained; he also complained to Lou Andreas-Salome that many of his colleagues had "derived little from analysis as far as their personal character is concerned." And then there was the growing roll of patients who bore the worrisome effects of long analysis—most notably the Wolf Man who began treatment with Freud in 1910 and from 1926 on was in and out of analysis with Ruth Mack Brunswick, who herself was in and out of treatment with Freud from 1926 and was resorting to dangerous drugs during the 1930s. Nor must we forget Marie Bonaparte, who, intermittently in analysis with Freud from 1925 to 1938, fancifully tried to cure her frigidity by undergoing two vain operations to move her clitoris nearer her urethral meatus. She saw her former lover Loewenstein take her son into analysis in 1930, and she herself went into analysis with Loewenstein for a while in 1932. Anna Freud was analyzed by her father from 1918 to 1922 and from 1924 to 1925; her persistent spinsterhood gave rise to his fatherly concern. [Mahony 1989, pp. 64–65]

This bewildering, overwhelming, and somewhat confusing list that Mahony compiles is more a list of analytic embarrassments than issues that Mahony could know were current concerns of Freud's. He doesn't explain, for example, why he includes Loewenstein's relation to Bonaparte as an aspect of Freud's condition before and during the writing of this work. One might ask why Mahony lists Freud's analysis of his daughter as part of the context for the present work. This analysis, Young-Bruehl tells us (1988), took place over a decade before the present work; is it to be considered part of the context of all of Freud's writings from that time forward? Perhaps one of the reasons Mahony gives such a long inventory of events is that this essay brings up so many of Freud's past associations that it is tempting to include the entirety of Freud's career as influencing it. Of course, in a general sense this is true, but normally when considering the influences on a particular essay, it is hoped that we can be more specific. Even though Mahony appears to be engaging in a bit of wild analysis, it is understandable that this paper elicits a veritable litany of categories, since so many of Freud's past associates and issues make their appearance in these pages.

It seems likely that Freud's cancer and the looming threat of the Nazi invasion (from within and outside of Austria) influenced Freud to take one of his final looks at the state of psychoanalysis. Freud was already considering leaving his homeland; the state of civilization as well as the state of psychoanalysis must have weighed heavily on his mind. The discovery of his letters to Fleiss had to be an event that brought him back to the earliest days of the psychoanalytic movement. In terms of intellectual issues in psychoanalysis, let me add to the speculative list of factors impinging on Freud. It was during this period that Heinz Hartmann published *Ego Psychology and the Problem of Adaptation* (1939), and Anna Freud published *The Ego and Mechanisms of Defense* (1936). Both of these now classic monographs began to depart from

Freud's view of the ego as a structure. In my opinion, Freud attempted to embrace this new conception of the ego but was unable to fully agree with the positions that were taken by Hartmann and by Anna Freud. How Freud experienced these slight, but significant, departures from his theoretical stance is unknown to me, but in this essay we can see evidence of his attempting to state that he also[2] saw the ego as an independent structure with its own independent energies; several pages later, however, we see him recanting this position. He returns to the position that the ego is a structure that emerges from the id and that in most ways remains dependent on the id and superego for the duration of our lives.

In ending these prefatory sections we can take note of one additional historical circumstance. An unnamed colleague, close friend, and former patient of Freud's appears in the second section of the essay (p. 322 in the *Standard Edition*). Ferenczi had died in 1933; toward the end of his life he had broken away from Freud's domination. This is the former patient that Freud refers to. Freud is seemingly without rancor, but the use of Ferenczi as a clinical example must be questioned. Gay quotes Jones as saying that Ferenczi was "the senior member in the tight circle of Freud's professional confidants and the one who 'stood closest' to him" (Gay 1988, p. 187). While it is true that Ferenczi had two brief analyses with Freud (approximately twenty to twenty-two years before this essay was published), he had also been Freud's friend before and after their clinical encounter. That was hardly a typical case and surely Freud knew this, yet still included Ferenczi in the essay. The question that he raises is interesting and important, and does not stand or fall on the basis of the clinical example. It is still ironic to see how Freud, in his economical writing style, remembers a past friend and colleague and simultaneously raises a crucial issue for psychoanalytic practitioners.

THE ESSAY

Now that we have looked briefly at the circumstances of his life, let us consider the themes that Freud develops in this epic work. This ruminative, at times brooding essay covers many topics, including the etiology of certain disorders, issues of termination, the very nature of human existence, and the forces of life and death[3] (Eros and Thanatos). As we have said, references to some of Freud's past associates, patients, friends, and closest collaborators appear in this work. It is as if Freud wished to set the record straight before his death. In addition, he was asking many of the questions that he wanted future analysts to consider.

---

[2]Hartmann hypothesized that infants have cognitive capabilities immediately from birth. These capabilities might include perception, motility, etc.
[3]Freud's drive theory was written in terms of the instincts that govern life and death. Modern analysts have translated this theory into the drives of sex and aggression. This is an inexact translation of Freudian theory.

Of course he could also have been contemplating not only his demise but the demise of the psychoanalytic movement, given the rise of the Nazis and the exodus that had already begun to the United States and England.

ATTEMPTS TO SHORTEN ANALYSIS, AND FORCED TERMINATIONS

Freud begins by telling us that *analysis is a lengthy business*, and thus various analysts have tried to speed up the process. He writes of Otto Rank (a former colleague), who had made a particularly determined attempt to shorten analytic treatment:

> His hope was that, if this primal trauma [birth trauma] [would be] overcome by analysis, the whole neurosis would clear up, so that this one small piece of analytic work, for which a few months should suffice, would do away with the necessity for all the rest. [The idea] was a child of its time, conceived under the stress of the contrast between the post-war misery of Europe and the prosperity of America. . . . The theory and practice of Rank's experiment are now things of the past—no less than American "prosperity" itself. [Freud 1937b, pp. 316-317]

In this quote, one sees Freud dispense with two irritants from his past: Otto Rank and the prosperity of America, both of which may well have been in a depressed state at the time Freud was writing this paper. From this beginning, he goes on to tell us that he himself has made attempts to speed up analysis. Freud introduces us to the Wolf Man (his most famous patient) and tells us that the analysis with the Wolf Man "was in danger of failing as a result of its partial success" (Freud 1937b, p. 317). Although the Wolf Man had improved in some areas, Freud saw the patient as resistant and not actively engaged in the analytic process. At the end of the third year of the analysis, Freud informed the patient that the next year of treatment would be the last one regardless of what happened in the treatment. This forced termination was Freud's own technique for speeding up analysis.[4]

In weighing the pros and cons of setting a termination date, Freud relates that this "blackmailing device . . . is effective . . . but it cannot be held to guarantee perfect" results in analysis. "On the contrary . . . while the force of the threat will have the effect of bringing part of the material to light, another part will be lost to our therapeutic efforts" (Freud 1937b, p. 319).

The Wolf Man represents a case in which Freud is not completely satisfied with the results of analysis. In this light, it is interesting to examine Freud's rationale; his lack of satisfaction is embedded in a theoretical context rather

---

[4]Freud's setting of the termination date (see Chapters 12 and 13) is a procedure that is, at times, still followed today. Most analysts (including Freud) would agree that it is not an optimum way to end an analysis.

than a statement about the patient's functioning. Freud tells us that "we made no progress in clearing up his childhood neurosis which was the basis of his later illness" (Freud 1937b, p. 317). Freud is certain enough about this formulation that he is willing to *blackmail* the patient into associating, remembering, or helping in the reconstruction of his childhood.[5] We can see that even in this late paper, Freud considered the recovery and understanding of the patient's childhood neurosis as essential to the psychoanalytic process. What I have called the pathogenic memory model is still an active part of his thinking as it had been in every era of his career.[6] In fact, we can see by the position the recovery of childhood conflict plays in Freud's thinking that it is not just an essential component of analysis but *the* essential component of psychoanalytic treatment.

CRITERIA FOR TERMINATION

Consideration of the Wolf Man helps lead Freud into a discussion of what is meant by the ambiguous term, "the end of an analysis." Surprisingly, this is not a central question for Freud. Rather, he goes on to ask another question that will lead him to the pivotal discussion of this paper: "Instead of inquiring how analysis effects a cure . . . we should ask what are the obstacles which this cure encounters" (Freud 1937b, p. 322). This question in one form or another will occupy Freud for most of the remainder of the paper. He does, however, quickly dispense with the issue of "the end of an analysis." Freud's irony is powerful when he jibes fellow analysts for deploring or excusing an imperfection of some fellow mortal by exclaiming that "He was not completely analyzed" (1937b, p. 320). Obviously Freud has detected a tendency on the part of analysts to explain a person's life solely in terms of analytic results. He is going to be more circumspect in his portrayal of the efficacy of psychoanalysis. Here he relates the point at which an analysis ends:

> First, the patient must no longer be suffering from his former symptoms and have overcome his various anxieties and inhibitions and, secondly, the analyst must have formed the opinion that so much repressed material has been brought into consciousness . . . that no repetition of the patient's specific pathological processes is to be feared. [Freud 1937b, p. 320]

[5]We have to remind ourselves that Freud's treatment of the Wolf Man was, by modern standards, reasonably successful. Most modern commentators have diagnosed the Wolf Man as a borderline personality, a type of person that many analysts (as well as therapists from other orientations) today have difficulty in successfully treating. If we add to this the fact that Freud had no conceptual synopsis for treating a borderline patient, we might say that the treatment was at least as successful as many contemporary treatments that last a good deal longer. The Wolf Man, of course, was in many ways in treatment for the rest of his life. Many psychoanalysts tended to him during the course of his residence in Vienna.

[6]See Freud's "Remarks upon the Theory and Practice of Dream-Interpretation" (1923b), "Beyond the Pleasure Principle" (1920), "Dynamics of Transference" (1912c), psychotherapy papers (1904–1905), and *Studies on Hysteria* (Breuer and Freud 1893).

It is the second condition that holds Freud's attention; in discussing this criteria, he talks about some of the limitations that he seems to think are inherent in a therapeutic analysis. Again, an old friend returns and this old friend brings up an issue that has been with us since the beginning of Freud's career.

Ferenczi is the old friend who appears as a patient whom Freud had analyzed. Ferenczi was one of Freud's earliest supporters and certainly one of the most brilliant and innovative of analysts. It is fair to say he was, at the least, one of Freud's several analytic sons. In 1914, and then again in 1915, he entered into two brief and intensive analytic encounters with Freud. In discussing this case, Freud states that this patient married "the woman that he loved and became the friend and teacher of men whom he regarded as rivals" (Freud 1937b, p. 322). He was also, and continued to be, a friend and colleague of Freud's, and a central figure in the psychoanalytic movement. His marriage and his relationships with his former rivals were understandably more complicated than Freud could describe in this paper. It is interesting that Freud uses Ferenczi as an example, given the twenty-year relationship they had outside the therapeutic analysis. Freud frequently commented on Ferenczi's transference toward him, but for most of their relationship the transference had been positive. He writes about Ferenczi's transference only when the negative transference becomes apparent. Ferenczi had become critical and disenchanted; clearly Freud was upset and defensive. Ferenczi complained that Freud did not provide a complete analysis for him. Specifically, Ferenczi thought that Freud did not allow, nor analyze, the negative transference. Freud asserts that "even if the latent negative feelings (transference) could have been aroused it would not have been wise to do so." Here (Freud 1937b, p. 322) Freud asserted that it is difficult if not impossible to arouse the transference if the person is not experiencing something in his present life circumstances that will stimulate the conflict. He maintained that if the analyst brings up an issue, the best that one can do is give a patient an intellectual understanding of his conflicts. Thus the negative transference can be subsumed under this general rule, but there is still something specific about the negative transference that lingers for us. Freud dispenses with Ferenczi's complaint and points out that the patient lived on for many successful and *happy* years. He tells us in effect that one can't touch on everything in a given analysis, and therefore we cannot expect an analysis to provide a complete prophylaxis for all of the patient's life conflicts. We see now with both the Wolf Man and with Ferenczi that, although analysis may be partially successful, Freud is pointing out some analytic limitations. More specifically, it may be that the analyst will have to induce the patient to associate (for the Wolf Man by setting a termination date) and by dint of this induction give up the possibility of a full analysis. Or it may be that in a given analysis (such as Ferenczi's), it may not be possible to reach all the person's conflicts because the patient's life circumstances are such that they do not stimulate these issues during the treatment.

At this point, Freud does not explore the possibility that he may have contributed to the limitations of these two treatments. He does not comment on having violated some of his own suggestions in treating Ferenczi.[7] He focuses only on a limitation of the analytic method as if the method existed independently of the analytic clinician. This defines the extent to which Freud has retreated to an early model of treatment; he sees the extirpation of pathogenic memories as his task. It is not the transference that leads to the understanding of memories, but rather the person's life circumstances that stimulate association and memories. The treatment, in effect, does not have a life of its own. I believe that Freud implicitly returned to a sophisticated version of the model he proposes in Chapter 4 of *Studies on Hysteria*.

We may metaphorically remark that Freud's consideration of the negative transference has helped induce his regression. In *Dynamics of Transference*, he tells us that, "The negative transference requires a more thorough elucidation than is possible within the limits of this paper" (Freud 1912, p. 320). We can recollect that Freud has never attempted this elucidation. Bird, as we have seen (1972), believes that Freud and many contemporary analysts as well slight the negative transference. We can infer from Bird that part of the prophylactic action of psychoanalysis lies in the analysis of the negative transference. Perhaps this is one of the directions that Freud should have explored to achieve the prophylactic action he was seeking. Despite the inadequacies of Freud's arguments, we cannot ignore the questions that he raises. Is it possible that over the course of an analysis, even given the length of a modern analysis, certain material simply cannot be reached in many or most cases? Is it true that if the patient's current life does not provide the stimulus for certain issues that the analysis will not generate a life of its own through the unfolding of the transference? Is the unfolding of the transference therefore restricted by the circumstances of the patient's life at the time of the analysis? These seemingly interminable questions must naturally be followed by others that Freud has proposed about the issue of prophylaxis. If one can't get to certain issues in a given analysis, is there still some way to inoculate the person against further outbreaks of symptoms or conflicts? Freud's answers to these questions are indirect in the remainder of the paper, but the answers lead him to intriguing paths that point in many directions and in varying degrees touch on the past, present, and even the future of psychoanalysis.

INDIVIDUAL DIFFERENCES AND
THE QUANTITATIVE FACTOR

Freud never seemed to lose sight of fundamental questions that verged on the borders of the psychobiological. In considering the questions we have enumer-

---

[7]He had previously stated clearly that analysts should not treat friends, relatives, or even relatives of friends.

ated, he is brought back to bedrock issues about the genesis of the drives and the relationship between drive and ego development. He is almost unable to consider the clinical issue of termination without considering general etiological questions. His clinical examples are highly abstract and are more theoretical conjectures than true clinical examples. He emphasizes aspects of his theory that have already (in 1937) fallen into some disfavor with Freudian analysts. He tells us again that, however tentatively he stated his ideas about Eros and Thanatos, these are concepts he believes in strongly. He also brings in a theme that winds its way through the rest of the essay: what Freud calls the quantitative factor.

At first the quantitative factor is considered in terms of the drives, then the ego and drives, and then the interactions between the ego and id. By the quantitative factor, Freud is referring to the intensity or magnitude of the drives in a given individual. He assumes that there are individual differences, or characteristic quantitative amounts of drive that are present in individuals. Analysis, he tells us, works best when the etiological factors are primarily environmental. If the drives are too intense, trauma is easily achieved in early development, and it is difficult to help the person leave a given libidinal position or fixation point. We can say that it is only when the environment is the primary determinant of conflict that analysis can be truly effective.[8] Freud maintains that, for analysis to take hold, the analysand needs an intact ego.

In part of this essay, Freud mentions that ego development should be considered separately from the id or the drives. This position is one that he doesn't maintain even for the length of this essay; he reminds us very soon after his assertion about separate ego development that he considers the ego to derive from the id. Therefore, not only is the strength of the drives a factor in terms of the ego taming the drives, but indeed the instinctual quantitative factor is important in the very development of the ego. We can contrast this position to that of Hartmann, who sees the ego as an independent structure from birth. Freud seems to be reminding younger analysts that psychoanalysis was first and foremost (and perhaps still should be) a depth psychology.[9]

We can take another look at Freud's shifting position on the efficacy of analytic treatment. In "Analysis Terminable and Interminable" Freud brings up a former patient who, many years after her analysis, has a symptomatic relapse. The circumstances in her life were such that most people would have had significant reactions to the events she confronted. That she reacted in a way that is reminiscent of her previous difficulties can be seen as a failure of analysis. On the other hand, the fact that she was preserved symptom-free for a number of years, in difficult situations, may be seen as the success of analysis. In using this example, Freud is telling us that the ultimate success or failure of analysis is partly in the hands of fate and partly a result of the relationship of

---

[8]This may seem like a strange position for the analyst whose name is so linked with the importance of drives or instincts in early human development.
[9]This despite the new theoretical innovations—that is, the structural theory that he has introduced.

the ego and id (quantitative factor), as well as being a function of the analysis itself. Implicitly he is telling us that conflicts are never completely done away with, but are rather brought, more or less well, under the control of the ego. Given that this is the case, there can be events in a person's life that will test the control of the ego; at times a former analysand ego will fail the test. This is a different view than Freud expressed previously in the *Introductory Lectures*: "A person who has become normal and free from the operation of repressed instinctual impulses in his relation to the doctor will remain so in his own life after the doctor has once more withdrawn from it" (Freud 1916/1917, p. 167). Another example is used in the same volume (p. 213), where Freud is comparing the effects of hypnotic suggestion and psycho-analysis: "An analytic treatment demands from both doctor and patient the accomplishment of serious work, which is employed in lifting internal resistances. Through the overcoming of these resistances the patient's mental life is permanently changed, is raised to a higher level of development and remains protected against fresh possibilities of falling ill."

Obviously Freud's views changed, and perhaps they changed because of a lack of clinical contact. As he mentions, after World War I he primarily conducted training analyses. As we will see in a later section in this chapter, his view of training analyses is substantially different from contemporary views. It is my contention that Freud's *real* clinical career was over by the time World War I ended.[10]

There is an important auxiliary theme introduced that we can consider an ultimate obstacle to analytic treatment. It is a theme that Freud hints at in this work and states clearly only in his book *Moses and Monotheism* (1939).[11] Freud seems to have been a Lamarckian. His views on the racial unconscious were somewhat mystical and strongly influenced by Jung's views on the racial unconscious. It is clear that in 1937 through 1938, Freud believed that certain acquired characteristics could be inherited.[12] One is born, according to this belief, with certain unconscious tendencies. In terms of psychoanalysis, it may be particularly difficult to analyze a tendency that the analysand has no memory of and that indeed was passed on from a prior generation.

Here is an extreme position on the difficulties and limitations of psychoanalysis, and it is, I believe, a fair measure of Freud's pessimism at the time of the writing of this essay. In fact, one could say that, given all of the difficulties faced by analysis, it is a wonder that Freud remained as optimistic as he did. Freud acknowledged that analysis was often useful and at times (even in the cases that he cited) decisive in helping the people turn their lives around and

[10]Really by the time World War I began.

[11]Freud's being a Lamarckian is a view substantiated by his recently published work, *A Phylogenetic Phantasy*. It was written in 1915 but remained unpublished until recent years. It seems that this work was suppressed by those around Freud.

[12]For example, if the Jews actually killed Moses and experienced guilt, according to Freud, this guilt could be passed through the generations in what might be called the collective unconscious (Freud 1939).

gain control over events that were previously beyond their control. However, we can see that for Freud the idea of a rapid, permanent cure was a vision that had faded and been replaced by a view of the species as destined to repeat the past unless both the individual and the group could come to understand the irrational forces imbedded in the unconscious.[13]

TRAINING ANALYSES

In this essay, Freud does not exclude analysts from the limitations of the analytic process. He tells us that "it cannot be disputed that analysts do not in their own personalities wholly come up to the standard of psychical normality which they set for their patients" (Freud 1937b, p. 351). We have already noted his use of irony in discussing analysts' view of human frailty in terms of incomplete analyses, but here he is making a stronger statement about the nature of the analytic process. He states that in this almost "impossible profession" the prospective analyst must gain the "ideal qualifications for his (or her) work . . . in his own analysis" (p. 352). This analysis must, for practical reasons, be *short and incomplete*, but it will provide to the learner "a sincere conviction of the existence of the unconscious." Obviously, Freud's idea of training analyses did not persist into the later half of the century, for they surely haven't remained short; whether they are incomplete is yet another matter. Still, he began a tradition of evaluating candidates during their training analyses, which must be one of the most effective ways of limiting free association. It is difficult to say honestly what you are thinking if you are worried that your analyst may tell you that you are not fit to be an analyst. It must also force the transference into relatively restricted areas. This, in my opinion, is one of the places in which Freud's legacy is most problematic. Freud, however, offers another suggestion that has not received a great deal of explicit attention. He advocates that the analyst should periodically enter an analysis at approximately five-year intervals.[14] Perhaps if analysts had followed Freud's prescription, the effect of the initial training (or pseudo-) analysis would be mitigated. His idea was to have an initial short analysis and periodic relatively short analyses. As far as I know, this has never been tried by any analytic institute. Freud's encouraging analysts to undergo periodic analyses is his attempt to tell future analysts that the analytic process will continuously stimulate conflict. He is reminding us that it is good to be aware that not only the patient, but the analyst as well, will be continuously affected by the analytic process. It is an interminable process for all concerned.

[13]Leaving aside the issue of the collective unconscious, it is my view that Freud is more correct than not and that humans grossly underestimate the extent to which repetition is a factor in our individual and collective lives.
[14]He may be offering this suggestion as an antidote to the initial short, incomplete training analysis that he proposes.

THE BEDROCK CORE OF ANALYTIC TREATMENT

Is Freud's final view that analysis by its very nature is an interminable process? The strong form of this view is that a finished analysis is an impossibility, and that there are factors beyond the reach of any individual that militate against being able to be completely analyzed. The more moderate form of this position, and I believe the one closest to Freud's view, is that analysis is a difficult process but one that can be of significant benefit to many and offers some (limited) prophylactic benefit. Even an incomplete analysis may have a decisive positive effect if the environment is kind and does not provide the conditions for what might be called adult trauma. Given human life, it is probable that most people will encounter traumatic-like circumstances in their adult life. Thus, while analysis may offer some prophylaxis, it is a quantitative question as to how much prophylaxis a given analysis can provide. Analysts should realize that this applies to them as well. Their profession makes them somewhat vulnerable to the stirring up of unresolved conflict, and they might need periodic analyses to deal with their conflicts.

In this essay (which is partially an historical overview), Freud reminds us that, try as he might to accommodate to the newer views of an independent ego, all energy is derived from the drives or the id. In his updated version, the environment may influence the drives, but it is the drives that are the psychic engine of the mind. He also gives his views on what are the basic or deepest issues that can be reached in terms of unconscious fantasies that can be understood in analysis. Once more, a former friend comes to the fore, when Freud tells us that it was Fliess who called his attention to the idea that, "it is the attitude belonging to the sex opposite to the subject's own which succumbs to repression" (Freud 1937b, p. 355). Here, Freud makes his journey more complete and mentions not only Fliess in this section, but Adler as well. By mentioning Fliess, he demonstrates that Adler's idea of masculine protest is only a derivative of ideas that he and Fliess had discussed many years before (between 1897 and 1902). He restates the centrality in his theory of the castration complex in the phallic stage.[15] Thus, penis envy for women, and a passive (feminine) attitude of a man toward other men, are the bedrock issues that analysis can reach. This position is a strong restatement of the importance of oedipal stage dynamics in analytic treatment and theory. It brings Freud full circle to some of the early positions that he takes in discussions with Fliess.

The importance of this statement can be extended not only to theoretical issues, but to issues of analyzability as well. For ten years (from 1907 to 1917), Freud discussed the importance of preoedipal issues (1911, 1913a,b, 1914a,b,c, 1915a,b, 1917). He had developed concepts that involved fixation points in the oedipal period for hysterics (1913b, 1915b), in the anal sadistic period for obsessive-compulsives (1913a), and at various points in the narcissistic period

---

[15]It is surprising to many people that Freud did not really formulate a phallic stage until 1923.

for people with paranoid and depressive disorders (1911, 1915b). Schizophrenics or paraphrenics bordered between narcissism and what he called autoeroticism (1911). Here he is returning to the idea that it is oedipal sexuality that most fundamentally determines the fate of conflicts. This has been perhaps the bedrock theoretical dispute in psychoanalysis over the last twenty years.[16]

In his discussion of "Analysis Terminable and Interminable," Mahony says:

> We realize only too well that it shares the limitations of its time. At the same time we can only imagine the additions and modifications that Freud would bring to the text if he were revising it today: preoedipal and postoedipal developmental issues, sexual and gender identity, structural aspects of the ego, the role of mourning and reparation, narcissistic and borderline pathology, termination as a phase of treatment, the pervasiveness of negative transference, the complications of countertransference, and so on. [Mahony 1989, p. 94]

Again there is an overwhelming list of possibilities and I will restrict myself, in completing this section, to considering only two of these elements.

As I have already stated, Freud spent a good deal of theoretical effort on the role of preoedipal developmental issues, and his earlier views are intriguing given our present discussion. Let us go back to Freud's paper, "On Narcissism," to look at his views in 1914; he is discussing Adler's position on the masculine protest, and the similarities of Adler's masculine protest to psychoanalytic ideas of the castration complex. Freud writes:

> I find it quite impossible to place the genesis of neurosis upon the narrow basis of the castration complex, however powerfully it may come to the fore in men among their resistances to the cure of a neurosis. Incidentally, I know of cases of neurosis in which the "masculine protest", or, as we regard it, the castration complex, plays no pathogenic part, and even fails to appear at all. [Freud 1914c, pp. 92–93]

This is quite striking, given what we have just read in "Analysis Terminable and Interminable." Freud is stating unequivocally that to place the etiology of the neurosis on what he calls the narrow base of the castration complex is not a satisfactory explanation of even the neuroses. What does he have in mind when he makes this assertion? As I have outlined above, in "On Narcissism" and a number of papers that surround it, Freud elaborately spelled out fixation points that occurred before the phallic stage[17] or the point of fulmination for the castration complex. One can say that, long before the oedipal stage takes on its central, almost exclusive importance in Freud's theorizing, preoedipal factors were actively considered by him to be important in the etiology of

---

[16]I must add that my bias is toward Freud's somewhat neglected work extending from 1907–1917. This period includes papers that spell out the beginnings of an object relations position.
[17]This is somewhat anachronistic since the phallic stage was not conceived of until 1923.

certain neuroses as well as narcissistic disorders.[18] It is interesting to wonder what happened to Freud's views on preoedipal development. Dr. Edoardo Weiss, a contemporary of Freud's, had the same question in 1926. Freud writes in reply to Weiss:

> Your question, in connection with my assertion in my paper On Narcissism, as to whether there are neuroses in which the castration complex plays no part, puts me in an embarrassing position. I no longer recollect what it was I had in mind at the time. To-day, it is true, I could not name any neurosis in which this complex is not to be met with, and in any case I should not have written the sentence today. But we know so little of the whole subject that I should prefer not to give a final decision either way. [Freud 1914c, p. 93]

Twelve years after his statement in "On Narcissism," Freud no longer remembered what he meant in these passages. One could have asked him much broader questions, questions about his theories of fixation points in pre-oedipal development, but of course we know the type of answer he might have given. By 1926, Freud had finished stating the major tenets of the structural model; with the statement of the structural model, the oedipal stage was established as the crucible of the neuroses. That there were many contradictory currents in earlier writings is not something that seems to have concerned Freud. In "Analysis Terminable and Interminable," Freud expressed the dominant position that he had held certainly after 1923, the writing of "The Ego and the Id" and "The Dissolution of the Oedipus Complex." This position has important implications, for many analysts have used derivatives of this position to determine criteria for analyzability.

We come to the end of our discussion of this fascinating paper with the realization that currents running through Freud's writings are deep and swift. Many things get stirred up and many get swept away. What remains is the enormous range of concepts, questions, and discoveries that he has left to the analytic community and to the world.

"Constructions in Analysis"

In this essay (Freud 1937a) we see the mirror image of Freud in "Analysis Terminable and Interminable": Freud is again asserting the importance of the patient remembering, but, in this rendition, the remembering is done via the construction or reconstruction of the patient's past by the analyst. He is writing this as a reminder to the analytic community and possibly as a re-

---

[18]Saying that if Freud were writing today he would be actively considering preoedipal development is quite an assumption. For a variety of reasons, Freud turned at least somewhat away from his earlier views, and there is no certainty that he would have returned to modern versions of his earlier (oedipal) views.

joinder to analysts who asserted at the Marienbad Congress (Strachey 1937) that, in analysis, all that could be analyzed is the transference. In fact, at the end of the previous paper, we see Freud writing "that the form of the resistance is immaterial: it does not matter whether it appears as a transference or not" (Freud 1937b, p. 356); all that matters is that the resistance prevents change from taking place. This is a different view of resistance than the one that predominates in the transference papers. Here Freud is asserting that when one reaches a certain content, it doesn't matter how one gets there or what form the patient's resistance takes. In the construction paper, transference is not really an issue; the issue is the validity of the construction and some general criteria on how to judge the validity of the construction. Moreover, Freud is writing here as if constructions are really at the heart of the analytic process; this is a return at least in spirit to the pathogenic memory model. How does one interpret this paper without losing Freud's previous views on the centrality of transference in treatment?

One possible answer to this question is that while Freud considered the transference and transference neurosis to be the way conflicts will be repeated in the analysis, constructions are the essential curative aspect of the treatment.[19] In this formulation, constructions can be derived only from an expression of the transference. Thus, whereas the patient repeats through transference, he gains insight through constructions. Freud is also implicitly stating that the adequacy of a construction is an important criterion in determining how completely the patient's conflicts are understood in the analysis. Inherent in making this argument a convincing one is the ability of Freud or any analyst to provide usable criteria for determining the adequacy of a construction.

One can consider this paper a sophisticated attempt by Freud to provide some criteria on how to judge the efficacy of construction. Although we can consider this paper an updated version of the pathogenic memory model, Freud characteristically adds a new element. In the last section of the paper, he draws a similarity between certain recollections and hallucinations. He then goes on to relate his experience with nonpsychotic patients who occasionally report hallucinations and likens these events to the *familiar* mechanism of dreams. Freud concludes by hypothesizing that there is "not only a method in madness . . . but also a fragment of historic truth (in madness)" (Freud 1937a, p. 370). The idea that he is proposing is that in the hallucination there is some element of childhood reality appearing. In talking about psychotic or psychotic-like phenomena, he is going into an area that he has generally eschewed in terms of analytic treatment. He gives extremely valuable clinical advice when he tells us that it would be a "vain effort" to convince the "patient of the error of his delusion and of its contradiction of reality" (Freud 1937a, p. 370). On the contrary, the therapeutic process would be "in liberating the fragment of

---

[19]While this formulation is a nice compromise construction, it ignores the quote on the previous page, which clearly downplays the importance of transference.

historic truth from its distortions and its attachments to the actual present day and in leading it back to the point in the past to which it belongs" (Freud 1937b, p. 337). He goes on to tell us that he believes that analysts would gain "a great deal of valuable knowledge from work of this kind . . . even if led to no therapeutic success" (p. 338). Obviously Freud is being cautious, but he is clearly encouraging analysts to begin (or for some analysts to continue) this type of work.

The insight about hallucinations and psychotic processes is in some ways a fascinating aside, since Freud had frequently said that he had no patience for treating severely disturbed patients. Why, at this late date, is he offering this insight (or hypothesis) and advocating that analysts treat psychotic (or border-line patients)? He had firmly stated in the past that analytic treatment should not be offered to patients with severe narcissistic disturbances. This question is particularly interesting, since in his previous paper, he is talking about the limitations of analytic treatment. Rather than try to answer these questions, I will simply point out that this is one more instance in which one should be cautious in attempting to narrowly define Freudian thought. In many ways, Freud defies all categorization and is a theorist who raises more possibilities than he and perhaps anyone could consider in a lifetime. In any case, we are thankful to Freud for this hopeful, interesting paper after the heavy and sobering "Analysis Terminable and Interminable."

12

*Freud's Termination
and Construction Papers*

Analysis Terminable
and Interminable[1]

(1937)

I

Experience has taught us that psycho-analytic
therapy—the liberation of a human being from
his neurotic symptoms, inhibitions and abnormal-
ities of character—is a lengthy business. Hence,
from the very beginning, attempts have been
made to shorten the course of analysis. Such endeavours required no justification: they could
claim to be prompted by the strongest considerations alike of reason and expediency. But there
probably lurked in them some trace of the impa-
tient contempt with which the medical profession
of an earlier day regarded the neuroses, seeing in
them the unnecessary results of invisible lesions.
If it had now become necessary to deal with them,
they should at least be got rid of with the utmost
despatch. Basing his procedure on the theory for-

[1]'Die endliche und die unendliche Analyse.' First published
Int. Z. Psychoanal., **23** (1937), 209; reprinted *Ges. W.*, **16**.
[Translation, reprinted from *Int. J. Psycho-Anal.*, **18** (1937),
373, by Joan Riviere.]

mulated in *Das Trauma der Geburt* (1924) Otto
Rank made a particularly determined attempt to
shorten analysis. He assumed that the cardinal
source of neurosis was the experience of birth, on
the ground of its involving a possibility that the
infant's 'primal fixation' to the mother might not
be surmounted but persist in the form of 'primal
repression'. His hope was that, if this primal
trauma were overcome by analysis, the whole neurosis would clear up, so that this one small piece of
analytic work, for which a few months should
suffice, would do away with the necessity for all
the rest. Rank's argument was certainly bold and
ingenious, but it did not stand the test of critical
examination. Moreover, it was a child of its time,
conceived under the stress of the contrast between
the post-war misery of Europe and the 'prosperity'
■ 1 of America, and designed to accelerate the
tempo of analytic therapy to suit the rush of
American life. We have heard little of the clinical
results of Rank's plan. Probably it has not accomplished more than would be done if the men of a
fire-brigade, summoned to deal with a house set
on fire by an upset oil-lamp, merely removed the
lamp from the room in which the conflagration
had broken out. Much less time would certainly be
spent in so doing than in extinguishing the whole
fire. The theory and practice of Rank's experiment
are now things of the past—no less than American 'prosperity' itself. ■ 2

Before the war, I myself had already tried
another way of speeding up analysis. I had under-
taken to treat a young Russian, a rich man spoilt
by riches, who had come to Vienna in a state of
complete helplessness, accompanied by physician
and attendant.[2] It was possible in the course of

■ 1
Although Freud writes about
his attempting to speed up the
analysis with the Wolf Man, in
point of fact we know that his
analyses were usually shorter
than the length of time he
actually spent with the Wolf
Man. It is interesting in this
context that, whereas Freud
mentions Rank's attempts, he
does not mention Ferenczi's attempts at changing analytic
technique. Later on in the
paper, he does refer to Ferenczi
with respect to a different
issue.

■ 2
Freud had written a critique of
Rank's work in "Inhibitions,
Symptoms and Anxiety." Freud's
anti-American attitudes were
well known, and he apparently
was unable to resist taunting
Americans at the same time
that he was criticizing Rank.

[2]Cf. my paper, published with the patient's consent, 'From
the History of an Infantile Neurosis' (1918). It contains no
detailed account of the young man's adult illness, which is
touched on only when its connection with his infantile neurosis requires it. ■ 3

several years to restore to him a considerable measure of independence, and to awaken his interest in life, while his relations to the principal people in his life were adjusted. But then we came to a full stop. We made no progress in clearing up his childhood's neurosis, ■ 4 which was the basis of his later illness, and it was obvious that the patient found his present situation quite comfortable and did not intend to take any step which would bring him nearer to the end of his treatment. It was a case of the treatment obstructing itself: the analysis was in danger of failing as a result of its— partial—success. In this predicament I resorted to the heroic remedy of fixing a date for the conclusion of the analysis. At the beginning of a period of treatment I told the patient that the coming year was to be the last of his analysis, no matter what progress he made or failed to make in the time still left to him. At first he did not believe me, but, once he was convinced that I was in dead earnest, the change which I had hoped for began to take place. His resistances crumbled away, and in the last months of treatment he was able to produce all the memories and to discover the connecting links which were necessary for the understanding of his early neurosis and his recovery from the illness from which he was then suffering. When he took leave of me at mid-summer, 1914, unsuspecting as we all were, of what was so shortly to happen, I believed that his cure was complete and permanent.

In a postscript to this patient's case history I have already reported that I was mistaken. When, towards the end of the war, he returned to Vienna, a refugee and destitute, I had to help him to master a part of the transference which had remained unresolved. Within a few months this was successfully accomplished and I was able to conclude my postscript with the statement that 'since then the patient has felt normal and has behaved unexceptionably, in spite of the war hav-

■ 3
See discussion of this case in Chapters 11 and 15.

■ 4
When Freud writes that "we made no progress in clearing up his childhood's neurosis," we can see that even in this late paper he is writing in a way that makes it clear that he believes it is necessary to understand the person's childhood in order to have a complete and efficacious analysis. Obviously Gill and, to some extent, Brenner would disagree with this view.

ing robbed him of his home, his possessions, and all his family relationships'. Fifteen years have passed since then, but this verdict has not proved erroneous, though certain reservations have had to be made. The patient has remained in Vienna and has made good, although in a humble social position. Several times, however, during this period, his satisfactory state of health has broken down, and the attacks of neurotic illness from which he has suffered could be construed only as offshoots of his original neurosis. Thanks to the skill of one of my pupils, Dr. Ruth Mack Brunswick, a short course of treatment has sufficed on each occasion to clear up these attacks. I hope Dr. Mack Brunswick herself will report on this case before long.[3] Some of these relapses were caused by still unresolved residues of the transference; short-lived though the attacks were, they were distinctly paranoic in character. In other instances, however, the pathogenic material consisted of fragments from the history of the patient's childhood, which had not come to light while I was analysing him and which now came away (the comparison is obvious) like sutures after an operation or small pieces of necrotic bone. I have found the history of this man's recovery almost as interesting as that of his illness.

Since then I have employed the method of fixing a date for the termination of analysis in other cases and I have also inquired about the experience of other analysts in this respect. ■ 5 There can be only one verdict about the value of this blackmailing device. The measure is effective, provided that one hits the right time at which to employ it. But it cannot be held to guarantee perfect accomplishment of the task of psychoanalysis. On the contrary, we may be quite sure that, while the force of the threat will have the

■ 5

The practice of setting a termination date is still used by some contemporary analysts. Recently, Dr. A. Cooper presented a case at the N.Y.U. Postdoctoral Program in which he felt that setting a termination date was the most effective way to treat a patient who was not able to make progress at a particular phase in his analy-

[3][One such report had already appeared: Brunswick (1928b).]
■ 6

■ 5 *continued*

sis. For Freud to say that a mistake once made cannot be rectified is interesting in light of
the Wolf Man's history. He
came back to Freud for further
consultation, and then Freud
sent him to Dr. Mack Brunswick for subsequent treatment.
Moreover, Freud offered the
Wolf Man various types of assistance after his analysis.
Freud, of course, is referring to
the idea that once the analyst
sets a termination date, it cannot be undone in the patient's
mind and because of that the

patient may never be able to
bring up certain issues to the
analyst. This was Freud's assumption, and while I personally think that he is right, it still
is an issue that might be studied.

■ 6

Muriel Gardiner has compiled
an extensive compendium of
reports on the Wolf Man including Freud's case report, Dr.
Ruth Mack Brunswick's case report and statements by the
Wolf Man and analysts who interviewed him. See also Kanzer
and Mahony.

effect of bringing part of the material to light,
another part will be held back and become buried,
as it were, and will be lost to our therapeutic
efforts. Once the date for discontinuing the treatment has been fixed we must not extend the time;
otherwise the patient will lose all his faith in the
analyst. The most obvious way out would be to let
him continue his treatment with another analyst,
although we know that a change of this sort involves a fresh loss of time and the sacrifice of
some of the results of the work already done. Nor
can any general rule be laid down as to the right
time for resorting to this forcible technical
method: the analyst must use his own tact in the
matter. A mistake, once made, cannot be rectified.
The saying that the lion springs once and once
only must hold good here.

II

The discussion of the technical problem of
how to accelerate the slow progress of an analysis
suggests another, more deeply interesting question: is there such a thing as a natural end to an

analysis or is it really possible to conduct it to such an end? To judge by the ordinary talk of analysts we should presume that it is, for we often hear them say, when deploring or excusing the admitted imperfection of some fellow-mortal: 'His analysis was not finished' or 'He was not completely analysed'.

Now we must first decide what is meant by the ambiguous term, 'the end of an analysis'. From the practical standpoint it is easily defined. An analysis is ended when analyst and patient cease to meet for the analytic session. This happens when two conditions have been approximately fulfilled. First, the patient must no longer be suffering from his former symptoms and must have overcome his various anxieties and inhibitions and, secondly, the analyst must have formed the opinion that so much repressed material has been brought into consciousness, so much that was inexplicable elucidated, and so much inner resistance overcome that no repetition of the patient's specific pathological processes is to be feared. If for external reasons one is prevented from reaching this goal, it is more correct to say that an analysis is imperfect than to say that it has not been completed.

The second definition of the 'end' of an analysis is much more ambitious. ■ 7 According to it we have to answer the question whether the effect upon the patient has been so profound that no further change would take place in him if his analysis were continued. The implication is that by means of analysis it is possible to attain to absolute physical normality and to be sure that it will be maintained, the supposition being that all the patient's repressions have been lifted and every gap in his memory filled. Let us first consult our experience and see whether such things do in fact happen, and then examine our theory and learn whether there is any *possibility* of their happening.

Every analyst will have treated some cases with this gratifying outcome. He has succeeded in

■ 7

In Freud's first statement on the end of the analysis, he gives the criteria for ending in terms of symptom relief or disappearance, the explication of unconscious material, and the overcoming of resistances. In the second statement, he mentions the same factors except in more absolute terms. All repressions have been lifted and every gap in the patient's memory filled. The difference in the second statement is that no further change would take place if the analysis continued. What is

■ *7 continued*

Freud referring to when he says no further change would take place if the patient continued in analysis? He is talking about the complete filling in of gaps in the patient's memory. We can note again how important the pathogenic memory model remains for Freud even at this late date in his career. More importantly in this context is whether he considers it possible or likely that all the gaps will be filled in. The answer to this question gives strong insight into Freud's thinking about the possibility of complete analyses and the relationship between external events in the patient's life and the transference in the treatment situation.

clearing up the patient's neurosis, there has been no relapse and no other nervous disturbance has succeeded it. We know something of what determines these results. No noticeable modification had taken place in the patient's ego and the causation of his illness was pre-eminently traumatic. The aetiology of all neuroses is indeed a mixed one; either the patient's instincts are excessively strong and refuse to submit to the taming influence of his ego or else he is suffering from the effects of premature traumas, by which I mean traumas which his immature ego was unable to surmount. Generally there is a combination of the two factors: the constitutional and the accidental. The stronger the constitutional factor the more readily will a trauma lead to fixation, with its sequel in a disturbance of development; the stronger the trauma the more certain is it that it will have injurious effects even when the patient's instinctual life is normal. There can be no doubt that, when the aetiology of the neurosis is traumatic, analysis has a far better chance. Only when the traumatic factor predominates can we look for what psycho-analysis can achieve in such a masterly fashion, namely, the replacement (owing to the strengthening of the ego) of the inadequate decision made in infancy by a correct solution. Only in such a case can one speak of a definitive end to an analysis. When such a result has been attained analysis has done all that can be required of it and need not be continued. If the patient who has made such a good recovery never produces any more symptoms calling for analysis, it still, of course, remains an open question how much of this immunity is due to a benevolent fate which spares him too searching a test.

The factors which are prejudicial to analysis and may cause it to be so long-drawn-out as to be really interminable are a constitutional strength of instinct and an unfavourable modification of the ego in the defensive conflict, a modification comparable to a dislocation or crippling. One is tempted to make the first factor—the strength of the instincts—responsible for the second—the modification of the ego ■ 8—but it seems that the latter has its own aetiology and indeed it must be admitted that our knowledge of these relations is as yet imperfect. They are only just becoming the object of analytic investigation. I think that here the interest of analysts is quite wrongly orientated. Instead of inquiring *how* analysis effects a cure (a point which in my opinion has been sufficiently elucidated) we should ask what are the obstacles which this cure encounters. ■ 9

This brings me to two problems which arise directly out of psycho-analytic practice, as I hope to show by the following examples. A certain man, who had himself been a most successful practitioner of analysis, came to the conclusion that his relations with men as well as with women—the men who were his rivals and the woman whom he loved—were not free from neurotic inhibitions, and he therefore had himself analysed by an analyst whom he regarded as his superior. ■ 10 This critical exploration of his own personality was entirely successful. He married the woman whom he loved and became the friend and teacher of the men whom he had regarded as rivals. Many years passed, during which his relation to his former analyst remained unclouded. But then, for no demonstrable external reason, trouble arose. The

■ 8
Freud extensively discusses the idea of ego alteration in later sections of this paper and in the last paper that he wrote, "The Splitting of the Ego." He uses the term *traumatic* to mean childhood experiences that were induced by the child's parents or other important figures in the child's life.

■ 9
Here Freud is maintaining that constitutional or physiological factors involved in psychological disorders are not amenable to psychoanalytic treatment. He goes on to say that analysts should study the obstacles to analytic success in such cases, and in the constructions paper he repeats this idea more concretely when he says that psychotic patients should be seen in analysis even if there is not much chance of success in such a treatment.

■ 10
Jones, Gay, and others report that this statement and what immediately follows was writ-

■ 10 *continued*

ten about Ferenczi the patient and Freud the analyst. Freud saw Ferenczi in "analysis" for three weeks in October 1914 and for another three weeks (with two sessions daily) in June 1916. Ferenczi died in 1933, and Freud wrote what might be characterized as a somewhat aloof obituary. Ferenczi's diary, written primarily between 1931 and 1933 and published recently, indicates Ferenczi's depth of feeling for Freud. He describes his analysis with Freud in somewhat different terms than Freud does in the above passages, and he is clearly somewhat bitter about his relationship with Freud. It has to be remembered that Ferenczi, when he wrote this diary, was undergoing a number of psychological and physiological changes. How much this affected him is difficult to answer, and certainly one should not judge an issue like this without sufficient study of what Ferenczi was experiencing. Still his criticism of Freud is one that has merit simply on the basis of the statement of Freud's technical papers. It is clear that Freud had difficulty dealing with manifestations of negative transference, and both his writing and his practice confirm this point. One might state that it was not just with Ferenczi that Freud insisted on dealing primarily or only with the implications of the positive transference.

man who had been analysed adopted an antagonistic attitude to his analyst and reproached him for having neglected to complete the analysis. The analyst, he said, ought to have known and to have taken account of the fact that a transference-relation could never be merely positive; he ought to have considered the possibilities of a negative transference. The analyst justified himself by saying that, at the time of the analysis, there was no sign of a negative transference. But, even supposing that he had failed to observe some slight indication of it, which was quite possible considering the limitations of analysis in those early days, it was still doubtful, he thought, whether he would have been able to activate a psychical theme or, as we say, a 'complex', by merely indicating it to the patient, so long as it was not at that moment an actuality to him. Such activation would certainly have necessitated real unfriendly behaviour on the

analyst's part. And, he added, every happy relation
between an analyst and the subject of his analysis,
during and after analysis, was not to be regarded
as transference; there were friendly relations with
a real basis, which were capable of persisting.

I now pass on to my second example, which
raises the same problem. A girl who had left her
childhood behind her had, since puberty, been cut
off from life by an inability to walk, owing to acute
pain in her legs. Her condition was obviously
hysterical in character and it had resisted various
kinds of treatment. After an analysis lasting nine
months the trouble disappeared and the patient,
whose character was truly sound and estimable,
was able once more to take her place in life. In the
years following her recovery she was consistently
unfortunate: there were disasters in her family,
they lost their money and, as she grew older, she
saw every hope of happiness in love and marriage
vanish. But this woman, who had formerly been
an invalid, stood her ground valiantly and in difficult times was a support to her people. I cannot
remember whether it was twelve or fourteen years
after the end of her analysis that she had to undergo a gynaecological examination on account of
profuse haemorrhages. A myoma was discovered
which made a complete hysterectomy advisable.
From the time that this operation took place she
relapsed into neurosis. She fell in love with the
surgeon and was overwhelmed by masochistic
phantasies of the dreadful internal changes which
had taken place in her—phantasies in which she
disguised her romance. She proved inaccessible to
a further attempt at analysis, and to the end of her
life she remained abnormal. The successful analytic treatment took place so long ago that we
could not expect too much from it; it was in the
first years of my work as an analyst. It is no doubt
possible that the patient's second neurosis sprang
from the same root as the first, which had been
successfully overcome, and that it was a different

manifestation of repressed tendencies which the analysis had only partially resolved. But I am inclined to think that, but for the fresh trauma, there would have been no second outbreak of neurosis.

These two cases, purposely selected from a large number of similar ones, will suffice to set going a discussion of the problems we are considering. The sceptical, the optimistic and the ambitious will draw very different conclusions from them. Sceptics will say that they prove that even a successful analysis does not prevent the patient who is cured for the time being from subsequently developing another neurosis, or even a neurosis springing from the same instinctual root, that is to say, from a recurrence of his former trouble. The others will maintain that this is not proved. They will object that both the cases I have cited date from the early days of analysis, twenty and thirty years ago, respectively, and that since then we have acquired deeper insight and wider knowledge and, in adapting our technique to our new discoveries, we have modified it in many respects. Today, they will argue, we may demand and expect that an analytic cure shall be permanent or, at least, that, if a patient falls ill again, his fresh neurosis shall not turn out to be a revival of his earlier instinctual disturbance, manifesting itself in a new guise. Our experience, they will say, is not such that we must limit so severely the demands which we may legitimately make upon psychoanalytic therapy.

Now, of course, my reason for selecting these particular cases as illustrations was precisely that they date so far back. It is obvious that the more recent the result of an analysis the less valuable is it for our theoretical discussion since we have no means of predicting what will happen later to a patient who has been cured. Clearly the expectations of the optimist presuppose a number of things which are not exactly a matter of course. In the first place he assumes that it is really possible to resolve an instinctual conflict (or, more accurately), a conflict between the ego and an instinct finally and for all time. Secondly, that when we are dealing with one such conflict in a patient, we can as it were, inoculate him against the possibility of any other instinctual conflicts in the future. ▪ 11 And thirdly, that we have the power, for purposes of prophylaxis, to stir up a pathogenic conflict of this sort, when at the moment there is no indication of it, and that it is wise to do so. I merely suggest these questions: I do not propose to answer them now. In any case a definite answer is perhaps not possible at the present time. ▪ 12

Probably some light may be thrown on the subject from the theoretical standpoint. But already another point has become clear: if we wish to fulfil the more exacting demands which are now made upon therapeutic analysis, we shall not shorten its duration whether as a means or an end.

[Sections III through VII of this paper have been omitted.]

▪ 11

The question of inoculating a patient against the possibility of further difficulties is a central issue in analytic teatment. One can say that some version of the idea of inoculation is necessarily present in psycho-analytic treatment. For analysis to be a different treatment than other therapies one would have to say that it is able to resolve more widespread issues than would other treatment modalities. It would also help the patient deal with circumstances later in his life that he would not have been able to handle as well without prior treatment. This is an important question today in evaluating psychoanalytic or psychodynamic treatments and comparing these treatments with either short-term or behavioral modalities.

▪ 12

Here Freud is considering again the issue that he has brought up in relation to his treatment of Ferenczi. Ferenczi chastised Freud for not analyzing the negative transference, and Freud's answer was how is it possible to analyze something that doesn't make an appearance in the course of the analysis? Freud was not considering in this answer the brief (although intense) nature of the analysis. It is difficult, of course, to think about this point in relation to Freud's dis-

cussion, since the reader doesn't know that the first patient that he refers to is Ferenczi. Today, since analytic treatments are a good deal longer, it certainly would be possible to see a wider range of issues appear than was the case with Ferenczi or a good many of the patients that Freud saw in treatment. Therefore, the issue of having to stir up a patient's conflict(s) is somewhat less pressing today than it was to Freud who conducted many relatively short treatments (Ferenczi was only one example).

VIII

Both in therapeutic and character-analyses we are struck by the prominence of two themes which give the analyst an extraordinary amount of trouble. It soon becomes clear that some general principle is at work here. These two themes are connected with the difference between the sexes: one is characteristic of men and the other equally characteristic of women. In spite of the difference in their content there is an obvious correspondence between the two. Some factor common to both sexes is forced, by the difference between them, to express itself differently in the one and in the other.

The two corresponding themes are, in women, envy for the penis—the striving after the possession of a male genital—and, in men, the struggle against their passive or feminine attitude towards other men. What is common to these two themes was singled out by early psycho-analytic nomenclature as an attitude to the castration complex. Subsequently Alfred Adler brought the term 'masculine protest' into current use. It fits the case of men perfectly; but I think that, from the first, 'repudiation of femininity' would have been the correct description of this remarkable feature in the psychical life of mankind.

Supposing that we now try to introduce this notion into the structure of psycho-analytical theory we shall find that, by its very nature, this factor cannot occupy the same place in the case of both sexes. In males the masculine striving is from the beginning and throughout entirely ego-syntonic; the passive attitude, since it implies an acceptance of castration, is energetically repressed, and often the only indications of its existence are exaggerated over-compensations. In females also the striving after masculinity is ego-syntonic at a certain period, namely, in the phallic phase, before development in the direction of femininity has set in. But later it succumbs to that momentous process of repression, the outcome of which (as has often been pointed out) determines the fortunes of the woman's femininity. A great deal depends upon whether a sufficient amount of her masculinity-complex escapes repression and exercises a lasting influence on her character. Normally, large portions of that complex undergo transformation and contribute to the development of femininity: the unsatisfied wish for a penis should be converted into a wish for a child and for a man, who possesses a penis. Very often indeed, however, we find that the wish for masculinity persists in the unconscious and, in its repressed state, exercises a disturbing influence.

As is plain from what has just been said, in both cases it is the attitude belonging to the sex opposite to the subject's own which succumbs to repression. I have stated elsewhere[13] that it was Wilhelm Fliess who called my attention to this point. Fliess was inclined to regard the difference between the sexes as the true cause and original motive of repression. I can only repeat that I do not accept this view: I do not think we are justified in sexualizing repression in this way—that is to say, in explaining it on a biological instead of a purely psychological basis.

The paramount importance of these two themes—the wish for a penis in women and, in men, the struggle against passivity—did not escape the notice of Ferenczi. In the paper that he read in 1927 he laid it down as a principle that in every successful analysis these two complexes must have been resolved.[14] From my own expe-

[13] '"A Child Is Being Beaten"' (1919), Collected Papers, 2, 172.
[14] '. . . in every male patient the sign that his castration-anxiety has been mastered must be forthcoming, and this sign is a sense of equality of rights with the analyst; and every female patient, if her cure is to rank as complete and permanent, must have finally conquered her masculinity-complex and become able to submit without bitterness to thinking in terms of her feminine role.' (Ferenczi, 1928, 8.)

rience I would observe that in this I think Ferenczi was asking a very great deal. At no point in one's analytic work does one suffer more from the oppressive feeling that all one's efforts have been in vain and from the suspicion that one is 'talking to the winds' than when one is trying to persuade a female patient to abandon her wish for a penis on the ground of its being unrealizable, or to convince a male patient that a passive attitude towards another man does not always signify castration and that in many relations in life it is indispensable. The rebellious over-compensation of the male produces one of the strongest transference-resistances. A man will not be subject to a father-substitute or owe him anything and he therefore refuses to accept his cure from the physician. There is no analogous form of transference which can arise from the feminine wish for a penis, but it is the source of attacks of acute depression, because women patients feel an inner conviction that the analysis will avail them nothing and that they will be none the better for it. We can only agree with them when we discover that their strongest motive in coming for treatment was the hope that they might somehow still obtain a male organ, the lack of which is so painful to them.

All this shows that the form of the resistance is immaterial: it does not matter whether it appears as a transference or not. The vital point is that it prevents any change from taking place—everything remains as it was. We often feel that, when we have reached the wish for a penis and the masculine protest, we have penetrated all the psychological strata and reached 'bedrock' and that our task is accomplished. And this is probably correct, for in the psychical field the biological factor is really the rock-bottom. The repudiation of femininity must surely be a biological fact, part of the great riddle of sex.[15] Whether and when we have succeeded in mastering this factor in an anal-

ysis is hard to determine. We must console ourselves with the certainty that everything possible
has been done to encourage the patient to examine
and to change his attitude to the question. ▪ 13

▪ 13

Freud's view of penis envy and
indeed his later view of the
centrality of the phallic stage in
human development are questioned today by many analysts.
One can say that classical analysts are classical in the sense
that they agree with this theoretical formulation of Freud's as
opposed to practicing analysis
in the way that Freud practiced
or prescribed. We can see that
Freud's criteria for reaching the
termination phase of analysis
are theoretical ones; when the
patient has understood the
basic or core conflicts, then at
that point the analysis is complete. If one accepts this formulation, then one can have definite criteria for the termination
phase of analysis. For one to
consider this as the appropriate
signpost, one would have to be
quite confident about the theory he was espousing. Today,
with the amount of emphasis
on preoedipal deficits or conflicts, it is possible to say only
that the criterion for termination of analysis must to some
extent be independent of one's
theoretical position. That is, it
should be possible to say that
the patient will have certain
changes in affect or perceptions
or behavior as criteria for analytic change and termination.

---

[15]We must not be misled by the term 'masculine protest' into
supposing that what the man repudiates is the *attitude* of
passivity, or, as we may say, the social aspect of femininity.
Such a notion is speedily contradicted by the observation that
the attitude such men display towards women is often masochistic or actually slavish. What they reject is not passivity in
general but passivity in relation to *men*. That is to say, the
'masculine protest' is in fact nothing other than fear of castration.

Constructions in Analysis[1]

(1937)

I

It has always seemed to me to be greatly to the credit of a certain well-known man of science that he treated psycho-analysis fairly at a time when most other people felt themselves under no such obligation. On one occasion, nevertheless, he gave expression to an opinion upon analytic technique which was at once derogatory and unjust. He said that in giving interpretations to a patient we treat him upon the famous principle of 'Heads I win, tails you lose'. That is to say, if the patient agrees with us, then the interpretation is right; but if he contradicts us, that is only a sign of his resistance, which again shows that we are right. In this way we are always in the right against the poor help-

[1]['Konstruktionen in der Analyse.' First published *Int. Z. Psychoanal.*, 23 (1937), 459; reprinted *Ges. W.*, 16. Translation, reprinted from *Int. J. Psycho-Anal.*, 19 (1938), 377, by James Strachey.]

less wretch whom we are analysing, no matter how he may respond to what we put forward. ▪ 14 Now, since it is in fact true that a 'No' from one of our patients is not as a rule enough to make us abandon an interpretation as incorrect, a revelation such as this of the nature of our technique has been most welcome to the opponents of analysis. It is therefore worth while to give a detailed account of how we are accustomed to arrive at an assessment of the 'Yes' or 'No' of our patients during analytic treatment—of their expression of agreement or of denial. The practising analyst will naturally learn nothing in the course of this apologia that he does not already know.

It is familiar ground that the work of analysis aims at inducing the patient to give up the repressions (using the word in the widest sense) belonging to his early life and to replace them by reactions of a sort that would correspond better to a psychically mature condition. It is with this purpose in view that he must be got to recollect certain experiences and the emotions called up by them which he has at the moment forgotten. We know that his present symptoms and inhibitions are the consequences of repressions of this kind: that is, that they are a substitute for these things that he has forgotten. What sort of material does he put at our disposal which we can make use of to put him on the way to recovering the lost memories? All kinds of things. He gives us fragments of these memories in his dreams, invaluable in themselves but seriously distorted as a rule by all the factors concerned in the formation of dreams. Again, he produces ideas, if he gives himself up to 'free association', in which we can discover allusions to the repressed experiences and derivatives of the suppressed emotions as well as of the reactions against them. And, finally, there are hints of repetitions of the affects belonging to the repressed material to be found in actions performed by the patient, some important, some trivial, both

▪ 14
This type of comment has been made persistently up to the present day. Philosophers like Hook and Nagel as well as modern philosophers such as Wisdom have made similar comments.

inside and outside the analytic situation. Our experience has shown that the relation of transference, which becomes established towards the analyst, is particularly calculated to favour the reproduction of these emotional connections. It is out of such raw material—if we may so describe it—that we have to put together what we are in search of.

What we are in search of is a picture of the patient's forgotten years that shall be alike trustworthy and in all essential respects complete. But at this point we are reminded that the work of analysis consists of two quite different portions, that it is carried on in two separate localities, that it involves two people, to each of whom a distinct task is assigned. It may for a moment seem strange that such a fundamental fact should not have been pointed out long ago; but it will immediately be perceived that there was nothing being kept back in this, that it is a fact which is universally known and even self-evident and is merely being brought into relief here and separately examined for a particular purpose. We all know that the person who is being analysed has to be induced to remember something that has been experienced by him and repressed; and the dynamic determinants of this process are so interesting that the other portion of the work, the task performed by the analyst, has been pushed into the background. The analyst has neither experienced nor repressed any of the material under consideration; his task cannot be to remember anything. What then *is* his task? His task is to make out what has been forgotten from the traces which it has left behind or, more correctly, to *construct* it. The time and manner in which he conveys his constructions to the person who is being analysed, as well as the explanations with which he accompanies them, constitute the link between the two portions of the work of analysis, between his own part and that of the patient.

His work of construction, or, if it is preferred, of reconstruction, resembles to a great extent an archaeologist's excavation of some dwelling-place that has been destroyed and buried or of some ancient edifice. The two processes are in fact identical, except that the analyst works under better conditions and has more material at his command to assist him, since what he is dealing with is not something destroyed but something that is still alive—and perhaps for another reason as well. But just as the archaeologist builds up the walls of the building from the foundations that have remained standing, determines the number and position of the columns from depressions in the floor and reconstructs the mural decorations and paintings from the remains found in the débris, so does the analyst proceed when he draws his inferences from the fragments of memories, from the associations and from the behaviour of the subject of the analysis. Both of them have an undisputed right to reconstruct by means of supplementing and combining the surviving remains. Both of them, moreover, are subject to many of the same difficulties and sources of error. One of the most ticklish problems that confronts the archaeologist is notoriously the determination of the relative age of his finds; and if an object makes its appearance in some particular level, it often remains to be decided whether it belongs to that level or whether it was carried down to that level owing to some subsequent disturbance. It is easy to imagine the corresponding doubts that arise in the case of analytic constructions.

The analyst, as we have said, works under more favourable conditions than the archaeologist since he has at his disposal material which can have no counterpart in excavations, such as the repetitions of reactions dating from infancy and all that emerges in connection with these repetitions through the transference. But in addition to this it must be borne in mind that the excavator is dealing with destroyed objects of which large and important portions have quite certainly been lost, by mechanical violence, by fire and by plundering. No amount of effort can result in their discovery and lead to their being united with the surviving fragments. The one and only course left open is that of reconstruction, which for this very reason can often reach only a certain degree of probability. But it is different with the psychical object whose early history the analyst is seeking to recover. Here we are regularly met by a situation which in archaeology occurs only in such rare circumstances as those of Pompeii or of the tomb of Tutankhamen. All of the essentials are preserved, even things that seem completely forgotten are present somehow and somewhere, and have merely been buried and made inaccessible to the subject. Indeed, it may, as we know, be doubted whether any psychical structure can really be the victim of total destruction. It depends only upon analytic technique whether we shall succeed in bringing what is concealed completely to light. There are only two other facts that weigh against the extraordinary advantage which is thus enjoyed by the work of analysis: namely, that psychical objects are incomparably more complicated than the excavator's material ones and that we have insufficient knowledge of what we may expect to find, since their finer structure contains so much that is still mysterious. But our comparison between the two forms of work can go no further than this; for the main difference between them lies in the fact that for the archaeologist the reconstruction is the aim and end of his endeavours while for analysis the construction is only a preliminary labour.

II

It is not, however, a preliminary labour in the sense that the whole of it must be completed before the next piece of work can be begun, as, for instance, is the case with house-building, where all the walls must be erected and all the windows inserted before the internal decorations of the rooms can be taken in hand. Every analyst knows that things happen differently in an analytic treatment and that there both kinds of work are carried on side by side, the one kind being always a little ahead and the other following upon it. The analyst finishes a piece of construction and communicates it to the subject of the analysis so that it may work upon him; he then constructs a further piece out of the fresh material pouring in upon him, deals with it in the same way and proceeds in this alternating fashion until the end. If, in accounts of analytic technique, so little is said about 'constructions', that is because 'interpretations' and their effects are spoken of instead. But I think that 'construction' is by far the more appropriate description. 'Interpretation' applies to something that one does to some single element of the material, such as an association or a parapraxis. But it is a 'construction' when one lays before the subject of the analysis a piece of his early history that he has forgotten, in some such way as this: 'Up to your nth year you regarded yourself as the sole and unlimited possessor of your mother; then came another baby and brought you grave disillusionment. Your mother left you for some time, and even after her reappearance she was never again devoted to you exclusively. Your feelings towards your mother became ambivalent, your father gained a new importance for you,' . . . and so on.

In the present paper our attention will be turned exclusively to this preliminary labour performed by constructions. And here, at the very start, the question arises of what guarantee we have while we are working on these constructions that we are not making mistakes and risking the success of the treatment by putting forward some construction that is incorrect. It may seem that no general reply can in any event be given to this question; but even before discussing it we may lend our ear to some comforting information that is afforded by analytic experience. For we learn from it that no damage is done if, for once in a way, we make a mistake and offer the patient a wrong construction as the probable historic truth. ■ 15 A waste of time is, of course, involved, and anyone who does nothing but present the patient with false combinations will neither create a very good impression on him nor carry the treatment very far; but a single mistake of the sort can do no harm. What in fact occurs in such an event is rather that the patient remains as though he were untouched by what has been said and reacts to it with neither a 'Yes' nor a 'No'. This may possibly mean no more than that his reaction is postponed; but if nothing further develops we may conclude that we have made a mistake and we shall admit as much to the patient at some suitable opportunity without sacrificing any of our authority. Such an opportunity will arise when some new material has come to light which allows us to make a better construction and at the same time to correct our error. In this way the false construction drops out, as if it had never been made; and, indeed, we often get an impression as though, to borrow the words of Polonius, our bait of falsehood had taken a carp of truth. The danger of our leading a patient astray by suggestion, by persuading him to accept things which we ourselves believe but which he ought not to, has certainly been enormously exaggerated. An analyst would have had to behave very incorrectly before such a misfortune could overtake him; above all, he would have to blame himself with not allowing his patients to have their say. I can assert without boasting that such an abuse of 'suggestion' has never occurred in my practice. ■ 16

It already follows from what has been said that we are not at all inclined to neglect the indications that can be inferred from the patient's reac-

■ 15
Freud's position on mistaken constructions is one that has many aspects. He seems relaxed about the possibility of mistaken constructions and seems to imply that occasional mistakes will be tolerated by the patient. One assumes that Freud's position is the same for mistaken interpretations as it is for constructions. Whether one agrees with Freud's position or not may well depend on both the type of patient one is considering as well as the point in treatment that is under discussion. At some phases in the analysis patients may well be tolerant of false leads, but at other times patients may well be intolerant of any mistakes and even find correct interpretations objectionable. Freud might consider these patients unanalyzable but this should be an empirical question. One might ask whether under some conditions a variety of patients are analyzable? It may be that one of those conditions is that the analyst be circumspect with both interpretations and constructions. Kohut, for instance, talks about the difficulty that certain narcissistic patients have in the early parts of treatment when the analyst interprets. Bach has made similar points. Glover in an early

■ 15 *continued*
paper on inexact interpretation
has a more severe attitude toward mistaken interpretations
than Freud does in the preceding paragraphs.

■ 16
Freud's assertion depends on
how one views the issue of sug-

gestion. In the case of the Wolf
Man, one may consider that the
setting of a termination date is
a strong suggestion both to
produce certain types of material and to associate
appropriately to this material.

tion when we have offered him one of our constructions. The point must be gone into in detail.
It is true that we do not accept the 'No' of a person
under analysis at its face value; but neither do we
allow his 'Yes' to pass. There is no justification for
accusing us of invariably twisting his remarks into
an assent. In reality things are not so simple and
we do not make it so easy for ourselves to come to
a conclusion.

A plain 'Yes' from a patient is by no means
unambiguous. It can indeed signify that he recognizes the correctness of the construction that has
been presented to him; but it can also be meaningless, or can even deserve to be described as
'hypocritical', since it may be convenient for his
resistance to make use of an assent in such circumstances in order to prolong the concealment of a
truth that has not been discovered. The 'Yes' has
no value unless it is followed by indirect confirmations, unless the patient, immediately after his
'Yes', produces new memories which complete and
extend the construction. Only in such an event do
we consider that the 'Yes' has dealt completely
with the subject under discussion.

A 'No' from a person in analysis is no more
unambiguous than a 'Yes', and is indeed of even
less value. In some rare cases it turns out to be the
expression of a legitimate dissent. Far more frequently it expresses a resistance which may have
been evoked by the subject-matter of the construction that has been put forward but which may just
as easily have arisen from some other factor in the

complex analytic situation. Thus, a patient's 'No'
is no evidence of the correctness of a construction,
though it is perfectly compatible with it. Since
every such construction is an incomplete one, since
it covers only a small fragment of the forgotten
events, we are free to suppose that the patient is
not in fact disputing what has been said to him but
is basing his contradiction upon the part that has
not yet been discovered. As a rule he will not give
his assent until he has learnt the whole truth—
which often covers a very great deal of ground. So
that the only safe interpretation of his 'No' is that
it points to incompleteness; there can be no doubt
that the construction has not told him everything.

It appears, therefore, that the direct utterances of the patient after he has been offered a
construction afford very little evidence upon the
question whether we have been right or wrong. It
is of all the greater interest that there are indirect
forms of confirmation which are in every respect
trustworthy. One of these is a form of words that
is used (almost as though there were a conspiracy)
with very little variation by the most different
people: 'I've never thought (or, I should never
have thought) that (or, of that).' This can be translated without any hesitation into: 'Yes, you're right
this time—about my *unconscious.*' Unfortunately
this formula which is so welcome to the analyst,
reaches his ears more often after single interpretations than after he has produced an extensive
construction. An equally valuable confirmation is
implied (expressed this time positively) when the
patient answers with an association which contains something similar or analogous to the subject-matter of the construction. Instead of taking
an example of this from an analysis (which would
be easy to find but lengthy to describe) I prefer to
give an account of a small extra-analytical experience which presents a similar situation so strik-
ingly that it produces an almost comic effect. It
concerned one of my colleagues who—it was long

ago—had chosen me as a consultant in his medical practice. One day, however, he brought his young wife to see me, as she was causing him trouble. She refused on all sorts of pretexts to have sexual relations with him, and what he expected of me was evidently that I should lay before her the consequences of her ill-advised behaviour. I went into the matter and explained to her that her refusal would probably have unfortunate results for her husband's health or would lay him open to temptations that might lead to a break-up of their marriage. At this point he suddenly interrupted me with the remark: 'The Englishman you diagnosed as suffering from a cerebral tumour has died too.' At first the remark seemed incomprehensible; the 'too' in his sentence was a mystery, for we had not been speaking of anyone else who had died. But a short time afterwards I understood. The man was evidently intending to confirm what I had been saying; he was meaning to say: 'Yes, you're certainly quite right. Your diagnosis was confirmed in the case of the other patient too.' It was an exact parallel to the indirect confirmations that we obtain in analysis from associations. I will not attempt to deny that there were other thoughts as well, put on one side by my colleague, which had a share in determining his remark.

Indirect confirmation from associations that fit in with the content of a construction—that give us a 'too' like the one in my story—provide a valuable basis for judging whether the construction is likely to be confirmed in the course of the analysis. It is particularly striking when a confirmation of this kind slips into a direct denial by means of a parapraxis. I once published elsewhere a nice example of this[2] The name 'Jauner' (a familiar one in Vienna) came up repeatedly in one of my patient's dreams without a sufficient explana-

---

[2][In Chapter V of *Zur Psychopathologie des Alltagslebens* (1904) (not included in the English translation of 1914).]

tion appearing in his associations. I finally put forward the interpretation that when he said 'Jauner' he probably meant 'Gauner' [swindler], whereupon he promptly replied: 'That seems to me too "jewagt" [instead of "gewagt" (far-fetched)].' Or there was the other instance, in which, when I suggested to a patient that he considered a particular fee too high, he meant to deny the suggestion with the words 'Ten dollars mean nothing to me' but instead of dollars put in a coin of lower denomination and said 'ten shillings'.

If an analysis is dominated by powerful factors that impose a negative therapeutic reaction, such as a sense of guilt, a masochistic need for suffering or a striving against receiving help from the analyst, the patient's behaviour after he has been offered a construction often makes it very easy for us to arrive at the decision that we are in search of. If the construction is wrong, there is no change in the patient; but if it is right or gives an approximation to the truth, he reacts to it with an unmistakable aggravation of his symptoms and of his general condition.

We may sum the matter up by asserting that there is no justification for the reproach that we neglect or underestimate the importance of the attitude taken up by those under analysis towards our constructions. ■ 17 We pay attention to them and often derive valuable information from them. But these reactions on the part of the patient are rarely unambiguous and give no opportunity for a final judgement. Only the further course of the analysis enables us to decide upon the correctness or uselessness of our constructions. We do not pretend that an individual construction is anything more than a conjecture which awaits examination, confirmation or rejection. We claim no authority for it, we require no direct agreement from the patient, nor do we argue with him if at first he denies it. In short, we conduct ourselves upon the model of a familiar figure in one of

■ 17
Freud's idea of indirect associations or confirmation of interpretations is an interesting and potentially testable idea. In fact, there have been some attempts to empirically study the effects of interpretation that lend some credence to Freud's examples and general views.

Nestroy's farces—the man-servant who has a single answer on his lips to every question or objection: 'All will become clear in the course of future developments.'

III

It is hardly worth while describing how this occurs in the process of the analysis—the way in which our conjecture is transformed into the patient's conviction. All of this is familiar to every analyst from his daily experience and is intelligible without difficulty. Only one point requires investigation and explanation. The path that starts from the analyst's construction ought to end in the patient's recollection; but it does not always lead so far. Quite often we do not succeed in bringing the patient to recollect what has been repressed. Instead of that, if the analysis is carried out correctly, we produce in him an assured conviction of the truth of the construction which achieves the same therapeutic result as a recaptured memory. The problem of what the circumstances are in which this occurs and of how it is possible that what appears to be an incomplete substitute should nevertheless produce a complete result—all of this is material for a later enquiry.

I shall conclude this brief paper with a few remarks which open up a wider perspective. I have been struck by the manner in which, in certain analyses, the communication of an obviously apt construction has evoked in the patients a surprising and at first incomprehensible phenomenon. They have had lively recollections called up in them—which they themselves have described as 'unnaturally distinct'—but what they have recollected has not been the event that was the subject of the construction but details relating to that subject. For instance, they have recollected with abnormal sharpness the faces of the people involved in the construction or the rooms in which something of the sort might have happened, or, a step further away, the furniture in such rooms—on the subject of which the construction had naturally no possibility of any knowledge. This has occurred both in dreams immediately after the construction had been put forward and in waking states in the nature of a day-dream. These recollections have themselves led to nothing further and it has seemed plausible to regard them as the product of a compromise. The 'upward drive' of the repressed, stirred into activity by the putting forward of the construction, has striven to carry the important memory-traces into consciousness; but a resistance has succeeded—not, it is true, in *stopping* that movement—but in *displacing* it on to adjacent objects of minor significance.

These recollections might have been described as hallucinations if a belief in their actual presence had been added to their clearness. The importance of this analogy seemed greater when I noticed that true hallucinations occasionally occurred in the case of other patients who were certainly not psychotic. My line of thought proceeded as follows. Perhaps it may be a general characteristic of hallucinations to which sufficient attention has not hitherto been paid that in them something that has been experienced in infancy and then forgotten re-emerges—something that the child has seen or heard at a time when he could still hardly speak and that now forces its way into consciousness, probably distorted and displaced owing to the operation of forces that are opposed to this re-emergence. And, in view of the close relation between hallucinations and particular forms of psychosis, our line of thought may be carried still further. It may be that the delusions into which these hallucinations are so constantly incorporated may themselves be less independent of the upward drive of the unconscious and the return of the repressed than we usually assume. In the mechanism of a delusion we stress as a rule only two factors: the turning away from the real world and its forces on the one hand and the influence exercised by wish-fulfilment upon the subject-matter of the delusion on the other. But may it not be that the dynamic process is rather that the turning away from reality is exploited by the upward drive of the repressed in order to force its subject-matter into consciousness, while the resistances stirred up by this process and the impulse to wish-fulfilment share the responsibility for the distortion and displacement of what is recollected? This is after all the familiar mechanism of dreams, which intuition has equated with madness from time immemorial.

This view of delusions is not, I think, entirely new, but it nevertheless emphasizes a point of view which is not usually brought into the foreground. The essence of it is that there is not only *method* in madness, as the poet has already perceived, but also a fragment of historic truth; and it is plausible to suppose that the compulsive belief attaching to delusions derives its strength precisely from infantile sources of this kind. All that I can produce to-day in support of this theory are reminiscences, not fresh impressions. It would probably be worth while to make an attempt to study cases of the disorder in question on the basis of the hypotheses that have been here put forward and also to carry out their treatment upon the same lines. The vain effort would be abandoned of convincing the patient of the error of his delusion and of its contradiction of reality; and, on the contrary, the recognition of its kernel of truth would afford common ground upon which the therapeutic process could develop. ■ 18 That process would consist in liberating the fragment of historic truth from its distortions and its attachments to the actual present day and in leading it back to the point in the past to which it belongs. The transposing of material from a forgotten past on to the present or on to an expectation of the

■ 18

Although it may be true that Freud's views on hallucinations may not be entirely new, it does show how even at an advanced age he was still contemplating how to understand the meaning of phenomena that

■ 18 *continued*

many other people had found completely inexplicable or meaningless. His advice about not contradicting the patient's view but rather finding some common ground on which to communicate is, to me at least, remarkably contemporary in its outlook. In some way, a number of current theorists including Kohut, Gedo, and Winnicott, to name just a few, are attempting to find common ground on which to communi-cate to patients who have frequently been considered unanalyzable. Freud, in Bach's terms, has perhaps talked about one way to enter a patient's world without making the patient feel extremely vulnerable or criticized. It is interesting at this late date in Freud's career that he would take this view particularly in relation to psychotic patients, since he found this type of patient so difficult to treat.

future is indeed a habitual occurrence in neurotics no less than in psychotics. Often enough, when a neurotic is led by an anxiety-state to expect the occurrence of some terrible event, he is in fact merely under the influence of a repressed memory (which is seeking to enter consciousness but cannot become conscious) that something which was at that time terrifying did really happen. I believe that we should gain a great deal of valuable knowledge from work of this kind upon psychotics even if it led to no therapeutic success.

I am aware that it is of small service to handle so important a subject in the cursory fashion that I have here employed. But none the less I have not been able to resist the seduction of an analogy. The delusions of patients appear to me to be the equivalents of the constructions which we build up in the course of an analytic treatment—attempts at explanation and cure, though it is true that these, under the conditions of a psychosis, can do no more than replace the fragment of reality that is being repudiated in the present by another fragment that had already been repudiated in the remote past. It will be the task of each individual investigation to reveal the intimate connections between the material of the present repudiation and that of the original repression. Just as our construction is only effective because it recovers a fragment of lost experience, so the delusion owes its convincing power to the element of historic truth which it inserts in the place of the rejected reality. In this way a proposition which I originally asserted only of hysteria would apply also to delusions—namely, that those who are subject to them are suffering from their own recollections. I never intended by this short formula to dispute the complexity of the causation of the illness or to exclude the operation of many other factors.

If we consider mankind as a whole and substitute it for the single human individual, we discover that it too has developed delusions which are inaccessible to logical criticism and which contradict reality. If, in spite of this, they are able to exert an extraordinary power over men, investigation leads us to the same explanation as in the case of the single individual. They owe their power to the element of historic truth which they have brought up from the repression of the forgotten and primaeval past.

13

Contemporary Views of Termination

Although Freud wrote about endings in analysis, he was not primarily concerned with what contemporary analysts have designated as the termination phase of treatment. Freud does point out that there are not always mutual terminations in analyses, but his interest is in understanding the obstacles that are frequently encountered in the analytic situation. Contemporary analysts have attempted more generally to study the way analyses end.

Jack Novick

Novick relates that mutually agreed-upon terminations are the exception in modern analytic treatment.[1] In a review of the termination phase of treatment (1982) he brings up six major termination issues:

1. He provides categories of terminations.

2. He discusses the goals of treatment, since the idea of a mutually agreed-upon termination implies that the objectives of treatment have been reached.

3. Since Novick (and others) consider there to be a terminal phase in analysis, he has to state criteria that can allow us to identify this phase of treatment. He also is interested in the preconditions that allow one to enter and successfully traverse the terminal phase.

4. If one can specify all of the above, then it is possible to ask some practical questions about this phase of treatment: for example, how is the date for termination set, and by whom is it brought up (by the analyst or analysand) or is it somehow a mutual process?

[1]This is a position that Freud certainly would agree with in "Analysis Terminable and Interminable."

5. During the termination phase, various analysts have reported that the patient's original symptoms reappear as a normal aspect of the analytic process. Novick questions this interpretation. It is also observed that analysands typically mourn the loss of the analyst in the termination phase of treatment. The factors determining these reactions is a question that Novick considers.

6. Novick, as a last point, reviews some issues that involve the patient (or ex-patient) after analysis. Various analysts have argued that major changes frequently occur after the treatment has ended. They have come to regard this as a normal aspect of the treatment. Novick raises some interesting questions regarding this interpretation of postanalytic change.

NOVICK ON SOME DEFINITIONS IN THE TERMINAL PHASE

Novick's review begins with consideration of the question of premature termination. This type of termination is divided into two clearly defined categories. Those that are decided on by the analyst are designated *forced terminations*, whereas those initiated by the patient are labeled *unilateral terminations*. Forced terminations may occur because the analyst moves away, contracts a prolonged illness, becomes pregnant, or even dies. Grouped with these reasons are the more common analytic issues, "a premature decision made by the analyst for countertransference reasons, such as dealing with entrenched preoedipal transference situations, especially those of the sadomasochistic kind, or dealing with seemingly interminable patients" (Novick 1982, p. 330). Similarly, unilateral terminations include such divergent factors as "geographic moves or physical illness, to intensive resistances to the transference" (Novick 1982, p. 330). Although the problem of premature terminations is certainly not limited to analytic treatment or to psychological treatments, there are obviously important reasons to understand the difficulties in the path of mutually agreed-upon terminations.[2]

A conclusion that Novick draws in his review is that the percentage of premature terminations is underestimated. For example, reviewing eight cases that Firestein presents in his book on termination (1978), Novick relates that, whereas Firestein refers to only one of the eight cases as a premature (forced) termination, in reading through the summaries it becomes evident (to Novick) that six others were prematurely terminated or forced by the analyst, and one termination was based on a unilateral decision by the patient.

---

[2]Part of the difficulty in understanding the reasons for premature terminations may lie in the way analysts conceive of or at least label the issue. The word *premature* in this context has a negative implication that colors the whole issue of the validity or success of the treatment in question. If a patient terminates prematurely, is it possible to think of the treatment as anything but a failure?

It is not our intention to reconcile these two markedly different views of these cases but only to comment on one possible reason for this strong disagreement. In making this assertion, Novick wasn't saying that these were poorly conducted analyses, but nevertheless, this is the common inference that many readers would make.[3] In his last articles, Freud attempts to say that the idea of successful mutual termination is perhaps a myth, yet his words are dismissed by many as a statement by the founder of a field who did not have the benefit of viewing modern developments in psychoanalysis. Perhaps we should say that the mutual termination is an ideal (like any other analytic standard) and that it should not be considered a necessary precondition for success in the analytic situation. If we do that, it may reduce the pressure on analysts to report that their cases were mutually terminated. I am suggesting that one possible reason for the above discrepancy is that analysts are reluctant to report premature terminations, since this implies a failed analysis.

ASSESSING CRITERIA FOR SUCCESS

Let us go back to Novick's statements and assume that he is warranted in his assumptions about Firestein's cases. Are we correct in proposing that if a case is prematurely terminated it can be a successful analysis? Before one can entertain such a question, there would have to be some statement of the criteria for analytic success. Once this question is broached, we see that we have entered into one of the murkiest of analytic regions. Freud's early criteria were seemingly straightforward; if the patient's symptoms were removed or dissipated, then the treatment could be considered a success. When Freud began to make pronouncements about making the unconscious conscious, or expanding the domain of the ego (in the structural model), he implicitly stated goals for analytic treatment that are difficult to unravel. It is hard to specify operational criteria for these statements, although I would venture that most analysts can come up with their own versions of what Freud meant.

Novick reports that, for many modern analysts, self-analysis is an important, if not an overriding, criterion for the success of analytic treatment.[4] Novick sees the roots of this idea in Sterba's discussion (1934) of the fate of the ego in analysis. In this article Sterba implicitly gave criteria for elucidating the concept of ego autonomy at the end of analysis. Hoffer is the first analyst cited as stressing "the importance of identification with the functions of the analyst" (Novick 1982, p. 358). Treatment can be terminated when the analysis can be turned over to the analysand. This idea, while meeting with a good deal of

---

[3]It may be that these analyses were of considerable benefit to the patient but for one reason or another the patient-analyst did not successfully or completely pass through the termination phase of treatment.

[4]Obviously, Freud (like modern analysts) still believed that patients needed to master the issues for which they originally came into analysis, as well as to develop a capacity for self-analysis.

explicit and implicit acceptance, has not stood without some criticism. Brenner sees this goal as one that is more appropriate for analysts-in-training as opposed to patients who are undergoing a purely therapeutic analysis. A number of other analysts have seen this goal as overly ambitious and unrealistic. Novick states that "it is not known to what extent the self-analytic function is retained after analysis or how important it is for the maintenance of the improvement" (1982, p. 358). He also says that "we know from our work with children that many of them can achieve and maintain positive results without developing a self-analytic function" (p. 358). This last statement is to me indicative of the difficulties of discussing this point as well as other related issues in psychoanalysis. We might ask Novick how he knows that children maintain positive results without developing a self-analytic function. We can ask the obvious question about whether he really has done a follow-up study to be able to make this type of empirical statement. More importantly, we can ask how he is conceptualizing the self-analytic function in children. Is it seen as appearing in the same way we would expect it to be manifest in adults? Is it possible that in children this function takes a different form? Is it possible that the analytic results of children are not a good model in a discussion of the psychoanalysis of adults? It is hard to discuss the autonomy of a young child, who is usually still living with his parents, in the same way we can discuss the autonomy of an adult who one hopes can develop a life of his own with the assistance of analytic treatment. Moreover, this brings up a more basic question: How are we conceiving of the self-analytic function in adults? Novick refers to Hoffer, but Hoffer at best gives us a concept of this function. There has been nothing approaching a study of how patients fare who have more self-analytic ability as opposed to patients who have less. It may not even be entirely clear what one would look at in such a study. Perhaps, before we could attempt such a study, we would have to clearly understand what we mean by the self-analyzing function.

We might ask what are the different functions of an analyst that the patient might come to internalize? Clearly, in the literature, most analysts in one way or another refer to the analysand's ability to self-interpret. This follows the premium that Freud and many modern analysts put on the role of insight in the analytic situation. There may, of course, be other functions of the analyst that are of equal importance. A possibility is that patients may internalize different analytic functions depending on what is important in a given analysis. The analyst's equanimity in the face of conflict may be an analytic attitude that is extremely important in the analysand's ability to face his postanalytic conflicts. The analysand may be able to call on this function at times of conflict, but it is questionable whether many analysts would call this a self-analyzing function. When Freud tells us that in analysis we extend the ego's control (over the id), one can imagine that this can be accomplished in a variety of ways. Analysts traditionally have seen the ability to formulate explanations in a verbal mode as the primary avenue of analytic cure and postanalytic prophylaxis. Perhaps we can formulate the goals of analysis in terms of the analysand's ability to be able to internalize, and then voluntarily call on those traits of the analysts that have been curative during the course of the analysis. One of the traits of the analyst may be the ability to formulate the patient's conflicts in verbal terms. This may be the prime trait that needs to be internalized, but other traits can be considered as important. The willingness to consider the patient's problems worthy of detailed consideration may be considered as a preliminary step to understanding the patient's conflicts, or it might with some patients have considerable importance in its own right. A child who is brushed aside and considered only in the context of the parent's needs is introduced to a new world with an analyst who can listen to her difficulties and pain.

Although Novick states that self-analysis is being increasingly emphasized as a goal of treatment, it is clear that he as well as others have some reservations about this goal. The definition of the goal remains to be fully explicated. A full explication of the goal may provide links between adult self-analysis and self-analytic modes in child treatment. As a preliminary step, if we define a goal of analysis as the internalization of those traits of the analyst that help the patient to face and understand his conflicts, we may consider that children do develop some self-analytic abilities after analysis. To state the central point in a more concise form, the difficulties that Novick sees in the goal of self-analysis may be due to a restrictive definition of self-analysis. This restrictive definition may also be related to his notions of the curative aspects of analytic treatment.

BEGINNING THE TERMINAL PHASE

Novick conceives of the preconditions for the terminal phase as being related to what he calls an adolescent pattern of premature termination. The pattern of adolescent-type resistance is in his view a "major resistance to a positive oedipal transference and thus to the start of a terminal phase," which resistance or pattern "must be interpreted before a true termination phase can begin" (Novick 1982, p. 339). The terminal phase is thus seen as a period during which conflicts around positive oedipal themes are manifested.

What is accomplished during the terminal phase of treatment? Most commentators agree that there is no prototypic pattern in this phase although certain themes seem to be commonly expressed. There are, according to Gitelson (1967), more

"good hours" when the therapeutic alliance (E. Ticho 1972) is at its maximum efficiency. The major tasks, as seen by most authors, are those of working through and synthesizing the insights gained (Ekstein 1965), turning insight into effective and lasting action (Greenson 1965), and, most important, doing the work of mourning—the final working through of a separation from the analyst as an object representative of drive derivatives from all levels of development, but especially the *oedipal level* (W. Granatir in Panel, 1975). The major defense during this phase is an attempt to avoid the painful work of mourning either by denying the importance of the analyst as a transference object (for example, by immediately displacing the transference wishes onto another object), or, as is more usual at this phase of treatment, by denying the irrevocability and inevitability of the loss. [Novick 1982, p. 347]

When contemporary analysts use the term "working through," the assumption is that working through is by and large performed during the terminal phase of treatment.[5] The term then connotes a solidification of the work that has been accomplished previously in the analysis, and the insights that have been obtained are translated increasingly into "lasting action." One has, of course, to accept the concept of therapeutic alliance to agree that it is at maximum efficiency, but my reading of the literature is that most authors would agree that that there are more "good hours" during this phase of treatment. Whether or not one agrees that oedipal themes predominate during this phase of treatment in part depends on your view of the etiology of various conflicts. Certainly Brenner would agree with this formulation but probably would not agree with Novick's contention that along with the need to relinquish oedipal themes it is also necessary to relinquish the analyst as an omnipotent and idealized mother (Novick 1982). This is quite a different formulation and there is an assumption that in all analyses patients develop fantasies about the analyst that are derived from early in their development. This idea is similar to Zetzel's conception (1966) of the therapeutic alliance as being derived from early fantasies emerging through mother–infant interactions.

THREE CONTROVERSIES

Analysts have often observed during the terminal phase of analysis that there is a revival of initial symptoms. Thus the patient repeats, in attenuated form, the symptoms or difficulties that originally brought him into analysis. Whereas some analysts have viewed this revival as a normal part of the terminal phase, Novick sees this as a sign that the termination is premature.[6] There is also a question of what the analysand relinquishes and works through during the terminal phase of treatment. Does the patient give up the analyst as a real as well as a transference object, or is what is given up purely a function of the transference even during the terminal phase of treatment? A third point of

[5]This is a somewhat different use of the term that Freud introduced. See Part II of this book.
[6]This may be part of the criteria he uses in assessing Firestein's cases as premature terminations.

controversy relates to observations of a number of analysts that there are major changes in the patient after the analysis has ended. These analysts have assumed that these changes are related to the continuation of analytic work that the patient is now carrying on by himself. They have also assumed that this is a natural aspect of the analytic process. Novick interprets these postanalytic changes as a result of treatments that are involved with unilateral premature terminations. Novick's interpretations of the terminal phase of treatment leads one to conclude that the work of analysis is by and large accomplished within the confines of the analytic situation and the transference relationship.

What are we to make of Novick's contention that the revival of symptoms during the terminal phase is related to premature terminations that are forced by the analyst? He cites as evidence his reading of Glover's cases (Glover 1955) in which there was both a revival of symptomatology and an admission by Glover that he gave notice of termination prematurely. This can be taken as a demonstration that it is possible to induce symptom revival, but it is also possible that, as Glover contends, there would have been symptom revival in any case. Novick's own clinical experience seems to yield contradictory evidence, since he does not find that patients demonstrate revival during the terminal phase. It is his contention that "this may be due to my own technique of picking up and analytically addressing adolescent terminal phenomena before broaching and setting the date for the terminal phase" (Novick 1982, p. 348). I must admit that in my experience I have seen both patients who did and patients who did not demonstrate symptom revival. Interestingly, in two patients who did relive symptoms there was a good deal of preparation, and in Novick's terms it certainly seemed as if adolescent terminal phenomena were addressed. However, these patients originally suffered from more intense conflicts and from my point of view it was not surprising to see a revival of conflicts during the termination phase. It seems to me that in Novick's review perhaps the most crucial issue is being left out; that is, individual differences in the way patients react to the analytic situation. These individual differences no doubt elicit different reactions (as well as different fantasies) on the part of the analyst, but it may be that these differences are a normal aspect of the analytic experience. It may be that we have to think of a range of normal experiences, rather than a prototypical analytic experience as Novick tends to relate. This range of experiences would have to take into account the different reactions that some types of patients both manifest and tend to elicit. Moreover, a truly sophisticated analytic discipline would take into account a range of responses that different styles of analysts tend to elicit in the terminal as well as in other phases of the treatment.

Novick writes: "In an earlier publication (1976), I presented material from a case which seemed to indicate that it is the analyst as a transference object who is mourned and transference wishes . . . that have to be relinquished" (1982, p. 350). He goes on to say:

It is my suspicion that when analysts refer to the loss of the analyst as a real object, they are talking about the functions that allow for the revival of (an) early infant-mother transference. For example, Stephen Firestein (Panel, 1975) remarks that the analyst is the "first person who really understood the patient. It is in this sense that the analyst is a real person to the patient and ending this relationship is bound to have an enormous impact." . . . What this statement represents is a countertransference fantasy, one frequently found in workers at all levels of sophistication in this field. . . . If, as Firestein contends, the analyst were the first person to really understand the patient, then the patient would be dead. No matter how bad the mothering person may have been in reality, if that maternal person had not understood and responded to the patient's infantile signals of need and distress, then the patient would, as Spitz (1965) has demonstrated, have died. No one has ever been or will ever be as important as the primary mother and it is only through the transference that we become, temporarily, a vital person to the patient. [Novick 1982, p. 350]

It is doubtful that Firestein expected that his seemingly innocuous remark would draw such a strong response. Clearly, although Novick is convinced of his position, he states his position in a type of *reductio ad absurdum* manner. The key to Firestein's remark is that the analyst is the first person to *really* understand the analysand. Surely Firestein couldn't have meant that the analyst was the first person to understand the patient when he or she signaled for food, water, or even affection. He must have meant "understood" in a more significant sense of the term. I must be pardoned for parodying Novick's position, but clearly I do not think he is addressing the issue that Firestein is raising. One version of this position is that the analyst has really listened to the patient in a manner that is different from what the patient had previously experienced. This difference is one in reality and is not simply the patient's fantasy or transference reaction. Thus, the mourning in the terminal phase is in part a recognition that a certain aspect of the patient's life is coming to an end. I suspect that many analysts would agree that a typical countertransference difficulty that is encountered in termination is one in which the analyst has fantasies of being irreplaceable, and necessary for the patient's continuing functioning. At the very least there may be a tendency to consider most of what goes on in the analytic situation as unique instead of placing it in the context of the transference. This I assume is at least related to Novick's statements, and I can certainly agree that there are difficulties encountered by the analyst in termination that are important to highlight. My reading of Firestein's statements do not lead me to conclude that he is maintaining that he is in fact the first maternal figure that his patients have encountered. I do think that there are some real aspects of the analytic relationship that should be dealt with in the termination phase of analysis. The relationship has not been solely a transference relationship, and a full analysis should deal with both the transference and the real aspects of the analytic relationship. This point is amplified in Chapter 16, where I discuss the issue of analytic trust.

We are now at the point of considering the postanalytic phase, and here again it seems to me that Novick is taking a position that is clear but somewhat overstated. His contention is that major changes that occur after the termination of treatment are a result of premature termination. This seems to be a reasonable hypothesis that would apply to many examples but certainly would not apply universally. Perhaps again the difficulty is in being able to descry what is meant by major changes? Since I have previously stated some reservations about the form of Novick's positions, I need say now only that some of these same reservations apply here in terms of the possibilities of important differences in which some patients experience the analytic situation. Rather than go on with my commentary about Novick's point of view, it is important to put into perspective the quality of his review and synthesis. It is an exemplary critique, in which he clearly presents the issues in the field and then in a separate, precise manner states his own opinions.

Charles Brenner

The goals of treatment for Brenner are certainly in line with Freud's formulations:

> In every case, the goal of psychoanalysis is to alter a patient's psychic conflicts in such a way as to eliminate or alleviate their adverse effects. The results of such an alteration will appear as symptomatic and characterological change, as an improved potential for "growth," as better object relations, as more pleasure, as less misery etc. [Brenner 1976, p. 170]

Most therapists would agree with these general goals, which are unexceptional as such. It is Brenner's belief in the role of insight and the power of interpretative efforts to achieve these goals that is notable. His view in terms of the timing of termination give more of a flavor to his views on the interaction between analyst and patient in the termination phase of treatment:

> The time must necessarily come when it seems to an analyst that his patient's conflicts have been beneficially altered as much as they are ever likely to be altered by analysis. Whether or not the patient reaches the same conclusion at about the same time, it is the analyst's responsibility to make his own decision and to present it as such to his patient. If both are in agreement, so much the better. [Brenner 1976, p. 179]

Brenner's view of the responsibility of the analyst is different from Novick's concept and certainly different from Kohut's ideas on the terminal phase of treatment. The decision is the analyst's and the decision is implemented whether or not the patient is in accord. Implicit in this formulation is the idea that the patient may resist the idea of terminating, and so the analyst must act whether or not the patient is in agreement with this action. We assume that the patient will not get any further benefit from continued analysis, since her conflicts have been reasonably well understood and worked through. One wonders why, if this is the case, the patient would not "reach the same conclusion" as the analyst in this decision. In Novick's analysis of Firestein's cases, it is possible that Firestein is applying Brenner's termination methods, and this may the reason that Novick has judged these terminations as premature. Clearly, from Novick's point of view, if there is not a joint decision about termination, the termination is premature. Brenner is clearly stating that his termination criteria are different and do not depend on the patient's stated readiness for termination.

Brenner and Novick do agree that the issues that are dealt with in the terminal are to be considered transference phenomena, and as such are similar to any other aspect of the treatment. Although Brenner states that often the patient may manifest a mourning reaction during the terminal phase:

> This is by no means always the case, however, as Arlow and I have shown. Whatever the reaction may be—and for most patients it is a mixed one—it should be analyzed as thoroughly as possible. One can be sure, also, that transference wishes and their consequences will figure prominently in the analytic material. [Brenner 1976, p. 179]

Since Brenner views the terminal phase as an important aspect of the treatment situation, he advocates that sufficient time be given to this phase of the treatment.

Although one can say that Novick and Brenner agree on various issues concerning the terminal phase of treatment, the one disagreement that I have highlighted is in my view quite crucial to how one conducts an analysis. It is not surprising that Brenner eschews the concept of the therapeutic alliance. The idea of the therapeutic alliance implies a type of mutuality between analyst and analysand that seems to be outside of Brenner's theoretical matrix. It is almost as if he still adheres to an aspect of Freud's pathogenic memory model; if one is able to extricate the memories' pathology (in the form of the transference), then there will be a relatively automatic relief in terms of the patient's symptoms. If this is the case, then the objective observer (the analyst) must determine that the analysis is over and will no longer be of benefit to the analysand.

Heinz Kohut

Kohut's view of termination begins from his concepts of the conditions that are necessary for a successful analysis. In his view:

A successful analysis is one in which the analysand's formerly archaic needs for the responses of archaic self-objects are superseded by the experience of the availability of empathic resonance, the major constituent of the sense of security in adult life. . . . In the analytic situation, these reactivated needs were kept alive and exposed, time and again, to the vicissitudes of optimal frustrations until the patient ultimately acquired the reliable ability to sustain his self with the aid of the self-object resources available in his adult surroundings. According to self-psychology, then, the essence of the psychoanalytic cure resides in a patient's newly acquired ability to identify and seek out appropriate self-objects both mirroring and idealizing—as they present themselves in his realistic surroundings, and to be sustained by them. [Kohut 1984, p. 77]

In this formulation, Kohut seems to be implying that the repeated identification of archaic needs coupled with the analyst's empathy is the curative aspect of analysis. To be sure, this must come under conditions of optimal frustration in the analytic situation, but if this is Kohut's version of insight it is markedly different from Freud's and Brenner's concept of insight. Kohut is clearly saying that the experience of empathy is the necessary and, in the appropriate situation, the sufficient cause for analytic change to occur. When empathic resonance can be experienced, under these optimal analytic conditions, the patient can seek the appropriate self-object(s) in his adult surroundings. From Kohut's perspective, it is not always necessary, in fact even desirable, to understand certain aspects of the patient's unconscious life in the analysis. In talking about a particular patient, Kohut says, "I believe he dimly recognized that the activation of certain aspects of the mirror transference would expose him to the danger of permanent psychological disruption through the reexperience of primordial rage and greed" (1977, p. 24). From Kohut's point of view this makes the treatment no less an analysis but defines the limitations of the role of insight at some points in an analysis. It is not necessary to understand or experience one's past completely, but rather to understand some aspects of it under the conditions of empathic resonance. Then one can search for appropriate and satisfying self-object resources in the environment.

What does Kohut mean by self-object resources? Kohut states that patients with narcissistic disorders develop transference states[7] in which the analyst and the patient are represented as self-objects. Thus, in a mirroring transference, the analysand is fantasized alongside an approving or mirroring analyst. The form of the joint representation may, of course, vary; the analyst may be perceived as similar or identical to or even as merged with the patient, but the main point is this linkage of analyst and analysand in the patient's representational world. When Kohut originally wrote about this self-object bond (1966, 1968), it was assumed that at the end of analysis this bond would

[7]See Part II of this book.

be dissipated and that relationships with people after analysis would no longer be self-object relationships. Kohut in later publications indicated that, at the end of analysis, it is not that self-object relationships are no longer in existence but rather that more appropriate self-object relationships are desired and established. The results of analysis, indeed the nature of relationships, are conceived by Kohut in later formulations in a fashion that differs markedly from Brenner and the analysts who came after Freud such as Hartmann and Anna Freud. Kohut initially expressed this difference in terms of different views of ego autonomy (1972); however, in his later works he has stated that his theory of object relations as well as his views on normal functioning have diverged from what is considered to be the classical position. Kohut's ideas about normal functioning are that the seeking of mirroring self-object relationships is a universal tendency. Thus, to end an analysis while still seeking a self-object bond is not a surprising state of affairs, or characteristic only of people with narcissistic difficulties. The question to be asked at the end of an analysis should concern the *quality* of the self-object bonds that a person attempts to establish. According to Kohut (1984), one should be able to "acquire the reliable ability to sustain (one)self with the aid of the self-object resources available in one's adult surroundings." The criteria for reaching that goal are indicated when

> one or the other of two specific tasks (are completed): (1) when after the analytic penetration of the defensive structures, the primary defect in the self has been exposed and via working through and transmuting internalization, sufficiently filled out so that the formerly defective structures of the self have now become functionally reliable. (2) . . . after the patient has achieved cognitive and effective mastery with regard to the defenses surrounding the primary defect in the self, with regard to the compensatory structures and with regard to the relationship between these—the compensatory structures have now become functionally reliable—independent of the area in which the success was achieved. [Kohut 1977, p. 4]

These two statements indicate that Kohut views analytic treatment as potentially providing compensatory structures for the patient. His final views on the search for the self-object bond are not limited to patients who have narcissistic disorders; rather, he also perceives that patients with oedipal disorders have difficulties that are "embedded in as oedipal self–self-object disturbances . . . that beneath the lust and hostility (of the oedipal stage) . . . there is a layer of depression and of diffuse narcissistic rage" (Kohut 1984, p. 5). Thus, in all disorders there are embedded narcissistic factors; narcissistic motives involve the deepest layers of human existence. Without the treatment of narcissistic issues, the compensatory structures that Kohut discusses will not be formed.

During the termination stage the analysand is exposed "to the impact of the realization that he has to face the ultimate separation from the analyst as a self-object" (Kohut 1977, p. 15). Kohut reports that during this phase regressions may take place, but that then, "without being pushed away by the analyst . . . the patient will spontaneously move towards new modes of sustenance . . . with an increasing variety of self-objects outside the analytic situation" (Kohut 1984, pp. 78–79). Before this movement takes place, mourning may occur, but Kohut sees various regressions as well as a mourning reaction as natural during the termination phase of treatment. If we compare this version of termination with Brenner or even Novick, we see quite different views of the termination process.

14

Contemporary Views
of Reconstruction

Although reconstruction is not a major aspect of Gill's—or, surprisingly, even Brenner's—ideas on technique, clearly Kohut sees reconstruction as an essential aspect of his analytic method. Again we can note that at least some classical analysts have not necessarily followed Freudian concepts in this area of psychoanalytic technique. The movement away from reconstructive work has been noted by Curtis (1979). In this article he maintains that classical analysts dwell on the here-and-now transference at the expense of what he considers to be necessary reconstructive work. Greenacre had made a similar observation several years earlier (1976) when she described a general turning away of classical analysts from reconstructing the patient's past. She also noted that analysts no longer seemed interested in, or able to deal with, a patient's presentation of screen memories. Interestingly, in a recent paper, Arlow has noted that there "has been a current revitalization of reconstruction as a concept and technical procedure" (1990, p. 2). This revitalization has occurred primarily in analysts like Kohut who have tended to see early development from a theoretical perspective that departs from the standard (American) or classical view. In our discussion of reconstruction in this chapter, we will concentrate on Arlow's paper and use his formulations to focus our attention on current issues in the use of reconstruction in the psychoanalytic situation. In this article Arlow contrasts his view of reconstruction with the views of analysts who are interested in early (preoedipal) developmental issues.[1] In

[1]These analysts tend to be associated with Self psychology, but there are many other analysts interested in early development who would consider themselves to be Freudian or Post-Freudian analysts. (See Chapter 7 of this book.)

particular, analysts like Valenstein and Lichtenberg are involved with relating new conceptions of development to psychoanalytic technique.

The Phenomenological Error

The *revitalization* of the concept of reconstruction is also related to the therapeutic challenges that occur as a result of analysts beginning to treat patients with borderline and narcissistic disturbances (Valenstein 1987). The developmental and clinical interests converge, since Valenstein and Lichtenberg propose[2] that narcissistic and borderline disturbances orginate in early, primarily preverbal phases of development. This has led Valenstein to state that we now have "analytic formulations and intersubjective transferential explorations of what had been thought of previously as the inchoate neonatal and infantile period of development" (1987, p. 1). Arlow comments that, "He (Valenstein) believes that the recent contributions from direct observations of neonates and the knowledge gained from infant psychiatry may enable analysts to effect reconstructions that previously appeared to be only speculative" (Arlow 1990, p. 4).

Arlow uses statements by Valenstein, Cooper (1988), and Lichtenberg (1989) as examples of what he calls the "phenomenological error, which is a variant of what Hartmann has termed the genetic fallacy." The phenomenological error leads him to further consider "the challenge of the nature, the meaning and the methodology of reconstruction" (Arlow 1990, p. 6). Here Arlow logically distinguishes a model or theory of psychoanalytic technique from the general content of psychoanalytic theory. Before we explore Arlow's views, let us more explicitly state the concepts that he is confronting. Cooper provides a clear commentary when he says that "each of us approaches the patient with a limited array of mental templates that predetermine the shape that we give to the communications we have received from the patient" (Arlow 1990, p. 6). Lichtenberg articulates a similar view when he maintains:

> Since Freud was forced by the associations of his patients to reconstruct the sources of adult psychoneuroses through an understanding of childhood, all psychoanalysts have worked with what I call 'model scenes' of infancy. These include the presumed oral bliss of the nursing infant or the incorrectly presumed autistic or narcissistic isolation or solipsistic state of the neonate, the conflict of the toilet-training toddler caught between retention and expulsion, and all the variants of the oedipal child's sexual pursuits and rivalries. These initial efforts to conceptualize the early infantile past of the adult are by contemporary consensus inadequate and, especially for the first two years of life, inaccurate. My premise is that research and direct observation provide us with a set of model scenes closer

[2]This proposal is by no means novel to either of these authors.

to the living experiences of the child, and that these normal and pathological prototypes facilitate the analytic process. [Arlow 1990, pp. 6–7]

Here is what Arlow calls the phenomenological error—that is, an analyst "foisting upon the patient's associations an interpretation based upon a model concept of pathogenesis" (1990, p. 7). Arlow argues that positions like Cooper's and Lichtenberg's "maintain that every analyst pattern the patient's associations according to his (the analyst's) inner vision of the infant's early life." His interpretation of the Lichtenberg–Valenstein–Cooper position is that the analyst interprets or reconstructs on the basis of theoretical concepts of development *rather* than on the basis of the patient's associations.

It is unlikely that any of the analysts that we have mentioned would deny that their interpretations are guided by their theoretical orientations. In fact, as we have just seen in the quotations, they affirm that their theoretical orientations are useful in understanding clinical phenomena. They advocate that analysts give up their old theoretical assumptions that have guided them in the past, and take on new theoretical concepts or templates. These analysts are also implying that Arlow too is influenced by a theoretical template, but that it simply is not the best template. Arlow, however, is addressing another issue that Freud has raised in his paper on constructions.[3] The subject that he is considering involves the determination of what constitutes appropriate evidence for an interpretation in the analytic process. From Arlow's point of view, the evidence must appear in the context of an analytic session and there must be certain aspects of contiguous associations that warrant an interpretation[4] by the analyst (1969, 1979, 1981, 1985). Arlow maintains that the analyst should not interpret until these criteria are met. If these criteria are not met, Arlow would contend that the analyst is no longer operating *within* an analytic process, but rather is imposing his theoretical views on the analytic process. For Arlow's arguments to have the force of logical necessity, one must accept his criteria of context and contiguity; more importantly, one must accept the centrality of free association or the associative process in analytic treatment. Arlow has thus made one element of Freud's technique explicit, he has shown the centrality of free association in analytic technique.

To understand Arlow's position, obviously one must know more fully what he means by context and contiguity. Let us take a look at Arlow's summary of his position:

In general there are certain criteria that transform what would seem to be random associations or disconnected thought into supportable hypotheses that

---

[3]Arlow, as we will see later, comes back to the issue that Lichtenberg raises, and—at least implicitly—defends the template that he utilizes.

[4]The reader may notice that I am presaging an aspect of an argument that I will present; namely, that reconstruction is to be considered one form of interpretation, and, as such, is to be considered in the same way that we would evaluate any interpretative effort.

can be entertained with conviction and buttressed by *fact* [italics mine]. . . . Most important is the context in which the specific material appears. Contiguity usually suggests dynamic relevance. The configuration of the material, the form and sequence in which the associations appear, represent substantive and inter-pretable connections. Other critiera are to be seen in the repetition and the convergence of certain themes within the organized body of associations. The repetitions of similarities or opposites is always striking and suggestive. Material in context appearing in related sequence, multiple representations of the same theme, repetition in similarity, and a convergence of the data into one compre-hensible hypothesis constitute the specific methodological approach in psycho-analysis used to validate insights obtained in an immediate, intuitive fashion in the analytic interchange. In actual practice, the aesthetic and cognitive compo-nents of the interpretive work proceed side by side. They do, however, have different relevance at various junctures in the analytic experience and are deter-mined not only by the flow of the material but by the nature of both the analyst's and the patient's characterological defenses and communicative styles. [Arlow 1979, p. 203]

We see in Arlow's statement actually three implicit comments about criteria for interpretation—what he calls *context and contiguity* and also what he refers to as *convergence of themes*. Before we discuss his ideas let us go to another quote relating the interpretation of the past (reconstruction) to the interpretative process in general:

What makes any interpretation of the past possible, what makes reconstruction possible, is the fact that the past is embedded in the present. Certain aspects of the past remain dynamically active in the patient's current life. They become apparent in many forms—character development, dreams, symptoms, para-praxes, fantasies, etc.—but they bcome understandable in the psychoanalytic situation by virtue of the persistent derivative manifestations as they appear in context, in patterns of contiguity, in repetition, figurative language, metaphor, similarities and opposites, etc. [Arlow 1990, p. 8]

Arlow's use of context and contiguity are ways of stating the influence of primary process in the analytic situation. Whereas Arlow has used convincing clinical examples for his ideas, and has presented important concepts, he has not given us completely interpreted rules for interpretative efforts.[5] Leaving this aside, we can ask whether—if one understands the context and the contiguous relationships involved in the patient's associations—an interpreta-tion will necessarily follow. From Arlow's point of view the probability of an interpretation is increased if there are a variety of sources that converge on the same thematic material. If the patient's fantasies, dreams, parapraxes, and the like all converge (i.e., yield similar themes), then naturally the analyst will have

[5]He has, however, talked about a range of factors that the analyst can use to understand when to interpret, including the analyst's own reactions to the patient's associations. It remains, however, for his ideas to be codified into fully operational rules of inference.

more confidence in his efforts at interpretation. Thus, from Arlow's point of view, while the transference is important it is too narrow a base on which to rest an analysis. Rather, all sources of associations are important in giving one confidence in attempting interpretations. Reconstructions are for Arlow one class of interpretations that are subject to the same guidelines as any other interpretive efforts. They are possible, he tells us, since it is part of the human condition to repeat one's past. Of course we should not expect to see the past presented in direct form. The past is dynamically embedded in the present, and, as such, is subject to the same possibilities of dynamic distortion as is any other type of mental representation.

In the analytic situation the patient's associations are the crucial data to be considered. "The patient is supposed to follow the fundamental rule, that is, he is expected to report without criticism whatever occurs to consciousness" (Arlow 1979, p. 194). The analyst is a participant-observer who at times disturbs the "equilibrium between impulse and defense" (Arlow 1979, p. 194). Arlow has followed Lewin (1955) in comparing the dream to the analytic situation. In this comparison, Arlow sees the analyst as at times interpreting to ease the defensive maneuvers of the ego so that the patient can continue to free-associate and allow unconscious derivatives to emerge. In effect, this type of interpretation says to the patient, "'Don't be so vigilant. Don't be so wakeful. Let yourself sleep and dream and produce derivatives of unconscious wishes'" (Arlow 1979, pp. 194–195). Alternatively, "An interpretation directed toward revealing an id impulse is tantamount to saying to the patient, 'Wake up. Observe the implications of what you have just been thinking or dreaming'" (Arlow 1979, p. 195). Clearly, in this formulation the ability of patients to free-associate and to observe the implications of their free associations is crucial.[6]

We have seen, however, that a number of analysts do not share this view of free association. Bird and Gill are two analysts who have either downplayed the significance of free association (Bird, see Chapter 4) or maintained that perhaps we should abandon the concept altogether (Gill, see Chapter 10). Both of these authors have replaced the emphasis of the associative process by accenting the importance of transference interpretations.

The lines of the competing arguments seem clear; if one accepts the use of a technique with free association,[7] one can interpret only under the conditions that Arlow has indicated. If these conditions can be clearly operationalized then Arlow has presented rules of inference about interpretation in the psychoanalytic situation. The clarity fades in this formulation when we consider the content as well as the structure of an interpretation. Here it is hard to conceive of any analyst who would not have to admit that his or her theoretical

---

[6]In the last chapter of the present volume I talk about patients who can do neither at the beginning of an analysis. The discussion is focused on the analytic possibilities for this type of patient. Obviously, in Arlow's formulations these patients would be considered not analyzable.

[7]Of course one must provide the conditions that are facilitative for the patient to engage in the associative process.

predilections will influence the choice of content in an interpretation. Moreover, it is the case that Arlow's criteria for interpretation are satisfied more often than one actually interprets; thus, the selectivity of the analyst in these instances is also guided or influenced by his theoretical position. This is not terribly surprising, for undoubtedly a number of things will influence the analyst's interpretations;[8] but if we follow Arlow's position to its conclusion we can say that the use of his technique will offer us the possibility of comparing alternate theoretical explanations of the patient's associations.[9] Thus, up to this point Arlow has presented us only with a rationale for how to time and evaluate interpretative efforts in psychoanalytic treatment. If one accepts this position, then the use of theoretical models to influence the content of an interpretation would not be a violation of the Freud–Arlow analytic method. The use of theory to tell us when to interpret would be a violation of the Freud–Arlow technique. The content of the interpretation is untouched by Arlow's criteria; we will see how he attempts to link form and content in the psychoanalytic process. It is important to note that whereas Arlow has given a rationale for interpretative efforts, he has not to this point stated why interpretations should at times take the form of reconstructions.

Reconstruction: One Form of Interpretation

To repeat a quote, we can say that reconstruction is one form of interpretation and that it is possible because "certain aspects of the past remain dynamically active in the patient's current life. They become apparent in many forms— character development, dreams, symptoms, etc. . . . they become understandable in the psychoanalytic situation by virtue of the persistent derivative manifestations as they appear in context, in patterns of contiguity, in repetition, figurative language, metaphor, similarities and opposites" (Arlow 1990, p. 8). In this quotation, transference is deliberately omitted; and, in Arlow's view, whereas transference is an important aspect of the analytic situation, "undue weight has been attached to the interpretation of the transference." It is his opinion that "transference represents [only] one of the ways in which the past impinges upon the present. By itself, however, without contiguous associative data, screen memories and derivatives of unconscious fantasy, transference phenomenology can only suggest a type of speculation." This is an interesting position since Arlow suggests that the past in one form or another *has* to be interpreted in analysis. This idea, while central to Freud, has strangely been diminished in contemporary analysis.

---

[8]Most prominently his or her character or personality style.
[9]This is true, of course, only if one accepts Arlow's assumptions about the importance of contiguity and context. Fortunately there are ways of empirically testing some of his assumptions, but these tests remain to be performed.

Freud—while acknowledging theoretically that the memories of the past are "sublimated" or changed by the person's active processing of his or her memories[10]—often translated a person's adult experiences directly into childhood scenarios seemingly without considering how the past might be altered in memory consolidation.[11] Arlow points out that what is reconstructed is not an objective event, as viewed by an outside observer. It is the historic dynamism that is reconstructed. Recollection and/or reconstruction become significant only when they are placed in direct connection with the persistent psychological consequences that ensued. This obviously includes the process of defense as well as any other ego or cognitive functioning that might affect memory processes. Reconstruction then involves the translation of the patient's dynamic unconscious just as any other interpretative work might perform this translation. One might still ask, Is reconstruction a necessary component of psychoanalytic treatment? Given Arlow's and Freud's assumptions, this is virtually a meaningless question. It may be more correct to state that in many, perhaps most, of Arlow's and Freud's interpretative efforts, there are reconstructive elements. This is true since the dynamic unconscious is conceived of in terms of the past being repeated in the present. In fact we can say that if one is making a transference interpretation within a Freudian model of analysis, then implicitly the past is always being considered.

When the formulations are put in these terms, many questions arise that involve basic theoretical assumptions.[12] However one defines transference, there is a difference between an analyst who overtly refers to the past (Arlow or Kohut) and an analyst who for the main part eschews this type of reference in his or her interpretations. The first question, then, that we may ask is the extent to which Arlow advocates referring to—and attempting to explain or account for—the analysand's present-day experience in terms of past experiences. Here I would argue that anyone who stays within Freud's assumptions of the dynamic unconscious would of necessity advocate explicating the patient's past. The patient's core conflicts in this conceptualization are embedded in terms of fantasies and memories (screen and otherwise) from the patient's childhood years. The objects (persons) who are used to displace and project from, come mainly from those years. For Freud it is a necessary piece of *converging* data to be able to reconstruct the patient's past and to understand the fantasies that were formed during the person's childhood. In fact for Freud (and I believe necessarily for Arlow) an important termination criterion

---

[10]By active processing I mean primarily that the person's fantasies will lead to the construction of a memory that is certainly not necessarily identical to the actual events. In addition, the person's cognitive style, defensive tendencies, and frustration tolerance will all affect the way a memory is consolidated.

[11]Obviously this is an overstatement since one can point to several instances in which Freud carefully considered the alteration of a childhood memory. In the case of the Wolf Man he explicitly considers this question (Freud 1918).

[12]We have not considered, nor will we, the philosophic questions that arise from the statements that involve reconstruction.

involves the adequacy of the analyst's reconstructive efforts. Put in other terms, both the analysand and the analyst must understand the conditions of pathogenesis before the conclusion of the analysis. This idea is tied to the concept of the transference neurosis: if the transference neurosis is displayed in full form then it will be possible to understand the pathogenic memories and fantasies that are involved in intrapsychic conflict. Alternatively, one can say that if the transference is manifested in a full enough manner, it will then be possible to reconstruct the patient's childhood.[13]

Reconstruction of Preverbal Experiences

I have already mentioned that our discussion of Arlow's views did not speak to the content of interpretive efforts. He has argued against what he has called the phenomenological error; that is, analysts making interpretations or reconstructions, without adequate *analytic* evidence. He has specified criteria for interpretations and specifically casts doubts on the possibility of meeting these criteria for events that occur in the preverbal era:

> The problem of reconstructing traumatic events from the preverbal period or, to put it more correctly, the analysis of the persistent effects of experiences during the earliest months of life becomes a problem of methodology. . . . Much of the difficulty resides in the fact that the child's capacity for symbolization, structuralization of memory and fantasy formation, is limited compared to how these capacities develop after the second and third years of life. The concept advanced by certain object relations theorists is that specific sets of early interactions with objects come to have a dynamic thrust of their own, so that they are compulsively repeated in later life in situations in which they prove to be inappropriate. To begin with, such formulations seem to deny the concomitant effect of drive derivatives. An object relationship without some drive investment is inconceivable. [Arlow 1990, pp. 21-22]

Arlow is committing the same type of error that he previously had argued against; he is imposing his theoretical template on the possible analytic experiences that one might encounter. He does this when he states that "an object relationship without some drive investment is inconceivable." It *is* conceivable to analysts such as Fairbairn, Guntrip, and Kohut, who have maintained that some or all object relationships are better understood without invoking the concept of drive. Arlow might maintain that he has a superior explanation, but object relations without drive manifestations are inconceivable only within certain theoretical frameworks. In fact the elegance of his ideas on technique allows for different theoretical positions to be compared

---

[13]I am putting the above sentence in this alternative form only to show that the concept of transference neurosis is not necessarily involved with viewing reconstruction as a criterion for termination.

within the analytic situation. At the very least, Arlow has stated criteria for
such a comparison.[14]

Arlow's position on the reconstruction of preverbal experiences seems as
biased and as prone to the phenomenological error as is the position that he is
criticizing. He states that "such reconstructions are hard to come by," but this
is obviously less true for analysts who believe in the importance of preoedipal
factors. His position on constructions of preverbal experiences is even less
convincing when he tells us that recall of past events is not an appropriate
characterization of reconstructive efforts; he quotes Blum (1980) in saying
that:

> "The reconstructive integration identifies patterns and interrelationships, rather
> than isolated conflicts and experiences, and the intrapsychic configurations,
> consequences and developmental influences are far more important than actual
> historical facts. The past is transformed to new meanings and reorganized on
> new levels of development." [Arlow 1990, pp. 28–39]

Arlow ends his paper by fully bringing reconstructions into the fold of
dynamic interpretations since a reconstruction "in effect does what any good
interpretation does . . . [it] serves as a base for the elaboration of the patient's
unconscious fantasies, facilitating the emergence of additional material, the-
matically associated or consonant with the nature of the reconstruction" (1990,
p. 29).

We have now come almost full circle in following Arlow's reasoning:
reconstructions, when appropriate, serve the same function as any interpretative effort. Many if not most interpretative efforts involve reconstruction.
Interpretations serve to demonstrate how the analysand has brought an aspect
of the past into the present. However, the past as an actuality is not the main
issue; rather, the dynamic meanings of the past are the important issue in any
interpretative effort. We can then say that reconstructions are not mainly
concerned with facts, but, as Blum states, with "patterns and interrelation-
ships." Why then be concerned if interpretations of preverbal experiences are
factually correct, or hard to come by? The important aspect of an interpretation is the way it integrates patterns and relationships, and, to paraphrase
Freud, how the analysis is deepened by the intervention. Arlow's argument
against attempts to interpret preverbal experiences falls by the wayside if one
takes seriously his differentiation between reconstruction and recall of actual
events. Lichtenberg, Valenstein, and Cooper can interpret from any theoretical
matrix if they follow the guidelines of context, contiguity, and convergence. If
they do then it may be possible to compare the effect of interpretations from
different theoretical viewpoints.

---

[14]This, of course, is true only if one accepts certain assumptions that I have alluded to earlier:
contiguity, context, and converging themes.

Reconstruction and Therapeutic Action

The main question that is debated about reconstruction, however, is not whether one can consider adequate reconstructive knowledge a criterion for termination, but rather what is the therapeutic efficacy of reconstructive efforts. Does the patient benefit from his or from the analyst's knowledge of the way he has encoded the past? Here I would hope that the answer could be based on some type of therapeutic study, but as of yet that study has not taken place. In the absence of a study I would state that minimally Arlow's position involves the importance of converging experiences in the psychoanalytic situation. The more areas of a person's life that converge in the same direction, the more likely that both analysand and analyst will have confidence in an interpretation that reflects these converging experiences. We can say that reconstructive efforts are one source of converging experiences, much in the same way that the transference, fantasies, dreams, parapraxes, and so on, are all such experiences in analysis. It is hard to believe that many patients aren't deeply interested in their past, and not simply as a defense against the transference. If we accept the converging experience idea we might further ask, does the understanding of one's past have a special significance that goes beyond other converging experiences in analysis? I can answer only that in my experience this seems to be the case; but obviously this is only one opinion, and, as we have seen, there are a number of opinions on this issue.

Conclusions

The issue of reconstruction raises a number of questions that have been side-stepped in the present discussion. In fact this issue as much as any in the contemporary literature raises questions about how the analyst conceives of the therapeutic process. Is the analyst referring to actual events in the patient's life when there is a reconstruction? In my view Arlow is ambiguous about this issue and would probably offer an answer that involves a mixture of positions. Clearly only the early Freud believed that reconstructions usually (or inevitably) referred to actual traumatic events in the patient's life. Most contemporary analysts have moved away from this view;[15] probably the most consistent recent stance in relation to this issue is one taken by Spence (1982) and Schafer (1977, 1982). These authors, from one or another perspective, view the patient's associations as a narrative that in many ways can be interpreted as can any text or narrative. Thus the criteria used to evaluate literary texts can be profitably applied to the psychoanalytic situation. The issue of reality is then replaced by internal criteria used to evaluate the text (or the patient's associa-

---

[15]Freud, as we have seen, attempted to move away from this view but inevitably came back to different versions of the pathological memory model.

tions). It may be that Schafer or Spence might offer patients reconstructions, but the reality of the reconstructions is beside the point. The issue can be stated solely in terms of how a given intervention either elucidates or furthers the unfolding of the text. Thus issues of consistency and parsimony are crucial from this perspective.[16] The issue of converging evidence, however, is less important; in addition, although it may be possible to develop a textual analysis of nonverbal behaviors, these authors do not frequently develop this issue. An extreme version of Arlow's position coincides with the narrative position. If Arlow is willing to say that the occurrence of an event in the patient's life is totally irrelevant to the analytic process, then his position logically coincides with the narrative position.

In some sense we might ask, How else are the patient's associations to be viewed? It is certainly possible to see associations in terms of a text; and whether one finds this a usual metaphor or not, the questions of consistency, adequacy of fit, and parsimony are all questions that one must consider in putting forth interpretations.[17] To fully explore the implications of the narrative position we would have to understand some of the assumptions on which this position is based. In the past I have attempted to characterize the philosophic basis of Schafer's position (Ellman and Moskowitz 1980). I believe that Spence's work rests on the same type of philosophic assumptions. However, in this context I will not attempt to discuss the adequacy of their formulations. I will note only that the extent to which one accepts a narrative position should be based on one's view of the extent to which the analyst and analysand can gain a veridical perception of the analysand's life. This veridical perception should include actual events in the past and present as well as the analysand's view of these events. Alternatively, I would say that the extent to which one differs with the narrative position is determined by the extent to which one finds it useful to employ a theory of reality in the analytic situation. In this formulation there is a distinction—at some points in the analysis—of subject and object, both between the analyst and analysand, as well as at times *within* the analyst and analysand.[18]

Rather than go on with this discussion, I would prefer to point out that the question of reconstruction is related to many issues that involve fascinating questions related to positions that attempt to formulate the psychoanalytic task within an intersubjective position. These positions rely, in my opinion, on certain positions made current by contemporary physics as well as certain trends in literature and philosophy. How these trends will intersect with conceptions of the analytic situation will be one of the more interesting future developments in psychoanalysis.

---

[16]Of course the issues of consistency and parsimony are criteria that are used to judge any theory. These criteria have been utilized by many philosophers of science.

[17]This is true whether the interpretations are intended as causal explanations or not.

[18]To provide a clearer understanding of what I have in mind, I will say that in this formulation the observing ego can be formulated as a cleavage between subject and object within the analysand.

PART VI

*Integrating Freud's Legacy with
Contemporary Views and Experience*

15

Freud's Actual Conduct of Treatment

It would seem that Freud's cases would be a natural place to turn in order to gain further insight into his ideas about psychoanalytic treatment. However, when one looks at Freud's behavior with patients, it is difficult to reconcile some of his conduct with his written work. If one takes some of the comments of Freud's former patients seriously, then it becomes even more challenging to integrate Freud's actions with his theoretical understanding. During the course of this volume we have not systematically looked at Freud's behavior with patients. In this chapter we will briefly discuss this topic and then more extensively focus on Freud's notes from the case of the Rat Man.

Freud as an Analyst

Although at times Freud may have seen himself first and foremost as the inventor of a new technique (Bernfeld 1949), this perception does not seem relevant to him at most points in his career. On occasion he is clearly concerned with this new technique (this new method of observation), while at other times the technique is quite definitely of secondary importance. In at least two of the three cases that we have mentioned, Freud's concern was not with the observational method that he was employing, but rather the theoretical issues that were driving him at the time.

Dora was of interest to him because of his revolutionary theory about dreaming and his continuing consideration about the etiology of hysteria.[1] In

---

[1] I believe that he eventually published this aborted case as a lesson for himself and future analysts about the importance of transference. (This is discussed in detail in Part II of this book.)

this instance we can say that his concern with treatment occurred after the case had been finished, when he had a chance to reflect on his experiences. At the time of Freud's analysis of the Rat Man we can assume that Freud was interested in technique, since he was planning to write a book at this point in time (Gay 1988). His discourse on the Rat Man involves a discussion of technical elements in psychoanalysis more than does any of his other cases. With the Rat Man he seems to have wanted to demonstrate the power of the method of free association and, to a lesser extent, the importance of transference.

On the other hand, in his rich and confused write-up of the Wolf Man, Freud rarely mentions technique. Clearly this is a letter to Jung and perhaps Adler as well. In this letter Freud is asserting the predominance of sexuality in the formation of psychological conflict. The exception to his avoidance of the subject of technique is the discussion of the technical innovation he employs in forcing the Wolf Man to terminate treatment. In discussing the Wolf Man in "Analysis Terminable and Interminable," Freud uses the famous phrase that the lion only springs once; this metaphor is intended to remind us that once the analyst sets a date in a forced termination, the action cannot (and should not) be reversed or repeated. Freud, however, did see the Wolf Man at a later date and was certainly involved in the Wolf Man's life at later points; Freud, in fact, found the Wolf Man another analyst.[2] Freud did not turn the Wolf Man away after his authoritarian pronouncement. Here, as at other times, Freud departed from his bold, military-like statements and behaved in a humane manner.[3] This case is a small example of the liberties Freud took with his own methods of psychoanalytic technique.

There are many such contradictions to be found in Freud, cases in which he tells us one thing about treatment, then goes on to do quite different things. He relates that it is a mistake to see friends in treatment—or even relatives of friends—since we can be sure that these actions will lead to undesirable results on all fronts. He then proceeds to see not only friends, but his own daughter, in treatment. What are we to make of these contradictions? He writes about the importance of transference, and yet it is clear that he never mastered working with the transference.[4] We do not need the mass of writings about what he did with his patients to know this; we can see his conflicts about transference in many of his technique papers and certainly in the case studies. As an analyst, Freud never fully left the pathogenic memory model, although as a theorist he began to depart from this model soon after he finished seeing Dora. We might say that Freud oscillated in his clinical interest in psychoanalysis, and we know that as he progressed he was a good deal more interested in the discoveries that the method yielded than in this new method of observation itself. He was not

---

[2]See Gardiner's book, *The Wolf Man* (1971), which contains Freud's case report, Brunswick's case report, and a memoir by the Wolf Man himself.
[3]There are, of course, other times when Freud did not behave in quite such a caring manner.
[4]At times, even late in his career, he did not even seem to value working with transference.

interested in being a modern analyst, even a modern analyst of his own era. One can almost say that, once Freud had experienced and seen the implications of his clinical experience, he was on to the next area of discovery. He did not wait around to develop or internalize his technique and understand the full implications of his own thoughts.

Freud's behavior, of course, must be understood in the context of his clinical experience. In the period after his treating Dora, his practice built up and, as he told Jung, he was certainly busy by 1906: ("At present I am devoting ten hours a day to psychotherapy.") This was perhaps the busiest clinical period of his entire career. By the time he wrote many of his technique papers, his practice was already beginning to diminish or had already diminished as a result of the war. During World War I, Freud was writing a great deal but doing relatively little clinical work. He was doing a great deal of work in organizing the psychoanalytic movement, but this is not the same as seeing patients in treatment. By the time he finished with his paper on transference love, his practice had been decimated and he was writing on the basis of his past cases.

At the end of World War I Freud resumed his practice, and, as Peter Gay tells us, he began to see patients who could pay him in foreign currency, preferably in dollars. He had to support his family and this was no simple task in post-war Vienna. Nor was his family a small one; there were many relatives who needed some degree of support, and Freud was sensitive to his role of provider. It is well known that he did not accept lucrative offers (Gay 1988, Jones 1955a,b, Schur 1972) that might have made life easier for him and his family. Still, he did feel he needed patients who could pay him in a currency that would not immediately be rendered worthless by the runaway inflation in Vienna. Who were the patients he saw after the war? He saw many foreigners, particularly those from the United States and England. Many of the people he took on for treatment had various time pressures and were seeing him for some version of formal or informal training analyses. To make this potentially long story somewhat shorter, we can say that after the war Freud's practice was quite different than it was before the war. After the war he was fully established as the leader of a movement that had already developed a significant worldwide structure. His writings had become influential in many areas of society, and although controversy still swirled around him, he had clearly established psychoanalysis as a discipline with a growing number of adherents. After World War I he was conducting mainly training analyses for people who were expressly interested in psychoanalysis, and not necessarily (or overtly) interested in a therapeutic analysis.

This description of Freud's patients finds its parallel in his stated views on performing analytic treatment. We learn from Ferenczi that Freud had said that "the therapeutic process is negligible or unimportant" (Ferenczi 1988, p. xiii). Another former patient of Freud's, Hilda Doolittle, quoted Freud as saying, "My discoveries are not primarily a heal-all. My discoveries are a basis for a very grave philosophy. There are very few who understand this, there are few who are capable of understanding this" (LaForgue 1973, p. 308). Freud made these statements as he was growing older and had endured a number of personal losses as well as contracted a life-threatening disease. Still, we can say that after the war he was not interested in analytic treatment the way he had been in the preceding years, during the writing of the technique papers. That he at times made disparaging remarks about his clinical endeavors is not astonishing. As LaForgue has said:

> Who could reproach Freud for having become bitter beneath the weight of the general incomprehension he met, often greater among his fervent enthusiasts than among his adversaries. . . . And let us not forget the painful illness which struck him in his sixtieth year, making it difficult for him to speak. [LaForgue 1973, p. 343]

De Saussure, a prominent Swiss psychoanalyst, was seen by Freud in treatment in the early 1920s. He comments that:

> Freud was not a good psychoanalytic technician. Since he was not analyzed himself, he tended to commit two kinds of errors. First, he had practiced suggestion too long not to have been materially affected by it. When he was persuaded of the truth of something, he had considerable difficulty in waiting until this verity became clear to his patient. Freud wanted to convince him immediately. Because of that, he talked too much.
>
> Second, one rapidly sensed what special theoretical question preoccupied him, for often during the analytic hour he developed at length new points of view he was clarifying in his own mind. This was a gain for the discipline, but not always for the patient's treatment. [De Saussure 1973, p. 359]

As we know, Freud did not write significantly about technique from 1919 (the end of his technique papers) until 1936 through 1937. His major writings after the war were concerned with his new theoretical concepts. This new method of observation was one he took somewhat for granted for a number of years. When he went back to writing about technique, he mentioned the importance of a training analysis, indeed even about the importance of periodic analyses for analysts. We may wonder about De Saussure's point that Freud was not a good technician because he never had an analysis. Clearly he was writing about the need for other analysts to enter into periodic analyses; could he himself have entered an analysis? Positing this issue leads us into anachronistic fantasies; it is almost impossible to fully imagine the circumstances that surrounded Freud and how he truly thought about various issues. One can say only that at times he behaved as if he, and perhaps some selected others, were not subject to the psychological influences of the unconscious that his genius had uncovered.

We can attempt at least a partial understanding of Freud's limitations as a clinician, and to some extent understand why Freud disregarded his own ideas about technique. Why, at times, did he not seem to value the therapeutic technique that he had labored so hard to develop? Why was he unable to apply the principles of technique that he wrote about and at least for some period of time understood and experienced? I would agree with Bird[5] when he contends that in many ways Freud moved away from his insights about transference as his career developed. If he had continued to develop these ideas, he might have come to the conclusion that a good many of his treatments involved suggestion and were what some might term "transference cures."

To repeat the main contention, I believe that Freud must have felt he was partially immune to the influences that psychoanalytic theory describes. One can imagine that he wanted to *defeat* the unconscious rather than admit he needed some assistance in understanding his unconscious fantasies. His self-analysis, while remarkable in many ways, was inevitably incomplete. His investment in individual patients (including himself) was attenuated by the growing realization that he had the possibility of presenting to the world a truly revolutionary theory of humans. If one is a man for the ages, it must be hard at times for him to listen to what he might consider only a confirmation of a previous discovery. It must have been hard to listen to "ordinary" cases.[6] He was, as an analyst, frequently a teacher, a lecturer, and an evaluator, and the lives he touched must have been the richer for it even though he was not always—or I suspect even usually—functioning as a therapeutic analyst.

FREUD'S MAJOR CASES

In discussing Freud's cases it is hard to restrict ourselves to his own writings in view of the vast amount of material that has been written by others about Freud's patients. For example, the literature about the Wolf Man, Freud's most famous case report, includes many accounts of his adult life, his childhood, and information about his subsequent treatments, as well as memoirs by the Wolf Man himself. Although the Wolf Man was certainly Freud's most scrutinized patient, all of Freud's patients have elicited a good deal of inquiry into their life circumstances. It is inevitable that there have been many attempts at modern interpretations of all the case material (Blum 1980b, Gardiner 1971, Kanzer 1980a,b, Langs 1980). Given this additional commentary, we will wander back and forth between Freud's statements and some of the modern interpretations. Hopefully, this oscillating will improve our vision as we look at the patients and the treatment that Freud immortalized in these now classic formulations.

The question arises as to how to approach Freud's case material. The cases typically considered to be Freud's major ones start from Dora[7] and end with

---

[5]However, I would give a different sequence than the one Bird has hypothesized.
[6]Perhaps the most fascinating aspect of psychoanalysis is that there are no ordinary cases. I have commented (Ellman 1985b) that this may be why doing psychoanalysis frequently seems like a completely creative endeavor.
[7]"From the History of an Infantile Neurosis," published in 1918; she was seen in treatment for three months in 1900.

the Wolf Man.[8] Between the publication of these cases, Freud wrote about Little Hans,[9] the Rat Man,[10] and Schreber.[11] Little Hans, a child at the time of treatment, was treated by his father, who was supervised by Freud. The Schreber case was an analysis by Freud of Schreber's memoirs. Since Freud did not directly treat either Little Hans or Schreber, we will not discuss these cases in this chapter. We will focus mainly on the case of the Rat Man, since it is in this case that we can most clearly see Freud in action. In addition, we will again briefly discuss some aspects of Dora and the Wolf Man.

THE ANALYTIC COMMUNITY AND FREUD'S CASES

It is a sign of Freud's dominating presence in psychoanalysis that Blum wrote in 1980: "When I was a candidate, the case (of the Wolf Man) was taught with almost unquestioned acceptance of Freud's formulations and adherence to his established early views (1914) and those of Brunswick (1928)" (Blum 1980, p. 342).

This statement is quite remarkable in its implications for psychoanalytic education. The Wolf Man was seen in treatment from 1910 to 1914. Freud himself anticipated that his explanation of the Wolf Man's childhood (with respect to a dream of the Wolf Man) would not be universally accepted by other psychoanalysts. He acknowledged that his interpretations of a dream of the Wolf Man were debatable. It is an exceptional circumstance that what Freud knew to be controversial in 1914 was accepted without question thirty to forty years later. This condition of analytic education is now (hopefully) a thing of the past. Blum's recollection is illustrative of a condition of public acceptance of Freud's ideas even though many analysts had private reservations about Freud's conclusions. This accounts for a certain type of conformity in the early literature concerning these cases; this conformity too is now relegated to the past.

A difficulty in looking at Freud's cases is determining from what perspective they are to be viewed. Should one try to reinterpret the cases, or review the evidence for the various reinterpretations that have been put forward by modern commentators? This is an interesting task, but it is not the present focus. In the discussion of the Rat Man, for example, I will go over some of the general characteristics of the case but will not systematically argue for one interpretation over another. Rather I will state my own preferences, and focus primarily on what Freud did with this patient. The questions raised here will center on Freud's actions, and the comparison between his behavior and his ideas on psychoanalytic technique. Since Freud saw the Rat Man between 1907

[8]"From the History of an Infantile Neurosis."
[9]"Analysis of a Phobia in a Five-Year-Old Boy," published in 1909.
[10]"Notes upon a Case of Obsessional Neurosis," published in 1909. He was seen in treatment from 1907 to 1908.
[11]"Psycho-Analytic Notes on an Autobiographical Account of a Case of Paranoia (Dementia Paranoidas)," published in 1911.

and 1908, and the technique papers were written from three to twenty-nine years after this case ended, one can legitimately ask whether this case is truly representative of Freud's later ideas on technique. Later we will discuss this question and again consider the extent to which Freud's ideas or clinical practices shifted during the course of his career.

The Rat Man

In an important discovery, a portion of Freud's daily notes on this case was found to have survived. Strachey reports that "it was Freud's practise throughout his life, after one of his works had appeared in print, to destroy all the material on which the publication was based" (Freud 1909b, p. 253). Thus it is rare to have even Freud's original manuscript available, and as far as is currently known, this is the only existing record of Freud's daily notes. Freud typically took notes each night after seeing patients (Jones 1954). The notes on this case that were found go from Freud's first contact with the patient on October 1, 1907 to January 20, 1908. The notes are informal, slightly disjointed accounts of the day's proceedings; in translation, Alix and James Strachey have put them into a smoother narrative. The consultation session (my term) and the first seven sessions are not included in the translation because the Stracheys felt that "approximately the first third of the original record was reproduced by Freud almost verbatim in the published version [of the case]" (Freud 1909b, p. 254).

Recently, Hawelka obtained the original notes from these sessions, published them, and produced a French translation (Mahony 1986). I have utilized these notes and occasionally provide my own translations. Why these notes have survived is unknown, but their discovery allows us to hear some of Freud's thoughts on how the treatment proceeded, and to gain some insight into Freud's reactions to the experience of being an analyst.

THE FIRST EIGHT SESSIONS AND THE FUNDAMENTAL RULE

Freud tells us that the Rat Man, or Dr. Ernst Lanzer, remained in treatment for a little less than a year. During that time "the patient's mental health was restored to him by the analysis" (Freud 1909b, p. 249). Freud saw the patient as a moderately severe to severe case of obsessional neurosis.[12] He also, at the same time, gave Freud the "impression of being a clear-headed and shrewd person" (Freud 1909b, p. 158). Ernst was 29½ when he came to see Freud in October 1907. He was the fourth of seven children from a nonobservant and assimilationist Jewish family. He had begun his law studies at the University of Vienna law school at 19, but had not yet completed his law degree when he

---

[12]In this case report Freud comments on different areas, but he most prominently takes this opportunity to write about the etiology of obsessional neurosis.

came to see Freud. His father had died nine years previously, and Ernst still had not recovered from his varied and powerful reactions to his father's death. Before his father died, Ernst had began a courtship that bewildered and perplexed him for a good part of the rest of his life. (He subsequently died in World War I while serving in the army.) Gisela was a woman of whom his father disapproved; naturally enough, this paternal prohibition and his choice in women strongly entered into Ernst's extensive obsessional network. After the first session (the consultation session) Freud related the following:

> The chief features of his disorder were fears that something might happen to two people of whom he was very fond—his father and a lady whom he admired. Besides this he was aware of compulsive impulses—such as an impulse, for instance, to cut his throat with a razor; and further he produced prohibitions, sometimes in connection with quite unimportant things. [Freud 1909b, p. 158]

It was, of course, noteworthy that Ernst's fear of his father undergoing dangers and even tortures did not decrease as a result of his father's death. We can see this in his most famous obsession; it involved rats and began when a story was told to him during military training or maneuvers. Another officer, whom he dreaded, told him of a specially horrible punishment used in the East. At this point, we might begin to get a sense of Freud's interaction with the patient. Ernst starts off the second session by saying:

> 'I think I will begin today with the experience which was the immediate occasion of my coming to you. It was in August, during the maneuvers in ——. I had been suffering before, and tormenting myself with all kinds of obsessional thoughts, but they had quickly passed off during the maneuvers. I was keen to show the regular officers that people like me had not only learnt a good deal but could stand a good deal too. One day we started from —— on a short march. During a halt I lost my pince-nez, and, although I could easily have found them, I did not want to delay our start, so I gave them up. But I wired to my opticians in Vienna to send me another pair by the next post. During that same halt I sat between two officers, one of whom a captain with a Czech name, was to be of no small importance to me. I had a kind of dread of him, for he was obviously fond of cruelty. I do not say he was a bad man, but at the officers' mess he had repeatedly defended the introduction of corporal punishment, so that I had been obliged to disagree with him very sharply. Well, during this halt we got into conversation, and the captain told me he had read of a specially horrible punishment used in the East. . . .' Here the patient broke off, got up from the sofa, and begged me to spare him the recital of the details. I assured him that I myself had no taste whatever for cruelty, and certainly had no desire to torment him, but that naturally I could not grant him something which was beyond my power. He might just as well ask me to give him the moon. The overcoming of resistances was a law of the treatment, and on no consideration could it be dispensed with. (I had explained the idea of 'resistance' to him at the beginning of the hour, when

he told me there was much in himself which he would have to overcome if he was to relate this experience of his.) I went on to say that I would do all I could, nevertheless, to guess the full meaning of any hints he gave me. Was he perhaps thinking of impalement?—'No, not that . . . the criminal was tied up . . .'—he expressed himself so indistinctly that I could not immediately guess in what position—'a pot was turned upside down on his buttocks . . . some rats were put into it . . . and the . . .' He had again got up, and was showing every sign of horror and resistance—'bored their way in . . .'—Into his anus, I helped him out. At all the more important moments while he was telling his story his face took on a very strange, composite expression. I could only interpret it as one of horror at pleasure of his own of which he himself was unaware. He proceeded with the greatest difficulty: 'At that moment the idea flashed through my mind that this was happening to a person who was very dear to me.' In answer to a direct question he said that it was not he himself who was carrying out the punishment, but that it was being carried out as it were impersonally. After a little prompting I learnt that the person to whom this 'idea' of his related was the lady whom he admired. [Freud 1909b, pp. 165–167]

So now we have a slight idea of the range of the patient's obsessions, but to return to the first session we might go over how Freud had started the analysis proper, since this beginning is relevant to Freud's interaction with the patient in the second session.

I made him pledge himself to submit to the one and only condition of the treatment—mainly, to say everything that came into his head, even if it was unpleasant to him, or seemed unimportant or irrelevant or senseless. I then gave him leave to start his communications with any subject he pleased. [Freud 1909b, p. 159]

We can see that in the first two sessions Freud is firm to adamant about the fundamental rule. He tells us that he "made him pledge" to obey the fundamental rule. When in the second session the patient has difficulty in saying all that is on his mind, Freud gives him little choice. Freud intones that he cannot grant the patient the right to withhold a train of thought. In fact, Freud tells him that he cannot accord what is outside of his power to give; this, of course, implies that both Lanzer and Freud are subject to laws of a higher order, laws of nature that neither can break. It takes the treatment somewhat outside the realm of the two-person field, and invokes more fundamental processes. Freud does help the patient in the second session by guessing that Ernst is referring to the criminal's anus. Why is he able to help him in this situation? In part, because Freud's concern with knowing overrides even the fundamental rule. In fact, if the correct information is gathered, Freud seems unconcerned that he is aiding him in avoiding the fundamental rule. We will see that Freud's helping the Rat Man will not stop at providing him with words. Freud will send Ernst a postcard, supply a meal for him, and in sessions compliment and, at times, shock him. Freud will find it permissible to attempt to influence the patient as long as the influence is directed toward understanding the patient's neurotic formation.

We can see even in this brief glimpse that Freud regards the fundamental rule as being in the service of uncovering pathogenic memories. We know from the Nunberg and Ferdern minutes of the Vienna Circle that, in Freud's discussion of this case, he maintained: "The technique of analysis has changed to the extent that the psychoanalyst no longer seeks to elicit material in which he is interested, but permits the patient to follow his natural and spontaneous trains of thought" (1962, p. 227).

As Mahony points out (1986, p. 90), others in Freud's circle who heard the case rapidly agreed; and Nunberg and Federn conclude: "Here, for the first time, we have a report of an analysis which was carried out with the help of free associations" (1962, p. 227n).

Modern analysts have not shared Nunberg and Federn's view, and Kanzer contends that Freud's technique in the Rat Man made use of suggestion while displaying "not a little bit" of argumentativeness. This, Kanzer reminds us, is similar to Freud's encounters with Dora (Kanzer 1980a).

Mahony (1986) observes that Freud had not yet mastered the technical requirements for encouraging free association. We can conclude that Freud's implicit fundamental rule involves overcoming what he deems to be the patient's resistance. Free association may be helpful in accomplishing this, but if the patient is still resistant, Freud will attempt to use pressure to overcome the patient's resistance.

THE FIRST SESSIONS AND THE EMERGING TRANSFERENCE

How does Freud view the issue of transference in this case? Let us take a look at these first sessions in terms of our view of the emerging transference:

> In the first session Freud notes that Ernst had two men who exerted considerable influence over him. One was a Dr. Guthann and the other a medical student Mr. Lewy. In his publication Freud writes that 'the medical student had subsequently become his tutor, and had at some point altered his behaviour and begun treating him as though he were an idiot.' The following is left out of Freud's account. One day when they were walking with a colleague of L., L. got his colleague to play a practical joke on him [Ernst] and when he took it seriously they both laughed at his stupidity. Freud includes that at length he [Ernst] had noticed that the student was interested in one of his sisters, and had realized that he had only taken him up in order to gain admission into the house. This had been the first great blow of his life. He then proceeded without any apparent transition: 'My sexual life began very early. I can remember a scene during my fourth or fifth year. . . .' [Freud 1909b, pp. 159–160]

What follows in this session is Ernst relating a series of experiences of sexual, more precisely voyeuristic excitement with several governesses. There is a scene when he was 7 years old and was humiliated while sitting with his younger brother and three female servants. One of the women said, "It could be done with the little one (his brother); but Ernst is too clumsy, he would be sure to miss it." This humiliating scene is followed by his remembrance of complaining to his mother that he suffered from erections. He also felt that his parents knew his thoughts and he imagined that he had spoken them out loud without having heard himself do it. When Freud asked him for an example of his fears, Ernst replied: "For instance that my father might die." Freud was astonished to learn at the end of the first session that his father had died several years previously. Freud's remarks about this session include only comments about the childhood etiology of the Rat Man's disorder and a conclusion that the patient's forgetting of a woman's first (Christian) name is a sign of Ernst's homosexual strivings.

In his notes on the second session Freud writes that he had already recognized the homosexual component after some remarks Ernst made in the first session. Thus Freud already assumes that he understands the genesis of Ernst's obsessional neurosis and is able to note his homosexual conflicts. What he does not include in his understanding of the case are Ernst's references to several humiliating current experiences with men. In addition, he does not comment on Ernst's childhood experience of his parents' knowing his thoughts. It may be that this experience is remembered at this point in the treatment, since Freud as his analyst is trying to understand Ernst's thoughts. Freud is also strangely lacking in curiosity concerning this patient's spending so much of the first session discussing his childhood sexuality. Clearly, as several commentators have pointed out (e.g., Kanzer 1980d, Mahony 1986), Ernst knew of Freud's interest in childhood sexuality; that he begins his treatment in this manner is possibly a manifestation of this knowledge, and perhaps an already formed transference to Freud, the reader of minds and expert in childhood sexuality. It is not at all surprising that Freud would not interpret any of this to the patient, but in his commentary (both published and in his notes) he seems uninterested in or unaware of the potential transference implications of the first two sessions. The fact that he leaves out the aggressive interplay between Ernst and his friends may have no particular meaning, but it is at least a coincidental harbinger of things to come. Freud will find it very hard to allow the patient to manifest negative transferential feelings and/or thoughts. The aggressive interplay between Freud and Ernst is almost always covert, and at times Freud actively attempts to suppress the full expression of the patient's anger. At least one commentator has viewed parts of Freud's actions as provoking some of the patient's aggressive responses (Langs 1980).

In the second session, the Rat Man expresses what Freud labels "The Great Obsessive Fear." It was during the patient's description of the torture as told to him by the captain, that Freud aided the patient in completing the vignette. Freud has been viewed as practicing an older form of treatment in his attempt to help the patient complete this thought. However, Kanzer says that:

> Where previously we have seen in Freud's helpfully "guessing" the thoughts of
> the patient . . . a transference gratification achieved through mutual acting out, it
> should also be acknowledged that it was a contemporary form of promoting the
> formation of a therapeutic alliance. [Kanzer 1980a, p. 235]

What Kanzer is referring to is the practice of some contemporary analysts
who attempt to demonstrate a certain attunement to or empathy with the
patient. They might achieve this by reflecting a patient's remark (Kohut), or by
restating a patient's experience or even completing a patient's sentence.
Through this type of intervention these analysts demonstrate an alliance,
establishing that they understand the analysand's communications. Another
related way of accomplishing this alliance is to help the patient express certain
difficult events, or at times even to synthesize certain experiences that are
difficult for the patient to express coherently. In talking about Freud's intervention, Kanzer is simultaneously criticizing Freud and the concept of therapeutic alliance (calling it a transference gratification). However, it is hard to
see Freud's intervention as an example of what contemporary analysts call the
therapeutic alliance (see Chapter 16).

As opposed to a contemporary analyst's version of therapeutic alliance, we
can say that at no point is Freud simply accepting of the patient's experience.
Rather, even the patient's facial expression is scrutinized, then taken as
evidence that something else is lurking below the surface. The Rat Man's facial
expressions therefore belie his avowed difficulty in relating the story. It is as if
the suffering that the patient is going through is somewhat less real than the
underlying (sadistic) fantasy. Freud again appears as the interrogator—as he
did with Dora, albeit in gentler form. This is clear when the Rat Man gives
Freud a clue that he thinks of the torture not only in terms of the women he
loves, but, to quote Freud: "He was now obliged to *admit* that a second idea had
occurred to him . . . namely, the idea of the punishment also being applied to
his father" (Freud 1909b, p. 167). Why was the patient obliged to admit this?
Because the laws of overcoming resistances must be met whatever the consequences. Readers familiar with the case will remember that the story of the
rats is combined with an obsessive and somewhat confusing account by the
patient of his attempt to repay a debt that he had felt he had incurred as a
result of receiving a package containing his glasses (pince-nez). He felt or
learned that someone had paid for this package, and his journey (at least his
mental journey) to repay this debt is one that takes him and Freud on far and
wide-ranging trips.

Freud's difficulty with the story is expressed when he says, "It would not
surprise me to hear that at this point the reader had ceased to be able to
follow" (Freud 1909b, p. 169). One must assume that he himself had some
difficulty, since in 1923 he and the Stracheys devised a map that ostensibly
makes the story less confusing. Here we have another sign of Freud as the
decoder of all communications, while the transference is left to play itself out.

The story, as Freud correctly states, is "full of self-contradictions and sounded hopelessly confused" (Freud 1909b, p. 169). Yet approximately fifteen years later, Freud is still trying to untangle the patient's story. Freud's desire to understand the unconscious significance of all communications is his dominating aim regardless of the interchange.

Before we go to subsequent sessions, we will take a look at some of the exchanges that Freud did not include in his notes on the second session:

> He interrupts himself here in order to complain about the lack of understanding of the physicians he had (previously) consulted. When he made some indications to Wagner Von Jauregg about the content of his obsessional thoughts, he answered with a pitiful smile and gave him the example that he had ideas that forced him to take an exam at a certain time despite the fact that he wasn't prepared for it. . . . "A beneficent obsession," says Wagner—Freud in his notes then lectures Wagner that he shouldn't make this statement to a patient. This is typical of psychiatry of the time. Later in the session Ernst feels the need for clarification. He must note that from the beginning, including all his earlier fears that something might happen to his loved ones, he had not limited these penalties to this earthly life but extended them to the hereafter, to eternity. . . . Freud notes "He takes advantage of the uncertainty of the understanding (of eternity) (particularly) after I had drawn his attention to the importance of the infantile element of his religiosity." [Freud 1909b, p. 161]

We can see that again Freud fails to note in his published text the patient's conflict with an authority figure. Ernst's complaints against his former physicians may well have been justified, but it may be worth detailing that, whereas there is little in these two sessions that is left out, in each of the sessions Freud omits elements of disputes that the Rat Man has been engaged in or fantasied about. The third session is spent with the patient telling more about the story of the pince-nez and the torture. In the fourth session the patient relates that he has "decided to tell you something which I consider most important and which has tormented me from the first" (Freud 1909b, p. 174). The Rat Man then recounts in detail the story of his father dying of emphysema nine years previously. Although he sat vigil, the patient was asleep when his father died; for this he has reprimanded himself. He recounts attempts to deny his father's death and then eighteen months later "the recollection of his neglect . . . had begun to torment him terribly" (Freud 1909b, p. 175). In writing of this case, Freud lectures that "a layman will say that the guilt is too great for the occasion . . . the (analytic) physician says 'No, the affect is justified.' The sense of guilt is not in itself open to further criticism . . . it belongs to some other content, which is unknown (unconscious) and requires to be looked for" (Freud 1909b, pp. 175–176).

Unfortunately, Freud also provided this lecture to the patient. He writes of the fifth session:

> The patient showed great interest in what I had said, but ventured, so he told me, to bring forward a few doubts.—How, he asked, could the information that the

self-reproach, the sense of guilt, was justified have a therapeutic effect? I explained that it was not the information that had this effect, but the discovery of the unknown content to which the self-reproach was really attached. Yes, he said, that was the precise point to which his question had been directed. I then made some short comments upon the *psychological differences between the conscious and unconscious*, and upon the fact that everything conscious was subject to a wearing away, while what was unconscious was relatively unchangeable . . . I illustrated my remarks by pointing to the antiques standing about in my room . . . their burial had been their preservation: . . . (Ernst inquired) Was there any guarantee of what one's attitude would be towards what was discovered? . . . He had said to himself, he went on, that a self-reproach could only arise from a breach of a person's own inner moral principles and not from that of any external ones—I agreed, and said that the man who merely breaks an external law often regards himself as a hero. Such an occurence, he continued, was thus only possible where a *disintegration of the personality* was already present. Was there a possibility of his effecting a re-integration of his personality, he asked? I replied that I was in complete agreement with this notion of a splitting of his personality. He had only to assimilate this new contrast, between a moral self and an evil one, with the contrast I had already mentioned, between the conscious and the unconscious. The moral self was the conscious, the evil self was the unconscious. . . . He then said that, though he considered himself a moral person, he could quite definitely remember having done things in his childhood which came from his other self. . . . Freud then compliments him on implicitly understanding the importance of infantile life, and the session ends when the patient again expresses a doubt whether it was possible to undo modifications of such long standing. . . . I told him I did not dispute the gravity of his case nor the significance of his pathological constructions; but at the same time his youth was very much in his favour as well as the intactness of his personality. In this connection I said a word or two upon the good opinion I had formed of him, and this gave him visible pleasure. [Freud 1909b, pp. 176–178]

What are we to make of Freud's remarking on his good opinion of the patient? From Freud's report, the patient seemed to be pleased with the compliment. He leaves out, however, that the patient was "jolted" (Kanzer's term) by Freud's proclamation that there was indeed justification for his self-reproaches. To quote Kanzer: "In addition to this accusation and assumption of the role of omniscience, Freud's response involved the use of imagery and metaphors that could not have but shaken the patient deeply" (Kanzer 1980a, p. 236).

Kanzer is referring to Freud's archaeological or what Mahony has called *cryptological* metaphor.[13] One may surmise that the patient is wondering what he can do with the overwhelming news that in fact he is guilty. He had, after all, been consciously attempting to ward off his feelings of guilt by rationally telling himself (when he could) that he wasn't truly guilty; here Freud is telling him that there must be something of which he is actually guilty or else why all

---

[13]Mahony has called it cryptological since Freud refers to the "buried" fantasies.

the storm, drama, and obsessions. It is no wonder that the patient comes to the next session feeling overwhelmed as well as defensive, and probably at least somewhat resentful. After this intervention Freud is both reassuring and complimentary, and yet at the same time he does not want to minimize the extent of the pathology. If the pathology can only be unearthed, then conscious and unconscious, the moral self and the evil self, can be joined in harmony. Freud here is replacing the early nineteenth-century view of childhood innocence with a more contemporary view of childhood demonology. A picture of childhood demons invading the patient emerges; these demons can be exorcised if both of them together stand firm and don't succumb to the sirens embodied in the resistances. Where are the heralded transferences that we are to read so much about? So far they are nowhere to be found and in gentler tones Freud seems quite like the nineteenth-century therapist that we thought we had left with Dora.

In the fifth session, Freud compliments Ernst, to undo the visible upset the patient is undergoing as a result of having been jolted in the previous session. In my opinion Freud was probably unconsciously responding to some aspect of the material that had provoked him.[14] This speculation aside, it is clear that Freud has already had some difficulty in relating to, and discussing with, the patient his aggressive interchanges with contemporary male figures in his life. This is not meant to imply that Freud should have confronted the patient or interpreted anything to the patient about these interchanges. Rather, they might have been explored and a forum for their expression might have begun to be established.[15] Thus it was not Freud's complimenting the patient that is problematic; it is what led up to his perceived need to compliment Ernst that is called into question.

How have others viewed this event? Zetzel (1965) has seen this interchange as a means of furthering what she has called the therapeutic alliance. Kanzer, on the other hand, maintains that a "more neutral approach, devoid of both the injurious as well as supportive aspects of [what he calls Freud's attempts at] human influence could surely have brought out and ultimately interpreted the current aspects of death wishes to the father as applicable to the analyst" (Kanzer 1980a, pp. 236–237).

Kanzer does not doubt that the patient is guilty about death wishes toward the father-analyst, but he emphasizes that the lack of neutrality in Freud's technique makes the transference implications unavailable for interpretative efforts. By the end of the seventh session, Freud is able to formulate interpretations of a good deal of the Rat Man's life. Clearly, Freud has not derived these formulations on the basis of the patient displaying a full-blown transference neurosis during the eight sessions that they have met. Yet he has been able not only to formulate a good deal about the patient's obsessions, but

---

[14]That is, I think that Freud sensed Ernst's difficulty with authority figures and was attempting to handle the patient's underlying conflicts by inducing guilt in him.
[15]Hopefully within a nonjudgmental atmosphere.

also to formulate a good deal about his childhood neurosis and the etiology of both the childhood and adult obsessions that plague the Rat Man. On the basis of Freud's notes[16] we can say that his understanding of the patient was fairly firm after the first eight meetings. He also transmitted a good deal of that understanding to the patient. Clearly, on the basis of Freud's notes and the case write-up, we can say that transference was not a central issue for Freud in the present case, at least during the first eight sessions. Freud was content to let the patient proceed, when he was associating and providing Freud with material to interpret. When Ernst stopped, Freud pressured him.

Freud, Ernst, and Dora

In many ways, we have seen that Freud's behavior with Ernst Lanzer bears a number of similarities to his conduct with Dora. His interest in both cases is with uncovering the meaning of the patient's verbalizations, dreams, and symptoms in terms of a model of childhood object relations in which these relations are mostly centered around fantasies of bodily functioning (childhood sexuality). He is quick to interpret, and one must admit—even if one disagrees with the interpretations—that they are brilliant constructions. There are, however, distinct differences in the way Freud is dealing with the present case.

We have emphasized the resemblance of Freud in the Dora case to the present one; the differences are just as striking. Freud does not try to insist on analyzing every dream so that he understands every element of the dream.[17] There are, in fact, dreams that he doesn't analyze at all, because he thought that the subject was covered in other material, or that the patient did not seem receptive to looking at the material covered in the dream. More importantly, he is actively aware of the transference even if it is not the main element of the treatment that he focuses on:

> Nov. 21—Next day he came in a state of depression, and wanted to talk about indifferent subjects. . . . The most frightful thing had occurred to his mind while he was in the tram yesterday. . . . His cure would not be worth such a sacrifice. I should turn him out, for it concerned the transference. Why should I put up with such a thing? None of the explanations I gave him about the transference (which did not sound at all strange to him) had any effect. It was only after a forty minutes' struggle—as it seemed to me—and after I had revealed the element of revenge against me and had shown him that by refusing to tell me and by giving up the treatment he would be taking a more outright revenge on me than by telling me—only after this did he give me to understand that it concerned my daughter. With this, the session came to an end.

[16]As well as on the basis of Freud's published case report.
[17]In the Dora case Freud presented two dreams that he analyzed in great detail. He also continued the analysis of the dreams across a number of sessions. There is no place in the present case that we see Freud do anything like that.

Nov. 22 (Next session)—Cheerful, but became depressed when I brought him back to the subject. A fresh transference—My mother was dead. He was anxious to offer his condolences, but was afraid that in doing so an impertinent laugh might break out as had repeatedly happened before in the case of a death. . . . Freud—Hasn't it ever occurred to you that if your mother died you would be freed from all conflicts, since you would be able to marry? Patient—You are taking revenge on me. . . . You are forcing me into this, because you want to revenge yourself on me. . . . He agreed that his walking about the room while he was making these confessions was because he was afraid of being beaten by me. . . . Moreover, he kept hitting himself while he was making these admissions. . . . Patient—Now you'll turn me out. . . . [Freud 1909b, pp. 280-284]

It seems evident just from the material that Freud is eliciting that something different is happening here than with Dora. Moreover, Freud is tolerating this material and attempting to deal with it as a manifestation of transference. We can see in the November 21 session that Freud recognizes the motive of revenge in the transference; after a forty-minute struggle he is able to communicate this to the patient.[18] Even though one might have different interpretations of the material Freud is presenting, it is being noted here as one illustration of how Freud was emerging at that point from a purely pathogenic memory model. Here he is observing transference manifestations as they are occurring, and attempting to interpret them or allow the transference to unfold. In the next session, when the patient continues an element of hostility in the transference, we see that Freud attempts to change the direction of the interaction and brings the patient's mother into the arena of the analysis. Nevertheless, when the patient feels this as an attack by Freud, the transference is again referred to, and Freud implicitly brings up the sadomasochistic elements of the patient's transference reactions. Ernst is still attempting to get Freud to beat him by forcing him to leave the treatment situation. This might be both a wish for a beating, as well as a striking back at Freud. Does Freud understand the full ramifications of the material? A number of analysts would answer in the negative, but one can't deny that Freud, at this point, is actively trying to decipher the transference meaning of the patient's associations. It also reaffirms Freud's continuous efforts to descry the significance of his own reactions. Here we see a definite departure from the pure pathogenic memory model. Freud seems on his way to understanding how transference is manifested in the treatment situation. In fact, as we have noted,[19] Freud continued to understand the importance of transference; whether he utilized this knowledge in the treatment room is a matter of conjecture. At any rate, I have chosen to use these illustrations of Freud's handling of the transference as illustrations of his new stance; there are a

[18]Freud's self-observation about the struggle he experienced reaffirms for us his difficulty with this type of material.
[19]See Part II of this book, particularly the paper "Recollection, Repetition and Working Through."

number of other illustrations that could have been chosen. What does not seem to be present is any example of Freud designating an aspect of the treatment as illustrative of the transference neurosis. This case, of course, occurred before Freud published the concept of the transference neurosis.[20]

Freud's Extra-Analytic Behavior

There are many other things that are worthy of note in this elaborate case write-up, but we will restrict ourselves to three topics. Two of these topics can be classified as events that Freud induced through extra-analytic behavior.[21] What are the two examples of extra-analytic behavior? Early in the treatment (session 8, October 11), Freud was frustrated that Ernst hadn't talked about Gisela, and requested that he bring in her photograph. Later (December 8), Freud sent him a postcard, suggesting that the patient bring in a picture of Gisela. At another point in the treatment (December 28) the patient expressed that he was hungry and Freud provided a meal for him. In his notes to the case, Freud wrote, "He was hungry and was fed" (Freud 1909b, p. 303). What are we to make of these two examples of extra-analytic behavior? In the first example Freud is inducing the patient to talk about a topic in a way that can be characterized as both intrusive, seductive, and certainly coercive. To take a brief look at Freud's notes of October 11: "Violent struggle, bad day. Resistance, because I requested him yesterday to bring a photograph of the lady with him—i.e., to give up his reticence about her. Conflict about whether he should abandon the treatment or surrender his secrets" (Freud 1909b, p. 260).

We can say again that Freud was obviously not concerned with keeping the transference in the forefront of the treatment. Rather, he was interested in decoding the significance of the various figures in the patient's life. The fact that the patient doesn't want to give this information is an example of resistance that both patient and analyst have to rally against. One might ask what Freud's rationale was for determining when a patient is ready to discuss certain topics. How did Freud consider elements of timing in his interventions? This type of question is related to the underlying logic of Freud's technique. Even if he practiced his brand of psychoanalysis imperfectly (as might be expected of the inventor of the technique), is there an underlying rationale to his technique that would allow others to perfect this version of psychoanalysis? Or, alternatively, are

---

[20]As far as I know, there are no published (or unpublished) examples of Freud calling a part of a treatment the transference neurosis.

[21]Eissler, in an important essay (1958), designates some behavior or interventions of the analyst as parameters. A parameter is a piece of nonstandard analytic technique that is introduced to facilitate the treatment. The intervention is considered a true parameter if the intervention or rather the effects of it can be subjected to analysis. It is possible to question whether Freud's behavior can be considered a parameter in this treatment.

we simply to put aside his actions as the embryonic attempts of the inventor of a new technique?[22] It is hard to see the rationale that Freud employed in this intervention. It seems that he was acting as a type of paternal figure, demanding to know who this woman was that Ernst was seeing.

What about the meal that he provided for Ernst? Did this provide for difficulties in the treatment? Here[23] there are markedly diverse opinions that one can sample from. In two interesting and engaging articles (1977a, 1979), Lipton contends that what is today depicted as the classical position[24] should not be considered Freud's position. Lipton cogently argues that if Freud is the creator of psychoanalytic technique, the classical position should be the one that is most closely related to Freud's position. However, he uses Freud's behavior with the Rat Man to establish that Freud was *not* a classical analyst in the modern sense of the term. His prime example for this argument is Freud's providing a meal for the Rat Man. Lipton could, of course, have used a plethora of examples to bolster this point. He does argue that Freud's providing a meal for the patient was acceptable under the circumstances.[25] What he deems as necessary is for Freud (or any analyst) to be sensitive to the transference implications of his actions. Freud's "natural behavior" with patients is perfectly acceptable from Lipton's (and Gill's) point of view. How one determines the limits of this natural style, of course, is an important question.

Lipton puts forth the following thesis:

> The essence of the difference between modern technique (and Freud's technique) is that modern technique has been expanded to incorporate aspects of the analyst's relation with the patient which Freud excluded from technique. Accompanying this expansion, there has been a tendency to evaluate technique on the basis of a standard which can be applied immediately to any intervention which the analyst makes without giving consideration to its effect, or lack of effect, on the course of the analysis. . . .
>
> The criticisms of Freud's technique show that modern technique places great weight on minor matters rather than major ones. Rather than impeaching the major interpretive work of the analyst, they focus on trivial matters: a meal, a postcard, a realistic clarification, the fact that the patient arose from the couch several times, the fact that Freud made some statements which may not have been mandatory, and so on. The undeniable fact that each of these trivial matters

---

[22]In my opinion Freud's interpreting of resistance should normally be restricted to interpreting the transference resistance. This, I believe, would follow from some of his ideas about transference and resistance. There would be exceptions to this formulation, but these would lead into a lengthy discussion. I would comment here only that I do believe that one can construct a fuller technique based on Freud's ideas than has been done up to this point.

[23]This is not meant to imply that one can't also obtain quite diverse views about Freud's sending a postcard to Ernst.

[24]Lipton prefers to call this position *standard analytic technique*.

[25]Lipton maintains that the patient would have had difficulty in obtaining a meal that night and that Freud was behaving courteously.

may become of importance to the patient seems to have led to the conclusion that any such interventions should be eschewed. [Lipton 1977a, p. 262]

Thus Freud is seen as distinguishing his real relationship to the patient from the transference relationship. This is seen as true, even though it is acknowledged by both Freud and Lipton that this real relationship may affect, even strongly affect, the transference relationship. One can say that Lipton is arguing against a sterile, impersonal technique. He is obviously stating that the focus of classical analysts takes one away from the central issues of meaning in the analytic situation.

Compare this point of view with these statements of Langs':

Freud's cordial postcard which apparently had a strong homosexual meaning for the Rat Man . . . evoked considerable anxiety, erotic fantasies, and anger. The postcard fostered fantasies that Freud wished to be more personally involved with the Rat Man and to have him as a member of the family. [Langs 1980, p. 221]

Langs interprets that:

The dream or fantasy of Freud's daughter with the patches of dung in place of eyes is to be viewed here as—among its many meanings—a reflection of the Rat Man's unconscious perception of Freud's blindness to the interaction between the two of them. [Langs 1980, p. 222]

Langs concludes that Freud was unaware of the powerful transferential meaning of his actions. In fact, he names his article "The Misalliance Dimension in the Case of the Rat Man" because of the manner in which Freud oversteps the boundaries of "normal" analytic behavior without being aware of the powerful implications of his actions. Langs' consideration of Freud providing a meal for the patient is equally critical:

Let us first detail the sequence that preceded this experience and the reactions that followed, after which he will be able to formulate the repercussions of this particular "deviation" in technique which took the form of a direct, noninterpretive gratification of the patient. In general, in the proceeding sessions, the Rat Man was concerned with his anger at his father in a way that suggested "transference reactions." In earlier sessions there were fantasies of his older male friend's death, as well as destructive thoughts about his father. . . . The material suggests that the Rat Man's moment of hunger occurred at a time when he was dealing with some very traumatic memories and some very disturbing feelings toward Freud. Some of this may have been evoked by the apparently seductive postcard sent by Freud to the Rat Man, the effects of which had remained unanalyzed. [Langs 1980, p. 223]

Langs concludes, at this point, that Freud had "no extensive clinical experience in distinguishing his patients' primarily intrapsychically determined fantasies about him (transferences) from their conscious and unconscious realistic, veridical perceptions (nontransferences)."

Both Lipton and Langs make convincing arguments that seem equally hard to refute. Intuitively, it appears that a theory of technique that focuses on minutiae cannot be helpful in capturing the essence of human experience. Alternatively, Langs' interpretations of the effects of Freud's interventions seem to provide convincing explanations. Although Lipton offers an interesting overview and rationale for the *natural analyst*, it is hard to completely accept Freud on this basis. Rather, one can say that Freud's natural behavior is positive within some defined limits; how one defines the limits will provide a crucial aspect of a theory of technique. Lipton presents as a linchpin for his contentions the fact that Freud's understanding of the case was correct. He also states that the case was obviously a successful one, and that this is further evidence that the focus of contemporary analysts is misplaced. It seems to me that Lipton is falling into the same dead end that Freud entered when he stated what is now called his *tally argument*.[26] Freud's results can be interpreted in a variety of ways and still the argument for his natural behavior stands or falls on its own merits. Let us say we agree with Lipton that Freud was successful with this case; it may be that we think he would have achieved greater therapeutic success if he had not been involved with the patient in various extra-analytic behaviors. Or we may think that Freud's success was due to these behaviors and had nothing to do with the efficacy of his interpretations. The permutations seem endless, and asserting that Freud was successful in the case does not lead us very far in understanding why natural behavior is desirable in the analytic situation. I think that Lipton provides a more cogent rationale when he states simply that the focus of psychoanalysis should be on understanding rather than on minutiae.[27] Still, Langs would argue that there are at least some boundary issues that must be stated if one is to have a theory of technique; and with this argument, I would say, it is impossible to disagree. How one defines those boundaries is the crucial issue.

---

[26]Freud argued that psychoanalytic theory must be correct since its therapeutic results tally or agree with the theory that generated the therapy. There are so many difficulties with this argument that it is difficult to know where to begin in a critique. As a first point there is not a necessary relationship between psychoanalytic therapy and psychoanalytic theory. Freud could have invented a number of therapies that would be compatible with his theory. The theory still has too much slack to be able to directly predict only one therapy that is compatible with, or is even the best fit for the theory. Given that this is the case it is difficult to argue that if the therapy has positive results the theory is correct, or alternatively if there are negative therapeutic results the theory is wrong. Thus to some extent the theory and the therapy are independent of one another. In addition it is always possible to get therapeutic results for reasons that do not relate to the reasons one is utilizing to explain the therapeutic results. For example, is Freud successful because he interprets correctly or because he has provided a transference cure? There are a number of arguments that one can make around this issue. For an alternative point of view see Grunbaum (1984).

[27]Moreover, I will argue that the minutiae are impossible to control beyond certain limits and that the ideal of an impersonal and therapeutic analyst are of necessity incompatible.

Freud as Educator

It would be easy to give three or four more different contemporary interpretations and evaluations of Freud's actions with Ernst Lanzer. These two almost diametrically opposed views should suffice to give the reader some indication of the spectrum of opinion that surrounds this case. We have looked primarily at dramatic elements of Freud's behavior with the patient. Freud's technique can be viewed in several other ways, however. We can observe the way Freud consistently gives the patient theoretical explanations during at least the early phases of the treatment. We can also examine how Freud differs from what a number of authors have termed the "silent analyst."

We encounter Freud consistently explaining unconscious motivation, resistance, and principles of childhood sexuality to the patient. There is little doubt that these theoretical interludes are of interest to the reader, but one wonders what impact they have on the patient. Kris (1951, 1956), in what Lipton considers to be the first major criticism of Freud, intimates that a good deal of what Freud accomplished was a kind of brainwashing of the patient. Clearly, Kris is concerned about the effects of suggestion in a way that did not concern Freud. If one were to build Kris's argument, it could be said that right from the beginning of treatment, Freud is attempting to convert the patient into becoming an advocate of the analytic method. Moreover, when the patient doesn't talk about what Freud considers to be important material, Freud certainly attempts to induce the patient to discuss those issues. Is this brainwashing, or does this behavior admit other interpretations? Certainly one could say that it is not unreasonable for the patient to be provided with some rationale as to why the analyst is making certain requests or utilizing certain techniques. It may be unreasonable for certain modern analysts to begin a treatment as if patients should know or understand why they are undergoing certain experiences. Thus what Kris calls indoctrination one might see as appropriately educative. This might be particularly relevant at a time in history when psychoanalysis did not enjoy its present popularity (or notoriety). Freud advocated providing the patient with a rationale, and insofar as he does this at the beginning of the treatment, this seems reasonable and appropriate.

One might question his timing in presenting some of his discourses on psychoanalytic topics. They come at times when the patient is resistant—or, put more neutrally, reluctant—to bring up some experiences that Freud thinks are important. At these delicate times, it might be possible for Freud to find alternate ways to help with the patient's internal struggles. Freud frequently appeals to the patient's intellect in trying to show his perspective about the issues that arise in the treatment. It always seems to have been his view that if the patient can gain insight into his condition, this insight can be ameliorative. Implicitly, Freud is saying that if insight is not ameliorative, then the patient is not analyzable. In this context it is easier to understand his view of the trial analysis. It may be that diagnosis was not the issue for Freud in accepting patients into treatment; rather, he was concerned with whether they could understand his point of view and where his theoretical perspective was leading them. One could say that along with the ability to maintain a positive transference, Freud valued those patients who interested him intellectually. He did not seem to tire of talking about psychoanalytic insights; he did seem to tire quickly of patients who displayed negative transference states. Today, the modern stereotype, or what Lipton calls standard technique, depicts the analyst as a silent listener who speaks mainly to deliver interpretative remarks. Although Freud certainly dispensed numerous interpretations, he was rarely silent at other times. He was an active questioner and commentator on virtually all facets of the treatment situation and the patient's life.[28] There is no question that Lipton is by and large correct when he states that Freud's technique at the time of the Rat Man was his final technique. There is no written record of Freud's views on technique changing,[29] nor is there any indication that this is the case, as Kanzer has indicated (see Chapter 17). However, it is true that Freud's newer conceptualizations of defense logically lead to different views of technique. If one has accepted the idea of unconscious defense, it makes little sense to exhort the patient to free-associate or discuss certain types of material, since the patient may well be unconscious of his reasons for not responding. Clearly, in a model that has defense as an unconscious process, one would have to have analyzed some aspect of the defensive process[30] before the patient would be able to talk about certain topics (at least in any meaningful way). One wonders if Freud wouldn't at least have been more of the silent analyst if he had taken his new model to heart. Leaving aside this speculation, it is clear that Freud did not see analytic behavior as markedly different from a variety of other types of professional behavior. As many authors have noted, he was not a different person as an analyst from who he was in a number of other settings. Freud's natural behavior in the analytic setting has not become a role model for the modern classical or standard analyst. Whether this is considered an advance in technique is a question that defines a good part of one's theoretical position; clearly, we can say that Freud's technique is not today's classical technique.

Termination Issues

How does the treatment end? We have already quoted Freud about the ending of the present case, but even the ending of the treatment raises divergent

[28]Although we will not present the research we have done, we have looked at many (perhaps all) of the published reports of former patients of Freud's; based on these reports, it is safe to say that Freud did not change in this respect during his lifetime.

[29]Freud did put forth the idea of transference neurosis after the analysis of the Rat Man. There is no record of his technique changing on the basis of this concept. It is possible to say that waiting for the transference neurosis to develop is a change in technique.

[30]It seems to me that a variety of analysts (Poland 1991, Schafer 1968) have correctly pointed out that one never analyzes defense in an abstract way, but rather that defense is bound up with a relationship of some kind.

voices. To paraphrase Freud, the patient's health was restored to him by the analysis, but like so many other men of promise, he perished in the Great War. Mahony disputes Freud's view of the treatment's end, maintaining that the patient actually ended it around January 21, the point at which Freud's notes for the case end. Mahony tells us that Freud overstated how long the treatment lasted,

> in order to make the Rat Man's treatment temporally and qualitatively superior to Dora's—hers, the only other previously published case that Freud himself conducted after his discovery of the Oedipus complex, ended as a failure in less than three months. Seemingly, therefore, Freud desperately wanted the appearance of a complete case to impress his recently won international followers and to promote the cause of the psychoanalytic movement. [Mahony 1986, p. 85]

The evidence for this allegation involves no new discovery of primary sources, but rather a reinterpretation of available sources. Mahony contends that the additional notes (beyond January 21) were not found because the intense (or analytic) aspects of the treatment ended at this time. Mahony considers the fact that additional notes were not found as evidence for his contention. He maintains that in the session notes written several weeks before January 21, the appearance of termination themes can be seen. Mahony also relates the following:

> My assumption about the brevity of an intense, regularly scheduled analysis receives unexpected support from a single isolated statement by James Strachey. In his editorial introduction to "Character and Anal Eroticism," first published in March 1908, he disclosed that the essay "was no doubt partly stimulated by the analysis of the 'Rat Man,' which had been concluded shortly before." Such an early dating confirms my conclusion that the Rat Man case, commonly regarded as Freud's only published, complete case, is nothing of the kind. [Mahony 1986, pp. 81–82]

Mahony concludes that Strachey's comment substantiates the view that Freud finished seeing the Rat Man by late January of 1908, as opposed to the summer (or early fall) of 1908. One can only wonder about Mahony's rules of evidence. Does this statement by Strachey confirm Mahony's contention that Freud lied about the length of treatment of the case? If this is true and Strachey's statement is taken as confirmation, then Strachey must have been an accomplice to this deception. Certainly Strachey knew Freud's claim, since he translated the case. So we must conclude, from Mahony's logic, that Strachey was in on the deception and carelessly provided a clue to the crime. The possibility of a misprint or mistake is excluded from this line of reasoning. Let us for a brief moment look at other mistakes in print. Mahony quotes Freud from "Analysis Terminable and Interminable" in the following manner: "It cannot be disputed that analysts in their own personalities have not thoroughly come up to the standard of psychical normality to which they wish to educate their parents" (Mahony 1986, p. 85n).

Now, Freud has written "patient," but in Mahony's translation the word is "parents." How should we interpret this mistake? Mahony is a writer who is attempting to show us that in many ways we have not correctly understood Freud, and that in various ways Freud has misled the analytic community. Is his mistake an example of his overpowering wish to educate those analysts (including Freud) that Mahony transferentially views as his parents? Does his overwhelming need to exhibit himself force him to make this mistake so that the analytic community will know about this dynamic? Or did a typesetter or editor make the mistake? The dangers of interpreting this type of mistake are obvious to all of us who are not involved with having to prove a given point. This danger was clearly not obvious to Mahony. It is interesting, however, that his allegation has brought no outcry from the analytic community. Recently (1984, 1985), Masson published several works with accusations that are trivial compared to the one that Mahony has put forth. Mahony alleges that Freud is lying about statements that are basic to the integrity of any reporter, whether that person is a clinician or researcher. I must again repeat that Mahony's evidence is virtually nonexistent, and termination themes are present in much of the material that is present in Freud's notes, including the sessions I have briefly quoted.[31] Those sessions occurred two months before Mahony's termination date. The patient did not settle into treatment easily, and expressed doubts about the treatment during the fourth session and periodically thereafter. This is not unusual for a patient. Nor is it uncommon for patients with obsessional traits to be uncertain and ambivalent about almost all the important events in their lives.

Leaving aside Mahony's assertions, how are we to judge the success of the present case? We know that the patient passed his examination during the treatment, and that shortly after the treatment ended, he married Gisela. Are these accomplishments to be considered a result of the treatment? It is difficult to be certain, but given the state of the patient, one can say that something positive seems to have happened during the time he saw Freud. Since the case lasted approximately eleven months, it is hard for contemporary analysts to believe that the patient was fully analyzed during this relatively short period of time. Should we then conclude that what Freud accomplished with Dr. Lanzer has to be considered less than a full analytic result, perhaps what many would call a transference cure? Does this render the case one that is of little interest in terms of contemporary analytic technique, and only of historical interest, since technique has advanced beyond Freud? Should we alternatively consider that perhaps Freud was able to accomplish things that are beyond contemporary analysts, and consider Freud's cases to be of interest as the product of a

---

[31]We have seen Freud struggling in the early sessions to keep Ernst in the treatment. We have also witnessed Ernst asking Freud to put him out of treatment.

singular genius? Or perhaps, as Freud seems to be saying in "Analysis Termi-nable and Interminable," we should think of the results of analysis in terms of a continuum rather than in dichotomous terms. In this context we might wonder what additional treatment the patient would have needed and what were the benefits and the drawbacks of the treatment he received.

Lipton does not question that the case was a success; he uses the success of the case to further his ideas about the benefits of Freud's analytic technique over classical or standard analytic ideas of technique. Mahony, on the other hand, seems to imply that even the way the patient died in the war was a product of his unsuccessful analysis. It is true that he labels the analysis a magnificent failure, but despite his attempts at undoing, he levels quite power-ful accusations against Freud. Most other commentators have seen the case as an interesting view of Freud's technique and have used the case to point out how analytic technique has evolved from that point in time. Although this point is not commented on by most analysts, Freud's diagnosis of the Rat Man is a question that might be considered in summarizing Freud's ideas. Is the Rat Man to be viewed as a severe obsessional disorder, or, in modern parlance, would he be labeled as some version of a narcissistic or borderline personality type? That Freud calls his obsessions deliria seems to indicate that at times some aspect of the patient's sense of reality or at times even his reality testing is impaired. This diagnostic question is implicitly relevant when we discuss the question of analyzability.

The Wolf Man and Dora

In discussing "Analysis Terminable and Interminable," Freud mentions his most famous patient, the Wolf Man. In this paper he limits his discussion to the implications of his intervention in setting a termination date. In publishing this case, Freud was primarily interested in illustrating the importance of childhood sexuality. His interest in the significance[32] of the primal scene led him to interpret a dream of the Wolf Man's as being stimulated by a memory of watching his parents having intercourse; to use Freud's terms, "he witnessed a coitus *a tergo* (from behind), three times repeated" (Freud 1918, p. 37). From our point of view, this case is notable in that Freud's handling of the dream is similar to his style in the Dora case.

We assume that this is not true of his behavior during much of his contact with the Wolf Man. The patient tells Freud about the dream after Freud has set the termination date. The dream is one that Freud continues to analyze for many sessions, and he uses his and the Wolf Man's associations to it inter-changeably to arrive at his interpretation. Freud's most memorable interpreta-

---

[32]This interest can be evidenced as he is supervising the treatment of little Hans (1909). Of course his interest in the primal scene dates back even before this case.

tion involves a reconstruction that receives relatively little support from the patient's associations. Nevertheless, this becomes Freud's most famous case and the patient becomes an analytic celebrity who, following his analysis with Freud, is visited by various analysts for the rest of his life. Freud's technique in dealing with the dream is to look at each segment of the dream and ask the patient for associations. Let us look at some aspects of the Wolf Man's dream: "I dreamt that it was night and that I was lying in my bed. . . . I know it was winter when I had the dream. . . . Suddenly the window opened of its own accord, and I was terrified to see that some white wolves were sitting on the big walnut tree in front of the window" (Freud 1918, p. 29). Freud then asks the patient:

> Why were the wolves white? This made him think of sheep, large flocks of which were kept in the neighbourhood of the estate. His father occasionally took him with him to visit these flocks, and every time this happened he felt very proud and blissful. Later on—according to enquiries that were made—it may easily have been shortly before the time of the dream—an epidemic broke out among the sheep. [Freud 1918, p. 30]

In this brief interchange we learn two things: Freud is asking the patient to associate to an element of the dream, and Freud is following up the patient's associations (to his questions) with further questions. He does this throughout the entire account of the dream. He asks such questions as: Why were there six or seven wolves? and continues until he has probed the patient for his responses to the entire dream. Why is it extraordinary that the analysis of the dream lasted through a number of sessions?[33] Freud has just told us a few years before this case was terminated that the dream no longer occupied a special place in psychoanalysis. However, in this case, the dream is the central piece of an elaborate reconstruction; the analysis of this dream is as crucial to this case as was the analysis of Dora's two dreams.

Freud understands intellectually that performing dream analysis as he did during the period of the Dream Book (around 1900) is no longer his (stated) method, but old habits are hard to break. This is especially true when the dream seems to fit in with a theoretical predilection of his.[34] It is necessary to remember that when Freud analyzed a dream in the case of either the Wolf Man or Dora he went way beyond either of the contemporary positions we have introduced here (see Chapter 7). The group that maintained the exceptional position of the dream would never have questioned a patient in the way that we see Freud doing in the case of the Wolf Man. It is of historical interest to see Freud abandon his technical suggestions when he is intrigued by the content of a dream.

[33]As an example Freud relates that "on another occasion an association which suddenly occurred to him carried us another step forward in our understanding of the dream. The Wolf Man states, "The tree was a Christmas-tree." This is the type of association by both the patient and the analyst that continues for some time in relation to the dream.

[34]That is the significance of the primal scene.

16

The Widening Scope of Psychoanalysis

As we have seen, there is virtually no aspect of technique (or theory) that was not of some interest to Freud. However, there were themes that Freud for the most part eschewed. Certainly, for the majority of his career, he maintained that narcissism was antithetical to psychoanalytic treatment. Late in his life Freud became more open to the idea of treating people with narcissistic difficulties. Despite this new attitude his suggestions for the initial stages of psychoanalytic treatment are not appropriate for therapy with narcissistic patients. In this chapter I will detail my reasons for this assertion and explore some alternative ideas on the opening phase of the analytic situation.

Freud's genius was such that he was able to perceive what his clinical experience barely allowed him to experience. In reconstructing his career, I imagine that he devised a number of concepts that he had only infrequently experienced, or at least attended to, in actual clinical situations. He gives indications in his case accounts and his other writings that he had little patience for resistant patients. Similarly, if a patient was interested only in *dumplings*,[1] this patient also did not capture Freud's attention for very long. The courageous discoverer often does not have time for what he considers to be details that are best left to others. It is in this context that I see Freud's suggestions for beginning the treatment. They are the counsel of someone who is eager to hear another story and more free associations, someone who wishes to know how new experiences relate to his revolutionary concepts. His proposals for beginning the treatment do not reflect the tactful, sympathetic clinician

[1]Freud's reference to those patients who were not able to elevate their thoughts beyond their everyday gratifications.

that Freud could be once the treatment was in progress.[2] Since in this chapter I will focus on the beginning phase of analytic treatment, I will also discuss the question of analyzability and the issues that come up around the concept of the unobjectionable transference.

Freud on Beginning the Treatment

This topic is one that has received relatively little attention in analytic literature, and yet to my mind it is the crucial phase of therapy in today's widening scope of psychoanalysis. That there is a widening scope today is partly due to the fact that analysts begin treatment in a manner that is different from the one Freud advocated. Freud's views on the beginning of treatment were dictated by his criteria of analyzability. He placed little confidence in psychiatric diagnosis, and instead was interested in the patient's ability to utilize interpretations. His concern involved the patient's ability to comprehend, and associate to, the analyst's interpretative efforts. Freud maintains that if a patient enters treatment with a negative transference, has reservations about treatment, or is too narcissistic, he is unable to benefit from analytic treatment. However, Freud tells us, if the patient is able to "show compliance enough to respect the necessary conditions of the analysis, we can regularly succeed in giving all the symptoms of the neurosis a new transference colouring, and in replacing his whole ordinary neurosis by a 'transference-neurosis' of which he can be cured by the therapeutic work" (Freud 1914b, p. 374).

Thus, for a patient who criticizes and provokes authority figures, or is not able to talk about certain difficulties, there is an implicit message that Freud sends: either you are able to comply (free associate) or you have to leave the analysis. Obviously some patients will be able to comply with Freud's demand for analytic material, but it can be that this type of compliance may lead to a pseudo-analysis. Then there are patients who are simply unable to comply with or tolerate the analyst's early interpretative efforts. Are these patients unanalyzable, or are there alternative ways of conceiving of the beginning phase of analysis to allow this type of patient the benefit of an analytic treatment.[3]

In Freud's vision of therapeutic change,[4] there is a distinct cleavage between patient and analyst that is closed by the analyst's interpretations.

---

[2]We have also seen that Freud is aware of analytic tact at the beginning of the treatment. He suggests that early interpretations are equivalent to flinging these remarks at the patient. This awareness does not seem to have carried over into the treatment room during most of his career.
[3]In what follows I am considering Freud's view of the beginning of the treatment, in contrast to my views and those of the authors I am citing. There are analytic authors who have advocated starting patients in psychotherapy and gradually moving them into analysis. Although these analysts come closer to the views I am considering, I will not refer to them in the course of this chapter since it would detract from the lines of the discussion.
[4]Implicitly, this is also Brenner's view of therapeutic change.

Through these interpretations the patient receives new insight that releases the analysand from his past conflicts and allows him to try activities or experience feelings that were previously inaccessible to him. To say this in another way, it is the analyst who puts the patient in touch with an aspect of his inner world that was previously unavailable to him. In this conceptualization, when the analyst is included in the patient's psychological world, it is as a transference figure. Interpretation aids the patient in understanding that the analyst is "really" outside of his world. In Freud's optimal treatment situation, there is an alliance between analyst and analysand that is mediated by the unobjectionable transference. The analyst is viewed as a helpful external figure, who is able to provide insight into problems that have been previously painful and inexplicable. The insight that the analyst provides is the therapeutic agent of change. When the analysand transfers onto the analyst, the analysand should be able to have enough distance to note that his reactions are occurring because of some as yet unknown internal, unconscious conflict, not because of something the analyst has done to him. This self-observing capacity is therefore deemed necessary to the performance of a successful analysis.

Bach, Kohut, and Winnicott

Bach, Kohut, and Winnicott have written about patients who are unable at the beginning of treatment to observe themselves in this manner. It is also difficult for these patients to hear or listen to interpretations. Bach writes that in order to have the conditions that Freud describes,

> [There] must . . . [be] a working alliance between the two parties and, even more fundamentally, one must have two parties who experience themselves as separately alive and functional. . . . Generally, in the transference regression with the narcissistic disorders, one or both of these conditions is not fully met. [Bach 1985, p. xii]

To illustrate Bach's point, a woman I was seeing in treatment would begin a low moaning sound whenever she felt I was beginning an interpretative remark. The moaning increased to a shrieking if it turned out that she was right and I was oblivious enough to have been making an interpretation.[5]

It is easy to understand that Freud would consider unanalyzable those patients who were unable to tolerate interpretative efforts. If interpretations are the active ingredients in therapeutic change, how is it possible to accomplish change with a patient shrieking during the interpretation?

Given Freud's assumptions, the idea of a trial analysis is not only a reasonable practice, it is a humane practice. It tells a patient quickly and in a

---

[5]The clinical examples that I use are my own, unless otherwise noted.

straightforward manner whether or not this procedure can be of benefit to him. But in one of his last papers, "Constructions in Analysis" (1937a), Freud suggested that analysts see patients whom he would previously have deemed unanalyzable. A number of analysts were doing exactly what Freud had suggested, and many of us have continued to expand our ideas of analyzability. Certainly Bach and Kohut tell us that narcissistic patients will frequently feel humiliated and shamed by early interpretations. Kohut indicates that for many people interpretations increase their sense of fragility, and that their experience is one of being intruded upon and assaulted.

Bach has taken this type of observation and has painted a compelling picture of the person's subjective world, in and out of analysis. In his view, narcissistic states are built as an *anti-world*, a way of keeping outside events from impinging on the person's subjective world. The anti-world also helps create a more satisfying internal world. These anti-worlds are constructed for protection, and to give the person some stable, continuous sense of self and, hopefully, sense of worth. The experience of being inconsequential and ineffective in the real (consensual or external) world is an overpowering one for people who are compelled to build these internal fortresses. This can happen despite the fact that the person is *successful* in various aspects of his life. The feeling of success is experienced like a non-nutritive filler, tasting good for a moment, but giving no lasting experience of satisfaction. It may not be experienced as success in any conventional sense, but may be felt as one way of keeping the external (what Bach calls the objective) world outside of the person's felt boundaries. Adopting Kohut's concept of self-object, one can say that narcissistic states[6] do not permit fully developed others from existing in the person's world. Rather, others are either incorporated into the person's world as part of these states (and part of the self), or expelled as alien objects, as in the following clinical example:

A hypochondriacal patient suffering from insomnia experienced the world as a continuing horror and nightmare that no other person could possibly understand. Her quest to find someone who could understand the torment that results from such continuous fatigue had been exasperatingly unsuccessful. This insomnia made the world an alien place in which she was forced to exist. Her diseased brain could not shut down and did not allow her to sleep but rather kept her in a fatigued, twilight state where she felt continuously depersonalized and derealized. Her disbelief that analysis could be of any help to her was matched only by her disillusionment with all medical forms of treatment. Before treatment could begin she had to fill me and the treatment room with the horror of her life.

This woman would not tolerate interpretations of why she felt this way. She needed to be able to completely saturate the treatment room with her pain

---

[6]Narcissistic states are not either/or situations, but rather continuous functions. They are states that are at times rapidly entered and left. Thus a person may feel narcissistically vulnerable at one moment and have little affective memory of this experience at another.

and suffering. She needed someone both to listen to her and to contain her despair. She knew that all active attempts to help her would be futile. It was important for someone to hear all this before she could in any way acknowledge the possibility of her being truly alive[7]—certainly before she could acknowledge the importance she placed in having another separate person in the room with her. The following is another clinical example that may be seen in terms of Bach's concepts:

In a more extreme example, a wealthy, bright businessman had constructed a world that had at the heart of it his unendurable odor. He perceived himself as being permitted to endure in the objective world only if he performed perfectly in a wide range of tasks, which he believed that anyone would be able to perform but that had been left to him. He felt that all others were laughing at him, even his wife and children, although through their kindness they tolerated him more easily than others (including his partner) could; he felt despised by all around him. Suicide was a constant preoccupation. His fantasies were the obverse of those in the recent novel *Perfume* (Süskind 1986); his odors were to be eliminated but he wasn't able to do so, and his world was one of putrefying smells that lingered throughout his day and night, wherever he went. The smells remained in his fantasies, in his dreams, and in his interactions with the external world. To tolerate his delusions was the first step in a long therapeutic road toward his goal of cleansing his psyche.

These brief illustrations are meant only to give a sense of what Bach calls *other worlds*. If the analysis of narcissistic, borderline, or nonclassical patients is to be a real analysis, these other worlds must be brought into the treatment. This may at first glance seem like an odd statement, for if these other worlds are important, what else would a person who enters these states talk about in analysis? Interestingly, the patient might talk about many other things, particularly in an analysis that is pleasant but that implicitly demands compliance.[8] The patient might talk about the external world in a manner that is intended to please the analyst. The businessman might, in an obsessional vein, talk about his life and business while never giving a hint of his inner reality. It may often be too difficult for the patient to bring this stultifying, but nevertheless precious and vulnerable other world under the "scrutiny" of the analytic situation. It may be that the start of a true analysis takes a long time. That is, it might be a long time before a person can share, or include the analyst, in his other worlds:

A patient who was quite quiet and introverted after four years of treatment began to have dreams about extraterrestrial beings living on earth. These dreams described in detail how difficult it was for these beings to communicate with earthlings. It took a

---

[7]It was her view that she was a "walking bag of protoplasm."
[8]This is at times implicitly and even explicitly how Freud's position leads one to conduct an analysis; the analysand must comply with the analyst's rules in the treatment.

surprising number of these dreams for me to realize that they were about our treatment. Just as importantly, the patient started to tell me about a fantasy of his being "the recorder." I finally found out that the recorder idea was based on a science fiction story that described another planet sending down human-looking organisms to record the activities of the earthling's society. This patient—a precocious child—saw himself as one of these beings, and in this vision found an identity that provided him with a *raison d'être* for his life. It was one of the few things in his tumultuous childhood that made sense to him. This fantasy was a central component of his sense of self, even later when I saw him as an adult. It took four years for him to begin to share these ideas with me, and to begin to include me in his complicated world that I had known very little about up to that point in treatment.

The patient in this example had difficulty in maintaining a continuous (transference) relationship with me. Some aspects of his conflicts would emerge, and would then again be submerged when his anxiety about our intimacy disrupted his sense of equilibrium. Unquestionably, homosexual themes were extremely troublesome for him, but the questions of intimacy and trust were central to his reluctance to let anyone view his secret labyrinthine world. Although it took four years for him to feel that he could utilize[9] me as a character in his world, it took an even longer time for him to allow me to have a separate existence. This occurred when he concomitantly acknowledged my separate existence, while becoming a part of the consensual world.

This person was able to allow another into his world after four years of therapy, but sometimes this fails to happen at all in analytic situations. Bach talks about a woman who attempted to commit suicide a week or two after finishing what her analyst felt was a successful analysis. Bach, her subsequent analyst, found that crucial issues in her life had not come up at all in her previous analysis. She reported that she had never discussed these things with her analyst, since for some reason she had seemed never to think about these topics in her previous treatment. We can interpret this to mean that there seemed to be no place in her first analysis for certain types of subjects, even though many of these subjects involved conscious, recurrent fantasies.

Analytic Trust

What is it in the treatment situation that will allow a patient to feel there can be room to bring up vital but secret and potentially threatening topics? To ask a related question, what are the conditions that have to be met with the unclassical patient that will allow him to enter treatment and eventually utilize

---

[9]The issue of object utilization is one that is an important theoretical concept in Winnicott's writings.

interpretative efforts? Winnicott talks about the formation of a false self[10] in which the real world can be experienced in a depersonalized state. The extent to which the person must protect his true self is correlated with the extent to which the world is experienced in a depersonalized and derealized manner. Winnicott conceives of the true self as the focus of the person's spontaneity and sense of creativity in the world. In Bach's notions of anti-worlds, he has given us a more elaborated version of the extent to which people must cover their true selves, and how they create these worlds to allow some sense of spontaneity in their psychological lives. In a variant on Winnicott's terms, we can say that until a patient can spontaneously feel that he can create his own world in the analytic situation, he will not be able to let aspects of his true feelings or self emerge in the analytic process. He will not be able to create the type of illusion that is necessary for an interpretable transference relationship. We can conceive of the anti-worlds that Bach has described as compromise formations in which limited aspects of the true self are expressed, while at the same time a defense is provided against the external (consensual) world.

How can the analyst be included in these anti-worlds? In less dramatic terms, how does the analyst form a bond with the narcissistically vulnerable patient, such that the analyst is seen as a helpful or facilitating person instead of one who poses a threat to the patient's sense of self? This question brings me back to the concept of the unobjectionable transference and the modern form of this concept, the working or therapeutic alliance. I find Brenner's (1979) arguments convincing, concerning the difficulties with the concept of the therapeutic or working alliance. I nevertheless think that authors who utilize these terms are attempting to describe something that has not been adequately articulated in psychoanalysis. Freud implicitly asked how the patient begins to trust the analyst, and answered this question by invoking the unobjectionable transference. His answer was that we must rely on our patients' trust and respect for authority, and their conscious, mildly sexualized attraction to the power and knowledge of the physician. Freud assumed that most people would naturally be attracted to and have respect for a person in the position of a therapist or doctor. Stated in this form, it is easy to see why Stein (1981) and Brenner (1979) argue that the unobjectionable transference should be analyzed as a form of transference. Patients should understand their respect for authority as they should understand any other form of transference. Brenner comes to the same conclusion about experiences in treatment, which analysts such as Stone, Zetzel, and Greenson

---

[10]It is his view that to some extent the development of a false self is a normal phenomenon. The false self is designed as a protective shield for a person's inner world where he can experience, or have the potential to experience, spontaneous creative impulses (true self)—in other terms, where a person can feel that he can create a world of his own. Whether one sees the false self as a metaphor or as a phenomenological statement depends on your reading of Winnicott. My reading is that, while at times Winnicott is talking about actual experiences that he labels as "false self experiences," in order to make sense of the range of his discussions about the false self one has to consider this term a theoretical concept.

label as examples of the therapeutic alliance. Brenner is convincing when he states that the clinical examples that were presented by these analysts are best explained by invoking the concept of transference.

The question that I am raising[11] is, how does the patient come to develop trust in the analyst and in the treatment? Is this simply a matter of the patient's respect for authority (or a form of suggestion), which I have agreed is most adequately seen as a form of transference? Or are there some elements of trust that are based on the reality of the analytic situation? To repeat a statement made earlier (Chapter 15), I think that in analysis patients are listened to and understood in a way that is new in their experience. The analyst's consistent empathic attitude is an unexplored (and unique) element for the patient. It is present in reality, and it is not simply a manifestation of transference. If the analyst can provide a consistent, empathic, facilitating environment, the analysand can begin to realistically trust that the analysis will be an environment that is not threatening to the survival of his sense of self. To be sure, this trust can be mixed with transference tendencies, but is there an element of trust that is not explained by the concept of transference?

To return to the beginning of therapy, we can say that most patients start treatment because of the pain they are suffering. The rational reasons for continuing the treatment depend on the trust that is developed as a result of one's experience in analysis. The mirroring that Kohut describes, the sensitivity to the suppressed and unexpressed that is detailed by Bach, and the facilitating environment portrayed by Winnicott, are all ways of developing what I would call realistic analytic trust. Some patients enter treatment with a respect for the analyst or analysis (Freud's unobjectionable transference) or with simply a respect for authority. This transference as I have stated should be analyzed; however, the feeling of being reliably understood is an achievable concomitant of an analysis. This experience paves the way for the person's willingness to entertain an interpretation. Analytic trust is nothing more than the patient's experiencing the analyst as being consistently understanding of their world, in a way that promises to (and hopefully eventually does) help the patient to comprehend and gain control of his life. The crucial element in establishing trust is the analyst consistently providing a framework of empathy. This involves the consistent ability to reflect and to synthesize the person's experiences, particularly early in the treatment. If the patient's reaction to the analyst is merely transference, then the analyst has not provided in reality what is necessary in the beginning phase of analytic treatment.[12]

[11]Or raising again, since I have already stated that Freud initially asks this question.
[12]What I mean here is that some patients may feel trust in their analyst despite the fact that adequate conditions for the analysis have not been established. Thus they find that they can't talk about certain crucial experiences but nevertheless trust their analyst. From my point of view this is an example of transference rather than analytic trust. From Freud's point of view it may be an instance of the unobjectionable transference; from my perspective, this transference may be quite objectionable. I should add that substantial analytic trust is not easily achieved, and is not fully achieved in my view until the end of the treatment. This again is an interesting topic that I cannot fully explore here.

The analyst must also maintain an atmosphere that is conducive to the expression of difficult material. To use another term of Winnicott's, it is important that the analyst be a willing container for the patient's feelings. At times this is extremely difficult, with patients who seem as if they can fill the room with their anger, accusations, and sense of betrayal. However, the atmosphere of freedom to express negative as well as positive affect is quite important. The analyst should not suppress, nor return, these negative states to the patient.[13] This freedom of patients to express anger, aggression, and doubts about the analyst as well as about themselves is an important facet of analytic trust. In my view, it is this aspect of analytic treatment that Freud found most difficult to tolerate. It seems to me that the handling of the negative affect and negative transference is the most difficult part of analytic treatment.[14] This is frequently accentuated in the early parts of treatment with the unclassical patient. I must repeat here[15] that if the analyst is not able to provide an environment that contains the patient's affective world, then the trust that the patient experiences may be an example of transference. The analyst in this instance would not have adequately provided the conditions for the patient to begin the treatment.

I have talked about the analyst being seen as a consistently empathic object for the patient, and I have also maintained that the unclassical patient does not easily tolerate interpretative efforts. One might wonder, when does the analyst display more understanding than when she or he makes an interpretation? Here we might turn to Kohut's account of an experience of his. He tells us what followed some initial difficulty in a treatment:

> After a prolonged period of ignorance and misunderstanding during which I was inclined to argue with the patient about the correctness of my interpretations and to suspect the presence of stubborn, hidden resistances, I came to the crucial recognition that the patient demanded a specific response to her communications, and that she rejected any other. . . . the patient could not tolerate the analyst's silence, but, at approximately the mid-point of the sessions, she would suddenly get violently angry at me for being silent. . . . I gradually learned, however, that she would immediately become calm and content when I, at these moments, simply summarized or repeated what she had in essence already said. . . . But if I went beyond what the patient herself had already said or discovered (something new), even by a single step only . . . she would again get violently

---

[13]Often, vulnerable patients experience interpretations about their negativity as retaliation by the analyst. This is one way that negative feelings may be experienced as being returned to the patient. There are a variety of implicit ways to return feelings to the patient, and, of course, at times the analyst may simply get annoyed and return the feelings more directly.

[14]I would agree with Bird when he says that it is the negative (or destructive in his terms) transference that is most frequently not dealt with in psychoanalytic treatments. I would also agree with recent commentators (Bach 1985, Stolorow et al. 1987) that frequently "borderline" patients are unnecessarily inflamed by analysts who do attempt to enforce analytic rules early in the treatment. These rules may be simply the tendency to provide interpretations when the patient is not ready for them nor wants to hear them.

[15]What may begin to sound like a mantra.

angry . . . and would furiously accuse me, in a tense, highpitched voice, of undermining her, that with my remark I had destroyed everything she had built up, and that I was wrecking the analysis. [Kohut 1968, pp. 108–109]

Here Kohut is telling us that the analyst must understand that unclassical patients find it offensive to hear interpretations that go beyond what they have expressed in treatment.[16] It interferes with their developing a self-object transference. The analyst, in reflecting, is sensitively repeating material that has already been stated in the analysis. When the analyst synthesizes state-ments that have been already made by the patient, here again the analyst is staying within the content that has been supplied by the patient. When the analysand is being appropriately reflected, he usually will not experience strong negative transference.[17] However, when there is a manifestation of negative transference, the analyst must, as I have already stated, be an appro-priate safe container, while allowing these feelings to develop. At times, when the patient displays strong masochistic or sadistic trends, the analyst may have to interpret aspects of the patient's behavior.

In my experience,[18] most nonclassical patients will not display extensive negative transference if they feel appropriately understood. Usually they will give treatment some chance to progress before displaying continuous negative affect. We may then conclude that the analyst must be understanding enough to know that analysands do not want to hear the analyst's conception of their unconscious fantasies at the beginning of treatment. This is especially true of narcissistically vulnerable patients.[19] Interpretative efforts may puncture patients' (defensive) grandiosity and may lead to acting out, and even to premature termination.

[16]Judging from the way Kohut relates this to us, he is still annoyed with the patient. His description of "her tense, highpitched voice" still rings with a sense of irritation. The paper that I am quoting from is an early one of Kohut's, and so the discovery that he made might still have been fresh in his mind as he related it to us.

[17]This, of course, is not always the case.

[18]This discussion is again a chapter in itself, but briefly I would state that, when analysts feel they must interpret, it is crucial that they be able to help patients understand the adaptive aspect of their present self-destructive or hostile behavior and not only focus on their destructive wishes. When the focus in the beginning of the treatment is only on patients' destructive wishes, there is a strong moralizing tone in the analytic interpretation. In my view, it is impossible for patients not to take this type of interpretation as criticism of themselves. It therefore is crucial to show them why they felt that this type of response was the only one available to them. If the analyst is not able to do this, then in my opinion it is best not to interpret but to attempt another type of intervention.

[19]Although I have stated that most nonclassical patients usually will give the treatment some chance to progress before displaying continuous negative affect, I wish to expand on this point. I said earlier that it is extremely important to state boundaries and to understand the meaning of boundaries for both the patient and the analyst. At times, it is necessary to state the boundaries emphatically, particularly if the analyst finds himself getting consistently irritated. A supervisee related that a patient would not pay on time and then would frequently bounce a check when actually paying. This began to prey on the therapist's mind and he offered constant interpretations to deal with this issue. When he dealt with the problem as a boundary issue instead, he was able to conduct the treatment without nearly as much conflict. (He put forth that as a condition of treatment the patient had to pay on time, and if checks bounced he had to pay with a money order.) It seems to me that these issues most frequently come up with patients who utilize projective identification as a main or primary defense.

When Freud cautions against early interpretation, he begins to travel in a similar direction. He relates that we shouldn't make our first disclosures to the patient until:

> A dependable transference, a well-developed rapport, is established in the patient. . . . It is not difficult for a skilled analyst to read the patient's hidden wishes plainly between the lines of his complaints. . . . I have heard that analysts exist who plume themselves upon these kinds of lightning-diagnoses and "express"-treatments, but I warn everyone against following such examples. Such conduct brings both the man and the treatment into discredit and arouses the most violent opposition, whether the interpretation be correct or not. [Freud 1913b, pp. 360–361]

When Freud makes this point he is not referring to patients with narcissistic vulnerabilities, but rather he is stating that anyone needs to develop a sense of trust to hear interpretative comments.[20] We can now ask, when is the nonclassical patient able to tolerate interpretative efforts? How does one determine whether analytic trust is established? In comparing the narcissistic neuroses to the transference neuroses, Bach states that:

> For the sake of exposition, [if] one could imagine a purely narcissistic neurosis or a purely object transference neurosis, then the therapeutic viewpoint for patients in the object transference neurosis would be some external objective viewpoint like that of the equidistant neutral analyst. But this presupposes that the patient has developed a subjective viewpoint so that the reality of the self is not an issue. The therapeutic viewpoint for patients in the narcissistic neuroses is a coherent, cohesive, and consolidated subjective viewpoint since the primary issue is precisely the reality of the self. [Bach 1985, p. 171]

The analyst as the objective decoder of meaning is replaced in the narcissistic neuroses by the analyst who becomes part of the patient's subjective world. When the patient gives some indication that the analyst is included in his subjective world,[21] the interpretative aspects of the analysis can begin. It is important to recognize that this acceptance is a fragile commodity. A patient in a mid-analysis retrospective commented that she knew the analysis had begun when she could refer to me as being the same as her father and a variety of other sadistic men in her life, without really believing it to be completely true.[22]

---

[20]I might state that in my view the beginning of treatment is not different in the main for neurotic (classical) and nonclassical patients. The question of analytic trust is an issue for all patients. For some patients, however, it is—for a reasonable amount of the analysis—the overriding issue.

[21]That is, the analyst is accepted in a way that does not *only* repeat the patient's past.

[22]She and I would set the date of this beginning at somewhat different points in time. From my perspective she had already begun to develop an observing ego when she made this comment. I believe that the analysis began when she allowed me to represent some fantastic elements of her father and to relate this to me—in short, when she began to include me (and to relate this to me) in her subjective world in the analysis.

"I feel that you hurt me, but I know that you don't want to." She trusted that the aggression she expressed and feared would not be coming back at her from the analytic chair. She was able to get to that point after her repeated attempts at provocation were contained in the treatment and her frequent regressions "were not looked down upon." She needed to establish an analytic world in which she was able to roam from the position of provocateur to that of victim and back again, without being stopped or hurt. In some occasional spaces it was possible to communicate to her the pain that this flurry of sadomasochistic activity either obscured or mechanized. The past relationships that were components of the pain were concealed by her creation of a stereotyped package of the world as a frightening, horrible montage of brutal, self-centered people. In a simplified version of what she went through we can say that, at first, this woman was able to create her vision of me, without my protesting my innocence, by pointing out that I was a product of her creation. We were gradually able to concentrate on the pain that was present outside of the stereotyped sadomasochistic behavior she exhibited. It was then that she slowly began to accept me as someone who could focus with her on the conscious experiences that she had some difficulty in acknowledging. It was important to allow these experiences to flow from her, and to put into words those experiences that she found difficult to state. Eventually she became able to acknowledge the inexplicable nature of the experiences. Simply stating the inexplicable often provided her with some relief and gradually paved the way for her trust in my understanding of what she was going through. It also led to her beginning to accept a formulation that didn't stay within the boundaries she had established in the treatment.

Conclusions

I can summarize the foregoing schematized example by saying that it is usually important to begin treatment by allowing patients to include the analyst in their world without protesting this inclusion.[23] It should be considered a worthy beginning for the analyst to be a part of this world, which the analyst might consider an anti-world.[24] This can involve relatively simple matters at the beginning of the treatment:

When I first began in private practice, a patient was referred to me who the referring analyst told me had made the rounds and had not been able to "connect" with anyone. After listening to this person for about thirty minutes I began to wonder why she had had such difficulty in finding an analyst. I thought that I must be missing some

[23]The patient's experience is one of the analyst protesting if the patient adds to, or tampers with, the analyst's version of this world.
[24]Occasionally the patient might also consider it to be anti-world; at other times this may not be the case.

important element of her difficulties. Shortly after I had these thoughts, she announced that she would start treatment only if she could address me by my first name. Although I was taken aback by her request, I was surprised that I was also annoyed by her. I stated (with some felt difficulty) that this decision was up to her and that—since in analysis there were no restrictions on what one could say—it would be inconsistent of me to place this restriction on her. She then recounted several encounters with other analysts about her concern. One analyst had said that he would consider this idea for several weeks and if he thought it was a good idea he would accede to her wish. I wondered about this response, for surely if a patient in treatment starts calling the analyst by his or her first name, how could one stop this behavior? Practically, the patient didn't have to ask for permission: she could have just begun to do it and then the analyst could respond as he or she might see fit. In my mind, this analyst as well as others (who had told her that it was a matter to further "analyze") sensed the extent to which she wanted to create her own environment in analysis, and this need of hers created anxiety in them. I suspect that they (and I) were worried that she might not let us be analysts, and that she would usurp our function or identity.

This issue was of relevance to this person because of her own and her family's long, complicated medical history, and the unexpected intrusions that a variety of illnesses had brought her from early in her life to the time of her consultation with me. Calling me by my first name magically gave her control of the doctor, the illness, and her frequently malfunctioning body. Interestingly, another analyst in consultation attempted to make an interpretation along these lines, only to be met with what I imagine must have been considered breathtaking rage. This patient needed to set these conditions for her analysis; an outside observer might have said this was a trivial issue, but the analyst's responses were based on what they sensed in her, rather than on the content of her specific conditions. As an aside, the responses that she elicited seemed to cut across theoretical boundaries; her analysts, ranging from the classical to the interpersonalists, were all offended by her request. I suspect that my own response to her was fashioned partly by the fact that I had been briefly warned by the referring analyst that she might be difficult, partly by my junior status, and partly by the fact that I was starting out in practice and had a different need for patients than did my more senior colleagues. Nevertheless, the issue was important to me, for it illustrated what small things could cause an analysis to flounder. It showed also how important it is to let analysands set up their own boundaries, within a context that the analyst can find comfortable.[25] In the consultation session, I try to state the conditions of treatment that I need to be comfortable. I do this so that the patient can initially understand the boundaries of the treatment and hopefully put these conditions into the background. When this is impossible, when the patient is unable to tolerate the initial boundaries, it may be that there is a bad analytic match. My experience is

[25]If a patient needs to control the temperature or the lighting in the room, it is something that I am comfortable in going along with, as well as analyzing, only when the patient indicates he can tolerate another separate person in the analysis.

that, if analysts are relatively unconflicted about their boundaries, it is very rare that initial boundaries are difficult even for nonclassical patients. It is hard to stress too strongly that, for nonclassical patients, the analysis as well as the analytic environment must be allowed to become part of their subjective world before another whole object can bring things to them from the external[26] world.

In the discussion of entering the patient's world, I posed the question as to how one would know when to interpret. This question was answered in terms of the patient beginning to accept the analyst as a separate object in the patient's object world. This may happen sporadically at first, and the representation of the analyst may periodically shift. I believe that often, when the nonclassical patient shifts transference states, there is a period of time in which the analyst is treated like a new person; it is as if the treatment is undergoing a new beginning. Whereas, of course, the patient is *not* the same at the beginning of treatment, this shift in transference does signal to him that another aspect of the world he has tried to conceal[27] is threatening aspects of his conscious world. Thus, when the content of the transference shifts, various patients can have responses that are reminiscent of the start of treatment. This is, at times, frustrating to patient and analyst alike, and if not accepted as a shortened version of the beginning of treatment, it can lead to disruptive results. If we assume that the nonclassical patient frequently splits his world into separate themes and experiences, then it is not surprising that the patient will not respond to analysis as a cohesive experience. This will gradually change as the analysis progresses, but during several transference shifts the analyst may have to regain the trust of the analysand. This new beginning is counterbalanced by the patient's experience with the analysis that will gradually spread and become dominant if these new beginnings can be tolerated and understood.

The issue of the beginning of the treatment highlights changes that I would advocate in the Freudian and classical or standard positions. Although I have accentuated these differences, there are as many or more points of agreement with Freud's positions that could be enumerated. It is my view that the idea of compromise formation is a crucial concept to understanding any person. The concept might well be expanded to include how aspects of the self and object are represented.[28] In my mind, it is proving easy to forget Freud's pioneering contributions to the understanding of how children internalize

---

[26]I am here neatly dividing subjective and objective world, and internal and external. This topic of course has received a great deal of discussion (throughout the ages), and here I will have to allow myself to make certain simple unexamined distinctions.

[27]Frequently by splitting the world into discrete contents.

[28]This would not be necessary if Freud had developed a way as a clinician to take his own views on the object relations into account when making interpretations. This was difficult for Freud, for he was tied so strongly to his discoveries of unconscious motivation and the role of sexuality that it was hard for him to include even his own views on the development of object relations and object love into his therapeutic technique.

experiences through their own bodily functions (childhood sexuality). Or how children fantasize about the world in an active manner, not simply in reaction to lack of parental empathy. It seems to me that Kohut's ideas about technique[29] involve assumptions about children being almost exclusively reactive to the state of parental empathy, as opposed to seeing them as active processors of fantasy and reality. To put it in Winnicott's language, healthy children create their reality; it is not presented to them. I differ with Kohut's mode of interpretation once the transference has been established. From my vantage point, Kohut does not take into account several aspects of the patient's internal world. However, it must be clear that Kohut's views about the beginning of treatment are to my mind important to integrate with aspects of Freudian thought. In addition, I believe that many facets of Kohut's attitude toward analysis are important and therapeutically sound.

The exciting aspect of reviewing Freud's writings on technique is that we can see how much ground he covered, how much he was able to envision about psychoanalysis as a therapy, while he was constructing a psychoanalytic vision in so many areas of human experience. The challenging aspect of Freud's legacy for contemporary analysts is to be guided by his vision while allowing other views and experiences to help shape our psychoanalytic perspective. I have tried, in reviewing the beginning aspects of treatment, to show how contemporary views might help in our integrative efforts.

[29]Particularly his assumptions about when to interpret the transference later in the treatment.

17

Freud's Positions

This chapter is intended as a summary statement of Freud's positions on technique.[1] It is as well a concluding comparison between Freud and some of the contemporary authors we have been following through the course of this volume. In discussing Freud's principles of psychoanalytic technique, questions inevitably arise about how Freud actually practiced psychoanalysis. I have attempted to partially answer this question during the course of this book (see Chapter 15), while at the same time endeavoring to avoid this question. The reason for this ambivalent reaction should be clear: Freud is difficult to categorize, and his actions vary both across and within the eras of his career. Thus it seems to me that we must content ourselves with Freud's ideas about technique, and take as historical accident his clinical practices.

Even when we favor some of his clinical practices, we must keep in mind that Freud did many things that most analysts would not support. Therefore, it is hard to argue that a given practice is correct because of the evidence that this was Freud's practice. Analysts who follow Freud can only evaluate his ideas and ask how well they have stood the test of time. His insights were derived in a way that it is difficult for the rest of us to understand, and so we are left with his writings; this is certainly not a small gift from the creator of psychoanalysis. Before we begin our summary I wish to point out the obvious: however Freud practiced, his ideas about technique logically stand apart from his actual behavior.

---

[1]Many of the points in this summary statement are contained in the body of this book. If one has read all of the previous chapters, parts of this summary may be redundant.

Survey of Freud's Positions

Since one of the questions we will discuss in this chapter is to what extent various analysts have continued Freud's method of treating patients, we will first have to form a view of Freud's technique as he stated it in his publications. This brief summary will thus utilize only the material that he published. During the course of the book, we have stated that Freud's technique can be divided into two different phases: one phase that lasted from 1890 to 1905 in which he considered the experiencing and understanding of pathogenic memories to be the prime focus of analytic technique; and a second phase in which he recognized and struggled with the importance of transference in analytic therapy. One can say that this second phase lasted for the rest of Freud's life. This arbitrary division leaves out so many aspects of Freud's thought that it is hard to make even a representative list of these topics.[2] At the very least we can say that Freud—whatever the changes in his theory—always believed that a successful treatment has to uncover and construct (reconstruct) the patient's childhood conflicts in an analytic treatment. At times he changed his views on what fixation points in development are crucial in the choice of neuroses, but his views on the necessity to recollect these points did not vary.

THE FUNDAMENTAL RULE AND THE DISCOVERY OF TRANSFERENCE

Free association was a concept or an ideal that was introduced in embryonic form early in Freud's experience as a psychotherapist, and one that was never abandoned during the rest of his career. Bird mentions (1972) that it is an insignificant concept next to the theory of transference. This was certainly not Freud's view. For Freud, free association was the cornerstone of his technique and the method by which he was able to make his startling discoveries.[3] His discoveries were primarily involved with understanding the developmental history of the patients he saw in treatment, and his technique always featured reconstructive efforts. Except for a brief time in his career,[4] he saw transference primarily as a form of resistance that had to be cropped away in order to get at pathogenic memories. If, in analysis, one was able to *crop away* the resistance, then the patient, through free associating, would inevitably lead the analyst back to the pathogenic conditions that were responsible for his disorder. For Freud, recovery of these memories was the goal, and free association was the path by which one could reach this goal. Thus free association was

[2]As I have said, Freud never fully left the pathogenic memory model; it may well be that many analysts would argue that the pathogenic memory model, insofar as it implies reconstruction, is an appropriate model for contemporary psychoanalysis.
[3]In my opinion, the use of the couch added greatly to his psychoanalytic technique, but Freud does not make the couch a significant issue in his ideas about psychoanalytic treatment.
[4]During the period that he wrote "Recollection, Repetition and Working Through."

always the fundamental rule, and while this rule changed over the decades,[5] the purpose for the rule—the recovery of pathogenic memories[6]—never changed.

Given that this is the case, those analysts who no longer think that reconstruction is an essential component of analysis have departed from a component of analysis that continued to be crucial for Freud during his entire life. To put this point in the terms we have been using, we can say that an extended version of the pathogenic memory model was in place for Freud even at the end of his career. Transference, however, was a major obstruction or resistance that Freud began to deal with after the Dora case and continued to grapple with for the rest of his career as an analyst. One might say that he never fully internalized the insights that he provided for the analytic community. Nor was he wholly consistent in his views on the role of transference in the analytic situation. We can see the progression of his views from Dora in 1900 through the three transference papers by 1915; this progression is what one would expect from a clinician who is becoming increasingly aware of the role of transference in the analytic situation. "The Dynamics of Transference" is really a fuller elaboration of views that he has already put into place either in *The Interpretation of Dreams* or in the postscript to the Dora case. In "Recollection, Repetition and Working Through," Freud not only introduces new concepts, but his discussion of transference has the ring of a clinician who has experienced the intensity of transference reactions in the analytic situation. He also seems at ease with the transference when he states that:

> The main instrument, however, for curbing the patient's compulsion to repeat and for turning it into a motive for remembering consists in the handling of the transference. . . . We admit it (the compulsion to repeat) into the transference as to a playground, in which it is allowed to let itself go in almost complete freedom and is required to display before us all the pathogenic impulses hidden in the depths of the patient's mind. [Freud 1914b, p. 374]

This was written at the time that I consider to be the height of Freud's valuing the importance of transference. He considered it essential to the treatment in curbing the patient's compulsion to repeat as well as in becoming the vehicle to enable the patient to remember. What Freud means by *curbing the patient's compulsion to repeat* is subject to some interpretation, since transference is a manifestation of the compulsion to repeat. One way of interpreting this passage is that it seems Freud was picturing the transference as "curbing" the patient's compulsion to repeat conflicts outside of analysis:

[5]Freud attempted during the course of his career to make the rule one that allowed the patient more freedom. To paraphrase him we can say that during the course of writing the technique papers he mentions that he no longer suggested a topic for the patient, in accordance with his new ideas about free association.

[6]It is important to remember that when we use the term *pathogenic memories* we are not necessarily referring to memories of actual events. These memories may often be fantasies, or fantasies in reaction to real events.

"We render it (the compulsion to repeat) harmless. We make use of the repetition compulsion, by according it the right to assert itself with certain limits" (Freud 1914b, p. 374). The patient is no longer acting or repeating outside of the treatment, but is repeating in the relative safety of the treatment situation. One can see that transference in the treatment for Freud "forms a kind of intermediary realm between illness and real life, through which the journey from one to the other must be made" (Freud 1914b, p. 374). This intermediate realm becomes the field of the treatment in which, at the zenith of its journey, it is possible to see a transference neurosis.

The concept of the transference neurosis indicates that the patient is repeating core or central conflicts in the treatment situation. This idea of central conflicts goes back to Freud's onion skin metaphor in the psychotherapy chapter of *Studies on Hysteria* (The idea of the *analytic surface* [Gray 1986] seems to be a derivative of Freud's onion skin metaphor.) In this onion skin model, core conflicts or memories are surrounded by intermediate memories and associations. In the journey to the central conflicts, there are many obstacles to be met and Freud labels these obstacles as resistance. Resistance, embedded for Freud in the concept of defense, is a central theoretical idea in and outside of the treatment situation. By labeling a patient's behavior resistance, Freud originally implies that patients, insofar as they do not follow the basic rule, are uncooperative and they are resisting the analyst's efforts to help them deal with their conflicts. This term at best is misleading when one considers that, in Freud's mature theorizing, defense is an unconscious process. Defense implies that most aspects of "resistance" are outside of the patient's awareness, while the term resistance connotes conscious intentionality. In addition, as several analysts have pointed out, the term *resistance* has a certain moralistic quality to it that some would see as antithetical to the analytic process.[7]

Freud appears unconcerned about such issues; however, we can bring up here the question of analytic neutrality or the position of the analyst with respect to the activities of the patient. In Freud's own terms, what should the analyst's position be in this impossible profession? Impossible, since one can ask how it is possible for the analyst to remain neutral or even objective, given the analyst's own predilections and reaction tendencies.

NEUTRALITY

How neutral *should* the analyst be, what are the constraints that Freud advocated, and how do these constraints affect the therapeutic process? When Freud invokes the surgeon as a standard of neutrality, he is using an interesting, impersonal metaphor. Yet he has also written about the sympathy and tact that the analyst should display. Moreover, we have his published account of

---

[7]I am one of those analysts.

how he provided the Rat Man, Dr. Ernst Lanzer, with a meal when he felt that this patient might have to go hungry for some period of time.[8] The issue of analytic neutrality is not only extremely important for the practice of analysis, but it is also the issue that frequently divides contemporary psychoanalysts. The issue of neutrality is often associated with the issue of the silent analyst (or "blank screen"), despite the fact that there is no necessary relationship between these two subjects.[9] Still, these topics are frequently coupled to present an analyst who is detached, silent, and offering insights without becoming affectively involved in the treatment situation. Perhaps, from one view, this is not surprising; if surgeons get involved with their patients it may be difficult, if not at times impossible, to perform the surgery. In a similar vein, some analysts would state that the analyst's job is to analyze, and there is nothing more that one can do as an analyst. It is hard to argue with this tautology; the key is, what would be considered as part of the analyzing function? Typically, in this hypothetical formulation, the analyst's function is only to interpret, and to help provide insight for the patient. Here then is another frequent correlation: the analyst who tends to see neutrality as an essential component of the analytic situation tends to see interpretation as the main avenue of analytic communication. Interpretation stimulates insight, and insight is the vehicle of change in the analytic process.

This is another area in which Freud's views harken back to the pathogenic memory model. Interpretation was then, and remained for him, the main task of the analyst. For Freud, this task involved deciphering symbols from dreams, symptoms, fantasies, and from the patient's associations. On various occasions Freud cautioned that the analyst should, particularly at the beginning of the treatment, employ analytic tact and not simply *fling* interpretations at the patient. Thus, although he thought that the curative aspects of psychoanalysis occurred through interpretative efforts, he suggested that, for an interpretation to be tolerated by the patient, there had to be some union between patient and analyst. The issue of some type of union, or working (or therapeutic) alliance, is another key area over which analysts are divided. If we continue to build up a hypothetical analyst, we can say that one type of analyst is firm about the issue of analytic neutrality, sees analysis as primarily an interpretative discipline, and does not see such concepts as the working or therapeutic alliance to be useful or explanatory in the analytic situation. Brenner is an analyst who, up to this point, would fit our hypothetical analyst almost perfectly. One can say that Brenner is an example of what has been called the classical position in psychoanalysis.

How other analysts view the term "classical" is well represented in two articles by Lipton (1977b, 1979). He begins by pointing out that classical

[8]As described in detail earlier in this book, we know from published accounts of his behavior with several patients that Freud departed from what many analysts would today describe as analytic neutrality.

[9]This is, of course, only one opinion on this subject.

analysis, in the way that the term is currently used, implies views deriving from Freud. It is Lipton's contention that many of the views of classical analysts are actually at some distance from Freud's positions. Lipton maintains that Freud never was concerned with analytic neutrality in the way modern classical analysts are, nor did his technique change after his analysis of the Rat Man.

RECONSTRUCTION IN THE STRUCTURAL MODEL

Up to this point in the overview, we have mentioned reconstruction in psychoanalysis as a residue of the pathogenic memory model. This is somewhat misleading, since it doesn't take into account how Freud integrated his views on reconstruction into the structural model. If we were to state Freud's position in a logically consistent manner, we would say that, after Freud recognized the importance of transference in the analytic situation, he gave up the idea of patients remembering their conflicts in the analytic situation and replaced this idea with the concept of patients *repeating* these conflicts there. Primal repression (or the initial repression) does not allow remembering but lays down the conditions for repetition of conflicts. It is only through the analysis of the transference that one can clear away the resistances so that patients can finally display their infantile or childhood neuroses in the transference (transference neurosis). The patient then never really remembers until the analyst is able to reconstruct the childhood conditions, through witnessing the transference neurosis in the safety of the treatment situation. Events are not remembered in analysis; they are reconstructed.

One might ask about the necessity of reconstruction. Why is it necessary for patients to understand the childhood conditions (the historical or genetic explanations) that were originally associated with their core conflicts? Why isn't it enough to understand how these conflicts are manifested in the person's present life, as well as to comprehend the unconscious significance of the person's transference reactions, dreams, fantasies, associations, and so on? In analytic terms, why isn't it enough to have a thorough dynamic understanding of the person without requiring a complete historical or genetic understanding? This is not a question that is in any way new to psychoanalysis; the answer that one gives to this question certainly affects the way one practices therapy.

TERMINATION AND CURE

Freud's criteria for termination[10] are by and large less ambitious than the criteria stated by today's analysts. Freud did not believe one could analyze everything that was potentially an issue for the patient unless there was something current in the patient's life that was stimulating a given conflict.

---

[10]At least the criteria he described late in his career. As I have pointed out, early in his career he was more hopeful.

Thus it could be that a patient might be better off, from Freud's perspective, in stopping an analysis and returning at a later date. This idea might be considered in opposition to the idea of waiting in analysis until the patient is able to transfer certain conflicts unto the analyst. In "Analysis Terminable and Interminable" (1937b) Freud lays out some issues concerning termination that a variety of analysts are studying today. He clearly recognizes that not all (or even most) analyses are terminated mutually, but while he recognizes the possibilities of various analytic outcomes, he is more concerned with the type of patient who will more likely have a successful analytic experience. He states the factors in a general way and maintains that analysis is much more likely to be successful when the etiological factors are environmental, as opposed to genetic or endogenous factors in the person. A patient who had difficulty with a sibling or conflicts with one or both parents, or who suffered a loss in childhood, is much more likely to benefit from analysis than someone who is constitutionally sensitive to the environment. The questions of analyzability and cure were more central for Freud than how to assess when the termination should occur. Freud's doesn't offer true criteria for termination, but rather offers ways of considering whether an analytic cure has been achieved.

His notion involves symptomatic relief and the possibility that analysis through the process of discovery provides reasonable prophylaxis in terms of future difficulties for the analysand. In modern literature, this has led analysts to discuss how well the patient has internalized the analyzing function. In other terms, how well can patients continue to analyze themselves after the analysis has been discontinued? This is one modern notion of the prophylactic aspects of the analytic process. If the patient is able to continue analysis without the analyst, this should provide a certain immunity to past conflicts overwhelming them and causing a repetition in their present life. One imagines that Freud would argue that it is still a quantitative question that one is asking in terms of the success of analysis. It may be that the strength of a person's conflicts may be overwhelming under some conditions no matter how well they have internalized the analyzing function. Others would contend that the self-analyzing function is not necessary for analytic success.

BEGINNING THE TREATMENT

We have talked about Freud's view of the endpoint of analysis but have said little about how he begins the process. We have seen in his writings that the idea of trial analysis is one that he favored. How did he begin to see patients during this trial period? Freud began analysis by a trial period during which he attempted to assess how well the patient was able to free-associate and tolerate interpretative efforts. Judging from his notes on the Rat Man case, his interpretations consisted of early attempts at reconstructive efforts. I believe that the Rat Man case is indicative of Freud's technique later in his career, and there are indications that early interpretation was frequently a feature of Freud's analytic stance throughout his career. In any case, Freud's idea of a trial analysis allowed for the analyst to test the patient's response to early interpretative efforts—despite the fact that Freud warns against flinging interpretations at the patient. His criteria for assessing analyzability involved attempting to rule out narcissistic patients as well as patients who were in some sort of immediate need of relief. Certainly, Freud tells us, patients in a life-threatening situation should not be considered for analysis. Most psychotic patients and what are today considered to be borderline patients would be ruled out of analysis by these criteria. This despite the fact that at least several of Freud's most famous patients would today be considered unanalyzable based on Freud's criteria for analyzability.

One aspect of his initiation at the beginning of treatment was to provide patients with educative statements. In all of Freud's published cases and in many cases of patients relating their experiences with him, we learn of Freud the educator. It was his style to inform patients of psychoanalytic tenets and try to help them understand why they were going through certain types of experiences during analysis. Although it appears as if this tendency was strongest during the beginning phase of treatment, Freud was the educator throughout the course of treatment. In fact, at times he entertained the idea that the first aspect of an analysis would be educative (Freud 1909), and only during the second half would transference reactions enter the treatment. This idea, while seeming artificial to modern analysts, must have seemed more pertinent to Freud who, for at least some period of time, was a solitary analytic voice.[11] Modern analysts have asked whether patients shouldn't be given a type of theoretical outline of analysis to provide them with the rationale of some of the travail that awaits them. It does not seem surprising to me that patients in Freud's time would have wanted some explanation of this new treatment. Freud, of course, gave much more than most had asked for, and his educative stance did not seem to be solely in response to patient's requests.

ANALYZABILITY AND BEGINNING THE TREATMENT

Although we have mentioned the notion of analyzability, we will restate Freud's position and the ambiguities in this position, since this topic is important in many contemporary debates. In several places, Freud tells us that insofar as patients are narcissistic they are unsuitable for analysis. The way he used the term *narcissistic* is subject to interpretation. We should begin by understanding that Freud's use of this terminology was not precise, nor was he overly concerned with standard diagnosis. In fact, we may have seen that he was somewhat disdainful of psychiatric diagnosis, believing that the psychiatric community of his time had little to offer in terms of treatment and thus focused on diagnostic issues to hide this obvious deficiency.

[11]This is overstated, since Freud always had some adherents and supporters of his point of view.

Given these considerations, how are we to interpret Freud's views on analyzability? We can look at a type of patient that Freud assumed has narcissistic difficulties, that is hypochondriacal patients. At the time he was writing the technique papers, Freud described hypochondriacs as patients with actual narcissistic problems (1914c). He likened hypochondriacs to actual neurotics in that there was an actual physiological basis to their disorder, but he saw them as different in that the libido involved in their disorder was narcissistic, as opposed to object libido.

It is my view that Freud resorted to this type of explanation for two reasons: (1) With both actual neurotics as well as hypochondriacal patients, he was unable to experience transference reactions in the way he experienced these reactions with other patients (i.e., with sexual overtones and a distinctive positive transference); and because of this he labeled these patients as actual disorders as opposed to psychological disorders. (2) He correctly saw that hypochondriacal patients had serious narcissistic difficulties (of course not all such patients do), and so he distinguished them from other actual neurotics who were somewhat more related in their reactions to him.

One way of interpreting Freud's reactions is that he saw patients as either narcissistic or actual neurotics when he was unable to sense a positive transference reaction to himself. It is important to remember that paranoids, patients who from Freud's point of view[12] want to destroy object relations, are also people with narcissistic problems. The stage of narcissism for Freud is relatively long and differentiated (Bergman and Ellman 1985), and those people who develop difficulties at this stage in their lives frequently have severe disorders. Thus, at times, Freud used the term *narcissistic disorders* when he was referring to psychotic and near-psychotic states. This is confusing, especially when he states that people with narcissistic disorders are not able to develop transference reactions. He meant that if such patients had experienced too few positive encounters with other people (object libido), it would be difficult for them to displace reactions onto the analyst based on past experience. We can see that transference for Freud is a displacement of unconscious fantasy, and the fantasy is one that involves other people. Freud thought narcissistic or self-directed fantasies (narcissistic libido) could not be utilized in transference reactions. His views on this changed somewhat, relatively late in his career, when other analysts (particularly from the Berlin school) reported that narcissistic patients did form transference relationships. Nevertheless, even though Freud's personal views (Gay 1988) may have changed, his published views had a powerful and long-lasting impact on the question of analyzability. To add to this somewhat confused situation, we can also state that the patients whom Freud analyzed would today be considered narcissistic. Certainly the Wolf Man would be considered to have a near-psychotic disorder; even the Rat Man would today be considered outside the neurotic range. Freud

---

[12]This, of course, is not just Freud's point of view.

didn't see either patient in these terms, and that, as we have said before, has to do with other than diagnostic considerations. He was interested in these two patients as bright, verbal men who were able to interact with him in interesting analytic adventures.

Freud had stated criteria for analyzability when he said (1905a) that patients must be of high intelligence and good moral character. These seem to be the essential criteria for him, as opposed to diagnostic evaluations. We can thus say in summary that Freud excluded psychotic patients (even though this was not always the case) from analytic consideration—but that, short of psychosis, if a patient was bright, worthy (by Freud's standards), and capable of a positive transference, he or she was a candidate for analysis. So that we don't completely leave the impression that Freud was arbitrary in his decisions, it should be remembered that, if a patient was capable of a positive transference, Freud believed that the patient was object related and at least not destructively narcissistic. Freud's view of analyzability certainly has not vanished from the analytic scene, and we will look at different views that, in one way or another, all start from his conceptualizations.

Freud's views on analyzability were directly related to the way he conceived of negative transference. In addition, the manner in which Freud conceptualized negative transference precluded an extensive analysis of this type of transference state. If a patient went into a prolonged state of negative transference, it signified to Freud that he was unanalyzable, and it might mean that either the analysis should be completely discontinued or that certain types of extra-analytic steps should be taken to help the patient out of this state. This enunciation of negative transference was consonant with Freud's practice and his writings. He mentioned in "The Dynamics of the Transference" (1912c) that the topic is an important one, but rarely wrote about the topic after this essay. We can see in the case of the Rat Man that the negative transference was the most difficult for Freud to deal with; in fact, he himself gave expression to this difficulty. Freud's difficulty is not unique; it probably is the case that negative transference states are the most difficult part of an analysis for many analysts. The way one conceives of the expression of negative transference will be of extreme importance in the way one conducts a treatment. It is interesting that, whereas positive transference admits of some theoretical elaboration, negative transference is seen as a unitary phenomenon.

Development of Freud's Technique

We have seen Freud's development of technique in two stages: (1) the pathogenic memory model, in which he attempted to unearth the early traumatic memories that he saw as causing neurotic states; and (2) the point at which he conceived of transference as an essential or at least important aspect of treatment—a view that culminated with the last of the transference papers.

Kanzer interpolates that Freud had another phase: "A third phase, embodied in the paper 'Recollection, Repetition and Working Through' . . . [that relied] essentially on neutrality and interpretation of the transference neurosis to achieve its results" (Kanzer 1980a, p. 233).

Kanzer's three stages of Freud's development do not stand up well to close scrutiny. While it is true that Freud's remarkable essay did introduce the concept of transference neurosis, the issue of neutrality certainly was not featured in this essay. Moreover, there is little in Freud's subsequent writings or behavior that indicate that the issue of neutrality was central for him.

Clearly the issue of neutrality is central to Kanzer; in his interpretation of the case of the Rat Man, he sees the use of human influence by Freud as a prime difficulty in Freud's approach to this case. Kanzer sees Freud's interventions with the Rat Man as "tacitly threatening and (alternatingly) cajoling." To be clear, it is not the *way* that Freud uses influence with patients but the fact that he attempts to use influence at all that Kanzer is criticizing. Although Kanzer states that the cases of the Rat Man and the Wolf Man are part of Freud's second stage of development, he gives no clinical examples of Freud's third stage of development. Moreover, there is ample evidence in Freud's writings (see the Preface to this volume) that Freud never left what Kanzer calls the second stage of development and in fact oscillated between the first and second stages for all of his career. If we turn to patients' reports of Freud as a clinician, it is clear that there is no evidence of Freud approaching a third stage of development. Thus, we conclude that when Lipton states there is no reason to think that Freud ever abandoned the ideas of technique he displayed in the Rat Man case, we have to concur. At another point I alluded to the possibility of considering a third phase of development in Freud's ideas, but there I was looking at the logical implications of Freud's thought, rather than referring to his writings.

Comparison of Freud's Positions with Those of Contemporary Analysts

We are now at a point at which we can compare Freud's positions with contemporary ones. We have seen that many of the terms and concepts that Freud introduced have been embraced by modern analytic writers, regardless of their theoretical orientation. Thus, for example, there are few analytic writers who are not concerned with the implications of transference in the treatment situation. We might say that the various metaphors introduced by Freud have provided us with dividing lines for different analytic positions. For instance, when he uses the surgical comparison, it is considered compatible with one theoretical position and not with others. Unfortunately the disputes that have grown up around psychoanalytic technique involve parodying different positions; therefore, if one considers the surgeon analogy to be compatible with the stance of a particular theorist, one is, in effect, labeling that theorist as one who is unconcerned with the patient's welfare. It seems to me unlikely that any theoretical orientation has a monopoly on compassion, but there are differences as to how one proceeds in treatment given a particular theoretical orientation. Although I am sure that my biases will be or have already become apparent, I will try to compare Freud's positions with those of three analysts we have followed throughout this book—Brenner, Gill, and Kohut—and then attempt to integrate some aspects of these positions.

THEORETICAL DIFFERENCES

The positions we have followed differ along several dimensions, and interestingly, as we have seen, none of these positions completely overlap with Freud's stance on technique. Our comparison will be primarily concerned with the authors' views on treatment, but here we will briefly mention some of their theoretical differences. If we were to compare these positions in detail, this might lead to yet another work that is longer than the present one; I will be content to note just a few of the most obvious differences and similarities with Freud's theoretical positions.

Brenner is the only avowed Freudian of the three authors we have covered. He is one of the modern analysts who has advocated and extended a version of Freud's structural model (Arlow and Brenner 1964). Kohut's theorizing, on the other hand, was strongly influenced by Freud's theory of narcissism (Kohut 1966, 1968), but in his later theorizing he significantly departed from several of Freud's basic assumptions.[13] Several authors (e.g., Kernberg 1975, Reed 1987) have noted that Kohut's theory leads to a limited motivational role for unconscious fantasy. While one may agree or disagree with this interpretation of Kohutian theory, there is no question that Kohut does not stress the understanding of unconscious conflict in treatment to the extent that it is stressed by Freud or Brenner.

It is more difficult to characterize Gill's position. We can say that Gill has, over his career, significantly contributed to psychoanalytical theory and held a variety of theoretical positions. Recently Gill has not taken a position on the status of psychoanalysis in terms of theory, but rather has concentrated almost exclusively on the treatment model. If one judges Gill's theoretical position by his comments on technique, it is clear that he has abandoned many Freudian assumptions and taken a position that is closer to a Sullivanian or interpersonalist stance.

---

[13]The importance of Freud's theory of psychosexual stages is greatly diminished in Kohut's work. Moreover, Kohut's view of aggression is different from Freud's, as well as that of those analysts who have stayed within Freud's assumption that some form of aggression has the status of an innate tendency, instinct, or drive.

Since our focus in the present work has been a discussion of psycho-analytic treatment, we will have to content ourselves with this superficial overview of these analysts' theoretical differences. Now we will turn to a review of some of the differences in their ideas on technique.

FREUD'S "NATURAL" BEHAVIOR
AND THE ISSUE OF NEUTRALITY

Freud, as Lipton has pointed out and Gill has echoed, was quite natural in his relationship with patients. He thought that his natural behavior would not interfere with the patient's transference manifestations. In this respect, Gill comes closest to Freud's position and believes that the idea of neutrality is an unobtainable ideal. Brenner's ideas clearly spell out the role of neutrality for the analyst and the importance of maintaining neutrality in order to be in a position to analyze the patient's transference manifestations. Kohut, while not advocating neutrality, certainly maintains that the analyst should not personalize the treatment, but should provide a situation that would allow the patient to feel appropriately mirrored. My interpretation of Kohut's view of analytic neutrality is that he comes close to advocating a position that is similar to Winnicott's idea of providing a facilitating or good enough environment.

Many authors besides Gill have criticized the idea of the neutral analyst. They have asked why a silent, relatively abstinent therapist should be considered neutral rather than, for instance, a depriving or a withholding analyst. The question of neutrality, however, should be understood not in terms of the degree of an analyst's interaction with patients, but rather in the analyst's ability to provide a nonjudgmental attitude so that patients are free to talk about what occurs to them regardless of the type of content. Brenner might contend that a Kohutian is tacitly encouraging the patient to provide certain types of associations or thoughts and inhibit other types. More specifically, with a Winnicottian or Kohutian approach, the analytic situation is one in which the patient is encouraged or influenced to bring up certain kinds of topics in analysis, and to inhibit topics that involve aggression or negative reactions. Various authors maintain that some patients can tolerate analytic neutrality, whereas other patients with more intense conflicts find the neutral analyst too depriving. Grunes has suggested (1984) that perhaps we should consider objectivity a goal for the analyst, but that neutrality for a variety of reasons is neither a possible nor desirable ideal. Neutrality implies that the analyst is devoid of values and is neutral in terms of anything the patient might do or become. Clearly, if the goal of analysis is conflict resolution, one might say that analysts are *not* neutral in terms of the results of the analysis, or the implications of certain types of acting out, or a variety of behaviors that would be detrimental to the health and welfare of the patient. Whatever one's view about the subject of neutrality, it is a post-Freudian issue that is actively debated in the analytic community. We can also say that the concept is most central in Brenner's version of psychoanalytic technique. Interestingly, a non-analyst writing in a popular magazine has presented some of the most compelling arguments for analytic neutrality, later to be published in the form of a book (Malcolm 1981).

TRANSFERENCE

Although Brenner differed from both Kohut and Gill on the question of analytic neutrality, this division shifts when the question arises concerning the handling of the transference. In fact, one can't talk about the handling of transference without briefly reviewing how these authors conceive of different components of transference. Interestingly, none of the authors offers a new theoretical definition of transference, and so, implicitly, we have to rely on aspects of Freud's conceptualization of the issue. While Gill does not comment on the content of the transference, clearly Brenner sees the content of transference as deriving from oedipal conflicts. Kohut highlights narcissistic issues and vulnerabilities.

Brenner's version of transference evolves out of Freud's theoretical emphasis on compromise formation. Dreams, symptoms, parapraxes, and a variety of other mental events and behaviors are seen as a compromise between defense and elements of unconscious fantasy. All transference is seen by Brenner as having not only elements of defense and wish but as being essentially ambivalent in nature. If the analyst encounters positive transference, Brenner maintains that there is a negative transferential element that at some point will be manifest in the analysis. While Brenner has not changed Freud's theoretical definition, he has systematically explored the implications of Freud's statements and demonstrated with great care what the implications for treatment are when one utilizes the concept of compromise formation. This is particularly relevant when we turn to the concept of transference. Brenner (1982), Bird (1972), and others have shown how we can conceive of transference as a ubiquitous phenomenon present in most of our activities and decisions. Although these issues were mentioned by Freud, they certainly were not part of a developed aspect of his theory. It is fair to conclude that, whereas the beginning threads of transference as a compromise formation and the ubiquitous nature of transference were present in Freudian thought, it remained for Brenner to spell out and cultivate these theoretical elements.

In my view, Kohut structures the treatment situation to facilitate (or encourage, depending on your bias) the manifestation and continuance of positive transference. He sees either the mirroring or the idealizing transference states as the important current running through a treatment, whereas he feels that negative transference states should be quickly and empathically dealt with. Transference as a compromise formation is thus not a relevant concept for him. Both Kohut and Freud divide transference states into three negative and two positive types of transference. This superficial resemblance is reinforced if we also remember that Freud's handling of transference states was at least in one way similar to Kohut's; it was Freud's intention to continue an underlying positive transference through as much of the treatment as was possible. The therapeutic importance of transference is, of course, quite different in Freud's and Kohut's theories of technique. Kohut's version of positive transference states is that they are necessary to create alternative psychological structures (transmuting internalizations), whereas Freud thought of the unobjectionable positive transference as an aid in keeping the analysand appropriately attached to the analytic process. Certainly Kohut's and Brenner's positions on the nature of the transference are not only dissimilar, but—in regard to the handling of the transference—they completely diverge.

Kohut conceives of the continuation of the positive transference states as helping to form adaptive structures for the analysand; Brenner sees the positive transference as embodying conflict. Kohut advocates that the positive transference should not be interpreted until there is a break in the patient's perception of the analyst as an empathic figure. Thus it is only when there is a perceived break in empathy that Kohut advocates interpreting the transference. Brenner and Gill, on the other hand, would advocate interpreting the transference whenever it appears prominently in the analysis. Freud, as we know, would agree with Brenner that the eroticized transference should be interpreted as it emerges in the treatment. But, as we have previously stated, Freud does not propose that one interpret the unobjectionable transference; here Brenner departs from Freud's ideas.

Gill interprets the transference in a more complete fashion than does Brenner. It is not clear that Brenner and Gill would always label the same behaviors in the treatment as transference. Gill's notions of transference appear to include a wider range of behavior than is the case with Brenner. This is, of course, an empirical question that would be interesting to understand and to resolve. It may be that Gill simply has different criteria about when to interpret and there might actually be agreement between them as to what is designated as transference. It may be, however, that Gill does have a more inclusive definition of transference than does Brenner.[14]

To be sure, as with any good theoretical concept, there is an empirical reference that one can point to; but *which* empirical reference one looks at depends on one's theory of transference. This is often forgotten in analytic circles, and transference is sometimes treated as an empirical definition rather than a theoretical concept. To remember momentarily, Freud defined transference as the transferring of energy[15] from an unconscious representation to one that is preconscious. The transfer from the unconscious to the preconscious is an assumption that is in principle not directly observable. What is directly observable is a wide range of behaviors, thoughts, and actions that this concept

---

[14]As an aside, we might remind ourselves that transference is a theoretical concept, and as such, the representation of certain behaviors or thoughts as transference depends on one's theoretical definition.

[15]I would maintain that Freud's definition of transference can be stated without the energy concept.

helps explain. How you define different elements of this concept will determine what behaviors you will attempt to explain. A variety of authors have used the concept of transference, but have not completely defined their theoretical assumptions. This leads to some difficulty in comparing the way transference is handled in the clinical situation.

Although I believe there are certain ambiguities that exist in talking about the concept of transference and the behaviors the concept refers to, these ambiguities seem to me to be amenable to resolution. This is not meant to imply that disagreements will be abolished, but rather that different analysts will be able to specify what they are referring to when they talk about transference. This may be the case because all of the authors discussed in this chapter accept the concept of transference as crucial to the psychoanalytic situation. Their ideas about reconstruction are not as easy to resolve.

RECONSTRUCTION

To begin with, not all authors agree that reconstruction is an important or even desirable part of analytic treatment. Even more fundamentally, some authors have doubted or have come close to doubting the possibility of reconstruction. We can only mention here that one interpretation of Spence's arguments about reconstruction (1982) is that he presents a case that there are logical difficulties in conceiving of psychoanalysis as a reconstructive effort. Although I believe Spence has raised many important issues about the nature of psychoanalytic work, I can only say here that I do not agree with this aspect of his thinking. For the readers interested in this issue, I refer them to Ellman and Moskowitz (1980). I would contend that Spence (1982), like Schafer (1976), has made certain philosophic assumptions that have not proven conducive to psychoanalytic theorizing.

Leaving aside the philosophic objections to reconstruction, we might ask why it is necessary to give an account of the patient's past when we can deal in the here and now with the transference. Is there something about capturing these memories that will lead to more efficacious psychoanalytic treatment?[16] Can we say that any reconstruction is an accurate statement of the person's history, or can we even say whether the patient's fantasy about his childhood is created during childhood or at a later point in life? Freud believed he was able to reconstruct the patient's life, even though he expressed some doubts about whether one should call these attempts constructions or reconstructions (Freud 1937a). Many analysts who followed Freud have had doubts about the possibilities of reconstruction.

We know that throughout Freud's career the recovery of memories was an essential aspect of his treatment. However, much of his emphasis changed to

---

[16]These questions leave aside considerations about whether what the analyst does is a construction or a reconstruction.

analyzing the transference and allowing for the possibility of a transference neurosis. This was always done in the service of being able to understand the patient's childhood conflicts. Interestingly, of the three authors that we have looked at in detail, none of them emphasizes the transference neurosis, and only one of them places a great emphasis on reconstruction. Kohut stresses reconstructive attempts, and there are frequently reconstructions in his clinical examples. Gill, of course, in his emphasis on the here and now transference, is opposed to concentrating on reconstructive interpretations. Brenner is surprisingly indifferent about the issue of reconstruction. In this aspect of Brenner's position, he is accepting of reconstructive attempts but does not consider them to be essential to his treatment technique. Interestingly, in a comparison of the reconstruction theories of Brenner, Gill, and Kohut (and even in the mention of transference neurosis), Kohut is most like Freud in terms of his ideas about treatment.

At this point I would state parenthetically that it seems to me that Freud's views on reconstruction are also implicit criteria for termination. Freud's view was that if one couldn't reconstruct the patient's childhood, then something crucial was omitted from the analyst's (or the patient's) understanding of the patient's life. One could state that termination criteria include not only amelioration of the patient's conflicts but also an understanding of the patient's life circumstances in a manner that is adequate for both analyst and analysand. Whether this reconstructive understanding is important therapeutically is an empirical question. Obviously Freud thought it was crucial. I believe that most complete analyses contain this type of understanding. I also believe that most patients would prefer to understand the reasons for their condition; to speculate for another moment, I would assume that all human beings are natural historians and want this type of self-knowledge. I am, of course, assuming that this type of self-knowledge is obtainable through analysis and this is by no means a small assumption.

INTERPRETATION

If we group together a number of issues such as the importance of dreams or the therapeutic alliance, Kohut and Freud seem to stand in closer proximity than any other grouping. It is almost as if Kohut has accepted a good deal of the structure from Freud's theory and is amending Freud's ideas in terms of providing a markedly different type of content. This closeness is turned asunder, however, when we consider some crucial aspects of the treatment situation such as the role of interpretation in analysis. Clearly, for Brenner as for Freud, interpretations are the ameliorative element in the analytic situation.[17] This is much less the case for Kohut, and it remains for a more

[17]Obviously we know at this point that one can't take a single element from the analytic situation and declare this element to be the crucial element, but for Brenner interpretations are certainly a necessary element in treatment.

extensive and penetrating examination to determine the extent to which interpretation is an important element in his ideas about treatment. (Certainly there has been a variety of opinions on this subject.) Gill sees the role of interpretation as pivotal in analysis, but for him it is less the conveyer of the curative element than it is for Brenner. Gill's allowing ideas like the therapeutic alliance in his conception of the treatment situation makes interpretative efforts slightly less central in his therapeutic conceptual milieu.

Conclusions

In this brief review of several concepts, we have seen that no single contemporary author has taken up all or perhaps even most of Freud's suggestions on how to conduct an analysis. All the authors reviewed in this book have accepted some aspects of Freudian technique and rejected others. Winnicott (1965) comments in another context that it was a footnote of Freud's that stimulated his pioneering interest in the mother–infant relationship. In a mere footnote Freud was, at times, able to foment analysts to whole new ways of looking at analytic material. Indeed, such footnotes and suggestions abound in Freud's writings. I hope I have been able to demonstrate in these pages how Freud's essays on technique have stimulated most of the modern analytic concepts that are now being considered and debated—and, hopefully, clinically and conceptually refined—in today's analytic world.

In Chapter 16 we looked at one aspect of Freudian technique that has undergone significant revision, a revision that has expanded the scope of analysis dramatically. The aspect to which I am referring has to do with how one envisions the beginning of analytic treatment. One important element of the beginning of any treatment is the analyst's view of the issue of analyzability. In my opinion it is primarily the consideration of this issue that has led to the widening scope of analysis (Stone 1961), which is discussed in detail in Chapter 16. It is often in the beginning of the treatment that the scope of treatment will either widen or diminish.

I have assumed that the widening scope of analysis is a positive development, but of course that is only one opinion. Hopefully, the scope of analysis does not widen without also deepening our understanding of human experience, and of the ways in which we can meaningfully intervene to help people overcome psychological pain and conflict.

References

Abend, S. M. (1982). Serious illness in the analyst: countertransference considerations. *Journal of the American Psychoanalytic Association* 3:365–380.

Abend, S., Porter, M., and Willick, M. (1983). *Borderline Patients: Psychoanalytic Perspectives*. New York: International Universities Press.

Abraham, K. (1953). *Selected Papers on Psychoanalysis*, ed. A. Strachey, trans. D. Bryan, A. Strachey. New York: Basic Books.

Altman, L. (1969). *The Dream in Psychoanalysis*. New York: International Universities Press.

—— (1975). *The Dream in Psychoanalysis* (revised edition). New York: International Universities Press.

Angel, K. (1971). Unanalyzability and narcissistic transference disturbances. *Psychoanalytic Quarterly* 40:264–276.

Anthi, P. R. (1983). Reconstruction of preverbal experiences. *Journal of the American Psychoanalytic Association* 31:33–58.

Arlow, J. A. (1969). Unconscious fantasy and disturbances of conscious experience. *Psychoanalytic Quarterly* 38:1–27.

—— (1979). The genesis of interpretation. *Journal of the American Psychoanalytic Association* 27:193–207.

—— (1981). Theories of pathogenesis. *Psychoanalytic Quarterly* 50:488–513.

—— (1985). Some technical problems of countertransference. *Psychoanalytic Quarterly* 54:164–174.

—— (1990). *Methodology and reconstruction in psychoanalysis*. Paper presented at the Institute for Psychoanalytic Training and Research, October 19.

Arlow, J., and Brenner, C. (1964). *Psychoanalytic Concepts and the Structural Theory*. New York: International Universities Press.

Bach, S. (1985). *Narcissistic States and the Therapeutic Process*. New York: Jason Aronson.

Balint, M. (1950). On the termination of analysis. *International Journal of Psycho-Analysis* 31:196–199.

Balkoura, A. (1974). Workshop: the fate of the transference neurosis after analysis. *Journal of the American Psychoanalytic Association* 22:895–903.

Baranger, W. (1974). Discussion of the paper by H. B. Vianna, "A peculiar form of resistance to psychoanalytic treatment." *International Journal of Psycho-Analysis* 55:445–447.

Barchilon, J. (1958). On countertransference "cures." *Journal of the American Psychoanalytic Association* 6:222–236.

Barglow, P., Jaffe, C. M., and Vaughn, B. (1989). Psychoanalytic reconstructions and empirical data: reciprocal contributions. *Journal of the American Psychoanalytic Association* 37:401–436.

Basch, M. F. (1981). Psychoanalytic interpretation and cognitive transformation. *International Journal of Psycho-Analysis* 62:151–172.

Benedek, T. (1955). A contribution to the problem of termination of training analysis. *Journal of the American Psychoanalytic Association* 3:615–629.

Beratis, S. (1984). The first analytic dream: mirror of the patient's neurotic conflicts and subsequent analytic process. *International Journal of Psycho-Analysis* 65:461–470.

Bergman, A., and Ellman, S. J. (1985). Margret S. Mahler: symbiosis and separation-individuation. In *Beyond Freud*, ed. J. Reppen. Hillsdale, NJ: Analytic Press.

Bergmann, M. S. (1982). Platonic love, transference love, and love in real life. *Journal of the American Psychoanalytic Association* 30:87–112.

Berman, L. E. A. (1985). Primal scene significance of a dream within a dream. *International Journal of Psycho-Analysis* 66:75–76.

Bernfeld, S. (1949). Freud's scientific beginnings. *American Imago* 6:163–196.

Bettelheim, B. (1982). *Freud and Man's Soul*. New York: Knopf.

Bibring-Lehner, G. (1936). A contribution to the subject of transference resistance. *International Journal of Psycho-Analysis* 17:181–189.

Bion, W. R. (1954). Notes on the theory of schizophrenia. *International Journal of Psycho-Analysis* 35:113–118.

Bird, B. (1972). Notes on transference: universal phenomenon and hardest part of analysis. *Journal of the American Psychoanalytic Association* 20:267–301.

——— (1973). *Talking With Patients*. 2nd ed. Philadelphia: Lippincott.

Blaustein, A. B. (1975). A dream resembling the Isakower phenomenon: a brief clinical contribution. *International Journal of Psycho-Analysis* 56:207–208.

Blum, H. P. (1971). On the conception and development of the transference neurosis. *Journal of the American Psychoanalytic Association* 19:41–53.

——— (1973). The concept of erotized transference. *Journal of the American Psychoanalytic Association* 21:61–76.

——— (1976). The changing use of dreams in psychoanalytic practice: dreams and free association. *International Journal of Psycho-Analysis* 57:315–324.

——— (1977). The prototype of preoedipal reconstruction. *Journal of the American Psychoanalytic Association* 25:757–786.

——— (1980a). The value of reconstruction in adult psychoanalysis. *International Journal of Psycho-Analysis* 61:39–52.

——— (1980b). The borderline childhood of the Wolf Man. In *Freud and His Patients*, ed. M. Kanzer and J. Glenn, pp. 341–357. New York and London: Jason Aronson.

——— (1982). The transference in psychoanalysis and in psychotherapy: points of view past and present, inside and outside the transference. *Journal of the American Psychoanalytic Association* 10:117-137.

—— (1983). The position and value of extratransference interpretation. *Journal of the American Psychoanalytic Association* 31:587-617.

—— (1989). The concept of termination and the evolution of psychoanalytic thought. *International Journal of Psycho-Analysis* 37:275-298.

Boesky, D. (1983). Resistance and character theory: concept of character resistance. *Journal of the American Psychoanalytic Association* 31:227-246.

Brenman, E. (1980). The value of reconstruction in adult psychoanalysis. *International Journal of Psycho-Analysis* 61:53-60.

Brenner, C. (1969). Some comments on technical precepts in psychoanalysis. *Journal of the American Psychoanalytic Association* 17:333-352.

—— (1976). *Psychoanalytic Technique and Psychic Conflict*. New York: International Universities Press.

—— (1979). Working alliance, therapeutic alliance, and transference. *Journal of the American Psychoanalytic Association* 27:137-158.

—— (1981). Defense and defense mechanisms. *Psychoanalytic Quarterly* 50:557-569.

—— (1982). *The Mind in Conflict*. New York: International Universities Press.

—— (1985). Countertransference as compromise formation. *Psychoanalytic Quarterly* 54:155-163.

Breuer, J., and Freud, S. (1893). Studies on hysteria. *Standard Edition* 2:3-305.

Bridger, H. (1950). Criteria for the termination of an analysis. *International Journal of Psycho-Analysis* 31:202-203.

Brodsky, B. (1967). Working through: its widening scope and some aspects of its metapsychology. *Psychoanalytic Quarterly* 36:485-496.

Bychowski, G. (1969). Social climate and resistance in psychoanalysis. *International Journal of Psycho-Analysis* 50:453-460.

Calef, V. (1954). Panel: training and therapeutic analysis. *Journal of the American Psychoanalytic Association* 2:175-178.

—— (1971). On the current concept of the transference neurosis: concluding remarks. *Journal of the American Psychoanalytic Association* 19:89-97.

Calef, V., and Weinshel, E. M. (1973). Reporting, non-reporting, and assessment in the training analysis. *Journal of the American Psychoanalytic Association* 21:714-726.

—— (1983). A note on consummation and termination. *Journal of the American Psychoanalytic Association* 31:643-650.

Casuso, G. (1974). Discussion of the paper by Angel Garma, "Aspects of the transference resistance in the final stages of psychoanalytic treatment." *International Journal of Psycho-Analysis* 55:377-378.

Cavenar, J. O., Jr., and Nash, J. L. (1976). The dream as a signal for termination. *Journal of the American Psychoanalytic Association* 24:425-436.

Clark, R. W. (1980). *Freud: The Man and the Cause*. New York: Random House.

Coen, S. J., and Bradlow, P. A. (1982). Twin transference as a compromise formation. *Journal of the American Psychoanalytic Association* 30:599-620.

Coltrera, J. T. (1979). Truth from genetic illusion: the transference and the fate of the infantile neurosis. *Journal of the American Psychoanalytic Association* 27:289-314.

Cooper, A. (1988). *Infant research in adult psychoanalysis*. Paper presented at The Workshop for Mental Health Professionals, Seattle, WA, March 12-13.

Crick, F., and Mitchison, G. (1986). REM sleep and neural nets. *The Journal of Mind and Behavior* 7:229-250.

Curtis, H. C. (1979). The concept of therapeutic alliance: implications for the "widening scope." *Journal of the American Psychoanalytic Association* 27:159-192.

Curtis, H. C., and Sachs, D. M. (1976). Dialogue on "The changing use of dreams in psychoanalytic practice." *International Journal of Psycho-Analysis* 57:343-354.

Dahl, H., and Teller, V. (1978). Countertransference examples of the syntactic expressions of warded-off contents. *Psychoanalytic Quarterly* 47:339-363.

Daniels, R. S. (1969). Some early manifestations of transference: their implications for the first phase of psychoanalysis. *Journal of the American Psychoanalytic Association* 17:995-1014.

Davanzo, H. (1962). A contribution to the analysis of resistances in neurotic dependence. *International Journal of Psycho-Analysis* 43:441-447.

Davies, G., and O'Farrell, V. (1976). The logic of transference interpretation. *International Journal of Psycho-Analysis* 3:55-64.

DeMonchaux, C. (1978). Dreaming and the organizing function of the ego. *International Journal of Psycho-Analysis* 59:443-454.

De Prado, M. P. (1980). Neurotic and psychotic transference and projective identification. *International Journal of Psycho-Analysis* 7:157-164.

De Leon-Jones, F. A. (1979). The role of the transference in mourning. *Journal of the American Psychoanalytic Association* 7:133-158.

De Racker, G. (1961). On the formulation of the interpretation. *International Journal of Psycho-Analysis* 42:49-54.

De Saussure, R. (1943). Transference and animal magnetism. *Psychoanalytic Quarterly* 12:194-201.

———— (1973). Sigmund Freud. In *Freud as We Knew Him*, ed. H. M. Ruitenbeek, pp. 357-359. Detroit: Wayne State University Press.

Dean, E. S. (1957). Drowsiness as a symptom of countertransference. *Psychoanalytic Quarterly* 26:246-247.

Decker, H. S. (1991). *Freud, Dora, and Vienna 1900*. New York: The Free Press.

Deutsch, F. (1954). Analytic synesthesiology: analytic interpretation of intersensory perception. *International Journal of Psycho-Analysis* 35:293-301.

Deutsch, H. (1939). A discussion of certain forms of resistance. *International Journal of Psycho-Analysis* 20:72-83.

Devereux, G. (1951). Some criteria for the timing of confrontations and interpretations. *International Journal of Psycho-Analysis* 32:19-24.

Dewald, P. A. (1976). Transference regression and real experience in the psychoanalytic process. *Psychoanalytic Quarterly* 45:213-230.

———— (1980). The handling of resistances in adult psychoanalysis. *International Journal of Psycho-Analysis* 61:61-70.

———— (1982). Serious illness in the analyst: transference, countertransference and reality responses. *Journal of the American Psychoanalytic Association* 30:347-364.

Dickes, R. (1967). Severe regressive disruptions of the therapeutic alliance. *Journal of the American Psychoanalytic Association* 15:508-533.

Edelson, M. (1975). *Language and Interpretation in Psychoanalysis*. New Haven: Yale University Press.

Eder, M. D. (1930). Dreams as resistance. *International Journal of Psycho-Analysis* 11:40-47.

Eisnitz, A. J. (1961). Mirror dreams. *Journal of the American Psychoanalytic Association* 9:461–479.

Eissler, K. R. (1953). The effect of the structure of the ego on psychoanalytic technique. *Journal of the American Psychoanalytic Association* 1:104–143.

—— (1958). Remarks on some variations in psychoanalytic technique. *International Journal of Psycho-Analysis* 39:222–229.

Ekstein, R. (1955). Termination of the training analysis within the framework of present-day institutes. *Journal of the American Psychoanalytic Association* 3:600–614.

—— (1965). Working through and termination of analysis. *Journal of the American Psychoanalytic Association* 13:57–78.

Ekstein, R., and Rangell, L. (1961). Reconstruction and theory formation. *Journal of the American Psychoanalytic Association* 9:684–697.

Ellman, S. J. (1985a). A comment on Bergmann's concept of Transference Love. *International Journal of Psychoanalytic Psychotherapy* 11:47–51.

—— (1985b). *Kohut and Freud: a comparison.* Paper presented at New York Academy of Medicine, New York City, November.

Ellman, S. J., and Antrobus, J. S. (1991). *The Mind in Sleep.* New York: John Wiley & Sons.

Ellman, S. J., and Moskowitz, M. B. (1980). An examination of some recent criticisms of psychoanalytic "metapsychology." *Psychoanalytic Quarterly* 49:631–662.

Ellman, S. J., and Weinstein, L. N. (1991). REM sleep and dream formation: a theoretical integration. In *The Mind in Sleep*, ed. S. J. Ellman and J. S. Antrobus. New York: John Wiley & Sons.

Escoll, P. J. (1983). Panel: the changing vistas of transference; the effect of developmental concepts on the understanding of transference. *Journal of the American Psychoanalytic Association* 31:699–712.

Etchegoyen, R. H. (1982). The relevance of the "here and now" transference interpretation for the reconstruction of early psychic development. *International Journal of Psycho-Analysis* 63:65–76.

—— (1983). Fifty years after the mutative interpretation. *International Journal of Psycho-Analysis* 64:445–460.

Ferenczi, S. (1988). *The Clinical Diary of Sándor Ferenczi.* Ed. J. Dupont. Cambridge, MA: Harvard University Press.

Firestein, S. K. (1969). Panel: problems of termination in the analysis of adults. *Journal of the American Psychoanalytic Association* 17:222–237.

—— (1974). Termination of psychoanalysis of adults: a review of the literature. *Journal of the American Psychoanalytic Association* 22:873–894.

—— (1978). *Termination in Psychoanalysis.* New York: International Universities Press.

Fischer, N. (1971). An interracial analysis: transference and countertransference significance. *Journal of the American Psychoanalytic Association* 19:736–745.

Fisher, C. (1953). Studies on the nature of suggestion—Part II: The transference meaning of giving suggestions. *Journal of the American Psychoanalytic Association* 1:406–437.

—— (1954). Dreams and perception: the role of preconscious and primary modes of perception in dream formation. *Journal of the American Psychoanalytic Association* 2:389–445.

———— (1965a). Psychoanalytic implications of recent research on sleep and dreaming: I. Empirical findings. *Journal of the American Psychoanalytic Association* 13:197–270.

———— (1965b). Psychoanalytic implications of recent research on sleep and dreaming: II. Implications for psychoanalytic theory. *Journal of the American Psychoanalytic Association* 13:271–303.

———— (1976). Spoken words in dreams: a critique of the views of Otto Isakower. *Psychoanalytic Quarterly* 45:100–109.

Fiumara, G. C. (1977). The symbolic function, transference and psychic reality. *International Journal of Psycho-Analysis* 4:171–180.

Fleming, J. (1972). Early object deprivation and transference phenomena: the working alliance. *Psychoanalytic Quarterly* 41:23–49.

Fliess, R. (1953). Countertransference and counteridentification. *Journal of the American Psychoanalytic Association* 1:268–284.

———— (1956). The deja raconte: a transference-delusion concerning the castration complex. *Psychoanalytic Quarterly* 25:215–227.

Fodor, N. (1945). The negative in dreams. *Psychoanalytic Quarterly* 14:516–527.

Fox, H. M. (1958). Effect of psychophysiological research on the transference. *Journal of the American Psychoanalytic Association* 6:413–432.

Frank, A. (1983). Id resistance and strength of instincts: clinical demonstration. *Journal of the American Psychoanalytic Association* 31:375–404.

Frankl, L. and Hellman, I. (1962). The ego's participation in the therapeutic alliance. *International Journal of Psycho-Analysis* 43:333–337.

Freeman, T. (1981). The pre-psychotic phase and its reconstruction in schizophrenic and paranoic psychoses. *International Journal of Psycho-Analysis* 62:447–454.

French, T., and Fromm, E. (1964). *Dream Interpretation: A New Approach*. New York: Basic Books.

Freud, A. (1936). *The Ego and Mechanisms of Defense*. New York: International Universities Press.

Freud, S. (1889). Translation with introduction and notes of H. Bernheim. *Standard Edition* 1:73–86.

———— (1894). The neuro-psychosis of defense. *Standard Edition* 3:45–61.

———— (1895). On the grounds for detaching a particular syndrome from neurasthenia under the description anxiety neurosis. *Standard Edition* 3:90–115.

———— (1897). Theory transformed. In *The Complete Letters of Sigmund Freud to Wilhelm Fliess: 1887–1904*, ed. J. Moussaieff Masson. London and Cambridge: The Belknap Press.

———— (1899). Screen memories. *Standard Edition* 3:303–322.

———— (1900). *The Interpretation of Dreams. Standard Edition* 4/5.

———— (1901). *The Psychopathology of Everyday Life. Standard Edition* 6.

———— (1904). Freud's psycho-analytic procedure. *Standard Edition* 7:249–254.

———— (1905a). On psychotherapy. *Standard Edition* 7:257–268.

———— (1905b). Fragment of an analysis of a case of hysteria. *Standard Edition* 7:7–122.

———— (1905c). Three essays on the theory of sexuality. *Standard Edition* 7:135–243.

———— (1909a). Analysis of a phobia in a five-year-old boy. *Standard Edition* 10:5–149.

———— (1909b). Notes upon a case of obsessional neurosis. *Standard Edition* 10:155–318.

———— (1910). "Wild" psycho-analysis. *Standard Edition* 11:221–227.

—— (1911). Psycho-analytic notes on an autobiographical account of a case of paranoia (dementia paranoides). *Standard Edition* 12:9-82.

—— (1912a). Recommendations to physicians on the psycho-analytic method of treatment. In *Collected Papers*, Vol. 2, pp. 323-333. New York: Basic Books, 1959.

—— (1912b). The employment of dream-interpretation in psycho-analysis. In *Collected Papers*, Vol. 2, pp. 305-311. New York: Basic Books, 1959.

—— (1912c). The dynamics of the transference. In *Collected Papers*, Vol. 2, pp. 312-322. New York: Basic Books, 1959.

—— (1913a). The disposition of obsessional neurosis (a contribution to the problem of choice of neurosis). *Standard Edition* 12:311-326.

—— (1913b). Further recommendations in the technique of psycho-analysis—on beginning the treatment. In *Collected Papers*, Vol. 2, pp. 342-365. New York: Basic Books, 1959.

—— (1914a). On the history of the psychoanalytic movement. *Standard Edition* 14:7-66.

—— (1914b). Further recommendations in the technique of psycho-analysis—recollection, repetition and working through. In *Collected Papers*, Vol. 2, pp. 366-376. New York: Basic Books, 1959.

—— (1914c). On narcissism: an introduction. *Standard Edition* 14:73-102.

—— (1915a). Instincts and their vicissitudes. *Standard Edition* 14:117-140.

—— (1915b). Further recommendations in the technique of psycho-analysis—observations on transference love. In *Collected Papers*, Vol. 2, pp. 377-391. New York: Basic Books, 1959.

—— (1916/1917). *Introductory Lectures on Psycho-Analysis. Standard Edition* 15/16.

—— (1918). From the history of an infantile neurosis. *Standard Edition* 17:7-122.

—— (1920). Beyond the pleasure principle. *Standard Edition* 18:7-64.

—— (1923a). The ego and the id. *Standard Edition* 19:12-59.

—— (1923b). Remarks upon the theory and practice of dream-interpretation. In *Collected Papers*, Vol. 5, pp. 136-149. New York: Basic Books, 1959.

—— (1925a). Inhibitions, symptoms, and anxiety. *Standard Edition* 20:87-172.

—— (1925b). Some additional notes upon dream-interpretation as a whole. In *Collected Papers*, Vol. 5, pp. 150-162. New York: Basic Books, 1959.

—— (1933). New introductory lectures on psycho-analysis. *Standard Edition* 22:5-182.

—— (1937a). Constructions in analysis. In *Collected Papers*, Vol. 5, pp. 358-371. New York: Basic Books, 1959.

—— (1937b). Analysis terminable and interminable. In *Collected Papers*, Vol. 5, pp. 316-357. New York: Basic Books, 1959.

—— (1939). *Moses and Monotheism. Standard Edition* 23:7-137.

Friedman, L. (1969). The therapeutic alliance. *International Journal of Psycho-Analysis* 50:139-154.

Fromm-Reichmann, F. (1939). Transference problems in schizophrenics. *Psychoanalytic Quarterly* 8:412-426.

Frosch, J. (1959). Transference derivatives of the family romance. *Journal of the American Psychoanalytic Association* 7:503-522.

Gabbard, G. O. (1982). The exit line: heightened transference-countertransference manifestations at the end of the hour. *Journal of the American Psychoanalytic Association* 30:579-598.

Galatzer-Levy, R. M. (1988). On working-through: a model from artificial intelligence. *Journal of the American Psychoanalytic Association* 36:125–151.

Gann, E. (1984). Some theoretical and technical considerations concerning the emergence of a symptom of the transference neurosis: an empirical study. *Journal of the American Psychoanalytic Association* 32:797–830.

Gardiner, M., ed. (1971). *The Wolf-Man.* New York: Basic Books.

Garduk, L., and Haggard, E. (1972). *Immediate Effects on Patients of Psychoanalytic Interpretations.* New York: International Universities Press.

Garma, A. (1974). Aspects of the transference resistances in the final stages of psychoanalytic treatment. *International Journal of Psycho-Analysis* 55:371–376.

—— (1975). Aspects of the transference resistances in the final stages of psychoanalytic treatment: a reply to the discussion of G. Casuso. *International Journal of Psycho-Analysis* 56:241–242.

Gay, P. (1988). *Freud: A Life for Our Time.* New York: Norton.

Gear, M., Hill, M., and Liendo, E. (1981). *Working Through Narcissism: Treating its Sadomasochistic Structure.* New York: Jason Aronson.

Gedo, J. E. (1975). Forms of idealization in the analytic transference. *Journal of the American Psychoanalytic Association* 23:485–506.

—— (1977). Notes on the psychoanalytic management of archaic transferences. *Journal of the American Psychoanalytic Association* 25:787–804.

—— (1979). *Beyond Interpretation: Toward a Revised Theory of Psychoanalysis.* New York: International Universities Press.

Geleerd, E. R. (1969). Introduction to panel on child analysis. The separation–individuation phase: direct observations and reconstructions in analysis. *International Journal of Psycho-Analysis* 50:91–94.

Gill, M. M. (1963). *Topography and Systems in Psychoanalytic Theory. Psychological Issues Monograph 10.* New York: International Universities Press.

—— (1979). The analysis of the transference. *Journal of the American Psychoanalytic Association* 27:263–288.

—— (1982a). *Analysis of Transference, vol. 1: Theory and Technique.* New York: International Universities Press.

—— (1982b). *Analysis of Transference, vol. 2: Studies of Nine Audio-Recorded Psychoanalytic Sessions.* New York: International Universities Press.

—— (1984). Psychoanalysis and psychotherapy: a revision. *International Review of Psycho-Analysis* 11:161–180.

Gill, M. M., and Hoffman, I. Z. (1982). A method for studying the analysis of aspects of the patient's experience of the relationship in psychoanalysis and psychotherapy. *Journal of the American Psychoanalytic Association* 30:137–168.

Gill, M. M., and Muslin, H. L. (1976). Early interpretation of transference. *Journal of the American Psychoanalytic Association* 24:779–794.

Giovacchini, P. L. (1961). Resistance and external object relations. *International Journal of Psycho-Analysis* 42:246–254.

—— (1969). The influence of interpretation upon schizophrenic patients. *International Journal of Psycho-Analysis* 50:179–186.

Gitelson, M. (1967). Analytic aphorisms. *Psychoanalytic Quarterly* 36:260–270.

Glover, E. (1926). A "technical" form of resistance. *International Journal of Psycho-Analysis* 7:377–380.

—— (1927). Lectures on technique in psycho-analysis: defense resistance. *International Journal of Psycho-Analysis* 8:504-521.

—— (1928). Lectures on technique in psycho-analysis. *International Journal of Psycho-Analysis* 9:7-46.

—— (1930). The "vehicle" of interpretations. *International Journal of Psycho-Analysis* 11:340-344.

—— (1931). The therapeutic effect of inexact interpretation. *International Journal of Psycho-Analysis* 12:397-411.

—— (1954). Therapeutic criteria of psychoanalysis. *International Journal of Psycho-Analysis* 35:95-101.

—— (1955). *The Technique of Psycho-Analysis*. New York: International Universities Press.

Goldberg, A. (1977). Some countertransference phenomena in the analysis of perversions. *Journal of the American Psychoanalytic Association* 5:105-120.

Goldberg, A., and Marcus, D. (1985). "Natural termination": some comments on ending psychoanalysis without setting a date. *Psychoanalytic Quarterly* 54:46-65.

Graff, H., and Luborsky, L. (1977). Long-term trends in transference and resistance: a report on a quantitative-analytic method applied to four psychoanalyses. *Journal of the American Psychoanalytic Association* 25:471-492.

Graller, J. L. (1981). Adjunctive marital therapy: a possible solution to the split-transference problem. *Journal of the American Psychoanalytic Association* 9:175-187.

Gray, P. (1986). On helping analysands observe intrapsychic activity. In *Psychoanalysis: The Science of Mental Conflict—Essays in Honor of Charles Brenner*, ed. A. Richards and M. Willick, pp. 245-262. Hillsdale, NJ: Analytic Press.

Green, A. (1973). On negative capability: a critical review of W. R. Bion's "Attention and Interpretation." *International Journal of Psycho-Analysis* 54:115-120.

Greenacre, P. (1954). The role of transference: practical considerations in relation to psychoanalytic therapy. *Journal of the American Psychoanalytic Association* 2:671-684.

—— (1956). Re-evaluation of the process of working through. *International Journal of Psycho-Analysis* 37:439-444.

—— (1959). Certain technical problems in the transference relationship. *Journal of the American Psychoanalytic Association* 7:484-502.

—— (1975). On reconstruction. *Journal of the American Psychoanalytic Association* 23:693-712.

—— (1981). Reconstruction: its nature and therapeutic value. *Journal of the American Psychoanalytic Association* 29:27-46.

Greenberg, J., and Mitchell, S. (1983). *Object Relations in Psychoanalytic Theory*. Cambridge, MA: Harvard University Press.

Greenberg, R., and Pearlman, C. (1975). A psychoanalytic-dream continuum: the source and function of dreams. *International Review of Psycho-Analysis* 2:441-448.

Greenson, R. R. (1958). Variations in classical psychoanalytic technique: an introduction. *International Journal of Psycho-Analysis* 39:200-201.

—— (1961). Panel: The selection of candidates for psychoanalytic training. *Journal of the American Psychoanalytic Association* 9:135-145.

—— (1965). The working alliance and the transference neurosis. *Psychoanalytic Quarterly* 34:155-181.

—— (1967). *The Technique and Practice of Psychoanalysis*. New York: International Universities Press.

—— (1970). The exceptional position of the dream in psychoanalytic practice. *Psychoanalytic Quarterly* 39:519–549.

—— (1972). Beyond transference and intepretation. *International Journal of Psycho-Analysis* 53:213–218.

Grossman, C. M. (1965). Transference, countertransference, and being in love. *Psychoanalytic Quarterly* 34:249–256.

Grunbaum, A. (1984). *The Foundations of Psychoanalysis: A Philosophical Critique*. Berkeley: University of California Press.

Grunes, M. (1984). The therapeutic object relationship. *Psychoanalytic Review* 71:123–143.

Gunther, M. S. (1976). The endangered self: a contribution to the understanding of narcissistic determinants of countertransference. *Journal of the American Psychoanalytic Association* 4:201–224.

Halpert, E. (1984). Panel: The value of extratransference interpretation. *Journal of the American Psychoanalytic Association* 32:137–146.

Harley, M. (1971). The current status of transference neurosis in children. *Journal of the American Psychoanalytic Association* 19:26–40.

Harnik, J. (1930). Resistance to the interpretation of dreams in analysis. *International Journal of Psycho-Analysis* 11:75–78.

Hartmann, E. (1976). Discussion of "The changing use of dreams in psychoanalytic practice." *International Journal of Psycho-Analysis* 57:331–334.

Hartmann, H. (1939). *Ego Psychology and the Problem of Adaptation*. New York: International Universities Press.

—— (1959). *Essays on Ego Psychology*. New York: International Universities Press.

Heimann, P. (1956). Dynamics of transference interpretations. *International Journal of Psycho-Analysis* 37:303–310.

Hobson, J. A., and McCarley, R. W. (1977). The brain as a dream state generator: an activation–synthesis hypothesis of the dream process. *American Journal of Psychiatry* 134:1335–1348.

Hoffer, W. (1950). Three psychological criteria for the termination of treatment. *International Journal of Psycho-Analysis* 31:194–195.

Holt, R. R., and Luborsky, L. (1955). The selection of candidates for psychoanalytic training. *Journal of the American Psychoanalytic Association* 3:666–681.

Hurn, H. T. (1970). Adolescent transference: a problem of the terminal phase of analysis. *Journal of the American Psychoanalytic Association* 18:342–357.

—— (1973). Panel: on the fate of transference after the termination of analysis. *Journal of the American Psychoanalytic Association* 21:181–192.

Ilan, E. (1977). The effect of interpretation in psychoanalytic treatment in the light of an integrated model of internal objects. *International Journal of Psycho-Analysis* 58:183–194.

Isaacs, S. (1939). Criteria for interpretation. *International Journal of Psycho-Analysis* 20:148–160.

Isakower, O. (1938). A contribution to the pathopsychology of phenomena associated with falling asleep. *International Journal of Psycho-Analysis* 19:331–345.

—— (1939). On the exceptional position of the auditory sphere. *International Journal of Psycho-Analysis* 20:340–348.

——— (1954). Spoken words in dreams. A preliminary communication. *Psychoanalytic Quarterly* 23:1-6.

Izner, S. M. (1975). Dreams and the latent negative transference. *Journal of the American Psychoanalytic Association* 3:165-178.

Jacobs, T. J. (1973). Posture, gesture, and movement in the analyst: cues to interpretation and countertransference. *Journal of the American Psychoanalytic Association* 21:77-92.

——— (1983). The analyst and the patient's object world: notes on an aspect of countertransference. *Journal of the American Psychoanalytic Association* 31:619-642.

Jacobson, E. (1954). Transference problems in the psychoanalytic treatment of severely depressive patients. *Journal of the American Psychoanalytic Association* 2:595-606.

James, M. (1964). Interpretation and management in the treatment of preadolescents. *International Journal of Psycho-Analysis* 45:499-511.

Jarvis, V. (1964). Countertransference in the management of school phobia. *Psychoanalytic Quarterly* 33:411-419.

Jekels, L., and Bergler, E. (1949). Transference and love. *Psychoanalytic Quarterly* 18:325-350.

Jones, E. (1954). *The Life and Work of Sigmund Freud, vol. 1: The Formative Years and the Great Discoveries, 1856-1900*. New York: Basic Books.

——— (1955a). *The Life and Work of Sigmund Freud, vol. 2: Years of Maturity, 1901-1919*. London: Hogarth Press.

——— (1955b). *Sigmund Freud: Life and Work*. New York: Basic Books.

——— (1957). *The Life and Work of Sigmund Freud, vol. 3: The Last Phase, 1919-1939*. New York: Basic Books.

Kantrowitz, J. L., Katz, A. L., and Paolitto, F. (1990). Followup of psychoanalysis five to ten years after termination: I. Stability of change. *Journal of the American Psychoanalytic Association* 38:471-496.

Kanzer, M. (1952). The transference neurosis of the rat man. *Psychoanalytic Quarterly* 21:181-189.

——— (1953). Past and present in the transference. *Journal of the American Psychoanalytic Association* 1:144-154.

——— (1966). The motor sphere of the transference. *Psychoanalytic Quarterly* 35:522-539.

——— (1980a). Freud's "human influence" on the Rat Man. In *Freud and His Patients*, ed. M. Kanzer and J. Glenn, pp. 232-239. New York: Jason Aronson.

——— (1980b). Dora's imagery: the flight from a burning house. In *Freud and His Patients*, ed. M. Kanzer and J. Glenn, pp. 72-82. New York: Jason Aronson.

——— (1981). Freud's "analytic pact": the standard therapeutic alliance. *Journal of the American Psychoanalytic Association* 29:69-88.

Kardiner, A. (1977). *My Analysis with Freud: Reminiscences*. New York: W. W. Norton.

Karush, A. (1967). Working through. *Psychoanalytic Quarterly* 36:497-531.

Kepecs, J. G. (1966). Theories of transference neurosis. *Psychoanalytic Quarterly* 35:497-521.

Kepecs, J. G., and Wolman, R. (1972). Preconscious perception of the transference. *Psychoanalytic Quarterly* 41:172-194.

Kern, J. W. (1978). Countertransference and spontaneous screens: an analyst studies his own visual images. *Journal of the American Psychoanalytic Association* 26:21-48.

Kernberg, O. F. (1965). Notes on countertransference. *Journal of the American Psychoanalytic Association* 13:38–56.

——— (1975). *Borderline Conditions and Pathological Narcissism.* New York: Jason Aronson.

Kestemberg, E. (1964). Problems regarding the termination of analysis in character neuroses. *International Journal of Psychoanalytic Psychotherapy* 45:350–357.

Khan, M. M. R. (1964). Ego distortion, cumulative trauma and the role of reconstruction in the analytic situation. *International Journal of Psycho-Analysis* 45:272–279.

——— (1976). The changing use of dreams in psychoanalytic practice: in search of the dreaming experience. *International Journal of Psycho-Analysis* 57:325–330.

Kitay, P. (1963). Symposium: "Reinterpretations of the Schreber case: Freud's theory of paranoia." *International Journal of Psycho-Analysis* 44:191–194.

Klauber, J. (1972). On the relationship of transference and interpretation in psychoanalytic therapy. *International Journal of Psycho-Analysis* 53:385–392.

——— (1977). Analyses that cannot be terminated. *International Journal of Psycho-Analysis* 58:473–478.

——— (1980). Formulating interpretations in clinical psychoanalysis. *International Journal of Psycho-Analysis* 61:195–202.

Kleeman, J. A. (1962). Dreaming for a dream course. *Psychoanalytic Quarterly* 31:203–231.

Klein, M. (1950). On the criteria for the termination of a psychoanalysis. *International Journal of Psycho-Analysis* 31:78–80.

——— (1957). *Envy and Gratitude: A Study of Unconscious Forces.* New York: Basic Books.

Kohler, L. (1984). On selfobject countertransference. *Journal of the American Psychoanalytic Association* 12:39–56.

Kohrman, R. (1969). Problems of termination in the analysis of adults. *Journal of the American Psychoanalytic Association* 17:191–205.

Kohut, H. (1957). Panel: clinical and theoretical aspects of resistance. *Journal of the American Psychoanalytic Association* 5:548–555.

——— (1966). Forms and transformations of narcissism. *Journal of the American Psychoanalytic Association* 14:243–272.

——— (1968). The psychoanalytic treatment of the narcissistic personality disorders: outline of a systematic approach. *Psychoanalytic Study of the Child* 23:86–113. New York: International Universities Press.

——— (1971). *The Analysis of the Self: A Systematic Approach to the Psychoanalytic Treatment of Narcissistic Personality Disorders.* New York: International Universities Press.

——— (1972). Thoughts on narcissism and narcissistic rage. *Psychoanalytic Study of the Child* 27:360–400. New York: International Universities Press.

——— (1977). *The Restoration of the Self.* New York: International Universities Press.

——— (1978). *The Search for the Self, vols. 1 and 2.* Ed. P. Ornstein. New York: International Universities Press.

——— (1984). *How Does Analysis Cure?* Ed. A. Goldberg with the collaboration of P. Stepansky. Chicago: The University of Chicago Press.

Krapf, E. (1957). Transference and motility. *Psychoanalytic Quarterly* 26:519–526.

Krause, M. S. (1961). Defensive and nondefensive resistance. *Psychoanalytic Quarterly* 30:221–231.

Kris, A. O. (1985). Resistance in convergent and in divergent conflicts. *Psychoanalytic Quarterly* 54:537-568.

Kris, E. (1951). Ego psychology and interpretation in psychoanalytic therapy. *Psychoanalytic Quarterly* 20:15-30.

——— (1956). The personal myth: a problem in psychoanalytic technique. *Journal of the American Psychoanalytic Association* 4:653-681.

Kris Study Group of the New York Psychoanalytic Institute, Reporter Herbert F. Waldhorn (1967). *The Place of the Dream in Clinical Psychoanalysis* (Monograph 2). New York: International Universities Press.

Kron, R. E., (1971). Psychoanalytic complications of a narcissistic transference. *Journal of the American Psychoanalytic Association* 19:636-653.

Kubie, L. S. (1968). Unsolved problems in the resolution of the transference. *Psychoanalytic Quarterly* 37:331-352.

LaForgue, R. (1934). Resistances at the conclusion of analytic treatment. *International Journal of Psycho-Analysis* 15:419-434.

——— (1973). Personal memoirs of Freud. In *Freud as We Knew Him*, ed. H. M. Ruitenbeek, pp. 341-349. Detroit: Wayne State University Press.

Langs, R. (1974). *The Technique of Psychoanalysis*, vol. 2. New York: Jason Aronson.

——— (1975). The therapeutic relationship and deviations in technique. *International Journal of Psycho-Analysis* 4:106-141.

——— (1980). The misalliance dimension in the case of the Rat Man. In *Freud and His Patients*, ed. M. Kanzer and J. Glenn, pp. 215-231. New York: Jason Aronson.

Leach, D. (1958). Panel: technical aspects of transference. *Journal of the American Psychoanalytic Association* 6:560-566.

Le Guen, C. (1982). The trauma of interpretation as history repeating itself. *International Journal of Psycho-Analysis* 63:321-330.

Lehrman, S. R. (1959). A note on two characteristics of transference. *Psychoanalytic Quarterly* 28:379-381.

Leites, N. (1977). Transference interpretations only? *International Journal of Psycho-Analysis* 58:275-288.

——— (1979). *Interpreting Transference*. New York: Norton.

Levin, M. (1930). Psycho-analytic interpretation of two statements from the Talmud. *International Journal of Psycho-Analysis* 11:94.

Levin, S., and Michaels, J. J. (1965). Incomplete psychoanalytic training. *Journal of the American Psychoanalytic Association* 13:793-818.

Lewin, B. D. (1946). Sleep, the mouth, and the dream screen. *Psychoanalytic Quarterly* 15:419-434.

——— (1949). Mania and sleep. *Psychoanalytic Quarterly* 18:419-433.

——— (1953). Reconsideration of the dream screen. *Psychoanalytic Quarterly* 22:174-199.

——— (1954). Sleep, narcissistic neurosis, and the analytic situation. *Psychoanalytic Quarterly* 23:487-510.

——— (1955). Dream psychology and the analytic situation. *Psychoanalytic Quarterly* 24:169-199.

Lewis, G. F. (1979). Screen memories as transference resistance. *Journal of the American Psychoanalytic Association* 7:159-170.

Liberman, D. (1966). Criteria for the interpretation in patients with obsessive traits. *International Journal of Psycho-Analysis* 47:212-217.

Lichtenberg, J. D. (1989). *Psychoanalysis and Motivation*. Hillsdale, NJ: Analytic Press.

Lifschutz, J. E. (1976). A critique of reporting and assessment in the training analysis. *Journal of the American Psychoanalytic Association* 24:43-60.

Limentani, A. (1966). A re-evaluation of acting out in relation to working through. *International Journal of Psycho-Analysis* 47:274-281.

Lipton, S. D. (1977a). The advantages of Freud's technique as shown in his analysis of the Rat Man. *International Journal of Psycho-Analysis* 58:255-274.

—— (1977b). Clinical observations on resistance to the transference. *International Journal of Psycho-Analysis* 58:463-472.

—— (1979). An addendum to "The advantages of Freud's technique as shown in his analysis of the Rat Man." *International Journal of Psycho-Analysis* 60:215-216.

Loewald, H. W. (1952). The problem of defense and the neurotic interpretation of reality. *International Journal of Psycho-Analysis* 33:444-449.

—— (1971). The transference neurosis: comments on the concept and the phenomenon. *Journal of the American Psychoanalytic Association* 19:54-66.

—— (1977). Transference and countertransference: the roots of psychoanalysis. Book review essay on "The Freud/Jung Letters." *Psychoanalytic Quarterly* 46:514-527.

Loewenstein, R. M. (1949). A posttraumatic dream. *Psychoanalytic Quarterly* 18:449-454.

—— (1951). The problem of interpretation. *Psychoanalytic Quarterly* 20:1-14.

—— (1968). Comment on Naiman's paper, "Short term effects as indicators of the role of interpretations." *International Journal of Psycho-Analysis* 49:356-357.

London, N. J., and Rosenblatt, A. D. (1987). Transference neurosis: evolution or obsolescence. *Psychoanalytic Inquiry* 7:4 (entire issue).

Lorand, S. (1957). Dream interpretation in the Talmud (Babylonian and Graeco-Roman period). *International Journal of Psycho-Analysis* 38:92-97.

Lossy, F. T. (1962). The charge of suggestion as a resistance in psychoanalysis. *International Journal of Psycho-Analysis* 43:448-467.

Macalpine, I. (1950). The development of the transference. *Psychoanalytic Quarterly* 19:501-539.

Maguire, J. G. (1978). The transference enactment of early body-image determinants. *Journal of the American Psychoanalytic Association* 6:181-208.

—— (1980). Empiricism, the transference neurosis, and the function of the self-object: a re-examination of the dynamic point of view. *Journal of the American Psychoanalytic Association* 8:93-109.

Mahon, E. J., and Battin, D. (1981). Screen memories and a termination of psychoanalysis: a preliminary communication. *Journal of the American Psychoanalytic Association* 29:939-942.

Mahony, P. J. (1977). Toward a formalist approach to dreams. *International Journal of Psycho-Analysis* 4:83-98.

—— (1982). *Freud as a Writer*. New York: International Universities Press.

—— (1986). *Freud and the Rat Man*. New Haven: Yale University Press.

—— (1989). *On Defining Freud's Discourse*. New Haven: Yale University Press.

Malcolm, J. (1981). *Psychoanalysis: The Impossible Profession*. New York: Alfred A. Knopf.

Malin, A. (1982). Panel: construction and reconstruction: clinical aspects. *Journal of the American Psychoanalytic Association* 30:213-234.

Marohn, R. C. (1981). The negative transference in the treatment of juvenile delinquents. *Journal of the American Psychoanalytic Association* 9:21-42.

Masson, J. M. (1984). *The Assault on Truth: Freud's Suppression of the Seduction Theory.* New York: Farrar, Strauss, & Giroux.

—— (1985). *The Complete Letters of Sigmund Freud to Wilhelm Fliess, 1887-1904.* Cambridge, MA: Harvard University Press.

Mayer, D. L. (1972). Comments on a blind spot in clinical research. A special form of transference in the psychoanalytic clinic. *Psychoanalytic Quarterly* 41:384-401.

McGuire, M. T. (1970). Repression, resistance, and recall of the past: some reconsiderations. *Psychoanalytic Quarterly* 39:427-448.

—— (1971). *Reconstructions in Psychoanalysis.* New York: Appleton-Century-Crofts.

McLaughlin, J. T. (1973). The nonreporting training analyst, the analysis, and the institute. *Journal of the American Psychoanalytic Association* 21:697-712.

—— (1981). Transference, psychic reality, and countertransference. *Psychoanalytic Quarterly* 50:639-664.

Meyerson, A. T., and Epstein, G. (1976). The psychoanalytic treatment center as transference object. *Psychoanalytic Quarterly* 45:274-287.

Moloney, J. M., and Rockelein, L. (1949). A new interpretation of Hamlet. *International Journal of Psycho-Analysis* 30:92-107.

Morris, J. (1983). Time experience and transference. *Journal of the American Psychoanalytic Association* 31:651-676.

Morse, S. J. (1972). Structure and reconstruction: a critical comparison of Michael Balint and D. W. Winnicott. *International Journal of Psycho-Analysis* 53:487-500.

Muslin, H. L. (1979). Transference in the Rat Man case: the transference in transition. *Journal of the American Psychoanalytic Association* 27:561-578.

Muslin, H. L., and Gill, M. M. (1978). Transference in the Dora case. *Journal of the American Psychoanalytic Association* 26:311-330.

Myers, W. A. (1980). A transference dream with superego implications. *Psychoanalytic Quarterly* 49:284-307.

Nacht, S. (1965). Criteria and technique for the termination of analysis. *International Journal of Psycho-Analysis* 46:107-116.

Naiman, J. (1968). Short term effects as indicators of the role of interpretations. *International Journal of Psycho-Analysis* 49:353-356.

Novey, S. (1961). Influences of anticipatory attitudes on the resolution of the transference. *Psychoanalytic Quarterly* 30:56-71.

—— (1962). The principle of "working through" in psychoanalysis. *Journal of the American Psychoanalytic Association* 10:658-676.

—— (1968). *The Second Look. The Reconstruction of Personal History in Psychiatry and Psychoanalysis.* Baltimore: Johns Hopkins Press.

Novick, J. (1976). Termination of treatment in adolescence. *Psychoanalytic Study of the Child* 31:389-414. New York: International Universities Press.

—— (1980). Negative therapeutic motivation and negative therapeutic alliance. *Psychoanalytic Study of the Child* 35:299-320. New York: International Universities Press.

—— (1982). Termination: themes and issues. *Psychoanalytic Inquiry* 2:329-366.

Nunberg, H., and Federn, E., eds. (1962). *Minutes of the Vienna Psychoanalytic Society,* vol. I, 1906-1908. New York: International Universities Press.

—— (1967). *Minutes of the Vienna Psychoanalytic Society,* vol. II, 1906-1908. New York: International Universities Press.

—— (1967). *Minutes of the Vienna Psychoanalytic Society*, vol. III, 1906-1908. New York: International Universities Press.

Oremland, J. D. (1973). A specific dream during the termination phase of successful psychoanalyses. *Journal of the American Psychoanalytic Association* 21:285-302.

Orens, M. H. (1955). Setting a termination date—an impetus to analysis. *Journal of the American Psychoanalytic Association* 3:651-665.

Orgel, S. (1977). A form of acting out in the narcissistic transference. *Psychoanalytic Quarterly* 46:684-685.

Ornstein, P. H., and Ornstein, A. (1980). Formulating interpretations in clinical psychoanalysis. *International Journal of Psycho-Analysis* 61:203-212.

Ornston, D. (1982). Strachey's influence: a preliminary report. *International Journal of Psycho-Analysis* 63:409-426.

—— (1985). Freud's conception is different from Strachey's. *Journal of the American Psychoanalytic Association* 33:379-412.

Orr, D. W. (1954). Transference and countertransference: a historical survey. *Journal of the American Psychoanalytic Association* 2:621-670.

O'Shaughnessy, E. (1983). Words and working through. *International Journal of Psycho-Analysis* 64:281-290.

Pacheco De, A., and Prado, M. (1978). On working through the psychotic elements in the analytic process. *International Journal of Psycho-Analysis* 59:209-214.

Parkin, A. (1981). Repetition, mourning and working through. *International Journal of Psycho-Analysis* 62:271-282.

Peto, A. (1960). On the transient disintegrative effect of interpretations. *International Journal of Psycho-Analysis* 41:413-417.

Pick, I. B. (1985). Working through in the countertransference. *International Journal of Psycho-Analysis* 66:157-166.

Plata-Mujica, C. (1976). Discussion of "The changing use of dreams in psychoanalytic practice." *International Journal of Psycho-Analysis* 57:335-342.

Poland, W. S. (1984). The analyst's words: empathy and countertransference. *Psychoanalytic Quarterly* 53:421-424.

—— (1988). Insight and the analytic dyad. *Psychoanalytic Quarterly* 57:341-369.

—— (in press). From analytic surface to analytic space. *Psychoanalytic Quarterly*.

Pribram, K., and Gill, M. (1976). *Freud's "Project" Re-assessed. Preface to Contemporary Cognitive Theory and Neuropsychology*. New York: Basic Books.

Racker, H. (1954). Notes on the theory of transference. *Psychoanalytic Quarterly* 23:78-86.

—— (1957). The meanings and uses of countertransference. *Psychoanalytic Quarterly* 26:303-357.

—— (1958). Counterresistance and interpretation. *Journal of the American Psychoanalytic Association* 6:215-221.

—— (1960). A study of some early conflicts through their return in the patient's relation with the interpretation. *International Journal of Psycho-Analysis* 41:47-58.

—— (1968). *Transference and Countertransference*. London: Hogarth Press.

Ramzy, I., and Shevrin, H. (1976). The nature of the influence process in psychoanalytic interpretation: a critical review of the literature. *International Journal of Psycho-Analysis* 57:151-160.

Rangell, L. (1982). Transference to theory: the relationship of psychoanalytic education to the analyst's relationship to psychoanalysis. *Journal of the American Psychoanalytic Association* 10:29-56.

—— (1983). Defense and resistance in psychoanalysis and life. *Journal of the American Psychoanalytic Association* 31:147-174.

Rank, O. (1921). Collective review: dream interpretation. *International Journal of Psycho-Analysis* 2:106-122.

Rapaport, D., and Gill, M. M. (1959). The points of view and assumptions of metapsychology. *International Journal of Psycho-Analysis* 40:153-162.

Rappaport, E. A. (1956). The management of an eroticized transference. *Psychoanalytic Quarterly* 25:515-529.

Reed, G. S. (1987). Rules of clinical understanding in classical analysis and in self psychology: a comparison. *Journal of the American Psychoanalytic Association* 35:421-446.

—— (1990). The transference neurosis in Freud's writings. *Journal of the American Psychoanalytic Association* 38:423-450.

Reich, A. (1950). On the termination of analysis. *International Journal of Psycho-Analysis* 31:79-183.

Reider, N. (1972). Metaphor as interpretation. *International Journal of Psycho-Analysis* 53:463-470.

Reik, T. (1924). Some remarks on the study of resistances. *International Journal of Psycho-Analysis* 5:141-154.

Renik, O. (1978). Neurotic and narcissistic transferences in Freud's relationship with Josef Popper. *Psychoanalytic Quarterly* 47:398-418.

—— (1981). Typical examination dreams, "superego dreams," and traumatic dreams. *Psychoanalytic Quarterly* 50:159-189.

Rickman, J. (1950). On the criteria for the termination of an analysis. *International Journal of Psycho-Analysis* 31:200-201.

Riviere, A. P. (1958). House construction play, its interpretation and diagnostic value. *International Journal of Psycho-Analysis* 39:39-49.

Robbins, W. S. (1975). Panel: termination: problems and techniques. *Journal of the American Psychoanalytic Association* 23:166-176.

Roheim, G. (1941). The psychoanalytic interpretation of culture. *International Journal of Psycho-Analysis* 22:147-169.

Roland, A. (1967). The reality of the psycho-analytic relationship and situation in the handling of transference-resistance. *International Journal of Psycho-Analysis* 48:504-510.

Rose, G. J. (1969). Transference birth fantasies and narcissism. *Journal of the American Psychoanalytic Association* 17:1015-1029.

Rosenbaum, J. B. (1961). The significance of the sense of smell in the transference. *Journal of the American Psychoanalytic Association* 9:312-324.

Rosenfeld, D. (1980). The handling of resistances in adult patients. *International Journal of Psycho-Analysis* 61:71-84.

Ross, D. W., and Kapp, F. T. (1962). A technique for self-analysis of countertransference: use of the psychoanalyst's visual images in response to the patient's dreams. *Journal of the American Psychoanalytic Association* 10:643-657.

Ross, M. (1973). Some clinical and theoretical aspects of working through. *International Journal of Psycho-Analysis* 54:331-344.

Rothstein, A. (1983). Panel: interpretation: toward a contemporary understanding of the term. *Journal of the American Psychoanalytic Association* 31:237-246.

Sachs, O. (1967). Distinctions between fantasy and reality elements in memory and reconstruction. *International Journal of Psycho-Analysis* 48:416–423.

Sampson, H. (1990). How the patient's sense of danger and safety influences the analytic process. *Psychoanalytic Psychology* 7:115–124.

Samuels, A. (1985). Symbolic dimensions of Eros in transference-countertransference: some clinical uses of Jung's alchemical metaphor. *International Review of Psycho-Analysis* 12:199–214.

Sandler, J. (1976). Countertransference and role-responsiveness. *International Review of Psycho-Analysis* 3:43–48.

Saul, L. J. (1962). The erotic transference. *Psychoanalytic Quarterly* 31:54–61.

Savitt, R. A. (1969). Transference, somatization, and symbiotic need. *Journal of the American Psychoanalytic Association* 17:1030–1054.

Schacter, J. S., and Butts, H. F. (1968). Transference and countertransference in interracial analyses. *Journal of the American Psychoanalytic Association* 16:792–808.

Schafer, R. (1968). Mechanisms of defense. *International Journal of Psycho-Analysis* 49:49–62.

——— (1973). The idea of resistance. *International Journal of Psycho-Analysis* 54:259–286.

——— (1976). *A New Language for Psychoanalysis.* New Haven: Yale University Press.

——— (1977). The interpretation of transference and the conditions for loving. *Journal of the American Psychoanalytic Association* 25:335–362.

——— (1982). The relevance of the "here and now" transference interpretation to the reconstruction of early development. *International Journal of Psycho-Analysis* 63:77–82.

——— (1985). Interpretation of psychic reality, developmental influences, and unconscious communication. *Journal of the American Psychoanalytic Association* 33:537–554.

Schimek, J. G. (1975). The interpretations of the past: childhood trauma, psychical reality, and truth. *Journal of the American Psychoanalytic Association* 23:845–866.

Schmale, H. T. (1966). Working through. *Journal of the American Psychoanalytic Association* 14:172–182.

Schmidl, F. (1955). The problem of scientific validation in psycho-analytic interpretation. *International Journal of Psycho-Analysis* 36:105–113.

Schur, M. (1972). *Freud: Living and Dying.* New York: International Universities Press.

Searles, H. (1979). *Countertransference and Related Subjects.* New York: International Universities Press.

Sedler, M. J. (1983). Freud's concept of working through. *Psychoanalytic Quarterly* 52:73–98.

Segel, N. P. (1969). Panel: narcissistic resistance. *Journal of the American Psychoanalytic Association* 17:941–954.

Shane, M. (1979). The developmental approach to "working through" in the analytic process. *International Journal of Psycho-Analysis* 60:375–382.

Shane, M., and Shane, E. (1984). The end phase of analysis: indicators, functions and tasks of termination. *Journal of the American Psychoanalytic Association* 32:739–772.

Shapiro, T. (1970). Interpretation and naming. *Journal of the American Psychoanalytic Association* 18:399–421.

Shevin, F. F. (1963). Countertransference and identity phenomena manifested in the analysis of a case of "phallus girl" identity. *Journal of the American Psychoanalytic Association* 11:331–344.

Siegman, A. J. (1963). A type of transference elation. *Journal of the American Psychoanalytic Association* 11:117-130.

Silverberg, W. V. (1948). The concept of transference. *Psychoanalytic Quarterly* 17:303-321.

Silverman, D. K. (1990). Extenders or modifiers: a discussion of Weiss and Sampson's control-mastery theory. *Psychoanalytic Psychology* 7:125-136.

Silverman, M. A. (1985). Countertransference and the myth of the perfectly analyzed analyst. *Psychoanalytic Quarterly* 54:175-199.

Smith, B. L. (1990). The origins of interpretation in the countertransference. *Psychoanalytic Psychology* 7 (Supplement):89-104.

Spanjaard, J. (1969). The manifest dream content and its significance for the interpretation of dreams. *International Journal of Psycho-Analysis* 50:221-236.

Spence, D. (1982). *Narrative Truth and Historical Truth. Meaning and Interpretation in Psychoanalysis*. New York: Norton.

Sperling, M. (1967). Transference neurosis in patients with psychosomatic disorders. *Psychoanalytic Quarterly* 36:342-355.

Sperling, M. (1950). Children's interpretation and reaction to the unconscious of their mothers. *International Journal of Psycho-Analysis* 31:36-41.

Stamm, J. L. (1974). A unique poetic sublimation of conflicts revived during termination. *Psychoanalytic Quarterly* 43:427-437.

Stein, M. H. (1958). The cliche: a phenomenon of resistance. *Journal of the American Psychoanalytic Association* 6:263-277.

———— (1981). The unobjectionable part of the transference. *Journal of the American Psychoanalytic Association* 29:869-892.

———— (1984). Rational vs. anagogic interpretation: Xenophon's dream and others. *Journal of the American Psychoanalytic Association* 32:529-556.

Stekel, W. (1944). *The Interpretation of Dreams: New Developments and Technique*. New York: Liveright Publishing Corp.

Sterba, R. F. (1934). The fate of the ego in analytic therapy. *International Journal of Psycho-Analysis* 15:117-126.

———— (1940). The dynamics of the dissolution of the transference resistance. *Psychoanalytic Quarterly* 9:363-379.

———— (1946). Dreams and acting out. *Psychoanalytic Quarterly* 15:175-179.

Stern, A. (1948). Transference in borderline neuroses. *Psychoanalytic Quarterly* 17:527-528.

———— (1957). The transference in the borderline group of neuroses. *Journal of the American Psychoanalytic Association* 5:348-350.

Sternbach, O. (1975). Aggression, the death drive and the problem of sadomasochism. A reinterpretation of Freud's second drive theory. *International Journal of Psycho-Analysis* 56:321-334.

Stewart, W. A. (1963). An inquiry into the concept of working through. *Journal of the American Psychoanalytic Association* 11:474-499.

———— (1967). *Psychoanalysis: The First Ten Years 1888-1898*. New York: Macmillan. London: George Allen and Unwin, 1969.

Stolorow, R. D. (1978). Themes in dreams: a brief contribution to therapeutic technique. *International Journal of Psycho-Analysis* 59:473-476.

Stolorow, R. D., Brandchaft, B., and Atwood, G. E. (1987). *Psychoanalytic Treatment: An Intersubjective Approach*. Hillsdale, NJ: Analytic Press.

Stolorow, R. D., and Lachmann, F. M. (1984). Transference: the future of an illusion. *Journal of the American Psychoanalytic Association* 12:19-38.

Stone, L. (1961). *The Psychoanalytic Situation: An Examination of Its Development and Essential Nature*. New York: International Universities Press.

—— (1967). The psychoanalytic situation and transference: postscript to an earlier communication. *Journal of the American Psychoanalytic Association* 15:3-58.

Strachey, J. (1937). Theory of the therapeutic results of psychoanalysis (symposium). *International Journal of Psycho-Analysis* 18:139-145.

Süskind, P. (1986). *Perfume*. Trans. J. E. Woods. New York: Knopf.

Tarachow, S. (1962). Interpretation and reality in psychotherapy. *International Journal of Psycho-Analysis* 43:377-387.

Taylor, J. N. (1959). A note on the splitting of interpretations. *International Journal of Psycho-Analysis* 40:295-296.

Ticho, E. A. (1972). Termination of psychoanalysis: treatment goals, life goals. *Psychoanalytic Quarterly* 41:315-333.

Tower, L. E. (1956). Countertransference. *Journal of the American Psychoanalytic Association* 4:224-265.

Valenstein, A. F. (1983). Working through and resistance to change: insight and action. *Journal of the American Psychoanalytic Association* 31:353-374.

—— (1987). Preoedipal reconstruction in psychoanalysis. Paper presented to the International Psychoanalytical Congress, Montreal, Canada, August.

Van Dam, H. (1966). Problems of transference in child analysis. *Journal of the American Psychoanalytic Association* 14:528-537.

Van Der Leeuw, P. J. (1979). Some additional remarks on problems of transference. *Journal of the American Psychoanalytic Association* 27:315-326.

Vianna, H. B. (1974). A peculiar form of resistance to psychoanalytic treatment. *International Journal of Psycho-Analysis* 55:439-444.

—— (1975). A peculiar form of resistance to psychoanalytic treatment: a reply to the discussion by Willy Baranger. *International Journal of Psycho-Analysis* 56:263-264.

Vogel, G. W. (1978). An alternative view of the neurobiology of dreaming. *American Journal of Psychiatry* 135:1531-1535.

Wachtel, P., ed. (1982). *Resistance: Psychodynamic and Behavioral Approaches*. New York: Plenum.

Wallerstein, R. S. (1967). Reconstruction and mastery in the transference psychosis. *Journal of the American Psychoanalytic Association* 15:551-583.

Wallerstein, R. S., and Sampson, H. (1971). Issues in research in the psychoanalytic process. *International Journal of Psycho-Analysis* 52:11-50.

Wasserman, M. D. (1984). Psychoanalytic dream theory and recent neurobiology findings about REM sleep. *Journal of the American Psychoanalytic Association* 32:831-846.

Weigert, E. (1955). Special problems in connection with termination of training analyses. *Journal of the American Psychoanalytic Association* 3:630-640.

Weinshel, E. M. (1971). The transference neurosis: a survey of the literature. *Journal of the American Psychoanalytic Association* 19:67-88.

Weiss, J., Sampson, H., and the Mount Zion Psychotherapy Research Group (1986). *The Psychoanalytic Process: Theory, Clinical Observation and Empirical Research*. New York: Guilford.

Werman, D. S. (1979). Methodological problems in the psychoanalytic interpretation of literature: a review of studies on Sophocles' "Antigone." *Journal of the American Psychoanalytic Association* 27:451–478.

—— (1985). Suppression of a defense. In *Defense and Resistance: Historical Perspective and Current Concepts*. Ed. H. P. Blum. New York: International Universities Press.

Wexler, M. (1965). Working through in the therapy of schizophrenia. *International Journal of Psycho-Analysis* 46:279–286.

Whitman, R. M. (1974). Panel: dreams and dreaming. *Journal of the American Psychoanalytic Association* 22:643–650.

Wilson, S. (1980). Hans Anderson's Nightingale: a paradigm for the development of transference love. *International Review of Psycho-Analysis* 7:483–486.

Windholz, E. (1955). Problems of termination of the training analysis. *Journal of the American Psychoanalytic Association* 3:641–650.

Winnicott, D. W. (1958). *Collected Papers. Through Pediatrics to Psychoanalysis*. New York: Basic Books.

—— (1965). *The Maturational Processes and the Facilitating Environment*. New York: International Universities Press.

—— (1971). *Playing and Reality*. New York: Basic Books.

Wisdom, J. O. (1967). Testing of a psycho-analytic interpretation. *International Journal of Psycho-Analysis* 48:44–52.

Young-Bruehl, E. (1988). *Anna Freud, A Biography*. New York: Summit Books.

Zac, J. (1972). An investigation of how interpretations arise in the analyst. *International Journal of Psycho-Analysis* 53:315–320.

Zeligs, M. A. (1961). The psychology of silence: its role in transference, countertransference and the psychoanalytic process. *Journal of the American Psychoanalytic Association* 9:7–43.

Zetzel, E. R. (1965). The theory of therapy in relation to a developmental model of psychic apparatus. *International Journal of Psycho-Analysis* 46:39–52.

—— (1966). The analytic situation. In *Psychoanalysis in the Americas*, ed. R. E. Litman, pp. 86–106. New York: International Universities Press.

Zulliger, H. (1950). Psychoanalysis and the form-interpretation test. *International Journal of Psycho-Analysis* 31:52–155.

Zwiebel, R. (1985). The dynamics of the countertransference dream. *International Review of Psychoanalysis* 12:87–100.

Credits

The editor gratefully acknowledges permission to reprint excerpts from the following:

Author Index

Abend, S., 88, 202
Abraham, K., 38*n**, 151, 156*n*, 202*n*
Adler, A., 70, 220, 221, 237, 286
Altman, L., 134, 135
Antrobus, J., 104
Arlow, J., 14, 85, 86, 266, 271
   on reconstruction, 271-281
Atwood, G. E., 88*fn***, 196*n*, 202

Bach, S., 28, 46*n*, 53*n*, 61*n*, 64*n*, 87,
   94*fn*, 119*n*, 121*n*, 151, 170, 202*n*,
   247*n*, 255*n*, 315-316, 317, 318, 319,
   320, 321*fn*, 323
Bergman, A., 337
Bergmann, M. S., 158*n*
Bernfeld, S., 3, 285
Bernheim, H., 7
Bion, W. R., 84*fn*, 202*n*
Bird, B., 20*fn*, 56*n*, 81-84, 198, 203, 216,
   274, 289, 321*fn*, 330, 342
Bleuler, E., 29, 48
Blum, H. P., 9, 279, 289, 290
Boesky, D., 53*n*, 56*n*
Bonaparte, M., 210, 211
Brandchaft, B., 88*fn*, 196*n*, 202
Brenner, C., 39*n*, 62*n*, 90, 92, 128*n*, 138,
   197, 227*n*, 260, 262, 267, 268, 269,
   271, 314*fn*, 319-320, 333, 340, 341
   on analytic practice, 201-206
   on dreams, 136, 137, 139

on interpretation, 194, 345, 346
on reconstruction, 345
on termination phase, 265-266
on transference, 46-48*n*, 49*n*, 85-88,
   93-94, 342, 343
Breuer, J., 3*fn*, 4, 5-6, 7, 8, 10, 11, 12,
   ·51, 100

Calef, V., 147
Charcot, J. M., 3*fn*, 100
Clark, R. W., 210
Cooper, A., 228, 272, 273, 279
Crick, F., 133
Curtis, H. C., 271

Dahl, H., 156*n*
De Saussure, R., 288
Decker, H. S., 14
Deutsch, F., 211
Deutsch, H., 211
Doolittle, H., 287-288

Eissler, K. R., 302*fn*
Ekstein, R., 147
Ellman, S., 100, 104, 133, 135, 281,
   289*fn*, 337, 344

Fairbairn, W. R. D., 278
Federn, E., 294

---

*   *n* refers to author's marginal commentary on Freud's papers.
** *fn* refers to footnotes.

Subject Index

Abreaction, 5, 6, 51, 52
Abstinence, rule of, 72
Acting out, 15, 55-56, 55-56*n**, 56-57*n*,
     128*n*
  protecting patients against, 60-61, 60-
     61*n*
Acting in, 57*n*
Actual neurosis, 26-28
  analyzability and, 30-31
Altered states, 100, 101, 148*fn***
Ambivalence
  dreams and, 123, 123*n*
  of transference, 29, 46*n*, 48
Analysis of the Self, The (Kohut), 91
Analyzability, 29, 30-31, 38*n*, 45-46*n*,
     91-92, 128*n*, 144-146, 148, 166-
     167, 166*n*, 201-203, 220, 247-
     248*n*, 306-307. *See also*
     Treatment, psychoanalytic
Anna O., case of, 11, 12
Anti-worlds, 316, 319, 324-325
Attention, evenly suspended, 151-152,
     154-155, 155*n*, 200

Bipolar self, 194
Birth trauma, 213, 226
Borderline disorder/patient, 38*n*, 88,
     119*n*, 121*n*, 196, 202, 317,
     336

Castration complex, 220, 221
Catharsis, 5, 51
Censorship, 105, 122, 130
Childhood amnesia, 53
Clinical Diary of Sándor Ferenczi, 68*n*, 169
Compromise formation, 86, 201, 319,
     326, 342
Conscious/Consciousness, 81, 298
  accessibility of ideas to, 5-6
  altered state(s) of, 100, 101
Constitutional factors, 35-36*fn*, 37*n*
Construction. *See* Reconstruction
Couch, 100, 148*fn*, 179, 179*n*, 185, 197,
     199, 203-204, 205
Countertransference, 31, 67, 67-68*n*, 69-
     70*n*, 72, 155*n*, 158*n*, 160*n*, 195,
     264. *See also* Transference love

Death instinct, 129-130*n*, 212, 217
Decisions, analytic injunction to
     postpone, 60-61, 147
Defense
  concept of, 7-9
  as conscious act of will, 9
  as unconscious process, 33, 86, 105-
     106, 152, 307
Delusions/hallucinations, 223-224, 252-
     256, 254-255*n*

---

*   *n* refers to author's marginal commentary on Freud's papers.
** *fn* refers to footnotes.

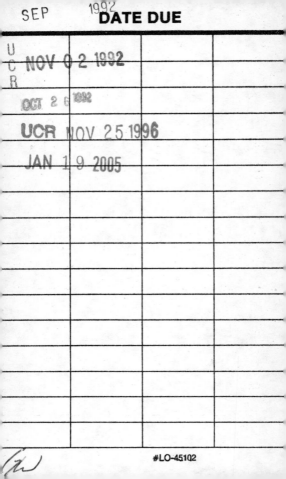